PILGRIMAGE
AND THE JEWS

PILGRIMAGE AND THE JEWS

DAVID M. GITLITZ AND LINDA KAY DAVIDSON

PRAEGER

Westport, Connecticut
London

Library of Congress Cataloging-in-Publication Data

Gitlitz, David M. (David Martin)
    Pilgrimage and the Jews / David M. Gitlitz and Linda Kay Davidson.
        p.   cm.
    Includes bibliographical references and index.
    ISBN 0–275–98763–9 (alk. paper)
    1. Jewish pilgrims and pilgrimages—History.   2. Jewish shrines.   3. Jerusalem in
Judaism.   I. Davidson, Linda Kay.   II. Title.
    BM729.P45G58   2006
    296.4'81—dc22   2005020953

British Library Cataloguing in Publication Data is available.

Library of Congress Catalog Card Number: 2005020953
ISBN: 0–275–98763–9

First published in 2006

Praeger Publishers, 88 Post Road West, Westport, CT 06881
An imprint of Greenwood Publishing Group, Inc.
www.praeger.com

Printed in the United States of America

The paper used in this book complies with the
Permanent Paper Standard issued by the National
Information Standards Organization (Z39.48–1984).

10 9 8 7 6 5 4 3 2 1

Copyright Acknowledgments

Laura Carboni, "Auschwitz Journal," http://www.bearingwitnessjournal.com (circa 2003).

Julie Golick, "March of the Living 1999 Diary," http://www.geocities.com/SouthBeach/1915/entry20.html.

Keith Grimwood and Ezra Idlet (Trout Fishing in America), "Mine!" Copyrighted Grimwood/Idlet, 1993 troutoons (BMI). From the CD **MINE!**, Trout Records, TR9.

Aaron Hass, "Survivor Guilt in Holocaust Survivors and their Children," in *A Global Perspective on Working with Holocaust Survivors and the Second Generation,* ed. John Lemberger (Jerusalem: JDC-Brookdale Institute of Gerontology and Human Development, AMCHA, and JDC-Israel, 1995), 163–184.

"Holocaust Museum of Richmond, Virginia: Tolerance through Education," http://www.va-holocaust.com.

Dara Horn, "On Filling Shoes," *Hadassah Magazine* (November 1992): 16–22.

David Margolis, "Ellis Island Revisited," *Los Angeles Jewish Journal* (1993), http://www.davidmargolis.com/article.php?id=51&cat_fp=0&cat_cc.

Moses Basola, *In Zion and Jerusalem: The Itinerary of Rabbi Moses Basola (1521–1523),* ed. Abraham David; trans. Dena Ordan (Ramat Gan: C. G. Foundation; Jerusalem Project Publications of the Martin [Szusz] Department of Land of Israel Studies, Bar-Ilan University, 1999).

Daniel Singer, "A Haunted Journey," *The Nation* 269, no. 9 (September 27, 1999): 18–25. Reprinted with permission from the September 27, 1999 issue of *The Nation* magazine. For subscription information, call 1-800-333-8536. Portions of each week's *Nation* magazine can be accessed at http://www.thenation.com.

Edith Turner, "Bar Yohai, Mystic: The Creative Persona and His Pilgrimage," in *Creativity/Anthropology*, ed. Smadar Lavie, Kirin Narayan, and Renato Rosaldo (Ithaca: Cornell University Press, 1993), 225–252. Used by permission of the publisher, Cornell University Press.

The Casale Pilgrim; a Sixteenth-Century Illustrated Guide to the Holy Places Reproduced in Facsimile. Trans., ed. Cecil Roth. London: Soncino Press, 1929.

Kobler, Franz, ed. *A Treasury of Jewish Letters.* 2 vols. Philadelphia: Jewish Publication Society, 1954.

Wilhelm, Kurt. *Roads to Zion: Four Centuries of Traveler's Reports.* Trans. by I. M. Lask. New York: Schocken, 1948.

Every reasonable effort has been made to trace the owners of copyright materials in this book, but in some instances this has proven impossible. The authors and publisher will be glad to receive information leading to more complete acknowledgments in subsequent printings of the book and in the meantime extend their apologies for any omissions.

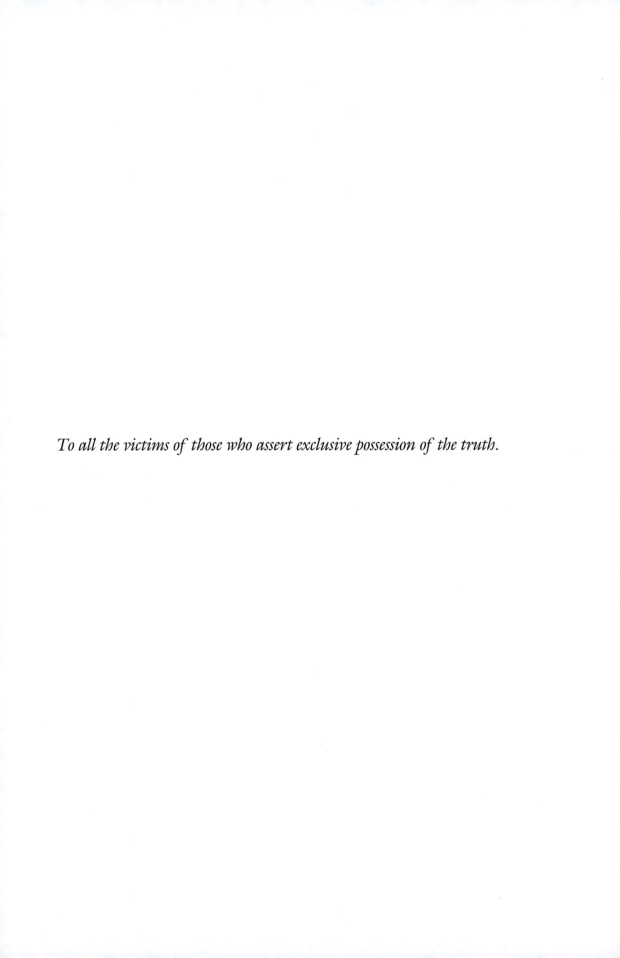

To all the victims of those who assert exclusive possession of the truth.

Hearing is not comparable to seeing.

Midrash Mechilta (Oral Tradition Shemot, 19:9)

I hear—I forget. I see—I remember. I do—I understand.

Chinese proverb

CONTENTS

ILLUSTRATIONS

PREFACE

We met on a pilgrimage road in Spain in 1974, little dreaming that the road would lead us to love, marriage, and—what is infinitely rarer—a collaborative career as writers.

Thirty years, five continents of travel later, our pilgrimage continues. Neither of us is very religious; we do not consider ourselves New Age seekers. But the theme of searching for the sacred, for finding answers, or perhaps just the questions, has taken us to India, Japan, most of the Americas, most of Europe, Israel, Turkey, and Morocco. It has led us to small caves, large cathedrals, and mountain tops. Our bumper sticker reads "My other car is a pair of boots."

This three-decade journey has changed our lives. In studying the paradigms of pilgrimage, we found that we have lived them.

When we speak publicly about pilgrimage—whether to Jewish or Christian audiences, or to academics—invariably someone asks, "Jews don't go on pilgrimage, do they?" We answer that indeed they do, that the Jewish people is a pilgrim people, with a rich and varied pilgrimage culture from biblical times right up to the present: pilgrimages to the holy Temple in Jerusalem and its remains; to the graves of the prophets and Matriarchs and Patriarchs; to saints' tombs all over Europe and in the Maghreb; to the Holocaust's theaters of destructions; to ancestral homelands that root immigrants in their ethnic heritage; to Israel and her shrines of nationalism and renewal. Pilgrimages to worship, to commemorate, to ask the deity for help, to shape a sense of identity. Moreover, in the past forty years, the number of Jews participating in pilgrimage activities increases with each passing year. And, as the evening news underscores, the battle over holy ground and access to it underlies much of the violence that poisons the relationships between Israel and her neighbors.

"We didn't know all that," comes the audience's reply, accompanied by surprised and frequently skeptical facial expressions. "You ought to write a book."

Four years later, one of them devoted to fieldwork in Eastern Europe, Morocco, and Israel, we are sending the manuscript of *Pilgrimage and the Jews* to the publisher. We would never have made it this far without the tolerance of our friends, our colleagues at the University of Rhode Island, and our daughters. We owe special mention to those who have helped us on the way, by offering suggestions, opening doors to special collections, giving advice. We are, as always, grateful to the InterLibrary Loan people at the University of Rhode Island Library and to Humanities Reference Librarian Jim Kinnie. We thank the University of Rhode Island Center for the Humanities for helping underwrite the cost of preparing maps and photographs for this project. We thank Dennis Skidds for preparing the five maps for this book. To Daniel Carpenter, "gratias agimus," and to Karry Sarkissian, "merci beaucoup," for helping with those pesky texts we couldn't decipher. Our research was made especially pleasant in Fez when we met Eva Orton and Danielle Mamane, gracious and warm people who shared their ideas and a lovely dinner with us. Hana Greenfield kindly related her remembrances of Holocaust times with us. To Suzanne Staszak-Silva, to Rebecca Homiski for working so cheerfully with the manuscript, and to Jeanne Fredericks for her unflagging enthusiasm for our project, our deep appreciation.

JEWISH PILGRIMS?

"Jews as pilgrims? Like to Lourdes or Fatima? Isn't that something that Christians do because they think it will cure them of some disease? Jews aren't superstitious like that."

"You might be surprised at the numbers of Jews who seek cures, or other favors from God, at places they consider holy. Rachel's Tomb and the tombs of the Patriarchs and Matriarchs are still drawing huge crowds today, in the twenty-first century."

"Jews as pilgrims? Like to Mecca? Huge crowds of Muslims from all over the world merging in some far-off city because their religion requires them to go? Jews would never do that. Who ever heard of any authority successfully ordering Jews to do anything?"

"You know, the Bible requires Jewish men to make three annual pilgrimages to Jerusalem. The Temple may be gone, but pilgrims still stream to the Western Wall."

"Jews as pilgrims to saints' tombs? Like to Saint Francis in Assisi, Saint Thomas à Becket in Canterbury? Or to the site of Husayn ibn 'Ali's martyrdom in Karbala, Iraq?"

"You don't think so? What about pilgrimages to the tombs of Hasidic rebbes like Elimelech of Lezhansk in Poland or Menachem Mendel Schneerson in Queens, New York? Or to the graves of Sephardic tzadiqim like 'Amram ben Diwane in Azjen, Morocco, or Baba Sali in Netivot in Israel? Complete with petitions that the holy men intercede with God on the pilgrim's behalf."

"Jews as pilgrims? Like the Hindus who go to Varanasi to die on the banks of the Ganges River because they think that will insure them a favorable afterlife? Not likely! Besides, lots of Jews aren't too sure about an afterlife anyway."

"Yet for hundreds of years old men have been journeying to Jerusalem to die and be buried on the Mount of Olives because they think that will hasten their resurrection at the end of days."

Anthropologists have defined *Homo sapiens* variously as the animal who laughs, or who makes tools, or who is capable of self-definition. Humans might also be characterized as the animal who goes on pilgrimage, for travel to holy places is a near-universal phenomenon among our species. Early Andeans went on pilgrimage to Chavín de Huántar; ancient Greeks to Delphi; Australian Aborigines to the Uluru Rock; South Asian animists to Mount Agung; Baha'i to Acre; Tibetan Bön to Lake Manasarovar; Buddhists to Bodh Gaya; Daoists to China's Five Holy Mountains; Ethiopian Christians to Däbrä Libanos; Hindus to Varanasi; Jains to Sravana Belagola; Mayans to Chichén Itzá; Native Americans to Bear Butte; Shinto to Tai Shan; Shi'ite Muslims to Karbala; Sikhs to Har Mandir; and Zoroastrians to Yazd. There are pilgrimages to innumerable tombs of saints and martyrs, places sanctified by the slaughter of innocents or by events seminal to the creation of ethnic, national, or religious identities. It should not surprise us, then, that Jews, too, are a pilgrim people, and have been so throughout both their mythic and historical pasts, and continue to be so today.

The terms "pilgrim" and "pilgrimage" are used so loosely in modern popular culture that someone is likely to label travel to anywhere for any reason a pilgrimage. America's Pilgrim Fathers landing at Plymouth Rock. Aunt Leah's annual excursion to Bloomingdale's. A neighbor finally taking his kids to Disney World. Mormon tourists in Salt Lake City. Aging hippies lighting candles at Jim Morrison's grave in Paris's Père Lachaise Cemetery the way their great grandparents did at Chopin's grave 100 yards from Morrison's. Or the way some of our gay friends do at Gertrude Stein's grave, 300 yards further still. Cape Verdeans by the thousands gathering in New Bedford, Massachusetts, one weekend each summer. Graceland. This breadth of definition is not only the province of the popular press. Novelists and poets have plumbed the human implications of these and hundreds of other journeys they call pilgrimages. We are not just talking of Chaucer's *Canterbury Tales*, but works as diverse as Robert Silverberg's *Kingdoms of the Wall*, Gao Xingjian's Nobel Prize–winning *Soul Mountain*, and Ruth Knafo Setton's *The Road to Fez*.[1]

Is there any meaningful content, then, to the statement that Jews are a pilgrim people, and have been so in the past, and continue to be so today?

First, it will help to set down some parameters for what we mean by pilgrimage. A pilgrimage can be broadly defined as "a (1) journey to a (2) special place in which both the journey and the destination have (3) spiritual significance for the journeyer."[2]

THE JOURNEY

The journey is most often literal, a physical movement from a place of normal, everyday existence, to some other place that is charged with meaning. There is no minimum distance requirement for a journey to be considered a pilgrimage, but people tend to focus attention on longer distances traveled rather than short jaunts. Pilgrimage journeys tend to have fixed end points—the holy site or special place—but they begin wherever one laces up one's boots or boards the airplane. Thus a visit to Jerusalem may be a pilgrimage whether it begins in Ramleh or in Seattle. Pilgrimages may even begin with the journey's planning stages, at the point where a person resolves to become a pilgrim. Some journeys start out as tourist travel and only become pilgrimages at the point where the spiritual aspects of the journey impact the traveler, perhaps even catching the traveler unaware. In addition to their point of departure, pilgrimages generally have a point of return. They are voyages to the special "there" and back again. Yet along the way something may occur to vitiate the need for return. Enlightenment may be reached, or the ties with one's pre-pilgrimage self may be cut definitively. The destination may be recognized as the new home, so that the pilgrim rips up the return ticket. For a Jew, the pilgrimage becomes *aliyah*.

There are also pilgrimage journeys that are metaphorical rather than literal. In those instances the journey is imagined, and the territory traveled, whether it is part of the physical or metaphysical world, exists only in the pilgrim's head. St. John of the Cross's journey through the dark night of the soul toward union with God exemplifies this sort. Furthermore, many Christians conceive of the span of a human life itself to be a pilgrimage. The soul departs from heaven to be incarnate in the human body, which then journeys—through time, rather than through space— toward its eventual return to God's presence. Or the return to heaven is aborted and becomes instead eternal damnation. Hindus and Buddhists tend to view the journey of human existence as cyclical: from birth, through time until death, and then rebirth again until eventually, if one accrues enough religious merit along the way, one is allowed to escape the cycle of journeys and join the great nothingness. In both of these traditions, life in this world is viewed as a test, a trial, in which the individual's proper behavior and attitudes earn merit toward a favorable disposition in the afterdeath. In both of these traditions, actual physical pilgrimages to holy sites in this world are considered meritorious acts to be toted up at a life's end in the calculus of salvation. None of these concepts carries much weight in Judaism.

A SPECIAL PLACE

Pilgrims point themselves toward a special place. If they do not have a particular place in mind, then they are wanderers, not pilgrims. The factors that make the place special are as varied as the human imagination. Religious pilgrimage tends to be based on three premises: that there is an unseen power greatly superior to ourselves that takes an active role in shaping our lives; that it is possible for humans to connect with that power; and that the power is especially approachable in certain privileged places. In religious pilgrimages, what most often privileges these places is their association with a deity. Thus the sites where a god appeared, or where he or she dwells, or worked a miracle are likely to be considered holy. The places associating a deity with a community's foundation myths are often holy: where the gods created our people, or where they promised us our land, or where they engaged our founding ancestors in their key experiences. The graves of certain special men and women—saints, marabouts, tzadiqim—are also often thought to be holy. Although the details and precise rationale for holiness vary from culture to culture, the underlying logic tends to be similar. Those places are privileged because at some moment the realm of the human and the realm of the divine came into contact there. They are touch points, portals, gateways between the here and now and the transcendent Other. If that connection happened there once, it follows that perhaps our relationship with the divine may also be more immediate, or more intense, or more propitious in such a place.

The pilgrimage experience may link the individual spirit with the transcendent, of course, but religious meaning is not the only kind of meaning that creates special places. Nations often enshrine the sites where key historical events occurred: battles won or lost, martyrs created, political systems founded. Commemorative monuments like Washington, D.C.'s Vietnam Veterans Memorial can be magnets for pilgrims, as can certain museums like the Holocaust Museum that is its neighbor. Immigrant peoples may enshrine the homelands they have left behind, and visits to such places are often thought of as pilgrimages. The tendency to idealize does not only work on places left behind. As we will see in Chapter 12, for modern secular Jews the State of Israel, resonant with historical past and pregnant with future promises, also functions as a very special place.

There are no limits on what may make a place special. Religious cultures may anoint certain places like Mecca and Jerusalem and Lourdes holy by consensus. Nations or peoples may sacralize places like Gettysburg, Pennsylvania, or Wounded Knee, South Dakota, or Masada, Israel, or Goree Island, Senegal. But any individual, as well, may hold some particular place special for reasons that are entirely personal: the old homestead, the place one's parents met, the cemetery where a treasured pet is buried. Pilgrimages to such places may in some fashion put people in better touch with themselves by connecting with ancestors or events from personal or communal history.

SPIRITUAL SIGNIFICANCE

The last components of this definition, the spiritual significance of both the journey and the destination, are bound up in one another. The goal of a pilgrimage is the satisfaction of a need. The journey is a quest for an experience that will have an important impact on the individual's life or spirit. To borrow a metaphor from science, pilgrimage is a catalyst, something that induces a transformation. Philosophers of religion sometimes call it an epiphany. In the words of Richard Niebuhr, pilgrims "are persons in motion—passing through territories not their own—seeking . . . completion, or . . . clarity . . . a goal to which only the Spirit's compass points the way."[3] Pilgrims prime themselves to expect change, and this helps make change happen. Sometimes change is a result of the ecstatic spiritual experience at the holy destination. In many cases it occurs during the pilgrim's journey to the special place. It may be triggered by the heightened sensitivity of the pilgrim toward matters of the spirit, the sense of strangeness or otherness derived from having left one's normal life and activities behind, or the newness of what the pilgrim experiences.

It is sometime difficult to distinguish between pilgrimage and tourism, for they have many characteristics in common. Both are temporary, non-ordinary interruptions in one's normal routine. Both involve a leave-taking, travel for some purpose involved with psychological or spiritual change, and reentry or reintegration into one's normal life.[4] And in practice, the two often mix. Pilgrims relegate time to visiting the secular wonders along their route. And tourists may find themselves moved, or even fundamentally transformed, by some site or experience along the way. Nevertheless, there are some essential differences between what Erik Cohen calls the "pilgrim-tourists, who travel toward the religious or cultural centers of their lives, and traveler-tourists who travel away from them to the periphery."[5] The distinction lies in the nature of the anticipated change. Tourists want to break with routine, to refresh themselves by experiencing something new: unfamiliar geography, different architecture, new foods, other lifestyles. Tourism frames experience as a form of recreation. Their itineraries may include sites of religious significance, but the visits are essentially secular in purpose. Their temporary break with routine is not intended to change the nature of that routine when they return to their normal lives. For pilgrims, on the other hand, the principal goals have to do with matters of spirit, of identity, of one's relationship with the divine. Tourists look outward; pilgrims look inward.

In struggling to discern the difference between pilgrims and tourists, observers of activity at a shrine rely on three sorts of data. One is personal testimony: memoirs, letters, and interviews in which travelers write or talk about their motives and attempt to evaluate their experiences. Given the wide variety of ways in which visits to special places can affect visitors emotionally or spiritually, as a general rule people who think of themselves as pilgrims, are. And even travelers who classify themselves as tourists often talk about their motives or their activities in language characteristic of pilgrimage. A second approach is observation of behavior. Visitors may engage in visible pilgrimage-like activities at a site. They may perform rituals that are drawn from religious experience. They may exhibit behaviors of reverence, worship, or memorialization that are typical of pilgrims. They may bond into groups that support each other in the evaluation of what they are undergoing, as pilgrims commonly do. Third, one may evaluate the physical traces left behind by pilgrim activity. Archaeologists who study ancient temples, ritual artifacts, and ex-votos, are adept at inferring pilgrim activity from the detritus left behind by long-vanished pilgrims.

Scholars, from historians, sociologists, and geographers to philosophers, theologians, and literary critics, have studied the pilgrimage aspects of everything we have mentioned so far. In the last few decades much attention has centered on the idea that pilgrims participate in two cultures: the one that for the moment they are leaving behind, and the culture of the pilgrim community on the road. According to some scholars, the pilgrim experience, especially in the large-scale pilgrimages that are emblematic of certain societies, helps individual pilgrims perceive and appreciate the characteristics that unify their culture despite its many local variants.[6] The Muslim hajj to Mecca, the Hindu Kumbh Mela gatherings at Allahabad, and the Jews' three annual pilgrimages to Jerusalem prior to the destruction of the Second Temple are good examples. Two of the most influential theorists of pilgrimage during the last half of the twentieth century were the anthropologists

Victor and Edith Turner. They probed the ways in which pilgrims step out of their home culture, crossing a threshold (which they call a *limin*) to join a new society based on classless shared experience (a state they refer to as *communitas*). The Turners found it useful to think of pilgrimages as divided into three parts: leave-taking, temporary otherness, and reentry. Change, in their analysis, tends to work its effects on pilgrims mainly during the middle phase of their experience. The pilgrims' challenge is to maintain the essence of their newly found perspectives during their reintegration into their former lives.[7] While the Turners' ideas have attracted much criticism, the categories that they devised set the framework for much of the subsequent theoretical discussion.

We have looked at pilgrimage through the lens of where people go. Now let us look through the other lens. What happens to people along the way? What sorts of changes and effects and differences do pilgrimages make in peoples' lives? What motivates people to set out on pilgrimage? What draws them to the special place?

Obviously pilgrims' motives vary in accord with the individuals' particular spiritual needs or with the patterns of behavior imposed by their culture. Yet there are some commonalities. Consider, for a moment, the religiously motivated journey, which is the most prevalent type of pilgrimage. In some religious traditions pilgrimage is mandated: Islam requires able males to make the hajj to Mecca, and biblical Judaism required three annual pilgrimages to Jerusalem. Religious pilgrims may also seek specific benefits from their journey. One common motive is to request the deity's intervention in personal or community affairs. This type of pilgrimage may be viewed as a transaction. The pilgrims offer devotion, emblematized by the resources of time and money they pour into the journey. The risks of death or disease attendant on the pilgrimage and the physical suffering occasioned by travel—at least in the pre-modern age—may be intended as offerings of self-mortification or asceticism that increase the pilgrims' worthiness to be rewarded. The benefits requested by the pilgrims are frequently material and temporal, such things as improved health, good fortune, fertility, or the recovery of lost property. Or the pilgrims may request transcendental favors: the purging of sin or a favorable afterlife. Mandates to go on pilgrimage can also be self-imposed. Some pilgrims journey to fulfill vows made in times of duress: save me from danger X and I will travel to shrine Y to give thanks. Or vows made in anticipation of a gift: grant me a son, and I will dedicate him to you as a priest. These kinds of reasons and their variants are common in many of the world's religions.

Some people become pilgrims for reasons other than religion. There are cultures that consider certain pilgrimages to be rites of passage from childhood to adulthood, as with some Native American tribes that send their pubescent male children on vision quests. There are pilgrimages designed to strengthen the participants' sense of ethnic, national, or cultural identity, such as the ethnic festivals that have become common summer pilgrimage events in the United States, or the annual reenactment of the civil rights march from Selma to Montgomery. Some immigrants or their children make a pilgrimage to the old country to connect with their families' roots. Another type of pilgrimage attracts crowds eager to see and hear a leader who is thought to embody, or channel, divine power, or at least to speak authoritatively about it: the Pope, Mother Meera, and the Dalai Lama are such figures. Some popular culture icons—Chopin, Elvis, Selena—were similarly magnetic during their lifetimes, and some of their graves continue to attract pilgrims.

With the exception of pilgrimage for the purpose of improving one's post-mortal state, all types of religious pilgrimages are well represented in Judaism. Mandatory pilgrimages? The biblical commandment to go to Jerusalem is unambiguous: "Three times in the year all thy males shall appear before the Lord God" (Ex. 23:17). Rites of passage? Look at the numbers of young Jewish boys who are taken to Meron for their first haircuts. Or on any Shabbat, the thirteen-year-olds who have been brought from Europe or the United States for their bar or bat mitzvahs at the Western Wall. Transactional pilgrimages? On any given day you can see childless women praying at Rachel's Tomb in the hopes that they will be able to conceive. Or during the annual *hillula* festivals of Moroccan Jews, villagers (or their children, on holiday from Israel or France) crowding around the tomb of their village rabbi-saint requesting the saint's blessing, or protection, or help with some particular problem. Identity pilgrimages? Tours to Israel; tours to New York's Lower East Side; tours to the *mellahs* of the Maghreb; tours to the Polish concentration camps. Pilgrimages to living beings? Think of the throngs of devotees who have traveled long distances to study or worship or just stand in the presence of certain renowned rebbes and tzadiqim.

Although Judaism shares the ancient and pervasive world culture of pilgrimage, we will come to see in the course of this book that Jewish pilgrimages tend to differ from those of other world religions in several ways. First, while Judaism has a long tradition of transactional pilgrimages and enthusiastically embraces identity pilgrimages, it has traditionally de-emphasized the more transcendental motives for pilgrimage, such as gaining favored status in an afterlife. Second, while many religions place great emphasis on the spiritual processes that pilgrims undergo during their journey to holy places, post-biblical Judaism tends to focus on the being there rather than on the getting there. As we will see in Chapter 2, the proto-pilgrimage migrations of Abraham's clan and the Israelites led by Moses may be considered exceptions. Even so, the journeys described in these foundation myths have had little impact on the behavior of later Jewish pilgrims. Unlike Christians on the Via Dolorosa retracing Jesus's route to Calvary, or Muslims in Mecca replicating Muhammad's steps in and around that holy city, Jewish pilgrims do not reenact their founders' journeys. Third, while many religions anticipate that pilgrimage will effect some fundamental transformation in the individual pilgrim, who may even be symbolically born again in the process, Judaism does not routinely expect this to happen. Jews tend to go on pilgrimage because it is a "good thing" for a variety of cultural reasons, not because they expect to be changed in some striking way. Fourth, while every religion's pilgrimage traditions are influenced by the contexts from which the religion emerged and by the religious cultures with which it coexists, Judaism—which through most of its history has been a religion of a minority people embedded within powerful and often attractive majority cultures—has been unusually susceptible to these influences. In the course of this book we will note the many ways in which ancient Middle Eastern religions, Christianity, and Islam, for example, have put their stamp on Jewish pilgrimage traditions. Fifth, while the pilgrimage traditions of many religions have evolved smoothly over time, those of the Jews have periodically undergone radical disjunctures and redefinitions. Diaspora and Holocaust will do that to a people. And lastly, while pilgrimage traditions within most religions tend to fit rather easily under a single conceptual tent, those of the Jews vary markedly from one Jewish group to another.

This book will consider the variety of pilgrimage traditions within three major groupings of themes corresponding roughly to the book's major divisions.

- The Center, Chapters 1–6. Jerusalem, and at its heart the Temple, as Judaism's holiest place and the central focus of both political and messianic yearnings. Judaism's centripetal force. The locus of the Shechinah. Why and how Jerusalem has become the navel, and why it still is after more than 2,500 years.
- Holy people, Chapters 7–9. Matriarchs, Patriarchs, rebbes, tzadiqim, *hahamim* (sages), and a variety of other holy figures whose tombs are the focus of pilgrimage activity. Tensions between the concepts of the diffuse Many and the unique central One. The variety of holy person traditions of Sephardim and Ashkenazim.
- Destruction, rebirth, and identity, Chapters 10–14. The Holocaust, the birth of the State of Israel, and—for many—the search for the meaning of Jewishness in a post-religious age. The violent displacement of modern Judaism from its traditional centers in Eastern Europe and the Muslim world, and the role of pilgrimage in the attempts to stem the erosion of this Jewish cultural diversity. Nostalgia pilgrimage and the shaping of modern Jewish identity. Shrine wars and the hopes for peace in the Middle East.

BEGINNINGS: CONVERGING ON JERUSALEM

Now this man used to go up year by year from his town to worship and to sacrifice to the Lord of hosts at Shiloh. (1 Samuel 1:3)

I made a sacrifice and poured out a libation on the mountain top. (*Epic of Gilgamesh*)[1]

Jerusalem's holiness to the Jews, the migration myths which recount its establishment, and early Judaism's concepts of sacred space must all be understood in relation to ideas and traditions current in the Middle East's Fertile Crescent in the second millennium before the Common Era.

In the Bronze Age world of Abraham, roughly eighteen centuries before the Common Era, tribal cultures prevailed. Each tribe—and the extended tribes that were becoming the region's first nation-states of Sumerians, Akkadians, Canaanites, Hittites, and others—worshiped its own protective deities who were immortal and invisible and possessed powers far beyond those of human beings. The worshipers of the deities comprehended them, for the most part, in human terms. The gods were plural. They were gendered. They expressed emotions both noble and base. They frequently arrayed themselves in families, and sometimes fought as rivals. While they could be capricious, they also controlled the heavens and the earth in accord with certain consistent laws and principles. The masculine deities tended to assume the roles of overlord or king with regard to their human subjects. Feminine deities oversaw the earth's fertility and the natural forces related to agricultural cycles and human reproduction.

Similar to the deities of the animist cultures that prevailed at the same time in East Asia, the Indian subcontinent, and parts of Europe and Africa, they were thought to dwell in caves and springs, trees and groves, or other salient features of the physical world. The gods of the Middle East's Fertile Crescent inhabited such places as well, but they were believed to prefer heights. These deities could best be accessed in high places such as mountaintops, and they were thought to take pleasure in humans' efforts to replicate them in symbolic cosmic mountains like ziggurats or pyramids. The places touched by the gods were also places where the gods could be touched. These places were sacred, in Mircea Eliade's sense that they manifested themselves as "something wholly different from the profane." Such places were simultaneously in this world and not of this world, since through the worshiper's belief their "immediate reality was transmuted into a supernatural reality."[2]

These deities took responsibility for the welfare of both the tribe as a collective and of the individuals constituting the tribal community. Their prevailing relationship to the tribe tended to be transactional: do this for me so that I will do that for you. They demanded fealty, devotion, and commitment expressed cyclically in both tangible and intangible ways. They required ceremonies of worship: daily, weekly, annually, and at key moments in the agricultural and the human life cycles. They demanded adherence to strict codes of behavior and to god-given precepts. The deities had to be lodged, generally in temples and shrines, and their dwellings or places of sojourn required ornamentation commensurate with their dignity and their worshipers' ability to contribute. They had to be nourished with both food and drink. They expected constant gifts, expressions of thanks for providing the necessities of life. Humans brought them the best of the flocks, the best of the fields, the best of the orchards. And, in some cases, the gods demanded the most heartfelt of sacrifices: human blood.

The pre-Davidic history of Judaism, as recorded in the Bible and glossed in the Jewish written and oral traditions, draws deeply from the surrounding religious matrix, as do its ideas about holy places and pilgrimage.[3] While purporting to relate stories of a succession of real individuals experiencing actual events in the literal geography of the Middle East, the narration also reveals the evolution of a nascent religious culture and the emergence of its theology, its modes of worship, and its moral code. Its binding theme is the interrelationship between a unitary, intangible, omnipresent deity and the community that worships that deity, including the rights and responsibilities of each individual.

Inherent in these narrations are some fundamental contradictions with regard to the nature of the deity, the definition of holiness, and the meaning of sacred place. If there is but one God, why command the Israelites to put no other gods before him (Ex. 20:3)? If that God is truly omnipresent, why are some places more holy than others? If God is intangible and everywhere, why does Jewish tradition so often localize him in a burning bush, an ark, a mountaintop, or a particular temple or shrine? Once God's presence has been manifest in a place, does holiness continue to adhere to that place? Must a holy place be as concrete and limited as a specific temple, or may it include the entire land? If God is approachable everywhere through prayer, why is prayer in some places thought to be more efficacious than in others? If God is always listening, why are certain dates thought to facilitate special access?

The traditional narrations of Judaism's foundation myths did not ignore these issues. The stories were written, many centuries after the presumed facts, from the perspective of theocratic monarchists who had a stake in and were committed to the concept of a unique, united Jewish people worshiping a single, unique God. Thus throughout the stories one notes a systematic distancing of the Jewish concepts of these matters from the other religious cultures of the Middle East. The postulation of the God of the Jews as the mightiest of many deities gradually gave way to that of a unitary deity, who does not have to be better than the others because there are no others. The notion of a God manifest in specific locations, one whose physical presence can be seen and heard and felt, one whose power emanates from some particular place or artifact, gradually ceded to the concepts of divine intangibility and omnipresence.

Even so, the ancient contradictions remain. Despite Judaism's generally held belief in God's omnipresence, many Jews revere certain places as holy and go on pilgrimage to those places. Special things are thought to happen at the sacred sites. In this chapter we will look at how the earliest Jewish holy places acquired their special cachet, what set them apart from the holy places of their neighbors, and how the paradigms of Jewish pilgrimage and the rules of how one is to behave at holy sites were established.

THE ARCHETYPES

ADAM

Many of the Bible's earliest stories—Adam, Noah, Abraham, Moses—are about travelers. Although the journeys they undertake differ greatly in their particulars, they exhibit some common themes that reflect the writers' fundamental notions about how God's designs for the Jews are bound up with the idea of holy place. Initially that holy place is Paradise, the Garden of Eden into which God set the new human beings. In its every detail Eden reflects the harmonious coexistence of all of God's creation. Yet its very perfection is oppressive, for it requires its human inhabitants to perfectly obey all of God's mandates. When they falter, as inevitably they must, the perfect world that houses them shatters. They are given the boot, thrust out on the road, condemned to wander. Though the consequences of exile are bleak for human kind, they are lightened by the fact that inherent in expulsion is the hope of return. Seen in this fashion, the wanderings of the children of Adam play out the three phases of the archetypal pilgrimage in reverse. It is not the classic leaving home → traveling to the holy place → and returning home, but rather it is exile from the holy place → wandering the paths of the world → returning to the holy place. This model of exile and return as reverse pilgrimage has asserted itself time and time again in Jewish philosophy and history.

NOAH

After seeing the mess that Adam and Eve and their children have made of the created world, God decides to start over. At God's command, Noah constructs an ark, gathers into it the procreative pairs of all living things, and floats off on the waters of the flood. No oars. No sail. Noah is clueless both about where they are going and how long the voyage will take. The destination and duration are chosen, but not by humankind. The choices represent humanity's best interests as determined by the closemouthed deity. The voyage to Mount Ararat is not a pilgrimage, but it establishes the parameters of the second archetype: God chooses special places and directs us there for reasons that, though veiled, are in our best interest. For Judaism this second archetype—wandering toward a holy place chosen by God—has been as potent a model as that of the pilgrimage of exile and return.

ABRAHAM

Tradition holds that Judaism actually begins with Abraham. An ancient exegetical current, reflected in the Christian Bible's Book of Hebrews (11:8–10), considers Abraham's long journey from Ur to Israel to be a pilgrimage, and that Abraham's Jewishness begins not with his self-circumcision but rather when he follows God's commandment to "go from your country and your kindred and your father's house to the land that I will show you" (Gen. 12:1), that is, to become a pilgrim making aliyah to Israel.[4] His was a transactional pilgrimage in reverse: not the supplicant's offering a pilgrimage, hoping God might grant his request, but God's making a promise and then requiring Abraham to undertake the journey in order to claim his reward.

The Bible suggests that Abraham follows a route in accord with two principles, one his and the other, God's. As head of a nomadic shepherd tribe, Abraham needs to find safe pasturage, leading him to establish his camps in the rural areas between cities like Bethel and Ai (Gen. 12:8). But, like Noah, Abraham's wanderings are not random, even though the long route from Ur to Haran to Canaan to Egypt and back to Canaan might have seemed so to him. The Bible relates that God's plan, reinforced through frequent apparitions, visions, and dreams, impels Abraham toward the place that God promised would be a homeland for him and his descendants (Gen. 12:7; 15:18). Along the way, Abraham seems to have avoided the urban cult centers of the sedentary nations[5] while expressing his devotion and keeping open the channels of communication with his deity by building stone altars at Shechem (Gen. 12:7), Ai/Bethel (Gen. 12:8, 13:4), and the oaks of Mamre at Hebron (Gen. 13:18, 18:1).

The key event in the Abraham saga, the encounter with God that confirms Judaism's rejection of the Middle Eastern traditions of human sacrifice,[6] is Abraham's willingness to sacrifice Isaac at God's command and God's providing a ram to be offered in his stead. Genesis does not identify with precision the site where this happens, stating only that it is a mountaintop in the land of Moriah, a three-day walk from Beersheba (Gen. 22:2–4). Abraham himself calls the site Adonai-Yireh, the mountain where "God is seen," a name that has persisted until this day (Gen. 22:14); the place is traditionally identified as Mount Moriah.[7] Some scholars speculate that this site, on one of the highest crests in the Judean Hills, with a relatively unrestricted view to both the coastal plain and the Dead Sea rift, must have already been venerated as a sacred place. Regardless, the logic of the biblical story is clear: Moriah became holy by being selected by God for this seminal event. It was there that Abraham's supreme gift of faithful obedience elicited the repetition of Judaism's fundamental covenant: "*Because* you have done this . . . I will indeed bless you, and I will make your offspring as numerous as the stars of heaven. . . . [A]nd by your offspring shall all the nations of the earth gain blessing for themselves, *because* you have obeyed my voice" (Gen. 22:16–18; italics ours).

Moses

The next great pilgrimage is the migration story of Exodus. It combines the archetype of the pilgrimage of exile and return, and the collective wandering pilgrimage of a people toward an unrevealed place of holiness designated by God. It is also, like Abraham's wanderings, a transactional pilgrimage in reverse. The story also encompasses Victor and Edith Turner's three phases of pilgrimage. The Israelites remove themselves from their everyday milieu in Egypt; they undergo a liminal or threshold stage when they encounter their God at Sinai in an experience clearly separated from the mundane; and they reaggregate themselves to normal life through an act of return. In this case, however, they return not to their place of departure but to the land long ago promised to Abraham.[8] This is the third archetype: Israel gathered from exile and guided by God-managed destiny in a pilgrimage of return.[9]

Curiously, none of theses stories leads to the creation of a sacred geography that might be retraced in pilgrimage. Exodus 12–14 and Numbers 33 purport to record the route by which Moses and the Israelites wandered from Egypt to the Promised Land, but many of the place names have an ambiguous relation to identifiable modern locales.[10] The Bible is imprecise with regard to the location of the burning bush. Likewise, it is vague about the location of the many miracles detailed in the book of Exodus (4:3–4, 4:6–7, 15:25, 16:4). Imprecise, too, is the location where the song of thanksgiving was chanted on the eastern shore of the Red Sea (Ex. 15:1–21) or where Moses erected a stone altar after the victory over Amalek (Ex. 17:15). Even the exact location of the mountain on which God gave Moses the law is a mystery to Jews, although Christian tradition, as early as the fourth century, asserts that the bush burned on the lower slopes of Jebel Musa, which it identifies as Mount Sinai, and that the tablets of the law were presented to Moses on that mountaintop. Since then, Saint Catherine's monastery in Sinai, which serves the two holy locales, has attracted steady small streams of intrepid Christian pilgrims.

While the Exodus saga minimizes the importance of the route, it presents a coherent view of the nature of sacred space. Moses's ongoing dialog with God runs through most of the book of Exodus, and the conversations take place almost anywhere. However, at certain times the apparition of the deity is so dramatic that it creates a holy place and establishes protocols of behavior that have become fundamental to the Jewish concept of sacred space. One such appearance is in the burning bush on Mount Horeb (Ex. 3:2–4:17). Another is the summit of Sinai, when God instructs Moses in the law (Ex. 19–23). The Bible is unambiguous in its assertion that the place of apparition is holy and that its holiness must be acknowledged and respected. God instructs Moses to remove his shoes before the burning bush (Ex. 3:5). He warns him not to approach too closely (Ex. 3:5), just as the Israelites camped at the foot of Mount Sinai are warned not to ascend the mountain or even to touch a boulder at its foot, under pain of death (Ex. 19:12–13). Its holiness must not be defiled by women or by a man who has had recent intercourse with a woman (Ex. 19:15). In this, the authors of the Bible portrayed Sinai as a proto-Temple. It is the high, majestic residence of God. It cannot be approached by ordinary folk, but requires that experience of the divine be mediated by a special someone who acts for and communicates to the group. The mediator, as is the case with anyone who would approach the deity, must undergo purification rites such as cleansing, refraining from sexual activity, and removing shoes.[11]

The Israelites of Exodus seem to have required constant physical reminders that their God accompanied them on their journey to look out for them. In the later part of Exodus, the Ark, or Tabernacle, is the locus of God's physical presence. It is built at God's express command and with precise detailed instructions as "a sanctuary, so that I may dwell among them" (Ex. 25:8). God's home on wheels is both holy and awe inducing. The Shechinah, the divine presence, manifest in the tablets of the law, requires layers of shielding—an Ark cover, a tent, a screen, curtains, railings—so that it may not be viewed directly or even approached too closely. Unlike the majority of Middle Eastern gods who were thought to be portrayed or even to reside in carved or cast images, the Israelites' deity is invisible and takes great care to insure that his presence is perceived without being seen. Thus he resides as a fire by night in the Tabernacle, which he envelops with the same luminous cloud that had covered Mount Sinai (Ex. 24:16–18). As always, God's presence requires his worshipers to keep a respectful distance. While the Tabernacle sits in the tribal council tent, the glowing cloud of God's glory envelops the tent and no one, not even Moses, can enter. The Ark seems to function in this period as a portable Sinai, a device by which the Israelites can make certain that the Shechinah travels with them as their guide, their protector, and their arbiter of correct behavior. It accompanies them in battle as a kind of talisman. No matter where they wander, the Tabernacle provides a vehicle for communication with the deity, almost like a kind of transcendent cell phone.

HOLY SITES OF THE SETTLING IN

In the dry, scrub-covered landscape of the Near Eastern tribal migrations, the occasional oasis or freestanding tree indicated the presence of water and confirmed people's faith in the proclivity of their deities to provide life-giving sustenance. In the pre-Israelite Mesopotamian cultures, trees appeared frequently as fertility symbols, and the tradition persisted into the classical age in the association of certain trees with the deities of fertility, such as the Phoenician and Greek consecration of cypress trees to Astarte.[12] To the early Israelites as well, trees and groves of trees were landmarks that projected holiness (Gen. 35:4, Deut. 11:30). They were places suitable for divine contact, as when Abraham received his angelic visitors under the oaks of Mamre (Gen. 18:1–2), where he had previously erected an altar (Gen. 13:18). Sacred trees could be places of assembly and judgment (Jud. 4:5, 9:6; Josh. 24:26), of oracle (Gen. 12:6;[13] Jud. 6:11, 9:37), or of burial (Gen. 35:8). To plant a tree in commemoration of an event, as did Abraham at Beersheba to seal his covenant with Abimelech (Gen. 21:33; Jud. 9:6), was an act of holiness. None of these practices seems to have been unique to the wandering Israelites, who most likely were echoing the attitudes and customs of their neighbors.

During the long migrations the Israelites often erected commemorative stelae, sometimes referred to as altars, as witnesses to important events. Moses built one after Joshua's defeat of Amalek (Ex. 17:15), and commanded that another be erected on Mount Ebal to record the details of God's law (Deut. 27:2–8; Josh. 8:30–32). The men of Reuben, Gad, and Manasseh commemorated their entry into Canaan with one (Josh. 22:10). Joshua built one to record his covenant with the tribes to stop worshiping foreign gods (Josh. 24:26). Their mode of construction and their often multiple purposes are detailed in the book of Joshua:

> Then Joshua built on Mount Ebal an altar to the Lord, the God of Israel, . . . "an altar of unhewn stones, on which no iron tool has been used" [i.e., their natural, unmediated appearance differentiated them from the carved idols of the neighboring peoples]; and they offered on it burnt offerings to the Lord, and sacrificed offerings of well-being. And there, in the presence of the Israelites, Joshua wrote on the stones a copy of the law of Moses. (Josh. 8:30–32)

In the desert it had been impractical for the wandering Israelites to think about constructing anything as grand as a permanent temple, or even a modest shrine, in which to worship their God. The best they could do was construct makeshift altars on which to offer their sacrifices. These altars might be used only once in passing, such as the one at which Jacob sacrificed in the mountains of Galeed (Gen. 31:54). Others might be reused during seasonal migrations, such as the altar between Bethel and Ai that Abraham revisited as he traveled south (Gen. 13:4), and the ones built by his son Isaac at Beersheba (Gen. 26:25) and his grandson Jacob at Shechem (Gen. 33:20).

They also used stone pillars to mark important graves—as is the case with Rachel (Gen. 35:19–20; 1 Sam. 10:2)—and eventually these too became important places of pilgrimage. The Bible distinguishes these grave markers from the stelae at the high places, called *bamot*, where the local pre-Israelite inhabitants of the land often worshiped (examples have been excavated at Megiddo, Gezer, and Taanach). For these peoples the cultic stone pillars, which the Bible terms *matzevot*, seem to have been male fertility symbols associated with Baal (2 Kings 3:2, 10:26). Wooden pillars, called *asherim* (1 Kings 14:23) or *asherot* (Jud. 6:25), appear to have represented a fertility goddess who was the consort of Baal (Jud. 3:7, 6:26; 2 Kings 23:4). Eventually, as the Israelites settled onto the land and became prosperous, they erected many more of these pillars and stone altars (Ex. 34:13; Deut. 7:5, 12:2–3; 1 Kings 14:23), either in imitation of their migrating ancestors or as an appropriation of the religious customs of their neighbors (Hos. 10:1; Mic. 5:12). It is not surprising that later, when the religion of the Israelites was being codified and formally distinguished from those of their neighbors, both the erection of altar stelae and the worship of—or at—trees were condemned as Canaanite practices (Hos. 4:13; Jer. 2:20, 3:6).[14]

Canaanite altar. Megiddo. Photo, Tim Bulkeley, University of Auckland Carey Baptist College (http://www.bigbible.org). http://www.ebibletools .com/Israel/Megiddo/DCP_0846.html. Used by permission.

PRE-JERUSALEM SHRINES

Once the Israelite tribes had wrested enough land from their agricultural neighbors to settle down and begin their own process of becoming an agricultural nation, their God settled in with them.

The Israelites who grazed their flocks and tilled the soil from the lush valleys of Galilee to the dry rolling hills around Beersheba, from the edges of the fertile coastal plain to the hardscrabble slopes of the central mountains, constituted a loose confederation of often fiercely competitive tribes. They worshiped the same God, but they rendered cult to him in different holy places, and they often fell prey to the temptation to worship the gods of their neighbors in addition to their own. This was the case with the violent, irresponsible actions of the tribe of Dan that established itself in the hill country of Ephraim in the northern Galilee. Judges 17–18 narrates a cautionary tale of how *not* to establish a place of worship. Micah stole silver from his mother and used a portion of it to cast an image. Acting wholly on his own, Micah put it in a House of God, set up his own son as priest, and hired a passing Levite to tend the altar. When the army of Dan swept through, they took Micah's household gods and his Levite and, after slaughtering the peaceful people of Laish, installed both gods and Levite in the temple in their new city. The Bible indicates that the heinous nature of this act was compounded by the fact that at the time the true House of God was located in Shiloh. Eventually the Danites set a statue of a bull, representing Baal, in their shrine, and the secessionist king Jeroboam made the village of Dan one of his two northern sanctuaries. Dan's temple seems to have functioned as a cult site, and most likely a pilgrimage center, until Tiglath-pileser III conquered the Galilee in circa 733 BCE and exiled its Israelite population to Assyria (2 Kings 15:29).

Shechem, high in the northern hill country, was a major Canaanite sanctuary, with a temple to El (or Ba'al Brit) in the city's fortified citadel (Jud. 9:46) and another worship site in a grove of oaks, or terebinths,[15] outside of town (Jud. 9:6). Israelite tradition held that Abraham had stopped at Shechem's holy place and, after having been granted a vision in which YHWH promised him the land of Canaan, erected an altar to his God (Gen. 12:6–7). Thus he complied with the archetypal conditions for the establishment of a sanctuary: a preexisting holy site, a manifestation of God's presence (theophany), a divine message, and the beginning of the cult.[16] Jacob, returning from Mesopotamia, set up camp at Shechem and purchased a plot of land on which to erect an altar stele (Gen. 33:18–20). Later he symbolically transformed his household's polytheistic worship to allegiance to the one God YHWH by having them bury the statues of their foreign gods under the terebinth of Shechem (Gen. 35:4). Legend also held that Joseph's bones were interred there when they were brought back from Egypt (Josh. 24:32). Shechem's citadel sanctuary remained in Canaanite hands and with its emphasis on fertility and divine support of agriculture[17] exerted no small attraction to the Israelite settlers (Jud. 8:33).

Joshua appropriated the oak grove for YHWH. He assembled the Israelites there and put up a stele engraved with the key points of God's law, including the injunction to "put away the foreign gods that are among you, and incline your hearts to the Lord, the God of Israel" (Josh. 24:23). Despite the monarchy's later attempts to centralize temple worship in Jerusalem, when the kingdoms split after Solomon's death, the sanctuary at Shechem gained prominence again as the cultic and political center of the northern tribes (1 Kings 12:1, 25).

Bethel, eighteen kilometers north of Jerusalem on the road to Shechem, was another noted cult site presumably of pre-Israelite origin. Abraham had built an altar near there to commemorate God's promise to assign him that land (Gen. 12:7); and Jacob, camping one night at a *maqom*, or holy place, dreamed of a stairway to heaven and in the morning erected a stone pillar there to give thanks to God for appearing to him at this House of God (Hebrew, *Beth-el*; Gen. 28:18, 35:1–7). This is probably the reason why in later years the Ark of the Covenant was housed there (Jud. 20:27), which in turn was why Bethel became a place of assembly, as when the eleven tribes rallied against Benjamin (Jud. 21:2). At this time it also functioned as a pilgrimage center (1 Sam. 10:3). As is the case with Shechem, when the monarchy split Bethel again rose to prominence.

Several other holy sites of this period are alluded to in the Bible.[18] Almost exclusively, these are places where things happened rather than grave sites. The place in Beersheba where Samuel's sons Joel and Abijah judged Israel was most likely a preexisting shrine (1 Sam. 8:2), probably in the place believed to be where Abraham had planted a tamarisk tree and built an altar (Gen. 21:33, 26:25),[19] and where Isaac, receiving confirmation of the promise made to his father, either rebuilt the ancient altar or erected a new one (Gen. 26:23–25). By the prophet Amos's time, in the mid-eighth century BCE, Beersheba had become a pilgrimage center (Amos 5:4, 8:14). The holy site of Mizpah was an assembly place for the tribes mustering for war against Benjamin (Jud. 20:1–3), for swearing oaths (Jud.

21:1, 5), and for judging (1 Sam. 8:1–2), and its altar of sacrifice (1 Sam. 7:5–12) undoubtedly attracted pilgrims. Gideon's homeland at Ophrah, with its ancient holy oak tree marking the place where he received an apparition and a promise and where he then built an altar, was undoubtedly another holy site (Jud. 6–9). So, too, was Ramah, where Rachel wept for her children (Jer. 31:15) and where Samuel sat in judgment (1 Sam. 10:2, 7:17).

There was a holy site in Hebron, where David was anointed king and where he made a covenant with Israel before the Lord (2 Sam. 2:4, 5:3), and where Absalom paid the vow he had made in Geshur (2 Sam. 15:7). Before the establishment of the Temple in Jerusalem, Jesse's family seems to have visited a holy site in Bethlehem to make its annual sacrifice (1 Sam. 20:6). The shrine at Nob, presided over by Ahimelech, housed Goliath's sword, carefully wrapped in cloth and stored behind the temple's ephod as if it were a holy relic (1 Sam. 21:1–10). There may also have been an ancient Israelite holy place on the summit of 600-meter-high Mount Carmel, given that Elisha was to be visited there (2 Kings 4:25) and Elijah summoned all of Israel to join him there to witness YHWH's defeat of the pagan gods (1 Kings 18:19).[20]

Gilgal, in the vicinity of Jericho, was probably originally a Canaanite open-air shrine marked by a circle of stones.[21] In addition to serving Joshua as a base camp for his campaign against Jericho (Josh. 6:11, 9:6), it was rendered holy for the Israelites by the presence of the Ark (Josh. 4:18–19, 6:6). Thus it was an ideal place for the covenant with God to be reaffirmed by circumcising the men who had wandered in the desert (Josh. 5:2–9) and for the first Passover to be celebrated (Josh. 5:10–12). Although Gilgal seems to have been frequented originally by the tribes of Ephraim and Benjamin, by Samuel's day it was in common use by all the tribes, making it a suitable place for Samuel to judge and for Saul to be proclaimed king of Israel (1 Sam. 11:15). By the time of the prophets of the eighth century, Gilgal, together with Bethel, was well-known as a place of pilgrimage, and was condemned by the prophets as an affront to the one true Temple in Jerusalem (Hos. 4:15, 9:15, 12:12; Amos 4:4, 5:5).

The most important Israelite shrine during the period of the judges seems to have been at Shiloh in the territory of Ephraim. Joshua assembled the tribes there to divide the newly conquered territories among them (Josh. 18:1). At some point the Ark of the Covenant that the wandering tribes had carried north out of Sinai was deposited in Shiloh (1 Sam. 4:3), which may be why that by the times of the judges, Shiloh was known as the locus of the one true house of the incorporeal God (1 Sam. 18:31). It was a place of oracle (1 Sam. 1:17). It hosted a popular autumn festival (Jud. 21:19–21). Its preeminence was noted by the psalmist who wrote that the Jews' sporadic recurrence to idol worship so angered God that "He abandoned his dwelling at Shiloh, the tent where he dwelt among mortals" (Ps. 78:60).

Of all the pre-Jerusalem shrines, Shiloh is the one we know the most about. Archaeologists have found cult artifacts there from the period of Israelite settlement in the twelfth century BCE that indicate Shiloh was a center of polytheistic worship.[22] Nonetheless, the biblical redactors portray it as a site important to Israelite monotheism and to the establishment of the monarchy. The opening chapter of 1 Samuel, for example, sets the key events of Samuel's birth at the shrine in Shiloh.

Local Israelites were expected to come to the shrine at least once a year to worship and presumably to pay some sort of shrine-maintenance fee. People might come at other times to ask God for help. Although some worshipers may have journeyed to the shrine alone, others brought their entire households. First Samuel 1 narrates how Elkanah had for a long time brought his household to the shrine annually and how, on this specific occasion that was independent of the annual cycle, he journeyed there with his wife Hannah to ask God to relieve her barrenness.[23] He also brought his wife Peninnah together with all her sons and daughters. Since the family stayed overnight, it seems likely that they brought tents with them to house their substantial numbers. The shrine seems to have been a solidly constructed building, perhaps the first temple of the Lord that the Israelites erected in their new land. Inside it was furnished with chairs or benches (1 Sam. 1:9). A stout door was shut tight at night and opened in the morning to worshipers (1 Sam. 3:15). Three priests, Eli and his sons Hophni and Phinehas, staffed the shrine, suggesting that shrine maintenance was a hereditary occupation. The chapter calls them *cohanim*, the word designating the descendants of Aaron who constituted the priestly caste. A building that screened the temple's holiest space and a resident priesthood to attend the deity and mediate the religious experience for the visiting worshipers were common in the religions of the agricultural peoples of the region.

Shiloh's central rite was animal sacrifice. Suppliants generally brought an appropriate animal with them.[24] The petitioner slaughtered the animal on the shrine's altar with the assistance of the priests. Some portion of the sacrifice was donated to the shrine's administration (1 Sam. 2:13–14), and these donations undoubtedly provided an important resource for maintaining the shrine's staff. The rest of the animal was distributed among the petitioners' family, who cooked and consumed it, evidently washing it down with great quantities of fermented beverage. These post-sacrifice feasts at Shiloh were joyous occasions with singing and dancing,[25] a party where teenagers might get to know one another and where marriages within or between tribes might be arranged (Jud. 21:21). Although the festivities might sometimes get out of hand, priests expected worshipers to behave decorously at the shrine. When Hannah prayed silently to God to grant her a son, Eli reproved her because he thought she was drunk, and then, when he learned the reason for her odd behavior, comforted her by reassuring her that God would heed her request.

First Samuel 1 also communicates a sense of the rules governing petitions. For maximum effect they required the petitioner to make pilgrimage to a holy place. The petition could be lodged only after normal worship activities had taken place, including animal sacrifice and donation of the appropriate portion to the temple administration. The petition could be buttressed with a vow in which the petitioner promised something contingent on the request's being granted: "if . . . [you] will give to your servant a male child, then I will set him before you as a nazirite until the day of his death. He shall drink neither wine nor intoxicants, and no razor shall touch his head" (1 Sam. 1:11). And the *quid* had to be followed up by the *pro quo*: "For this child I prayed; and the Lord has granted me the petition that I made to him. Therefore I have lent him to the Lord; as long as he lives, he is given to the Lord" (1 Sam. 1:27–28).

The Ark of the Covenant was a key to Shiloh's potency as a holy place. The deity who granted Hannah's petition was believed to reside physically in some way in the Ark inside the shrine at Shiloh. Pilgrims journeyed to visit him there. The Ark was an agent of power and protection. Thus when the Israelite fighters were losing to the Philistine armies, the elders suggested, "Let us bring the ark of the covenant of the Lord here from Shiloh, so that he may come among us and save us from the power of our enemies" (1 Sam. 4:3). The Philistines reasoned that if the Israelites' Ark were removed, presumably their God, too, would be absent. This is precisely what happened next. Philistines killed two of Shiloh's priests and made off with the Ark, with the result that "the glory has departed from Israel" (1 Sam. 4:21–22). Enraged, the Israelites' God quickly expressed his anger, his vengefulness, and his preeminence among the region's other deities. When the Philistines set the Ark in their main temple in Ashdod next to an idol of their principal god, Dagon, the Israelite God knocked down the idol and the next day cut off its hands and head. He then massacred the Philistines with a plague of tumors.

The Philistines' solution? Get rid of the Ark. They tried sending it to Gath, but the plague followed the gift. They carried it to Ekron, but the Ekronites clamored to have it sent back to the Jews, which, after seven months of debate and bureaucratic delay, they did, trundling it into the hills on a cart weighed down with jewels and golden figures. The Jews in Beth-Shemesh, overjoyed to see the Ark, built an impromptu altar and offered sacrifices of thanksgiving. God's response? Slay 50,000 men of Beth-Shemesh for the sacrilege of looking at the Ark. Not surprisingly, the people of Beth-Shemesh shed themselves of the Ark as quickly as they could, dispatching it to Kiriath-jearim, where under Samuel's orders it was stashed in the house of Abinadab for the next twenty years. The citizenry of Israel begged for access, but Samuel required that first they cease worshiping Ashtaroth and Baalim, the gods of their neighbors.

The message, and its implications for the Jewish traditions of pilgrimage, could not have been clearer. Israel's God was conceived as a monarch. He required a physical home. He demanded that his people protect that home and devote themselves exclusively to him with the proper respect. If they could not or would not do so, he denied them access to his person and his blessings. He brooked no comparisons. He was supreme among the gods, and in that way unique, and was prepared to lash out in violence at any encroachment on his prerogatives. If the Jewish people were to prosper, they had to find him a permanent home, adorn it according to his merit, and come to visit him at appropriate times. If they wanted something from him, they had to couch their petitions as transactions, offering fealty, devotion, and gifts, either in advance, as offerings, or upon delivery of the favor, as in the payment of a vow.

Jerusalem was calling.

JERUSALEM, THE STATE CULT, AND THE THREE HARVEST PILGRIMAGES

Countless multitudes from countless cities come, some over land, others over sea, from east and west and north and south at every feast. (Philo Judaeus of Alexandria, circa 40 CE)[1]

Oh send out thy light and thy truth; let them lead me, let them bring me to thy holy hill and to thy dwelling! (Psalms 43:3)

For the last three millennia, the number one pilgrimage destination for Jews has been Jerusalem. Jerusalem's preeminence in the heart of the Jewish people cannot be overestimated. Many believe that it is the mythical locus of the first solid ground created by God (BT Yoma 54a), the place where God scooped up the dust to make Adam,[2] the point from which Noah's flood began to flow and from which the earth's waters are controlled (BT Sukkah 53b; Psalms 29:10). It is a traditional site of Abraham's offering of Isaac in sacrifice, and of Jacob's dream.[3] Both as the sum of these pre-historical events, and as the historical city of David and Solomon, Jerusalem evokes Judaism's glorious past and the Israelites' evolution from nomadic herders to a settled agricultural nation. Because it was the promised reward for Israel's keeping God's new covenant (Jer. 31:31, 4:38), Jerusalem is fundamental to the concept of the Jews as the chosen people. Throughout the Bible the city is used repeatedly as a synonym for Zion, Israel, the Jewish nation, and the Jewish people.

As the symbolic mother of Israel, Jerusalem weeps at her children's misfortunes in exile and will rejoice at their return (Isaiah 65:19, 66:10–13). As the presumed locus of God's righteous kingdom on earth after the ingathering of Jews from the Diaspora, it represents what Joseph Dan terms the "eternal future utopia," the place of both individual and national redemption. As a privileged touch point between the human and the divine, it is the focus of Jews' yearning for renewed direct contact with their creator and the ecstatic joy of mystical communication with the divine. For traditional Judaism the world revolves around Jerusalem; it is the Jews' *axis mundi*[4]: "Thus says the Lord God: 'This is Jerusalem; I have set her in the center of the nations, with countries all around her'" (Ez. 5:5).[5] Jewish tradition holds that the earthly city of Jerusalem is so beloved by God that it is the model for the heavenly Jerusalem.[6]

But it was not always so.

During the 1,000 years between Solomon's opening the Temple doors and Rome's razing them, Israelites from near and far made pilgrimage to Jerusalem to offer their sacrifices at Judaism's holiest place. This chapter looks at how Jerusalem rose to such importance, how pilgrimages were formalized through legislation, and how the agricultural festivals became rites of nationhood. It reconstructs what it must have been like to be a pilgrim bringing offerings to Jerusalem for the three harvest festivals, the Shalosh Regalim.

DAVID AND SOLOMON

David's vision of a religious nation-state was shaped by the political and religious environment in which he found himself. David's new nation would thus require a capital city, a monarch, and a formal state religion identified with and defended by the monarchy. God's Shechinah had traveled with the Ark that the tribes brought north with them from Sinai. When the Ark ended up in Abinadab's house in Kiriath-jearim, it sat for two decades. Jewish nationhood probably began with David's decision to bring the Ark from there to Jerusalem. Second Samuel chapter six describes in colorful detail the procession and the installation of the Ark. David gathered 30,000 men (the number is probably a hyperbole for "many") in front of Abinadab's house on the hill at Kiriath-jearim. Abinadab's two sons placed the Ark ceremonially on a brand new cart and started off for Jerusalem, led by marching musicians. An unfortunate incident along the way interrupted the process, but eventually David brought the Ark into the city with joy, "with shouting, and with the sound of the trumpet." The king himself led the procession, leaping and dancing all the way. They installed the Ark in a tent that David had pitched for it, and the king distributed sweet cakes to everyone.

Once David had brought the Israelites' God symbolically—or perhaps the people thought literally—into his city, he had taken an important step toward making Jerusalem the center of the Israelite world. Nonetheless, David had to deal with the fact that the population of the Jebusite city he had taken over was religiously and ethnically mixed, conditions which continued at least into Solomon's day. Moreover, Israelite tribal loyalties and reliance on the supernatural powers of regional shrines were still strong. Rather than trying to restrict the city to an exclusively Israelite polity and religion, David attempted a policy of pluralism and synthesis. He appointed two priestly families as the keepers of the national sanctuaries: Abiathar, an old ally related to the priestly family of Eli at Shiloh, and Zadok, who may well have been head priest of the Jebusites before David's takeover. The so-called "threshing floor" that the Bible says David purchased from

Araunah the Jebusite (1 Chron. 21:22) was likely the site of the Jebusite temple that David's party reappropriated for the worship of YHWH.[7]

Solomon followed his father's conservative path of building on local religious traditions. He continued to allow the religious practices of Jerusalem's diverse population of Sidonians, Ammonites, and Moabites (1 Kings 11:5, 11:7, 11:33; 2 Kings 23:13).[8] The new Israelite Temple that Solomon erected (or the Jebusite temple that he enlarged and adorned) was not innovative, but rather followed architectural and conceptual patterns familiar throughout the region. In shape it resembled the longhouse temples common in Syria from the third millennium onward. The lateral walls extended to form a courtyard, separated from the enclosed holy of holies by a sumptuously decorated door. The longhouse was compartmentalized into three chambers that successively restricted access so as to protect the deity from being approached by the common folk or profaned by any impurity.

While David's transference of the Ark from Kiriath-jearim to Jerusalem was a cause for general rejoicing, Solomon's formal installation of the Ark in the new Temple projected the sense of power and gravitas that were appropriate to his sumptuous new palace-Temple. This procession was not composed of 30,000 members of the general populace, but rather a hierarchy of "the elders of Israel, and all the heads of the tribes, the leaders of the ancestral houses of the Israelites" (1 Kings 8:1). Priests and Levites installed the Ark in the Temple's inner throne room. Access for the common people now was to be mediated by the tribal leaders. Solomon himself, the priest-king, prayed on the people's behalf.

David's decision to make Jerusalem his capital and Solomon's creation of the Temple of YHWH changed the nature of Judaism in fundamental ways. For one thing, they institutionalized the links between political and spiritual power in a pattern that was common in the surrounding states. The messages conveyed by both architecture and cult were consistent. The palace and the Temple were physically linked. The priests served the monarchy (2 Sam. 8:17–18), and the monarch himself could function as a priest by making sacrificial offerings in the name of the people (1 Kings 8:62). The combined efforts of David and Solomon to centralize worship, political power, and military might in Jerusalem were designed to counteract the centrifugal forces inherent in the scattered geography and the individual clan traditions of the Jewish tribes. Fixing the cult center in Jerusalem helped undermine the pilgrimages to local deities and weaken the tithe-collecting abilities of regional shrines at places like Shiloh and Shechem. It helped legitimize the monarchy by associating it with the presence of the divine essence in the monarch's city, which became then, by definition, holy.

This in theory; in practice, the center could not hold. Solomon's death in 922 BCE precipitated the revolt of the northern tribes that had never fully accepted the centralization of power and cult in Jerusalem. For a while, pilgrimage to Jerusalem from the northern regions, now calling themselves the kingdom of Israel, all but ceased. Still, with the passage of time and the lessening of tensions the pilgrimages resumed. This situation was only barely tolerable to northern monarchs like Israel's secessionist King Jeroboam, who opposed the Jerusalem pilgrimage as a move toward reunification (1 Kings 12:27). Jeroboam's strategy was to attempt to wrest pilgrim traffic from Jerusalem, capital of the southern kingdom of Judah, by building rival temples in Dan and Bethel, adorning them with golden calves,[9] staffing them with his own priests, and dedicating them not to the God of Israel but to the gods who led the Israelites out of Egypt (1 Kings 12:28–30). Apparently unsuccessful in this bid, but still unwilling to throw in the towel, Jeroboam instituted a new festival at Bethel, at a date just after the Jerusalem pilgrimage, so that pilgrims from the northern kingdoms could avoid a having to choose which temple to support and instead could visit both shrines (1 Kings 12:33). During this period Shechem, too, regained prominence as a cultic and political center of the northern tribes (1 Kings 12:1, 25).

Most of what we know of this period comes to us in the words of the later redactors of the Bible, the so-called Deuteronomists, strict YHWH-ists who felt their monotheistic, Jerusalem-centered religion threatened by the attractiveness of the surrounding religious milieu. In numerous ways the Bible they composed testifies to the tension between their single, central, government-endorsed Temple and the Israelites' devotion to local shrines honoring local deities, sometimes even in conjunction with devotion to YHWH. The YHWH-ist reform movement, led by Hosea and Hezekiah toward the end of the eighth century, built a program around the slogan "Hear, O Israel, The Lord [YHWH] is our God, the Lord alone" (Deut. 6:4) to insure the Israelites' exclusive adherence to the YHWH-ist religion and to armor them against dangerous foreign influences. All local sanctuaries were to be abolished. Pilgrimage to the traditional high place shrines was forbidden. Altar stones, the *matzebot* and *asherot* that for hundreds of years had attracted Israelite worshipers, were to be torn down. Tithes had to be paid in Jerusalem alone. Even so, in periods of weak central government, such as the reign of King Manasseh (697–642 BCE), shrines and altars proliferated in the high places and in the groves of Palestine (2 Kings 21:2–3). This provoked outrage among the strict monotheists and the political centralists like Manasseh's grandson King Josiah (640–609 BCE), who according to the account in 2 Kings 23:19–20 destroyed the altars in the high places and groves of sacred trees. Josiah insisted that Jerusalem's Temple could no longer to be merely the first among many. It was to be the one and only, just as Israel's God had evolved from being mightier than the neighboring gods to being uniquely one.

THE THREE PILGRIMAGE FESTIVALS

The three annual agricultural festivals were appropriated by the new state. All three have origins that antedate recorded history, and all were widespread throughout the Middle East. The spring festival for the herders celebrated the birth of the first lambs. After the lambing of the ewes and before setting out for the summer pasturage, each family sacrificed a young lamb and smeared its blood on the family tents as a talisman of protection.[10] The festival served a similar purpose for the farming societies, and in the Bible is called the feast of *matzot* (Ex. 12:17) or unleavened bread. W.O.E. Oesterly and Theodore H. Robinson explain the emphasis on the avoidance of leaven this way:

> Bread was leavened with sour dough, a small piece from each baking being
> left to ferment and used for the next batch. There is thus a continuity in the

successive generations of the bread, and . . . some contamination may be transmitted throughout the year. The ill-effects of this can be avoided only by breaking the chain, and so for the first days during which the new crop is being used leaven is prohibited, being resumed only when the new dough has begun to ferment of itself.[11]

For herders or farmers, the pre-Davidic festival was focused on the home or camp, with only a secondary emphasis, if any, on journeying to an appropriate shrine.

The second event, the early summer festival celebrating the end of the wheat harvest, receives the least attention in the Bible, although it seems to have been observed by the Canaanites even before the Israelite invasion (Jud. 6:25). It was an occasion for feasting and carousing (Jud. 21:19). The last and most important of the three celebrated the successful harvest of fruit and grapes and the end of the agricultural season in early autumn. Evidence suggests that it was truly ancient. Egyptians celebrated a harvest festival as the marriage and death of the vegetation god. The tenth-century BCE Hebrew language agricultural calendar found in 1908 at Gezer documented a grain harvest festival.[12]

We have no precise indication about how the Israelites celebrated the festivals in preexilic times beyond the fact that they made three offerings a year in Jerusalem (1 Kings 9:25), with that of the Feast of Tabernacles being the most important (1 Kings 8:2).[13] It is also unclear when the pilgrimages became mandatory, but the practice was well-established by at least the time of Jeremiah (628–586 BCE), and the pilgrimages proved to be an effective tool in the centralists' drive to concentrate political and religious power in Jerusalem. The Bible clearly laid out the divine authorization for the pilgrimages and their ground rules:

> Three times in the year you shall hold a festival for me. You shall observe the festival of unleavened bread; as I commanded you, you shall eat unleavened bread for seven days at the appointed time in the month of Abib, for in it you came out of Egypt. No one shall appear before me empty-handed. You shall observe the festival of harvest, of the first fruits of your labor, of what you sow in the field. You shall observe the festival of ingathering at the end of the year, when you gather in from the field the fruit of your labor. Three times in the year all your males shall appear[14] before the Lord God. (Ex. 23:14–17)

The three times are specified in Deut. 16:16 as Passover, Shavu'ot, and Sukkot. This simple injunction introduced the key elements that characterized Judaism's annual pilgrimages. The pilgrimages were mandatory, but the mandate applied only to males.[15] They required a personal appearance in Jerusalem (i.e., at the Temple, "before the Lord God"). They were pegged to key moments of the agricultural cycle. They required pilgrims to bring a portion of their harvest with them as a gift for the Temple, and this tithe, or tax, was to be "the choicest first-fruits of your ground" (Ex. 23:19). Moreover, they provided three celebratory festivals each year in which the tribes could get to know each other, to forge friendships, and to amalgamate their diverse customs.

As the reference to the departure from Egypt indicates, by the time Exodus 23 was written the three pilgrimage festivals had come to have important symbolic as well as practical functions. They recalled the myths of tribal migrations and the Israelites' evolution from a nomadic pastoral people, who propitiated their deity and assured his blessing with a sacrifice of the firstborn of their flocks, to a sedentary agricultural people contributing a portion of their early harvest of grain and fruit to the Temple. In time the ancient spring festival of matzot, with its offerings of young lambs and sheaves of the first cut barley, became an occasion for recounting the events of the exodus from Egypt. Shavu'ot, the festival of the wheat harvest seven weeks after Passover, came to recall the forty-year period of wandering in the desert. And, Sukkot, in early autumn, when the first fruits and grapes were gathered, commemorated God's giving the Law to Moses at Mount Sinai.

THE BABYLONIAN HIATUS

The destruction of Solomon's Temple in 586 BCE, together with the relocation of a sizable portion of the Jewish people to Babylonia, rendered impossible strict adherence to the traditional Temple-centered cult or to the three annual pilgrimages. Compliance with the Law required shifts in emphasis that created institutions and established new patterns of thought and behavior. These, in turn, influenced the second, much longer Diaspora that followed the Roman destruction of the Temple in 70 CE, as we will see in the next chapter. Suffice it to note for now that when in 536 BCE Cyrus II permitted the Jews to return and rebuild the Temple, in the prophet Ezra's attempts to revive the ancient customs we can see the imprint of the exiles' emphasis on observances that did not require their physical presence in Jerusalem. For Sukkot the emphasis now fell on spending the seven days of the festival dwelling in booths, emphasizing that part of the festival that did not require bringing grain offerings to Jerusalem. In the disorder that accompanied the half-century of exile the Ark had disappeared, so that Ark-focused observances had to be reshaped to contemporary circumstances. The Babylonian community redirected their religious fervor into study of the Law, an activity that could be carried out anywhere, even becoming part of the normal religious experience in Jerusalem among those who returned from Babylon. By the time of Herod (37–4 BCE), the Diaspora community had multiplied enormously and communal synagogues had taken root all over the Mediterranean and the Middle East. For these late Roman Jews, study of the Law had become so prominent a part of the Jewish pilgrims' experience that a courtyard of the Jerusalem Temple was reserved for this synagogue function.[16]

RESUMPTION OF THE SHALOSH REGALIM AFTER THE BABYLONIAN EXILE

The completion of the Second Temple in 515 BCE and the return to Palestine by a sizable portion of the Babylonian Jewish community permitted a resumption of the ancient pilgrimage practices. Once again the roads of Palestine thronged with worshipers making one or more of the annual treks to Jerusalem to sacrifice, pray, study, and party at the Temple. These practices continued through Persian, Greek,

Hasmonean, and Roman times. It is this half millennium from which we have the most descriptive data and the closer we get to the present the more data we have. In fact, the most vivid descriptions are of pilgrimages to Ezra's Temple as reconstructed by Herod. This is not surprising, given the extent to which the Roman Empire was a record-keeping enterprise and that the seminal events of Christianity occurred in Palestine during this period. The amalgam of sources from that time—the Jewish and Christian Bibles (including the apocryphal books and other contemporary Christian writings), the Talmud, the rabbinical commentaries, the writings of Josephus, Philo of Alexandria, and their Greek and Roman contemporaries—cumulatively give us an idea of what the three pilgrimage festivals, the Shalosh Regalim, were like.

PILGRIM TRAVEL TO JERUSALEM

While the First Temple stood, pilgrims came to Jerusalem from all the lands occupied by the twelve tribes. Although the Bible mandated all males to appear three times each year, the size of the Israelite population and the limited physical spaces of Jerusalem make it very unlikely that this requirement was strictly observed. Instead, it seems probable that while some Israelites made the pilgrimage three times annually, some came once a year, and others only when economic or other circumstances made the trip feasible or when they felt it personally necessary. Much later, those Jews who returned from the Babylonian exile seem to have settled mainly in the area of Jerusalem; for them the festival pilgrimages to the Second Temple involved little more than a day trip and we can surmise a fairly high rate of participation. But not every Mesopotamian Jew elected to return to Palestine. From among those who remained in Babylon, a few hardy souls traveled long distances to participate in the Jerusalem ceremonies. Although it is impossible to calculate with any precision how many pilgrims journeyed to Jerusalem each year in late Second Temple times, it must have been several thousand.[17] It is also clear that even though the halakhic mandate applied only to men, women, too, journeyed to Jerusalem as pilgrims and played an active part in the ceremonies there.

From some nearby areas the majority of the population made the pilgrimage. Josephus, for example, says that when the Roman general Cestius reached Lydda [Lod] he found only fifty people: the rest of the population had gone up to Jerusalem for the Sukkot festival.[18] The catchment area for the pilgrimage was much broader, of course, encompassing not only the various regions of Palestine, but the whole of the Jewish Diaspora. The numbers increased dramatically toward the end of the Second Temple period, due in part to the great increase in the population of Jews in the Diaspora—both émigrés and converts—as well as the relative security for travel that the Roman Empire imposed on the eastern Mediterranean.[19] Contemporary writers like Philo were impressed by the diversity of the crowds.

> [Jerusalem is] the mother city not of one country Judaea but of most of the others in virtue of the colonies sent out at divers times to the neighbouring lands [of] Egypt, Phoenicia, the part of Syria called the Hollow and the rest as well and the lands lying far apart, Pamphylia, Cilicia, most of Asia up to

Bithynia, and the corners of Pontus, similarly also into Europe, Thessaly, Boeotia, Macedonia, Aetolia, Attica, Argos, Corinth, and most of the best parts of Peloponnese. And not only are the mainlands full of Jewish colonies but also the most highly esteemed islands Euboea, Cyprus, Crete.[20]

The writer of the Christian book of Acts, too, marveled at the geographic and linguistic range of the visitors: "[There are] Parthians and Medes and Elamites and residents of Mesopotamia, Judea and Cappadocia, Pontus and Asia, Phrygia and Pamphylia, Egypt and the parts of Libya belonging to Cyrene, and visitors from Rome, both Jews and proselytes, Cretans and Arabians" (Acts 2:9–11). Moreover, the Jerusalem Temple was a magnet not only for Jews. There is ample evidence that by Roman times at least the Temple was visited by gentile pilgrims as well, including many who came from far away to make their sacrifices in Jerusalem.[21]

In any period, the pilgrims who traveled from afar were likely to find the journey both long and arduous. Pilgrims who trekked the dry, waterless hills of Palestine (Ps. 84:6) required special provisions. Their progress was likely to be slow, as they were burdened with the offerings they were bringing to the Temple and with the animals that they would sacrifice there. Most of the pilgrims to Jerusalem came on foot, although some, like Jesus, rode donkeys (Matt. 21:5–6), and the wealthy who came from distant lands might ride camels. In later times, when Diaspora pilgrims were likely to travel to the coast of Palestine by boat, ocean travel exposed them to great risk.

Although some pilgrims traveled to Jerusalem as individuals, most—for reasons of clan affinity, or concerns for security, or for logistical convenience—must have traveled in formal or informal groups. Pilgrims carried cash. Prudence led them to seek safety in numbers, to gather in caravans to protect themselves against the bandits who preyed on travelers in the rough hill country surrounding Jerusalem. The physical condition of the pilgrim roads and issues of pilgrim security were the purview of the officials responsible for the area. During Second Temple times, the Jewish Sanhedrin was responsible for planting shade trees along the route, keeping fountains and cisterns in good repair, and marking important holy sites along the way.[22] Officials tended to look out for the interest of pilgrims since the economic prosperity of Jerusalem depended in large measure on the pilgrim-tourist trade.[23]

PILGRIM LODGING IN JERUSALEM

Housing so many pilgrims was difficult. There were inns and guesthouses that accommodated the normal flow of travelers during most of the year, providing beds and food for the humans and stables and fodder for their animals. But the several thousand pilgrims pouring into the city for the major festivals far exceeded the capacity of Jerusalem's commercial hotel industry. Inns in nearby towns, such as the one in Bethlehem sought out by Jesus's parents (Luke 2:7), supplemented hostelries of the capital city. Private citizens routinely lodged pilgrims in their houses. This was considered an obligation and thus required no payment, but by tradition pilgrims had to compensate their hosts with a gift of the hides of the animals they had brought with them for sacrifice (BT Yoma 12a). By the beginning of the Common Era, some Diaspora communities had acquired buildings in Jerusalem that served their members as synagogues, social centers, and guesthouses. The administrators of these hostelries undoubtedly knew their guests' local languages, and could help them negotiate the unfamiliar geography and ceremonial aspects of the pilgrimage.[24] To reduce the stress of groups having to search out lodgings during each subsequent visit to Jerusalem, communities from distant regions within Palestine seem to have entered into arrangements with villages near Jerusalem to lodge their pilgrims during the festivals. Jesus's group from the Galilee, for example, seems to have been based in Bethany, only three kilometers from the Jerusalem Temple, from which they could enter and leave the city at ease (Mark 11:11–12; Luke 24:50). Even so, most pilgrims seem to have brought their own lodging with them, erecting tent cities on the nearby hills.[25] Jewish Law required each pilgrim to spend at least one night in Jerusalem, and for festival periods the boundary of Jerusalem was deemed to include the surrounding hills and villages (BT Bezah 5a).

WHAT THE PILGRIMS ATE IN JERUSALEM

Jewish sources during both the pre- and post-exilic periods suggest the wide range of food products available to pilgrims. Many were sold to pilgrims by Jerusalem's merchants. There was an abundance of meat and fish. Vegetables like leeks, vetch, and fenugreek were available. The women of the pilgrim camps could purchase baking supplies to prepare bread. The children snacked on nuts and dried fruit. In addition to regular fermented grape juice, there was wine made from pressed grape skins and wine laced with honey (Mishnah Ma'aser Sheni 1:3–4, 2:1). Leviticus 23:13 underscores the importance of wine and strong drink at these festivals. Sukkot, which followed the grape harvest and brought the annual cycle of agricultural labor to a close, must have functioned as a blowout, a time of communal ebullience and excess. Observers like Josephus chronicle the commercial underpinnings of this riot of consumption[26]; he also makes clear that non-Jews, whether as tourists, observers, or active worshipers, took part in some aspects of the Temple ceremonies and the subsequent parties.

PURCHASES AND THE ECONOMICS OF THE PILGRIMAGE

Travelers spend money. Pilgrim families may have traveled with their tents to Jerusalem, and they may have brought some food and wine with them, but, likely, it would never have been enough. They would also have required such hard-to-transport staples as firewood to cook their ritual meals. All these goods formed part of the bustling commerce of pilgrimage. By tradition, sanctioned in Deuteronomy, pilgrims from afar were exempted from the burden of transporting their first fruits, young lambs, and pressings of oil to Jerusalem, and were allowed instead to sell those products at home for cash which they were obliged to use in the holy city for a feast of rejoicing: "spend the money for whatever you wish—oxen, sheep,

Souvenir oil lamp. 4 inch diam. 50 BCE–50 CE. Authors' collection.

wine, strong drink, or whatever you desire. And you shall eat there in the presence of the Lord your God, you and your household rejoicing together" (Deut. 14:26). Since many of the coins that pilgrims brought with them from their diverse lands bore the likenesses of their rulers, they were considered graven images and could not be used for paying Temple taxes or for purchasing animals to be sacrificed. Moneychangers in the Temple forecourt exchanged these coins for the local shekels that bore no human images.[27] No physical representation of the human form was permitted in the city: even the Roman legions were not allowed to carry insignia depicting the human form. Pilgrims did not spend money on food only. There must have been a lively trade as well in clothing and kitchen supplies. No wonder that the first Jerusalemites that arriving pilgrims would see were the swarms of vendors vying for their attention (Mishnah Bikkurim 3:3).

By the late Second Temple period, the impact of the massive pilgrimages on Jerusalem required a number of changes in the city's infrastructure, both concrete and symbolic. There were so many pilgrims that it was impossible for them all to consume the ritual foods within the Temple precincts as the Law required (Ez. 46:24), so the boundary of the sacred precinct was symbolically extended for this purpose to include all of Jerusalem and its environs.[28] In the suburbs, corrals for the sacrificial animals and storage facilities for fodder, as well as slaughterhouses and kitchens were built. Dovecotes to raise sacrificial birds for the Temple dotted the Mount of Olives.[29] The half-shekel tax supported the Temple infrastructure itself, including the salaries of judges and scribes and presumably of the engineers, masons, and cleaners who kept the Temple in repair.[30]

Cleanliness was a problem. Cisterns were dug in the city, ritual bathhouses were built, and the flow of wastewater was controlled. Market stalls were required to be cleaned daily. The quantity of animals sacrificed in the Temple each day produced masses of blood and offal. A Hellenic Jewish visitor sometime in the third or second century BCE noted that the Temple's "entire floor is paved with stones and slopes downward . . . to admit of flushing with water . . . to wash away the blood of the sacrifices."[31] Even though the number of fresh animal hides produced daily must have been enormous, for reasons of sanitation the city banned tanneries from the immediate area (Mishnah Bava Batra 2:9). Despite the need for large quantities of clay vessels for food and water, pottery making, too, was forbidden in the environs. Although the resident citizenry died at a presumably normal rate, the numbers of people who came to Jerusalem to spend their final days in the holy city augmented the number of corpses. To reduce the chance of contagion, Jerusalem prohibited burial within the city limits. Ritual purity was also of concern to the authorities, both religious and civil. Royal edict banned any nonkosher food from the city.[32]

PILGRIM RITES AND OTHER PILGRIM ACTIVITIES

The descriptions scattered through the book of Psalms enable us to glimpse the rites in Jerusalem that were the heart of the festival pilgrimages in the preexilic period.[33] In the morning, the pilgrim crowds gathered in some large open space below and at some distance from the Temple where, coordinated by priests, they performed their initial communal acts of adoration and sang songs such as Psalm 95. As the priests conducted them toward the Temple, they led them in hymns such as Psalm 132 that underlined God's choice of Jerusalem as his holy city and the house of David as his designated rulers. At the same time it focused their fervor on the holy site itself: "Let us go to his dwelling place; let us worship at his footstool" (Ps. 132:7). At the boundary of the holy precinct, the priests seem to have led the pilgrims in a responsive hymn that stressed adherence to the Law's ethical precepts as a precondition for the state of purity required to enter the Temple area:

> O Lord, who may abide in your tent?
> Who may dwell on your holy hill?

To which the assembled throngs replied:

> Those who walk blamelessly, and do what is right,
> and speak the truth from their heart;
> who do not slander with their tongue,
> and do no evil to their friends,
> nor take up a reproach against their neighbors;
> in whose eyes the wicked are despised,
> but who honor those who fear the Lord;
> who stand by their oath even to their hurt;
> who do not lend money at interest,
> and do not take a bribe against the innocent.
> (Ps. 15; see also Ps. 24:3–6)

After this cautionary recitation had been completed, the pilgrims were led in a liturgy of entering, again probably sung or chanted responsively. The priests called for the Temple gates to be opened so that the King of Glory might enter, and then asked the pilgrims: "Who is the King of Glory?" to which they responded: "The Lord, strong and mighty, the Lord, mighty in battle" (Ps. 24:8). Then, as they streamed into the Temple court, the pilgrims invoked and adored God with many of his titles and attributes: Creator, Judge, High King, Lord of Hosts, etc.

Worshipers who had had contact with the dead or other sources of contamination had to cleanse themselves with water, and this often took place in the Temple, particularly with pilgrims from abroad who had no other sources of cleansing ritual water available to them. Foreign Jews were also expected to cleanse themselves for seven days from the impurity of the Diaspora. By at least Second Temple times, everyone who entered the Temple itself, from common people to the priests, had to wash themselves ritually at one of the water sources in the Temple courts before entering the sacred precincts. As a gesture of purity most Temple visitors wore white clothing, and all removed their shoes and deposited their cloaks, bundles, staffs, and money belts before going in.[34]

Once inside the Temple, the pilgrims presented their various offerings and paid their dues to the priesthood. At some time during the day individual pilgrims lodged their personal prayers, echoes of which are recorded in the Psalms. They sang out their emotions of thanksgiving (Ps. 22:23–26), asked for better health (Ps. 6:2, 41:4), for freedom from false accusations (Ps. 7:9, 26:1, 43:1), or for forgiveness of guilt (Ps. 51:7–9). Much later, toward the end of the Second Temple period when Jewish delegations from the Diaspora had erected synagogues and guest houses in Jerusalem to serve pilgrims from their distant communities, pilgrim men would gather in them to study Torah together as part of their religious festival observances.[35]

During the postexilic period, and probably in earlier times as well, pilgrims remained in the holy city for the full length of each of the three holidays: seven days for Passover, one for Shavu'ot, and seven for Sukkot plus an eighth day of solemn assembly.[36] At the end of each festival, the priests would bid the pilgrims farewell with a prayer or hymn (such as that recorded in Ps. 121) that reassured them that God would stand as the protector of their interests in all of life's possible trials.

Pesach

The offerings and ceremonies varied somewhat for each of the three pilgrim festivals. For the Passover, most groups of pilgrims brought their live sacrificial lambs with them. So many pilgrims crowded the Temple that attendants had to work all evening to clear out the ashes from the previous day's burnt offerings. At midnight the priests opened the Temple gates and by dawn the courtyards were jammed. Officials had to hold three separate sacrifice sessions to cope with the multitudes (Mishnah Pesahim 5:7). A second century BCE Greek visitor was impressed with the serious tone of the ritual: "So great is the silence everywhere that one would suppose that there was no one in the place although the priests number seven hundred and they who bring the victims to the Temple are many; but everything is done with awe and reverence for its great sanctity."[37] When the first group had filled the Temple court, the priests closed the doors. After three sharp blasts on the shofar, each group—generally consisting of ten or more men, but sometimes including women—slaughtered its lamb. The priests, who stood waiting in a line with their round silver or golden bowls, caught the blood and passed it up the chain of priests to be poured on the base of the altar. Levite musicians sang the Hallel Psalms (Ps. 113–118) while the pilgrims skinned their animals and cut out the sacrificial portions (as detailed in Lev. 3:3–4) to be left as peace offerings. When they were done, they filed out, taking the rest of the meat and the animal skins with them, and the next shift surged into the courtyard where the ceremony was re-peated (Mishnah Pesahim 5).

The second major Temple ceremony of Pesach, which occurred late in the day, was the waving of the newly-cut barley sheaves that had been brought to Jerusalem from nearby farms. Afterward, the pilgrims retired to their camps to roast and eat the remaining portions of the lambs.[38] The other ritual foods re-quired for the Passover—the four cups of wine, the bitter herbs, and the haroset—were generally purchased from the many vendors who counted on the trade with pilgrims for their livelihood. After the families had feasted and drunk their fill, the ceremonies seem to have continued into the nighttime. Additional hymns were sung (Ps. 8 and 134). Some groups marched in procession around Mount Zion (Ps. 48:12–14).

Shavu'ot

Most of what we know about this festival's celebrations comes from late Roman times. People who lived relatively near Jerusalem would assemble in the largest vil-lage in their district. Following a night of presumably little sleep, they would set off for Jerusalem in the morning carrying their baskets of first fruits. Their pro-cession was led by an ox whose horns were painted or sheathed in gold and whose head was adorned with an olive wreath. Flute-playing musicians met them at the outskirts of the holy city and conducted them to the Temple, where a chorus of Levites welcomed them with more songs. Priests led the pilgrims in a recitation of Deuteronomy 26 that deals with first fruits (Mishnah Bikkurim 3:2–5).

The principal ceremony of Shavu'ot was the offering of two loaves of bread at the Temple, bread made from the newly harvested wheat. The ceremony rendered the new wheat crop licit for human consumption. Also presented as offerings were farm produce and doves, purchased in the outer court of the Temple Mount from the Temple treasurers.[39] Even though the festival lasted for only a single day, so many pilgrims wanted to make their sacrifices and present their offerings that this was permitted during the six days following as well.

Sukkot

Sukkot, often referred to as *the* feast (Ex. 23:16; 2 Chron. 7:8), was the most joyous of the three pilgrim festivals. It was characterized by almost continuous singing and dancing. Priests sang the Hallel Psalms to the accompaniment of flutes during all eight days of the festival. At the conclusion of the first day's sacri-fices, priests performed the water libation ceremony in the Temple's Court of the Women.[40] People deemed this ceremony so crucial to insuring an appropriate amount of rain at the proper season that the prophet Zechariah warned that nations that did not make the pilgrimage to Jerusalem on Sukkot would be denied rain during the ensuing year (Zech. 14:19). In the evening of the first day, bonfires and torches were lit, and, as the women looked on from the galleries, the men danced in the courtyard to singing and the music of "harps, lyres, cymbals, trumpets, and various instruments." The revels lasted all night. At dawn the pilgrims trooped down from the Nicanor gate to the Siloam spring to draw water to pour on the Temple altar. On the last day of the holiday celebrants marched around the altar shaking palm and willow branches and carrying fruit in their hands (Mishnah Sukkah 4:5).

THE SPIRITUAL COMPONENTS OF THE SHALOSH REGALIM

Victor Turner's seminal work on pilgrimage asserts that in the course of the journey to the holy destination the pilgrim enters a liminal state, crossing a threshold between the profane and the sacred, the natural human world and the supernatural.[41] In this liminal state experiences of all sorts tend to be infused with a heightened spiritual awareness. The pilgrim feels exalted. The journey and the experiences at the holy site are charged with a meaning that leaves the pilgrim transformed in some important way.

Hints of this supercharged emotional state run through the biblical Psalms, many of which seem to have been sung by or to the Jerusalem pilgrims.[42] The Psalms make clear that the pilgrims' exalted emotional state began with their decision to go on pilgrimage, whether this decision was motivated by a sense of obligation to fulfill the precepts of the Law or by a personal call in response to their yearning: "How lovely is your dwelling place, O Lord of hosts! My soul longs, indeed it faints for the courts of the Lord" (Ps. 84:1–2). "My soul thirsts for God, for the living God. When shall I come and behold the face of God?" (Ps. 42:2). "I was glad when they said to me, 'Let us go to the house of the Lord!'" (Ps. 122:1). This sense intensified as the individual joined with others in the pilgrim caravans streaming toward Jerusalem: "Happy are those whose strength is in you, in whose heart are the highways to Zion" (Ps. 84:5). Not only do the pilgrims' souls resonate with the glory of the Lord, the parched landscape of Palestine joins them in exultation: "As they go through the valley of Baca they make it a place of springs; the early rain also covers it with pools" (Ps. 84:6). The pilgrims' arrival at the holy city occasioned another outburst of joy: "Our feet have been standing within your gates, O Jerusalem!" (Ps. 122:2). Arrival at the Temple, the house of God where the Shechinah was believed to dwell physically and where his glory could be visually perceived, was likely to be a moment of extreme exultation. In the Temple the pilgrim could "behold the beauty of the Lord" and "see the goodness of the Lord" (Ps. 27:4, 13). To experience the Temple under these circumstances was to have a foreglimpse of heaven, or the idyllic world of Eden, a feast blending splendid surroundings with an abundance of food and drink, all of which flowed from the nurturing presence of God the Creator: "All people may take refuge in the shadow of your wings. They feast on the abundance of your house, and you give them drink from the river of your delights. For with you is the fountain of life; in your light we see light" (Ps. 36:7–9).

The culmination of the pilgrimage to Jerusalem was a visual experience: "I have looked upon you in the sanctuary, beholding thy power and glory" (Ps. 63:2). The symbol chosen over and over again by the psalmist to express this transforming glory is light, a supernatural radiance that sears and changes the soul. This light is the focus of the distant psalmist's yearnings: "Let the light of your face shine on us, O Lord!" (Ps. 4:6). "Let your face shine, that we may be saved!" (Ps. 80:3; 31:16). Even when it is directly perceived, God's light exceeds the imagination and must be expressed in metaphor—"The Lord God is a sun" (Ps. 84:11)—or by referencing its transforming power: "Look to him, and be radiant; so your faces shall never be ashamed" (Ps. 34:5). The concept of God's physical radiance infuses the Jewish Bible; yet the psalmist makes clear that the perception of this radiance is a key part of the pilgrimage experience: "Happy are the people who know the festal shout, who walk, O Lord, in the light of your countenance" (Ps. 89:15).

Once the pilgrims had returned home, the afterglow of their experience left many with a longing to repeat the pilgrimage: "These things I remember as I pour out my soul: how I went with the throng, and led them in procession to the house of God, with glad shouts and songs of thanksgiving, a multitude keeping festival. . . . My soul is cast down within me; therefore I remember you from the land of Jordan and of Hermon, from Mount Mizar. . . . Oh send out your light and your truth; let them lead me, let them bring me to your holy hill and to your dwelling! Then I will go to the altar of God, to God my exceeding joy" (Ps. 42:4, 42:6, 43:3–4).

In the descriptions of the Shalosh Regalim pilgrimages there is no mention of pilgrimage as penance, or of pilgrimage as an ascetic act for the purpose of purifying the soul or purging sin. There is no calculus of absolution, no accumulation of religious merit to ease one's way into a favorable afterlife. As we have seen, there was some evidence of intercessional prayer, but this was clearly not the prevailing motive. One went to Jerusalem as a pilgrim because one was required to go. One's sense of Jewish identity was bolstered by fulfilling the commandment in the company of one's peers. The awe and majesty of the Temple and the elaborate ceremonies of devotion and sacrifice evoked, as was intended, the fear of God. But the overriding emotion was joy communally shared. Philo of Alexandria captured the mood exactly:

> They take the temple for their port as a general haven and safe refuge from the bustle and great turmoil of life . . . released from the cares . . . to enjoy a brief breathing-space in scenes of genial cheerfulness. Thus filled with comfortable hopes they devote the leisure, as is their bounded duty, to holiness and the honouring of God. Friendships are formed between those who hitherto knew not each other, and the sacrifices and libations are the occasion of reciprocity of feeling and constitute the surest pledge that all are of one mind.[43]

OTHER CONTEMPORARY PILGRIMAGES

As we have seen, despite the enormous popularity of the Shalosh Regalim pilgrimages, the YHWH-ist advocacy of a single, central shrine and a rigidly controlled style of worship never completely eradicated the affinity that many Is-raelites had for regional shrines, and sometimes for competing gods. For example, shrines to Asherah, the consort of the chief Canaanite deity and, in all probability, consort of the Israelites' YHWH as he was originally conceived, continued to at-tract pilgrims and worshipers, some of them in the highest circles of government. Traces of the persistence of this cult are scattered through the Bible. Judah's King Asa (913–873 BCE), for example, took away his mother's Queen Mother status because she had erected a statue of Asherah, but he does not seem to have been willing or powerful enough to destroy the goddess's high places (1 Kings 15:13–14).Two centuries later God punished King Manasseh (circa 692–639) for rebuilding the high places and installing statues of Asherah in the Jerusalem Tem-ple (2 Kings 21:3–7). Not long after, King Josiah (639–609) won praise for de-stroying those statues (2 Kings 23:6–7).[44] There were other officially sponsored pilgrimages besides those of Pesach, Shavu'ot and Sukkot. Information scattered throughout the Bible's prophetic books indicates that in times of national calamity, when the Israelites felt themselves under threat of plague, drought, or attack, the priesthood might convoke a pilgrimage of petition. This was accompanied by a general fast requiring abstention from certain foods, sexual intercourse, and other pleasurable acts.[45] As during the tri-annual pilgrimage festivals, priests led the pro-cessions and other ceremonial rites. As physical expressions of their depth of emo-tion, the people tore off their regular clothes, donned sackcloth, hacked off their hair, marked their skin, and fell to the ground and rolled in the dust, moaning and lamenting aloud. Sometimes the priests offered sacrifices on the Israelites' behalf (Jer. 14:12; 1 Sam. 7:9). Later, when the danger had passed or had been averted, songs of thanksgiving were sung at the Temple.

When the Temple was destroyed by Nebuchadnezzar in 586 BCE and a large portion of the Israelite populace was dispersed to Babylon, a special category of lamentation pilgrimage was devised to mourn the devastated holy sanctuary. Not only were memorial hymns sung in the Diaspora (e.g., Ps. 137), the small popula-tion remaining in Jerusalem and those who had traveled from Babylon for the purpose (Jer. 41:5) would gather at the Temple ruins to proclaim their grief in laments such as that recorded in the second chapter of Lamentations.[46] As we will see in a moment, these were not the only changes wrought by the Diaspora.

PILGRIMAGE IN THE
EARLY DIASPORAS

By the waters of Babylon—there we sat down and there we wept when
we remembered Zion. (Psalms 137:1)

The period of dispersion began with the conquest of the northern kingdom
of Judea by the Assyrian kings Tiglath-pileser III (circa 733 BCE) and
Sargon II (721 BCE) and continued through the Babylonian king Nebuchadnezzar's destruction of Jerusalem and Solomon's Temple and his exile of the
Jews to Mesopotamia (586 BCE). It formally ended with Persian King Cyrus II's
edict permitting the Jews to return to Palestine (536 BCE). The Babylonian Diaspora changed the Israelites' concept of sacred space and its role in worship, as well
as the nature of the Jewish sense of identity. From at least Solomon's time until
Nebuchadnezzar's, God's essence, the Shechinah, was thought to be physically
present in the Temple's holy of holies. Legitimate worship of God was Temple-
centered, and the main vehicle for communication with the deity was priest-led
sacrifice. Three annual pilgrimage festivals helped bond the tribal Israelites into a
Jewish people.

But in the mid-sixth century BCE exile period there was no Temple in Jerusalem
and the Jews in Babylon did not even have easy access to its ruins.[1] The few who
attempted the pilgrimage risked their lives circumventing the Babylonian guards
(BT Ta'anith 28a).[2] Ezekiel's vision—in which the radiant splendor of God appeared to the Babylonian Jews as a glowing heavenly chariot (Ezek. 1:1–28)—was
interpreted to mean that the Shechinah had accompanied the Jews in their dispersion, and that God could be worshiped legitimately in their current home far
from Jerusalem. Even so, the Jews' leaders conceived of exile as punishment and
dreamed of a return to Jerusalem once the Jews had completed their atonement
and served the God-imposed sentence of exile. They envisaged a restoration of

Jerusalem and its Temple and their ancient forms of worship. But in Babylonia, the maintenance of Jewish identity required other forms. The most important was an increased focus on the Law. This is the period during which most of the Torah was being assembled by the learned scribes, and, in practical terms, its study replaced Temple worship. It acquired a value both in and of itself and as a means of learning what God required the Israelites to do to atone for the sins that had brought about the current catastrophe and to avoid future ones. After a time these first Diaspora Jews even may have constructed special buildings—synagogues or proto-synagogues—for study of the Torah.[3] It was during this period that Jews became the people of the book.

As the Israelites' worship of the deity gradually disassociated itself from Jerusalem, new forms of communication with God were devised. The practice of ritual sacrifice diminished and was replaced, paradoxically, by study of the minutely recorded details of its former observance. Although individual or congregational prayer is rarely mentioned in the books of the Bible that narrate events prior to the exile to Babylonia, it was now given prominence. In a way these new practices began to democratize Judaism by liberating worship from a reliance on tribal or national leaders or a hierarchical priesthood. Scribes learned in the Law and able to explain it to the people—the forerunners of what Jews would come to call rabbis—rose to prominence because of their skills. Because many Jews were attracted by the enveloping majority culture, the leadership increasingly emphasized practices that erected defensive barriers between the Jews and the peoples of their surrounding milieu. These included practices such as circumcision, scrupulous observance of the Sabbath, and the complexities of kashruth.[4]

During this period, communal ceremonial rites focused increasingly on mourning what was lost when the Jews were exiled. The book of Lamentations and Psalm 137 appear to record mourning rituals to be recited—literally or symbolically—among the ruins. The fall of Jerusalem was commemorated by a fast on the ninth of Tammuz, as was the burning of the Temple on the ninth of Av, the beginning of the siege of Jerusalem on the tenth of Tebet, and the murder of Gedaliah on the day after Rosh Hashanah.[5] These memorial observances helped keep alive the passion for return when what was lost would be regained. In the popular imagination the nature of Jerusalem's holy places changed from being the physical locus of worship to the symbolic icon of a strengthened covenant with God and the desire that he forgive them and allow them to return to their homeland.

The Shalosh Regalim, the three mandated annual pilgrimages, had to be recast as well. Prior to the dispersion, the Passover lamb could be sacrificed only at the Temple in Jerusalem and the Passover banquet consumed in the near vicinity of the Temple. During the years in Mesopotamia the home- or community-centered Passover seder, emphasizing the retelling of the saga of Exodus and consumption of the ritual foods in familial groups, had come to replace the Temple ceremonies. Sukkot now centered not on the physical journey to Jerusalem, residence in the holy city for seven days, and strict observance of the rituals of sacrifice and celebration that could only be performed there, but rather on fulfillment of the biblical command to build booths and to dwell in them for seven days.[6]

In the Diaspora, pilgrimage to Jerusalem or other holy places in its vicinity was at best very difficult. But there were other outlets for the urge to go on pilgrimage.

There were prophets in Mesopotamia who were considered holy, and some of the Jews who harkened to their voices when they were alive also seem to have visited their graves after they died. The reputed tombs of Ezekiel at Kefil near Birs-Nimrud and Ezra on the Tigris River, both in modern Iraq, and Daniel in Susa and Esther in Hamadan, both in Iran, all attracted pilgrims.[7]

THE RETURN

Many Babylonian Jews returned to Palestine in 538 BCE after Cyrus II's edict, with the bulk of them settling in Jerusalem and its environs. Even so, a substantial number remained in Mesopotamia, preferring life in its highly-developed cities to their ancestors' hardscrabble existence in the dry Judean hills. When the Second Temple was completed in Jerusalem circa 515, and Temple sacrifice was reinstituted, the Babylonian religious innovations of the generation of dispersal did not disappear. At some point during the years of exile, the ancient Ark had disappeared, and those parts of the Temple ritual that centered on the Ark now had to be discontinued or reshaped. Nonetheless, people continued to believe that God's Shechinah inhabited the new structure as it had the old. In the new Temple the sacrifice of live animals again became the dominant form of worship, but it was no longer the only one. The three annual pilgrimages to the Jerusalem Temple resumed, but with changes. Torah study now also held value among the Jews, and by Herod's time a space in the courtyard of the Temple had been designated for

Model of Second Temple. Jerusalem. Photo, D. Gitlitz, 1967.

reading and discussing the Law.[8] At Passover, lambs were sacrificed again at the Temple, but some of the people's attention remained fixed on the retelling of the story of Exodus. On Sukkot, pilgrims still flocked to Jerusalem, but, as Nehemiah 8:17 makes clear, "all the assembly of those who had returned from the captivity made booths and dwelt in the booths; for from the days of Joshua the son of Nun to that day the people of Israel had not done so."

NATURE OF THE DIASPORAS

From the sixth century BCE, an important consequence of the Diaspora was that multitudes of Jews chose to live outside of Palestine, with little or no intention of migrating to their ancestral homeland.[9] Although with each successive banishment Jews had been forcibly exiled from their homes, in each case the exile proved temporary; yet after the bans were lifted large numbers of Jews chose voluntarily to remain in these centers of high culture and economic opportunity. These were not the only foreign Jewish communities, of course. Even a hundred years before Alexander the Great's conquest of Egypt in the late fourth century BCE, which resulted in many Jews migrating to Alexandria and the thriving cities along the Nile, there had been an active Jewish community at Elephantine. Almost all of the Hellenic trading centers in the eastern Mediterranean attracted Jews, as did the cities of North Africa. Some Jews settled as far away as Spain. The number of Palestinian Jews living in foreign communities and their descendants was swelled by substantial numbers of pagan converts, who were attracted by the monotheistic religion of their new neighbors.

Some Roman writers recognized that the Diaspora invited Jews to focus on God's universality and to de-emphasize Jerusalem as the only place in which God could be fully and appropriately worshiped. Both Josephus and Philo of Alexandria, for example, stressed the Jews' destiny as a universal people.[10] Josephus, glossing Balaam's prophesy, related God's promise that "those numbers now are small and shall be contained by the land of Canaan; but the habitable world, be sure, lies before you as an eternal habitation, and your multitudes shall find abode on islands and continents, more numerous even than the stars in heaven."[11] Philo, commenting on Num. 9:6–14 in which God instructs Moses that people who, because of some ritual impurity, are unable to celebrate the Pesach at the appropriate time should be allowed to celebrate it a month later, went so far as to recommend modifying Halakhah to accommodate the special needs of those living abroad.

> The same permission also must be given to those who are prevented from joining the whole nation in worship . . . by absence in a distant country. For settlers abroad and inhabitants of other regions are not wrongdoers who deserve to be deprived of equal privileges, particularly if the nation has grown so populous that a single country cannot contain it and has sent out colonies in all directions.[12]

Another consequence of the Diaspora was that it required the Jewish communities living abroad to engage in a certain amount of doublethink. On the one hand, some of their traditionalist rabbis were telling Jews that the dispersal was God's punishment for their communal sin. They preached that when the Jews finally rectified their ways and adhered to a path of righteous behavior as defined by Halakhah, the return to Israel for which they presumably longed would at last be possible, and that only with this return could Jewish destiny be fulfilled.[13] On the other hand, most members of the dispersed communities seemed quite happy where they were. These Jews were not interested in returning to Palestine. Some were members of families that had resided in Persia, Greece, Carthage, Egypt, or Rome for several generations, so that they personally had no recollection of Jewish life in Palestine, nor could they imagine the surge of emotions experienced by pilgrims to the Jerusalem Temple. Some of these Jews took comfort from a view expressed in the book of Jeremiah (29:4–7) that a certain amount of assimilation to the customs of one's host country was not sinful, and might even facilitate a prosperity under which Judaism might thrive. After all, they reasoned, for the most part the specific halakhic observances were not incompatible with the prevailing culture of the Greek and Roman world.

Many Diaspora Jews felt a bond with Israel, but they also harbored patriotic feelings for Cyrene or Alexandria or Rome or wherever they found themselves. Some made a festival pilgrimage to Jerusalem, particularly during the years before the Romans destroyed the Temple in 70 CE, but rarely with the intention of remaining there. Distance and expense dictated that pilgrimage be undertaken only once a year, or even once in a lifetime, rather than three times annually. When the ceremonies were over, most returned to the lands which they now thought of as home.

Diaspora Jews whose feelings for the Temple were strong, though not strong enough to motivate them to pilgrimage, could still maintain a symbolic bond by contributing the annual half-shekel tax to support the Jerusalem Temple. In a way, this payment legitimized the Diaspora by providing a way to meet one's Jewish obligations from afar. It meant that return to Palestine was not a precondition of Jewishness.[14] After the 70 CE revolt and the destruction of the Temple, the emperor Titus Vespasian punished the Jews by co-opting the half-shekel tax for imperial purposes. It provided resources to enlarge Jerusalem's walls and aqueducts.

Even after the Second Temple was destroyed in 70 CE, its ruins continued to be an important holy magnet, and at least some Jews continued make pilgrimages to Jerusalem. After the Bar Kokhba revolt (132–135), Hadrian banned any circumcised person from entering the city—renamed Aelia Capitolina—under pain of death. Yet even then Jewish pilgrimage traffic never entirely ceased. Various passages in the Mishnah, for example, indicate that in the early third century pilgrims from the Diaspora like the rabbis Hanina, Jonathan, and Joshua ben Levi made visits to Jerusalem.[15] In the latter half of the same century, Rabbi Yohanan stated, "Anyone who wants to go [to Jerusalem], can go" (BT Bava Metziah 75b), showing that the ease of pilgrimage had increased. Festival pilgrims are chronicled from Alexandria, Babylon, Antioch, and other places.[16] The formal ban remained in effect and was for the most part enforced,[17] yet even after the Byzantine Christian emperor Constantine accepted possession of the city in 324, Jewish pilgrimage persevered.

As during the earlier Diasporas, if Jerusalem was a forbidden goal, there were other places that pilgrims could visit. The first-century CE guide written by a Jew,

Miracle scene: "Elijah Revives the Widow's Child." Third-century synagogue. Dura-Europos, Syria, Panel WC1. In Carl H. Kraeling, *The Synagogue* (New Haven: Yale University Press, 1956), Plate LXIII. © 1956 Yale University Press. All Rights Reserved. Used by permission.

entitled *The Names of the Prophets, and whence they were, where they died, and how and where they were buried*,[18] shows how important the grave sites of the ancient prophets had already become. The short text contains information on twenty-three of them, and each section, no matter how brief, says where the burial place is located. Although several prophets are only briefly commented on (Joel receives a bare two sentences), others get relatively long biographies that focus on their prophecies and miracle-working abilities. Jeremiah, for example, is credited with banishing snakes from Egypt while he was alive (*Names* 35). Ezekiel, whom the author calls a saint (Greek *hosios*), drew crowds while he was still alive. Once, to protect the Jews from Chaldean forces who wished to kill them, he controlled the river's waters, holding back the water so the faithful could get away and then releasing the water so the Chaldeans would drown (*Names* 37). The author's description of Ezekiel's tomb is vivid: "[it] is a double cave. . . . It is called 'double' because it has a winding (stairway) and there is an upper chamber hidden from the main floor, hung in the rock above the ground-level" (*Names* 37). He hints at the talismanic power of souvenir relics when he observes that pilgrims to Jeremiah's tomb in Egypt took away dust from the area to cure snakebites (*Names* 35). The author also includes information about prophets' tombs in the vicinity of Jerusalem, suggesting that Jewish pilgrims were not unknown in that area after all. Isaiah must have been a personal favorite, because directions to his tomb in Jerusalem are unusually specific: "near the tomb of the kings, behind the tomb of the priests on the side toward the south" (*Names* 34).

LIFE ON THE PILGRIMAGE ROAD

I have prayed for you and for myself on the sepulcher of our mother Rachel, and I have prayed and wept for the health of my sick son on the tomb of the prophet Nathan. (Isaac ibn Chelo, 1334)[1]

I was possessed by a violent and insatiable desire to visit the places of God, to set out for Mount Moriah and the chain of Lebanon, there to render homage to the supreme King of all things, in the bosom of Jerusalem. (Samuel Jemsel, 1651)[2]

To-day, Tuesday, the 12th June [1481], we left Alexandria, I and my companion Raphael, with the suite of Monsieur Antonio. We obtained a permit from the Gran Maestro and the Queen of Cyprus to go to Misr [Cairo]. We rode on donkeys and took . . . a mameluke to protect us on the way. . . . But when we were about three miles away from Alexandria the said mameluke rose up to slay us, for he had found excuse and he carried bow and arrows and a sword and we had no weapons. He compelled us to give him eight ducats. (Meshullam ben Menachem, 1481)[3]

All through the Middle Ages Jews went on pilgrimage to Jerusalem, to the area today called Israel, and to the broader region that stretched from the Euphrates in present-day Iraq to the Egyptian Nile. For the most part these were not mass movements of Jewish pilgrims, certainly nothing like the throngs of Christians trekking to Jerusalem or Muslims caravanning to Mecca. But Jewish pilgrim traffic was reasonably steady over more than a millennium and a half, the period stretching from the destruction of the Temple in 70 CE through the Jewish enlightenment of the mid-eighteenth century. In the aggregate there is enough information for us to glimpse what medieval Jewish pilgrimage must have been like. The data tells us who went on pilgrimage, what moved them, where they

The Holy Land

went, some of what they saw and felt, what difficulties they had to overcome, and, occasionally, what effect the pilgrimage had on their lives.

THE PILGRIMS AND THEIR WRITINGS

What sources tell us about medieval Jewish pilgrimage, and who were the informants who wrote them? For one thing, the authors were all men, even though some Jewish women did go on pilgrimage. We find some references to women in legal documents relating to other matters. For example, we know that at the end of the sixteenth century a man named Ma'ir ibn Shamwil made the pilgrimage to Jerusalem with his family, as did the Moroccan rabbi Ya'qub ibn Ibrahim.[4] Their contemporary Elijah of Pesaro cautioned would-be pilgrims to "always remember to keep your womenfolk and servants and little ones together."[5] But it is not until the 1830s, when Judith Montefiore wrote a diary about her trip to the Holy Land, that we hear a woman's voice.

Where were the pilgrims from? The narrations, itineraries, letters, histories, and account books all give the same answer: they came from wherever there were Jews. There were Ashkenazi pilgrims from Northern Europe and Sephardic pilgrims from the Maghreb. Pilgrims set out from the British Isles, the Iberian Peninsula, and what are now France, Italy, the Czech Republic, Poland, and Germany. The Cairo Genizah[6] harbors documents of pilgrims from Morocco, Egypt, Syria, and points in between.

What did they write? The most condensed accounts are itineraries, succinct, geographically organized lists of tombs of Jewish holy figures that circulated from the thirteenth century through the end of the Middle Ages. Some itineraries include sketchy data about the distances between sites and the places that pilgrims should not miss. But most, like this example from the twelfth-century European pilgrim Jacob ben Nathaniel ha Cohen, are bare bones:

> I saw the graves of our righteous Patriarchs in Hebron and the grave of Abner the son of Ner (near the well of our father Abraham), and of Jonah ben Amittai, the prophet, in Kiriath Arba, which is Hebron, and the grave of Hannah and the grave of Rachel at Ephrath, on the Jericho road on the way to Bethlehem. From these two villages it is a parasang and a half to Jerusalem.[7]

Much more lively are the pilgrim narratives. These include journals, autobiographical memoirs, and reports written after the fact by the people who listened to the travelers' stories. Some take the form of letters home that their authors intended to be widely circulated, the equivalent of e-mailed vacation letters to friends and family. Pilgrim narratives may incorporate details about the travelers' daily activities, their impressions of places and situations, and anecdotes that flavor their experiences.

Of course, information about Jewish pilgrims and their holy places does not come solely from Jewish sources. Other snippets of information about medieval Jewish pilgrimages may be found in the laws and regulations that govern them, in account books and tax reports, and in contemporary historical accounts of events that touched the lives of pilgrims. Sometimes marginal comments of Christian and Muslim writers add interesting details. In the eleventh century, the Persian Muslim Naser-e Khosraw wrote that, in addition to the many Muslims who go to Jerusalem in pilgrimage, "from the Byzantine realm and other places too come Christians and Jews to visit the churches and synagogues located there" (21).[8]

With regard to sources, we must keep in mind that tastes in travel literature change over time, particularly as to what sorts of things are important to include and whether the author's personal voice is permitted to shape the narrative. Writers write in accord with what they read, that is, by the prevailing norms of the genre. If contemporary travel literature emphasizes tomb lists, then they list tombs. If the popular mode is to record the travelers' extremes of religious emotion—rapture or lament—that is how their ink will flow. If the travel genre prizes picturesque anecdotes emphasizing hardships, their narration may as well. Thus we should not be surprised that Jewish pilgrim narratives only begin to meet our modern Western expectations in the late fifteenth century, after the European

Renaissance legitimized the exercise of curiosity and personal observation. But even after this genre shift, most travelers' accounts remain thin on detail, and much of our curiosity goes unsatisfied.

CHANGES IN JEWISH PILGRIMAGE OVER TIME

One way of looking at medieval Jewish pilgrimage to the Holy Land is chronologically. It makes perfect sense. Empires—Roman, Byzantine, Muslim, Christian Crusader, Seljuk, Ottoman—have come and gone in the Holy Land. Over the years mystics and scholars, false messiahs, and pre-Zionist visionaries have all inspired pilgrims to leave their homes and journey to the Holy Land. Expulsions and pogroms have pushed Jews onto the road. Successive wars have disrupted travel; successive despots have harassed travelers; successive governments have protected them, built roads for them, welcomed them, and also circumscribed their movements with restrictive laws and strangled them in red tape. And, of course, taxed them. In periods when travel was relatively easy and secure, the word got out, and the numbers of Jewish pilgrims increased; when it was tough, the stream of pilgrims dwindled to a trickle.

CONTROL BY CHRISTIAN ROME AND BYZANTIUM (325–638)

The Emperor Galerius legalized Christianity in 311, and in 324 Emperor Constantine made it the official religion of the Roman Empire. With Christianization, the attitude of the Roman-Byzantine ruling class changed significantly. Jews ceased being perceived as a rebellious political entity, a potential military threat to Roman authority over its distant provinces. Now Jews were evaluated principally in terms of their relationship to Christianity while Jerusalem, Judaism's holiest city, was now revered as the mystical center of the Christian world, the locus of its most important historical events and the heart of its theology of resurrection.

After the Byzantine Christian emperor Constantine accepted possession of Jerusalem in 324, the formal Roman ban on Jews in Jerusalem remained in effect, and was for the most part enforced. Since many of the early Christian converts were drawn from the Jewish population which, in turn, strove to attract them back, the competition between the established and the nascent faiths was strong. In the minds of early Christian theologians such as Origen (185–254), Eusebius (260–circa 339), and Gregory of Nyssa (335–394), Christianity had supplanted the older religion and abrogated many of its commandments. Replacement theology held that Jews had once been the chosen people, but that the deity had switched alliance and now favored the religion inspired by his son. Within this framework, the destruction of the Second Temple was an emblem, a clear sign of switched allegiance. Christians could use Jewish pilgrimage to the Temple's ruins as an effective tool to hammer home that point. With this in mind, Constantine, while remaining steadfast in banning Jewish settlement and even visits to Jerusalem, relaxed the ban one day each year on the ninth of Av, the traditional date of the Temple's destruction. On that day Jews were permitted to visit the remaining Western Wall of the Temple platform for the express purpose of showing their grief at its ruin and demonstrating in their lamentations the triumph of the Christian Church.

For a brief period the Emperor Julian I, who reigned from 361–363 and who withdrew imperial support for Christianity, relaxed the ban altogether, permitting Jewish settlers to reenter the city and to build a house of prayer and study, a synagogue, near the Temple Mount. In 363 an earthquake, a disastrous fire, and Julian's death made patent the folly of his position, and the all-but-one-day-a-year ban was reinstated. It was rescinded again, briefly, in 438 by the Empress Eudocia, but, from then until the early seventh century, Jews could make only one visit each year to Jerusalem.

Jews who participated in these annual visits to Jerusalem soon established ritualized routes and activities. The Bordeaux Pilgrim, a Christian who visited Jerusalem circa 333, chronicled his impressions of the lamenting Jews at the cleft stone now covered by the Dome of the Rock: "The Jews come every year and anoint it, bewail themselves with groans, rend their garments, and so depart."[9]

EARLY MUSLIM CONTROL (638–1099)

Muslim rule of Jerusalem dates from 638 when Caliph Umar I conquered the city. Circumstantial evidence indicates that Jews once again were permitted to enter the city as pilgrims. In the eighth century, we know of some Karaite pilgrims,[10] and by the early ninth century there was a resident Karaite community in Jerusalem and Karaite pilgrims from the eastern Mediterranean frequently visited the city. The most popular day for their pilgrimage was Hoshanah Rabah (the seventh day of Sukkot). They would gather on the Mount of Olives. Praying and singing, they would circle the mountain seven times before converging at a stone at the mountain's center from which, they believed, the holy essence (Shechinah) had ascended to heaven after the Temple's destruction.

Pilgrims came from the Crimea, too. The gravestone of Moses haYerushalmi in the Ukraine, dated 1002, reports that "good luck followed him and his companions to the tomb of King David and of his son Solomon, which no other persons heretofore had been permitted to enter." Moses haYerushalmi had evidently led a group of pilgrims from Chufut-Kale in the western Ukraine. His inscription indicates that at least some pilgrims took the name of Jerusalem when they returned home.[11]

Pilgrimage to Jerusalem during this period served as a mechanism for resolving communal issues of interest to the widespread communities of the Jewish Diaspora. Jerusalem rabbis would discuss controversial points of the law and fix the liturgical calendar for the upcoming year. The last notice of the annual pilgrimage during this period is from 1062; eleven years later the Jerusalem yeshiva was relocated to Tyre in the Lebanon.[12]

THE CRUSADES (1099–1250)

When Christian forces conquered Jerusalem in 1099, the Muslim residents who were not able to flee the city were either killed or sold into slavery. Records do not indicate clearly what happened to the Jewish residents of the city. The contemporary Muslim writer Ibn al-Qalanisi posits that they were executed: "A number of the townsfolk fled to the sanctuary [of David], and a great host were killed. The Jews assembled in the synagogue, and the Franks burned it over their heads."[13] Latin documents of the time and a Jewish letter found in the Cairo Genizah intimate that Jews were forced to clean up the Temple Mount and then were either enslaved or deported.[14] Another letter, dated summer 1100, asks Cairo's Jews for donations to ransom captives and to help Jews in Ashkelon pay the living expenses for Jews who had escaped from Jerusalem.[15] No wonder that Jewish documents of the period tend to express a hope that the Muslims would win the struggle: by now there was ample evidence that Jews fared far better under Muslim rather than Christian control.

Although the Crusades caused widespread destruction, they seem not to have dampened pilgrimage traffic to the Holy Land, at least from the Christian West. The crusaders spoke of themselves as pilgrims, and their control of the Christian holy sites spurred many adventurous religiously-motivated Christian pilgrims to set off in their footsteps. Travel was dangerous and especially so for Jews, but that did not deter men whose hearts were focused on Jerusalem. Several important Jewish figures set off for Zion during the twelfth century, such as Petachia of Ratisbon, who traveled from 1170–1187. Some of the most prominent came from the Iberian Peninsula, where the wars between Christians and Muslims had turned many Jews into semipermanent refugees who were alienated from both sides; they were increasingly persuaded that the future of the Jews lay not in the West but in the East. The list includes Judah Halevi, the well-known Iberian poet, prior to 1141; Maimonides, the important Andalusian theologian, who came from Morocco in 1165 and stayed two years before settling in Egypt; and Benjamin of Tudela, on his travels throughout the world, 1165–1173.

When Saladin and the Turks reconquered Jerusalem in 1187, this opened the way for Eastern pilgrims to visit the holy places again in greater numbers, and many came from Babylonia, Egypt, Syria, and elsewhere. But the area seethed with war. Christians retook coastal Acre in 1191 and carved out an uneasy coexistence with the Turks. Saladin's death in 1192 destabilized the region. Emperor Frederick of Germany recaptured and held a good part of Jerusalem from 1229 until 1244 when the Turks retook and sacked the city. In 1250 the Egyptian Mamelukes routed the Turkish forces. Despite the chaos, Jewish pilgrims kept coming, including some intending to stay.

MAMELUKE CONTROL (1250–1517)

Jerusalem's fortunes and the living conditions of her resident Jews fluctuated over the next several centuries. Some times pilgrims characterized the Jewish community as healthy; other times they reported it to be nearly nonexistent. There were famines and droughts, and prices swung wildly. The Mamelukes spent little to develop the city, with the exception of a few Muslim religious buildings. Jerusalem's Jewish community struggled to survive economically and to keep out of the way of the periodic outbreaks of violence, such as in 1260 when many Jerusalem Jews were massacred. But they kept coming. In 1268 Nachmanides wrote in a letter that many came to lament the destruction of the holy places. Eastern Jews, such as those from Babylon and Kurdistan, continued the custom of yearly pilgrimage.[16]

In Western Europe, the beginning of the Renaissance coincided with the mass expulsions of Jews from lands where they had lived for centuries: Castile, Aragon, Sardinia, and Sicily (1492); Portugal (1496); Navarre (1499); Naples (1511); Venice (1527); Milan (1540); and so forth. Not surprisingly, among the refugees were some who saw in their displacement an opportunity to make a pilgrimage to the Holy Land and, in some cases, to settle there.

TURKISH OTTOMAN CONTROL (1517–1920)

Suleyman's takeover of Jerusalem from the Mamelukes in 1517 augured a change for the city and, indeed, for the entire region. Suleyman underwrote construction of Jerusalem's walls in 1537 and began to rebuild the city and to stabilize its water supply. Jerusalem was not central to Turkish interests, but the firm Ottoman hand served to maintain order and create a climate favorable to pilgrims. In 1538, 300 pilgrims entered Jerusalem from the north, more than half of them Jews, predominantly North Africans and Damascenes. In 1574, 191 pilgrim Jews came from North Africa.[17] Many Sephardic refugees from Spain and Portugal settled in Palestine during the sixteenth century, some in Jerusalem, but more in Galilean cities like Tiberias and especially Safed, which was booming as a center of kabbalistic studies.

Despite this historical ebb and flow, the overall pattern of medieval Jewish pilgrimage does not seem to have changed that much over time. Jewish pilgrims never had many rights. They were at best tolerated and were always exploited by the prevailing powers. For the most part they made the journey for two reasons: to lament the destruction of Jewish Jerusalem and to worship at the tombs of Jewish holy men and women. In the bulk of this chapter, then, we will consider medieval Jewish pilgrimage not chronologically but as a relatively coherent phenomenon that in its most significant characteristics changed little over time.

MEDIEVAL PILGRIMS' MOTIVATIONS

What moved medieval Jews to become pilgrims, to leave their loved ones and take their lives in their hands on the long and difficult journey to places where Jews were unwelcome?

One reason was to fulfill a vow made during a time of stress. Sometime in the tenth or eleventh century, for example, a Jewish traveler nearly died when his boat sank near the Egyptian city of Alexandria. Then and there, he later wrote, "I took a vow to go to Jerusalem." Israel ben Sahlun, a book copier in the Egyptian city of Fustat, promised to move to Jerusalem if God would help him resolve certain intractable problems. He settled there in 1051.[18] Likewise Meshullam ben Menachem of Volterra traveled to the Holy Land in 1481 to fulfill a vow he had made when he was in great need.

Other Jews, believing that God would be more attentive to their prayers in the Holy Land, went to make a request. As we saw in one of the opening quotes of this chapter, this is why in the fourteenth-century Isaac ibn Chelo was moved to visit Rachel's grave. People believed that pilgrimage conveyed merit that might be rewarded with preferential treatment. A letter from a Spanish or Maghrebi pilgrim written about 1100 from Alexandria expressed faith that God would improve the writer's fortune because he had become a pilgrim: "Many years ago I left our country to seek God's mercy and help in my poverty, to behold Jerusalem and return. . . ."[19] In the twelfth century, Petachia of Ratisbon made his extended Holy Land tour to pray at tombs (through Syria, Babylon, and Iraq as well as Jerusalem and its environs). He characterized the act of praying with the Hebrew verb *lehishtateah*, which Josef Meri interprets to mean to "prostrate oneself in prayer or supplication."[20] Obadiah Jaré da Bertinoro used the same verb in 1488 to underscore his belief in the efficacy of making requests at a holy person's tomb.

Some Jews went to the Holy Land to die there. Some religions share the belief that the favorable disposition of one's soul is enhanced by dying or having one's mortal remains deposited in proximity to that religion's holiest sites. Aged Hindus, if they are able, journey to Varanasi, on the Ganges River, to await their deaths. Even more common is for surviving family members to faithfully transport the deceased's body to Varanasi for cremation or to take their ashes to be set adrift in the holy river. Similarly, since at least the eighth century CE many Jews of the Diaspora have aspired to die, or at least be buried, in Jerusalem, preferably on the Mount of Olives, which tradition holds is where the resurrection of the dead will begin at the end of time. This is a special category of pilgrimage, not a round trip journey through physical geography from home to shrine to home, but a metaphysical journey through time from human life to eternal home with God. Both Jacob ha Cohen in the twelfth century (98–99) and Nachmanides in 1268 expressed a strong desire to die in the Holy Land.[21] In 1626 the will of the Cretan Jew Abraham Balanzas noted his intention to go to the Holy Land to die.[22] Some Diaspora Jews, who were unable to make the journey during their lifetimes, wanted their bones buried in the Holy Land. The Christian pilgrim John Sanderson in 1601 reported that on his journey from Constantinople to Sidon there had been some (wool) sacks in which, "it was most certaynelie tould me, weare Jewes bones in two or three little chests, but unknown to us."[23]

Other Diaspora Jews who were unable to make this journey sought to reference it symbolically in their burial customs. Pilgrims to the Holy Land might carry home with them bags of soil from the Mount of Olives, and these were sometimes buried under the head of the deceased. Others were said to bring potsherds from Jerusalem to keep as family treasures until they were used to cover the eyelids of the deceased.[24] The yearning to die in the Holy Land was not necessarily pervasive, however. One eleventh-century pilgrim to Jerusalem, for example, wrote to his family in Egypt that he wanted to be back home with them when he died.[25]

THE HUNGER FOR MIRACLES

Many medieval Jews, similar to the adherents of other religions both then and now, believed that God's power was most likely to be made manifest to them at the graves of holy persons and at other holy sites. Modern secularists tend to write off seemingly inexplicable events as happenings whose physical causes we do not yet understand. Our medieval ancestors—and some people today—interpreted these events as tangible signs of God's interventions and labeled them miracles. Miracles justified belief. Miracles held out hope. The desire to witness or receive the benefits from a miracle launched many a pilgrimage. Elijah of Ferrara (1434) was of this frame of mind when he wrote, "I will not speak to you now of the miracles and marvels constantly manifested at the tombs of the prophets and of the pious men of Galilee and beyond Jordan, as well as in other places of the country of Israel, because, with God's help, I hope to go there and see them for myself. I will make them known to you next year."[26]

While medieval pilgrim narratives are generally short on personal observations and anecdotes, they can be quite expansive when it comes to recounting miracles. Many of these were legends recounted to visiting pilgrims to underscore a site's holy power. At the grave of Rabbi Judah bar Ilai and his son Rabbi Yose, a short distance from Safed in Ein Zeitun, Moses Basola (1521) found an old dead almond tree. The story?

> They say that once a Muslim woman climbed the almond tree on the grave in order to gather almonds, upon which the other women told her to first ask the hasid's permission. But she showered them with curses. She fell off the tree, breaking all her limbs. She then pledged the gold bracelets on her hands to the *zaddik*, purchasing olive trees with them. Subsequently others made pledges as well, and at present he has four hundred olive trees. This episode of the woman took place about sixty years ago.[27]

Medieval Jewish pilgrims tended to accept without question a particular grave's miraculous properties. Isaac ibn Chelo (fourteenth century) told a story related to a town called Ma'on:

> There was here a learned man known as Rabbi Sa'adiah. He was a man who was a worker of miracles. One day during the hour of prayer a wall of the synagogue was filled with great flames, flaring up in all directions. Then a great number of stars, remarkable for the beauty of their colour and for their brilliancy, made a sort of writing, which said: *Here lies Bar Cocheba [Kochba] (the son of the Star) the anointed Prince.* Rabbi Sa'adiah, when he knew whose tomb this was, threw himself on the ground, praying and weeping for a long time, until this vision had disappeared. (136)

At times Petachia of Ratisbon's twelfth-century narrative resembles a compendium of miracle stories. When he visited Daniel's room, he was shown "a very deep lion's den, and also a furnace half filled with water. Whoever is attacked by fever bathes therein and is healed."[28] In Polos, not far from Baghdad (perhaps the Greek city Seleucia), he found a grave with a beautiful building built over it, and wrote down the locals' explanation: A rich man had had a dream in which a Jew named Brosak appeared to him and promised him children if he would erect the building. When it was finished, children were born to the family (24). In Shushan, Petachia was shown Daniel's coffin "suspended . . . by iron chains on high iron pillars, erected in the middle of the river. . . . The Jews told him that any vessel passing underneath the coffin will proceed in safety if those in it be pious, but will founder if this not be the case" (39, 41). At Yavne, Petachia visited a miraculous spring that "flows for six days of the week, but on the Sabbath not a single drop is found in it" (57).[29] Nearby, in the lower Galilee, in the cave in which Shammai was buried with his disciples, he found "a large stone, hollow like a cup. . . . When men of worth enter, the stone appears full of sweet water. . . . The water doesn't appear to those not worthy" (57). The caves around Meron, near Safed, had long been associated with water miracles. One late medieval pilgrim reported that "on the three *Regolim* the Jews come to the burial place of the *tzadiq* Rabbi Shimon Bar Yochai and beseech with prayers, *selichos* and *tachanunim* to Hashem [God] that He grant them rain to enable them to stay there for a few days. And rain follows immediately."[30]

Medieval Jewish pilgrims not only recorded past miracles, they often saw miraculous intervention in events in their own lives, particularly their narrow escapes. Meshullam ben Menachem (1481) interpreted a boating accident near Candia (today's Iraklion, Crete) this way. While attempting to board a small boat, it slipped out from under him and he fell into the sea where he "sunk more than ten cubits with all my clothes. . . . Thank God the master of the ship saw that I had fallen into the water and ordered his sailors to jump into the water and get me out. . . . Then they got me on to dry land and God saved me" (202). Narrow escapes seem to have been Meshullam's specialty. Another time he was seated under a mast aboard ship and for no apparent reason decided to get up. He moved a step away and a mast timber crashed down where he had just been. "Another great miracle was wrought to me by the Almighty" (202).

Petachia of Ratisbon, writing about Ezekiel's grave near Damascus, reported that he had gone to visit the holy man's grave with some gold grains, but that the grains fell from his hands and were lost. When he arrived at the grave, he explained to Ezekiel that he had lost the grains and added, "wherever they may be they are thine." At that moment Petachia saw a bright light at some distance, and when he went to look, he found the grains, which he then placed on the holy man's grave (27, 29).

Not every Jewish pilgrim was so credulous. The Italian pilgrim Obadiah Jaré da Bertinoro, for example, answered an inquiry from home in 1481 in this way: "You ask me about the miracles which are said to take place at the temple-mountain and graves of the pious. What can I tell you, my brother, about them? I have not seen them."[31]

PREPARATIONS FOR THE JOURNEY

Pilgrimage always involved sacrifice. It was expensive. It took a long time, and the pilgrims were likely to be out of touch with home during much of the journey. Like any lengthy travel in the Middle Ages, it was risky, and there was a chance that the pilgrims would never see their loved ones again. The pilgrims might die along the road, or be taken prisoner. Their journey might become *aliyah*, with the pilgrim settling in the Holy Land and never returning home.

Thus the decision to become a pilgrim weighed heavily. Judah Halevi, who died en route to Jerusalem around 1141, told God in his poem, "His Pilgrimage to Zion," that to make the journey he had to leave behind the love of his family and the joy of being with his young grandson.[32] The Italian pilgrim Obadiah Jaré da Bertinoro regretted having left his father behind: "My departure has caused you sorrow and trouble, and I am inconsolable because I have left you at a time when your strength is failing; when I remember, dear father, that I have forsaken your grey hairs, I cannot refrain from tears" (209). Elijah of Pesaro concluded a letter to his brother in 1563 with these words: "my eyes and my heart are there with you day and night, and I constantly think about all I have left behind. I am with you even in my dreams, and awake crying, only to perceive that I am alone here, and that none of you is standing at my side" (56).

Like the Hindu sadhus who renounce every aspect of their former lives to wander the roads of India devoid of family, clothes, or even names, some Jewish pilgrims cut themselves loose from life with a single-minded determination that must have seemed cruel to those whom they left behind. In 1602, when he was twenty-eight years old, Solomon Shloemel ben Hayyim Meinsterl of Lundenberg decided to make a pilgrimage to the Holy Land:

> I sent my wife away with a divorce as she did not want to go with me. I also paid her all that was due her in accordance with her marriage contract, and also left our one daughter who was at that time thirteen years old with her. So, of all that had been mine not so much as a hair was left, not even my clothes and books, for I left them behind for her alimony and for the dowry of my daughter; but I trusted in the God of Jacob and entrusted my welfare to him. So I did depart from the land of my birth, in complete destitution.[33]

Sometimes the pull of the Holy Land conflicted with familial duty. In 1798, when the great rabbi Nachman of Breslov yielded to his obsession to go on pilgrimage to Israel, he dealt with his family abruptly.

> [The Rebbe's wife] sent her daughter, asking how it was possible for him to leave them without means of support. The Rebbe answered his daughter, "You can travel to your fiancé's parents. Someone will take your older sister in to live as a nursemaid. Another will take your younger sister in out of pity. Your mother can find work as a cook. I will sell everything in the house for travelling expenses." When the Rebbe's family heard this, they all burst into

tears. They wept bitterly, but he had no pity on them. He said, "It is impossible without this. No matter what happens, I must certainly go. For most of me is already there, and the minority must follow the majority."[34]

Once the medieval Jew had decided to become a pilgrim and had crossed the emotional bridge leading him away from his former status, he had to decide what to take with him: first and foremost, money or other portable assets like jewels. Normal travel was expensive, requiring outlays for transportation, food, tolls, taxes, bribes, and the like, and pilgrims were bound to encounter emergencies that also required cash. Pilgrims were obligated to perform acts of charity along the way and once they had reached the Holy Land. And, since many medieval Jews made their living as businessmen, they budgeted for acquiring items that could be sold back home.

In 1601 a group of Jews traveled to the Holy Land with a Christian pilgrim named John Sanderson. Sanderson's narrative provides some insights into his companions' activities. For example, they all stayed ten days in Damascus so that Abrahim Coen, whom Sanderson calls "a ritch [sic] . . . Jewe," could do some business. Coen spent 10,000 to 12,000 gold ducats ordering merchandise that he would pick up on his return. Sanderson notes that the moneys were quilted into the Jew's clothing. Sanderson was impressed that Coen had brought another 3,000 ducats, or perhaps more, to buy books to take to the Holy Land or to give in alms once he had arrived. Upon arriving in Safed, his party joined a "solemn Sabbath" celebration, and then stayed six more days. Coen gave away books—two fully-loaded mules' worth—alms, and food, including bread, porridge, and meat, one piece to each poor person. Sanderson calculated that Coen gave away at least 2,000 ducats-worth of goods in Safed, and another 1,000 in Jerusalem (96). Meshullam ben Menachem also combined pilgrimage with business. Once on his sea journey he nearly drowned, in part because "in my girdle I had all the jewels and precious stones which I had bought in Egypt . . ." (202).

Other than occasional hints such as these, there is little data about precisely what Jewish pilgrims carried with them. In addition to listing foods to take on a sea journey, Elijah of Pesaro (1563) recommended packing "wax, tapers, one lantern, [and] a copper vessel for your bodily needs" (49). We don't find a specific pilgrim packing list until 1650, when the Prague pilgrim Moses ben Israel Poryat (also known as Moses Praeger) advised potential immigrants and pilgrims in his book *Vademecum for Palestinian Travelers*. He insisted pilgrims pack their own bedding for the trip, even though bedding was cheap in Jerusalem, because they would need it on the road. He also instructed travelers to bring all their clothing, linen goods, and leather goods with them, because these were in short supply in Jerusalem and thus expensive. He cautioned travelers not to carry many books because transportation costs were high, but then listed an obligatory selection of volumes that would cripple six mules.[35]

MEANS OF TRAVEL

Most journeys to the Holy Land required both land and sea travel. Pilgrims from northern Europe had to travel south or southeast to get to a port. Spanish or

Portuguese Jews sailed from Mediterranean cities like Barcelona or Valencia; Italians departed from Venice or Bari or another of the Adriatic ports. Maghrebi Jews willing to brave the pirates sailed from Algiers or Oran. Boats disembarked at Antioch, Tripoli, Tyre Sidon, Acre, Jaffa, or Askelon and pilgrims traveled the rest of the way to Jerusalem by land. The route they chose depended on a number of factors, not the least of which was the availability of transportation. Generally, pilgrims tried to avoid places in conflict. Particularly during the Crusades, when various port cities were at times under siege, they tended to choose routes that skirted the battling armies or the ruins they left in their wake. Jaffa, for example, was twice taken by the Christians, in 1126 and 1191, was each time destroyed, and was subsequently rebuilt by the Muslims. Ashkelon, too, changed hands many times, and after its destruction in 1270 ceased to be a viable port of entry. During these centuries pilgrims seemed to have preferred sailing to the Lebanese or Syrian ports and caravanning south. Mesopotamian Jews might come from Baghdad or Damascus by caravan, as might Jews from Egypt or the Yemen.

Calculating the potential risk, expense, and convenience of the various routes and means of travel must have been a nightmare. Some of the pilgrims and traveling businessmen who wrote in the later Middle Ages assumed that it was their duty to counsel their readers about travel strategies. Their words allow us a glimpse of their authors' own travel experiences. Moses Basola (1521), for example, recommended where to find a good ship berth and cautioned against bunking in the cargo hold. If two people were traveling together, he advised taking a cabin, even if the cost of four or five ducats was a little pricey. For a family traveling together, he recommended reserving the purser's cabin, which should book for about five ducats. Passengers evidently could prepare food for themselves, for Basola suggested paying the ship's cook something to let them warm their pot on his fire. He also stressed the importance of acquiring fresh water at each port. Basola acknowledged that Jews, given the prevailing attitudes against them, were likely to find expenses a little higher: "The Jews usually collect the sum of a ducat among themselves for the deck officer so that he will look after them and deliver them from the ill-disposed ones among them, for it is in his power to do harm or good. It is essential to make this promise at the beginning of the voyage and to keep one's word at its conclusion. A word to the wise is sufficient" (116).

Elijah of Pesaro got as far as Famagusta (in Cyprus) before halting his pilgrimage in 1563 because of news of a plague in the Holy Land. His letter back home detailed his ideas about the costs and rigors of travel by sea. He described the Venetian galleass (a rapid passenger boat developed in the sixteenth century) and how the passengers' belongings, merchandise, and moneys were carefully registered before setting sail. Elijah must have traveled on a fairly luxurious galleass, since he recorded that, in addition to the normal sailing crew, the boat carried "two doctors . . . , a barber, a scrivener, a priest, a carpenter, a smith, a harness-maker, a butcher, and a herdsman to look after the beasts" (41). He detailed the various sleeping spaces, and insisted that pilgrims trust no one and get everything in writing.

Ferrying pilgrims could be a lucrative venture, and we know that some ports—Venice is a good example—specialized in such trade. In the 1480s Obadiah Jaré da Bertinoro wrote to his brother that he had received three letters from him

Pilgrim boat? "Colonia" [Cologne]. Hartmann Schedel, *The Nuremberg Chronicle*, 1493.

"through the master of the pilgrim ship," noting that "every year Jews come in the Venetian galleys and even in the pilgrim ships, for there is really no safer and shorter way than by these ships." He lamented that "I wish I had known all this while I was still in those parts [Italy], I would not then have remained so long on the journey. The galleys perform the voyage from Venice here in forty days at the most" (243). It seems likely that these boats carried Christian pilgrims primarily, but that paying Jews were welcome.

Moses ben Israel Poryat advised pilgrims to go to the Holy Land through Constantinople. He suggested that one should head to Vienna to link with a traveling merchant group. From there one should buy a riverboat passage to Budapest and from there three people should get together to hire a wagon (paying extra for baggage) for the journey to Constantinople. Once there, the pilgrim had to choose a boat: "Every new Moon of Elul, many ships set out together from Constantinople, so one can proceed comfortably and also be secure, thank God, from pirates" Traveling by caravan, on the other hand, may have been safer but it was clearly more uncomfortable, as it "usually remains stationary by day and travels during the night because of the great heat" (66–67).

Some journeys were less complicated. In 1621 Rabbi Isaiah Hurwitz of Prague wrote home to his family that his twenty-two-day sea journey had been relatively uneventful—despite the fact that his ship had been pursued for a time by a warship. He was pleased to note that "even the captain on the sea was well inclined to us so that we had a special room which was set aside for the study of the Torah and for prayers."[36]

Meshullam ben Menachem (1481) focused his advice on the overland routes from Gaza to Jerusalem:

> It is all desert, and every man must carry on his beast two sacks, one of biscuits and the other of straw and fodder, also water skins, for there you cannot find sweet water, but only salt. You must also take with you lemons because of the insects, . . . and you must go in a big caravan because of the robbers who frequent the desert, and you must go slowly for two reasons; the one because in the desert there is much dust and sand and the horses sink in it up to their knees and go with difficulty, and secondly because the dust rises and gets into a man's mouth and makes his throat dry and kills him with thirst, and if he drinks of the hot brackish water he is troubled worse than before (181).

FEAR IS THE PILGRIM'S COMPANION

Jewish and Christian pilgrims in the Middle Ages must have felt like characters in one of those video games—pardon the anachronism—where in every passageway dangers lurk to annihilate the traveler. Pilgrims carried cash, or its equivalent, to meet the expenses of their journey, and cash invites theft. Wealthy pilgrims could be captured and held for ransom; indigents were sold as slaves. Pilgrims to the Muslim Middle East were apt to be viewed as infidels whose murder, even if not immediately profitable, was likely to be rewarded in the afterlife. Pilgrim writing, therefore, includes a litany of cautions.

Battles disrupted traffic. Solomon ben Yehuda (about 1035), in a letter to the head of the Babylonian community in the Egyptian city of Fustat, complained: "I cannot hide from you the fact the even those pilgrims who used to come every year were prevented from doing so by warring armies and impassable roads."[37] A Western pilgrim, most likely from Spain or the Maghreb, wrote from Alexandria around 1100 that the Crusaders' attack on Jerusalem had brought pilgrimage traffic to a standstill (he had actually begun his pilgrimage about five years earlier, but had to stay in Alexandria because of the violence). He made clear that he was rooting for the Muslims to win, and if they did he promised to go straight away to visit Jerusalem and then return home.[38]

Brigands were a constant threat. In 1047, before journeying into the mountainous lower Galilee to visit the holy tombs, the Persian poet Naser-e Khosraw deposited all his valuables at the mosque in Acre for safekeeping because rumors of theft and robbery were rampant (17).[39] Meshullam ben Menachem advised travelers to be particularly wary of the bands of robbers who prey on the smaller caravans. These brigands rush at the pilgrims with "horses swift as leopards, with bamboo lances topped with iron in their hands, which are very hard. They also

Rachel's Tomb. Postcard, circa 1910. Authors' collection.

carry a pirate's mace in their hands and bucklers made of parchment and pitch; . . . they come upon the caravans suddenly and take everything, even the clothes and horses, and sometimes they kill them" (182). In the late fifteenth century the stretch of road through the mountains north of Jerusalem was considered particularly dangerous. Tax collectors were often in league with the brigands and sometimes they killed pilgrims who would not pay. In 1495 the party of one of Obadiah Jaré da Bertinoro's disciples was attacked outside of Shechem, taken back to the city, and held prisoner. The pilgrims spent a night in panic, wondering what would happen to them. The next day the donkey drivers, who were a multireligious group (and may well have collaborated in the extortion), worked out a deal. The pilgrims coughed up fourteen ducats, of which the narrator's contribution was fourteen silver pieces. Even after they had paid and gone on their way, the pilgrims were still worried that the bandits would recapture them.[40] The disciple also related that the roads were not safe going to and coming from Hebron and the tomb of Rachel. To illustrate the dangers, he told about another Jew who had come from Hebron to Jerusalem and the Arabs stole everything he had. Yet, hope reigned, for in the very next sentence he said, "I have heard it said that Jews come here from Egypt and Damascus for the Passover festival and go to Hebron quite safely," so he decided to wait to visit Hebron then (27).

Pirates, corsairs, and other maritime thieves were equally dangerous. In the twelfth century, Judah Halevi's list of potential threats included sea attacks by Crusaders, Muslims, sea monsters, and pirates, the last of which were probably responsible for his death. On the way he suffered seasickness, hunger, and thirst. Halevi was eloquent, and quite reasonably frightened, at the dangers of an ocean voyage. But his positive feelings about the Holy Land outweighed the discomforts, dangers, and deprivations that he catalogued in his verses:

> But all this is a light thing when set against Thy love,
> Since I may enter Thy gates with thanksgiving,
> And sojourn there, and count my heart
> A burnt offering bound upon Thine altar;
> And may make my grave in Thy land,
> So that it be there a witness for me.
>
> ("On the Sea, No. 3," 22–23)

Pirates were a hazard to sea travel to the Holy Land for the next several centuries. They were so thick along the North African coast that many pilgrims preferred the arduous—but safer—inland route across Algeria, Tunisia, Libya, and Egypt. In the sixteenth century, the Knights of Rhodes, based in Malta, found it lucrative to capture and hold for ransom Jewish pilgrims and businessmen.[41]

Some pilgrims must have felt that human enemies and the forces of nature were both allied against them. Obadiah Jaré da Bertinoro (1480s) certainly had reason when his boat anchored at Alexandria and the captain refused to put ashore out of fear for his life. While representatives of the emir at Alexandria shuffled back and forth from the anchored boat to their court in Cairo in order to negotiate the captain's safe landing, provisions aboard ship began to run out. Obadiah complained, "Our victuals began to be exhausted, we had no water, and would already have preferred death to life." As if that were not enough, that night a large storm arose. As waves washed over the deck, "the ship threatened to be wrecked every moment, for it was old and damaged. . . . For about twenty-four hours we were in such danger that we expected death every moment" (219). Fortunately Obadiah lived to tell the tale: the passengers were given pails and instructed to bail as fast as they could, and they managed to stave off disaster until the storm abated. Others were not so fortunate. When Elijah of Ferrara went with some of his family to Palestine in the early 1430s, two of his sons and a grandson all died on the journey.

Trivial things upset the pilgrims as well. The caravans were uncomfortable, and travelers needed to be attentive to their animals. For example, the group of Jews and John Sanderson who left Jerusalem for Shechem, on July 9, 1601, had to spend the night outside the town because "our horses, cambles, myles, and asses [were] very hott and weary" (113). The annoyance could be something as minor as not finding familiar food, as when Solomon ben Moses Sfaxi (i.e., from Sfax, Tunisia) in 1059 whined that "I am . . . in need of chickens."[42] Many pilgrims, faced with the unfamiliar, suffered from what today we call culture shock. Writers like Meshullam ben Menachem (1481) show this in their emphasis on the negative aspects of what they were viewing or experiencing. Listen, for example, to Meshullam about dinner: "The Moslems and also the Jews of this place are pigs at their eating. They all eat out of one vessel with their fingers, without a napkin, just as the Cairenes do" (194). Yet other pilgrims, like Meshullam's contemporary Obadiah Jaré da Bertinoro, take these same circumstances in stride, seeing them as normal and not at all unsettling. Here is Obadiah at a Shabbat dinner in Alexandria: "After all have drunk to their heart's content, a large dish of meat is brought, each one stretches forth his hand, takes what he wants, and eats quickly, for they are not very big eaters" (221).

Since Jews were rarely welcomed, except by other Jews, it was prudent to carry letters of introduction that attested to the pilgrim's bona fides. In that way, the pilgrims had the hope that they would be well received, and the receiving communities could feel more comfortable about opening their homes to these strangers. One such letter, probably dating from the eleventh century, was written in Salonica for a Russian pilgrim:

> We send greetings to you and feel it our duty to inform you about the request of Mr. . . . . He is a Jew from Russia and stayed with us here in Salonica, where he met his relative, Mr. . . . , who returned recently from the holy city of Jerusalem. . . . He [the Russian pilgrim] asked us to give him these few lines in order to use them as means of introduction. Please help him to reach his goal by the proper route, with the support of reliable men . . . for he knows . . . only Russian.[43]

His contemporary, a man named Reuben from Rodez (France), beset by terrible problems at home (a son and servants had been killed by bandits and he had been robbed by the area's governor), decided to go to die in Jerusalem. He asked a congregation for a letter "in order that it should be my mouthpiece in all the holy communities on the other side of the sea, because I am ignorant of their language."[44]

It is clear from this representative sample of reports that pilgrims had to remain alert to danger at every moment if they expected to survive their experience. But Jewish travelers had an added burden: they knew that the response to any unintended faux pas would likely be more severe because they were Jewish. It was wise to keep the lowest profile possible. Thus Meshullam ben Menachem advised that Jewish pilgrims who did not know Arabic should dress like Turks so that the Muslim residents would not assume they were Jews or Christian Franks (181).

Sometimes Jewish pilgrims let their guard down and luck, or providence, took care of them anyway. Moses Basola (1521) was one such. Early one morning he was riding on his camel through a valley. As Moses was preparing to put on his phylacteries, a tree branch whacked him in the face, throwing him off the camel and onto his back on the ground. He suffered several injuries, and may even have been knocked unconscious for some time. He reported the incident in his book without the slightest chagrin, concluding that God had granted him two miracles. The first was that he didn't die from the fall, and second, that the Muslims he was traveling with did not take advantage of his state to kill him but instead wrapped up his rib cage and took him to Safed.

TOLLS

If bandits were likely, tolls were certain. Travelers had to pay to get off a ship, enter a city gate, or use a highway. Pilgrims passing through Nablus had to pay a tax to support the military garrison there. When they entered Jerusalem, if they could not show a Nablus receipt they had to pay again.[45] Tolls were the bane of existence for all pilgrims, but particularly for Jewish pilgrims, who seemed always to be required to pay something extra. Fifteenth- and sixteenth-century pilgrim authors seem to have obsessed about tolls, considering it their responsibility to let their readers to know where and how much they would have to pay to officials whom, for the most part, they considered little better than thieves.

When Moses Basola sailed from Venice to Lebanon in 1521, he landed at Tripoli and his party had to pay four dirhams per person and ten dirhams for each piece of luggage or container of goods with them (57). Jewish men disembarking in Beirut, he wrote, had to pay seventy dirhams. Apparently in Beirut there was no charge for Jewish women or children, and personal luggage entered without charge. On the other hand, as soon as Basola got out on the highway he was hit with more tolls (the local term was *khafars*). Near Beirut, Jews were taxed ten dirhams. At Sidon there were three tolling places, and he had to pay ten dirhams at each. To pass Tyre he had to pay another ten dirhams. On the return journey from Safed to Damascus, Basola paid a total of thirty-five dirhams at three different collection points. With ironic understatement he cautioned his readers that there are a lot of opportunities to pay khafars in the Holy Land (57–60, 85).

According to Obadiah Jaré da Bertinoro (late 1480s), toll collectors also plagued the road from Cairo to Jerusalem. He counted twenty separate toll posts, and in total had to pay out a ducat to be allowed to pass. At the end of the road, with his goal in sight, it got worse. He reported that Jews, be they pilgrims or ordinary travelers, who entered Jerusalem from Cairo were required to pay "ten silver denarii at the city gate, while, . . . those who come by way of Jaffa have to pay a ducat" (242). Jewish residents in the city had to pay special taxes as well. John Sanderson (1601), observed that non-Jews, both travelers and residents, paid less (242). Writing about his visit to Joshua's tomb, he noted that all of the sacred sites were controlled by Muslims, and that "the Jewes at all pay pole pence, some more, some lesse, to the Moores before they be permitted to say thier ceremonies" (99).

By Ottoman times the toll business seems to have become extraordinarily corrupt, particularly in the environs of Jerusalem. Pilgrims visiting the tombs of the Patriarchs in Hebron and the tomb of Samuel the prophet near Jerusalem had to open their purses at several checkpoints. The Ottoman government in Istanbul regulated tolls and specified that a portion of what was collected should go toward the expenses of protecting pilgrims on the highways. But Jerusalem's governors paid little attention, instead considering pilgrims an inexhaustible source of cash. Rather than extending protection, they devised various schemes for extorting even more money from pilgrims. Featherbedding was common, with pilgrims required to hire an extra mule handler or two. Toll takers in the villages were encouraged to inflate their rates, with an implied kickback to the governor. Sometimes pilgrims had to pay to keep from being beaten or imprisoned for some minor or contrived infraction. If they could not pay cash, merchandise would do. In 1535, when a group of Jewish pilgrims were guided from Jerusalem to Hebron by an Ottoman government representative from Hebron, they paid him and the taxes with eleven arms' length of cloth.[46]

Some writers tried to cheat the toll takers by avoiding the toll stations. Meshullam ben Menachem (1481), for example, chose a roundabout way from Hebron to Jerusalem in order to avoid paying the taxes at the seven tollhouses on the road between the two cities. Was it worth the effort? Probably not, because off the main road Meshullam was attacked and nearly killed by robbers. He managed to stave them off with the assistance of two Mamelukes with whom he was traveling, but ended up having to pay them two ducats for their help (189).

PLAGUES AND PUDDLES

As modern travelers know, changes in diet and water can produce rumbling side effects. And with the unsanitary conditions that prevailed in most of the medieval world, pilgrim globetrotters were always at risk. Illness is mentioned often enough in pilgrim reports to suggest it was the rule and not the exception. In late December 1059 Tunisian pilgrim Solomon ben Moses Sfaxi wrote home from Jerusalem, where at that time of year it was likely that not a warm spot was to be found: "I arrived yesterday in Jerusalem . . . in sound health, after terrible suffering" (169). Obadiah Jaré da Bertinoro remarked that everyone else with whom he had traveled to Jerusalem had fallen ill. He attributed the bouts of sickness to climate changes (243). Meshullam ben Menachem complained, "I was ill in Jerusalem from the day I arrived until I left to go to Damascus, and I was near to death's door. . . . It is not to be wondered at that the foreigners who go there get ill; the wonder is that they do not all die. This is caused by the troublesome journey and the great heat one has to endure on the way" (195). Meshullam attributed his survival to the diligent attentions of an Ashkenazi family, who fixed him the comfort food he was used to from home. Unfortunately, once he left their care his health problems started up again. He wrote that from Jerusalem to Beirut he suffered from the heat. Then he had an attack of ague, and later a bad headache (196).

Since no traveler likes to swelter, or worse, to be wet, cold, and miserable, we are not surprised to find that Jewish pilgrims often whined about the weather. Solomon ben Moses, the eleventh-century pilgrim from Sfax whom we quoted above, got hammered by the weather in Ramleh: "the city is beset by terrible rain and snow, the rain having continued now for four days" (169). Meshullam ben Menachem carped that the deserts were uncomfortably hot, while "in Jerusalem there are draughts every day, summer and winter, different winds from the four corners of the earth such as I have never seen. They get into a man's limbs and kill him" (195). Moses Basola (1521) lamented that it took his group eight days to make the journey from Jerusalem to Safed "for the roads were washed out by the heavy rains" (84).

Travelers were likely to spread diseases as they journeyed. The men who guarded the walled cities' gates were alert for signs of illness and, at the first glimmer of a pustule, the doors slammed shut and the travelers had to sleep outside. In 1579, for example, some Jewish pilgrims from Cairo were barred entry to Jerusalem because officials feared they were bringing the plague with them. Of course, money could open closed doors and this well-known fact bred abuse. One favorite extortion tactic was to accuse pilgrims arriving from Syria or Egypt of carrying disease and to deny them entrance until the appropriate palms were crossed with silver.[47]

THE COMPANY OF PILGRIMS

We can assume that for safety's sake most pilgrims, at least until modern times, traveled in groups. The other reason Jewish pilgrims preferred group travel, of course, was to have a minyan of ten men in order to conduct religious services.[48] Yet early pilgrim accounts rarely give us specifics about the people with whom the narrators were traveling. It is only when the Renaissance currents of the late fifteenth century swept into the travel genre that writers began to flesh out their narratives with details that give them depth and perspective.

Obadiah Jaré da Bertinoro's letters to his father (1480s) describe his surroundings in fascinating detail. We know, for example, that his companions on the voyage from Messina to Rhodes included a Jewish merchant from Sucari (probably Palermo, Italy) traveling with a servant, "three Jewish leatherworkers from Syracuse, and a Sephardic Jew with his wife, two sons and two daughters." In all there were fourteen Jewish people on board (214–215). From Alexandria to the Nile he traveled with a man, his wife, and two sons because the father had made a vow to be in Jerusalem for the Passover feast (223). Ma'ir ibn Shamwil made the pilgrimage in the late sixteenth century with his entire family. The Jerusalem community persuaded him to remain there as rabbi.[49] Moses ben Israel Poryat, whose *Vademecum* (circa 1650) provided useful information for potential immigrants to the Holy Land, advised Jewish women about what books they should take with them, and encouraged them to pack Spanish sewing needles as well (69).

Yet most information about traveling companions is at best sketchy. A Jewish pilgrim group arriving in Jerusalem in 1538 included twenty-one Arabic-speaking men and women and twenty-four Europeans.[50] Moses Basola was accompanied on the land portion of his journey by some Muslims and at least two other Jews. The caravan had three camels roped together, so it seems likely that some of the travelers walked (60–61). The documents suggest that pilgrims attached themselves to a group or left it according to their personal circumstances. Obadiah Jaré da Bertinoro reported that when he sailed from Palermo, he joined a group that included Meshullam ben Menachem and his servant. One day a sailor acted crassly with Meshullam, who complained to the ship's master. Although the master reprimanded the sailor and wrenched an apology from him, Obadiah reported that the crew was displeased about the situation. At the next opportunity, Meshullam left that ship for another, even though it meant changing his proposed route through Alexandria to the Holy Land to one that took him through Chios and Constantinople (215–216).

The most detailed medieval list of Jewish traveling companions was provided by the Christian pilgrim John Sanderson. He sailed with a group of four Europeans to Sidon, where he (or they) joined a group of eight Jews on their way to Damascus. He lists seven of these Jews by name, and tells a little something about them: Abram Coen, son of Isack Coen, from Tirria et Sio (perhaps Chios); Rabbi

Salamon Marabi, from Terria; Jacob ben al David, from Smyrna; Isake, son of Jacob (about twenty-two years old at the time of the pilgrimage); Abram Alvo, from Constantinople (he cooked throughout the journey); Mose Rosino, from Damascus (he left the group in Damascus); Salamon di Urbino, from Constantinople. The eighth Jew was the father-in-law of Abram Coen. It appears that he desired to go to Safed to die and the group left him there. On the whole Sanderson's attitude toward the Christians and the Muslims he met was negative. But, surprisingly, he had both good and bad things to say about his Jewish traveling companions and some other Jewish people whom he met in Jerusalem. He seems to have valued them for their friendship and help: "My companion Jew, merchant and a dweller in Sio and Smirna, was so respective, kind and courteous that never in any Christians company, of what degree soever, I ever did receive better content." He was critical of a Jerusalem Jew who got him into trouble with a local Turk. However, in another situation when the Jerusalem Turkish ruler threatened him with imprisonment—Sanderson stupidly had worn his sword when he entered Jerusalem and then refused to pay the fine demanded of him—he was quite thankful when his Jewish companion successfully begged the ruler for Sanderson's release (120–121, 122, 124).

Jews from around the world came together along the pilgrimage roads. Their home languages might be Frankish, Persian, German, Arabic, Spanish, Italian, or one of the Slavic tongues, but their knowledge of Hebrew, which in the Middle Ages was the near universal language of Jewish prayer and study, allowed them to communicate with each other with some ease. Over the centuries more than one chronicler has noted the beneficial effects of the group pilgrimage culture on the communal psyche of the Jews. The first-century historian Josephus, for example, wrote that the pilgrimage to Jerusalem fostered appreciation, tolerance, and "mutual affection" among the Jews.[51] Fifteen hundred years later Meshullam ben Menachem reflected on the diverse community of Jewish pilgrims who were united by their common religious culture. In Ramah, a village not far from Jerusalem, he visited the small cave revered as the tomb of Samuel, Elkanah and Hannah:

> The Jews gather there every year and come even from Babylon, from Aram Zobah, which they call Aleppo, from Hamath, and from Gaza, and from Damascus, and Misr [Egypt], and other places, so that the foreigners by themselves are more than one thousand in number who come there every year on the 28th of the month of Iyar to mourn and to pray in this cave. . . . And all the Jews who come there are accustomed to buy oil to light in that Synagogue, and I, poor man, prayed in that place and put oil there as is the custom. (193)

And what of the larger, multireligious community that trekked to Palestine's holy sites in the Middle Ages? Jewish pilgrims often traveled in the company of Christians, and some of the holy places they visited were revered by Muslims as well. Since during most of the Middle Ages the holy places lay in Muslim-controlled lands, all pilgrims had to depend on Muslims for food, lodging, travel arrangements, and information. The Disciple of Bertinoro, in 1495, suggested that the safest way to travel by land was in large caravans and that camels or donkeys made the best mounts. He met up with some Christian Sicilian pilgrims in Safed, and they contracted a caravan of donkey drivers of all religions, Jews, Christians, and Muslims, to take them to Jerusalem for one set all-inclusive price (21). Guides were drawn from each of the three religious communities. Paula, a fifth-century Christian pilgrim from Italy, engaged at least one Jewish guide in the Galilee. Eleven hundred years later the Jewish cloth merchant 'Azar ibn Ibrahim acted as interpreter for a group of Catholic pilgrims.[52] When the Protestant pilgrim John Sanderson (1601) wanted to visit exclusively Christian sites, he hired a "Greekish preest," but engaged a poor Jewish resident of Jerusalem to accompany them, primarily to help translate, since the priest spoke mostly Greek and Sanderson only a little Italian. Sanderson made clear that he preferred the company of the Jewish pilgrims, and stuck with them for the rest of his visit in the Holy Land (102–103, 112).

Jewish travel accounts make clear that, although Jewish pilgrims often had pleasant interactions with their Christian or Muslim companions, they did not enter into a state of communitas with them. Again, Meshullam ben Menachem's experiences in 1481 are representative. Meshullam took passage on a fishing boat with other pilgrims, but the owner did not tell the Christian passengers that Meshullam and his companions were Jews. Both knew that the underlying tensions between the religions could flare into open conflict at any time. Meshullam was nervous from the first moment, so he was especially kind and courteous to the Christian group, whom he later wrote were "all wicked Germans and Frenchmen, but strong nobles and lords." Eventually the Christians learned that Meshullam was a Jew, but by then they had grown to like him so much that they did him no harm (198). Even when a Jewish pilgrim's interactions with his Christian and Muslim companions were entirely positive, he tended to report them in a way that suggested that the prevailing cultural tensions rendered his experiences exceptional. Meshullam's contemporary Obadiah Jaré da Bertinoro came to this conclusion about the Arabs in his travels in and around Jerusalem: "The Jews are not persecuted by the Arabs in these parts. I have traveled through the country in its length and breadth, and not one of them has put an obstacle in my way. They are very kind to strangers, particularly to anyone who does not know the language; and if they see many Jews together they are not annoyed by it" (235).

LODGING AND FOOD

Medieval Jewish pilgrims did not write very much about where they found lodging. Perhaps they believed that their audiences were so familiar with sleeping and eating arrangements that they did not need to record the details. Nothing about fleas, or the advantages of fresh straw over week-old straw in mattresses. Nothing about five to a room, or three to a bed—except for the sick or the very wealthy. Nothing about cold, dirty water. Nothing about the lack of laundry facilities, and the general medieval practice of wearing one's clothes for weeks on end. But from other sources we know enough about medieval travel to have a reasonable idea of how they must have spent their nights. At sea, the poorest travelers slept on deck. The better-off bunked in one of the holds, with the cargo hold being the least prestigious, since even the cleanest of ships also transported rats. As we saw earlier, pilgrims at the top of the economic ladder might reserve a cabin. Elijah of Pesaro (1563) recommended that sea travelers take certain foods with them for the journey: "for each person a half scudo of biscuit, a marcello's worth of bread, one barrel of wine, three bottles of vinegar, dried meat, cheese in brine, oil, . . . cooking pots and covers, all of copper; also peas, beans and the like, pulses, garlic and onions." He also suggested bribing the ship's baker to let them use his fire to prepare their meals (49).

On land the choices were greater, but so were the dangers and discomforts. Pilgrims had to protect themselves, their belongings, and their animals. Lodging inside the city walls was by far preferable to having to stay outside, where banditry was a curse. Most inns provided a variety of sleeping options, with the most common and basic being several people to a room sleeping on straw piled on the floor. In Western countries, whether inside or outside the walls, most had adjacent stables. In the eastern lands, the caravansaries, often with walls as thick as those of a fort, provided sleeping space arranged around a central patio where the animals could be kept for the night. Unfortunately, pilgrims often found them in a state of disrepair. The Disciple of Bertinoro (1495) complained that from Beirut to Damascus "there are no inns to be found on the road that have rooms—beds and tables; but at the end of a day's journey a tumbledown roofless caravansary . . . may sometimes be found" (18). When there were no sleeping rooms, he had to sleep outside with the animals. Most pilgrims kept their meager belongings beside them or sewn into their clothes.

In places where Jews lived, some community member generally lodged the Jewish travelers. In addition to providing a bed, the locals were sources of kosher food, news, and comradeship. Travelers could pray with the local minyan. On his pilgrimage, Petachia (twelfth century) went to Babel and conferred with the head of the academy there. He was given a sealed document to act as a safe-conduct and to introduce him to the other Jewish communities along his route. The document proved useful: In Shushan, he found only two resident Jews, and when he showed them the document, they took him to see Daniel's coffin (13, 23, 39). Obadiah Jaré da Bertinoro (1480s) reported that when he arrived in Rhodes, the leaders of the Jewish community went to the boat to greet him. They lodged him in "a fine room, provided with all necessities" and the other Jews on the boat were all "accommodated as well as it was possible," which was somewhat difficult, since the Rhodians' houses had all been destroyed in a Turkish siege (216). In Alexandria, Obadiah was lodged in the home of Rabbi Moses Grasso, the dragoman to the Venetians, who had rescued him and his companions from the Arabs. He invited Obadiah and a Sephardic pilgrim to Sabbath dinner (220). The trip by the Disciple of Bertinoro included a stay in Safed: "There we took a small room in the house of an extremely poor and needy Jew. In his house we remained for more than a month" (19). They paid him two silver coins daily for rent and food, including bread. At the caravansaries he could often purchase bread, fruit, and eggs. Or, as he reported in another passage, they could buy pareve provisions like "bread, cheese, grapes, and peaches" (16).

Jerusalem's Jews were not always pleased with the pilgrim traffic. Local residents tended to believe that pilgrims exhausted the local support systems and drove up prices. In 1579 the governor of Jerusalem went so far as to try to prohibit pilgrims from entering the city. He alleged that "they ride horses, change their clothing [to resemble Muslims], follow in Muslims' footsteps, seize Muslim women and employ them as [their] servants, [and] upset the local residents by causing prices to rise."[53] On the other hand, they could be good customers since pilgrims require everything, from food and lodging to translation services and souvenirs.

Relatively little evidence remains of Jewish pilgrimage souvenirs, except for some hexagonal mold-blown glass vessels, which may have been used to transport oil or dirt from the Holy Land back to the pilgrim's home. The lack of reference to them in the written accounts leads us to conjecture that they were fairly common items. They seem to have been made in Jerusalem in a workshop that also made similar objects for Christian pilgrims. The difference is the pressed decorative motifs: for Christian pilgrims, a cross; for Jewish pilgrims, a menorah, a lulav, a shofar. The earliest Christian bottles date

Pilgrim souvenir bottle. 4 inches high; mold-blown green glass. 500–700 CE(?). Authors' collection.

from the end of the sixth century. It is probable that the Jewish-motif items were not made after 629, when the Byzantine emperor Heraclius forbade the presence of Jews within a three-mile radius of Jerusalem.[54]

We have dozens of other questions we would have liked to ask these pilgrims. Who cooked the food and what did it cost? What material goods were in the houses they visited? What were the Jewish women like that they met along the way, and how did they occupy their lives? Where did the pilgrims wash themselves and their clothes (presuming that they did)? What sorts of souvenirs did they buy to bring home? Did they sing as they marched or sailed or swayed on the backs of their camels? But of these things the pilgrim chronicles are silent.

OH, ZION: JERUSALEM IN THE CENTER

When I saw the desolate and ruined city from a distance, and Mount Zion lying waste, a habitation for jackals and a lurking place for young lions which foxes traverse, my spirit overflowed, my heart mourned, and my eyes were filled with tears. I sat down and wept. . . . (Disciple of Bertinoro, from Italy, 1495)[1]

Jerusalem's sanctity has never terminated, for pilgrims flock to it from Egypt and other countries . . . and the very same miracles that occurred in Jerusalem during Temple times recur at the present. . . . The synagogue which has just enough room for its regular worshipers is filled to overflowing with more than three hundred pilgrims on Shavuot, all who find ample room and are seated comfortably. (Simon ben Zemah Duran, fourteenth–fifteenth century)[2]

Most medieval Jews and Christians conceived the world to be a large flat place whose holy center was Jerusalem. Jews considered other sites holy in part according to their proximity to the center. The concentric topography of Jewish holiness is nowhere more clearly put than in the Mishnah:

There are ten [degrees of] holiness:
(1) The land of Israel is holier than all lands.
(2) The cities surrounded by a wall are more holy than it [the land].
(3) Within the wall [of Jerusalem] is more holy than they.
(4) The Temple mount is more holy than it.
(5) The rampart is more holy than it.
(6) The court of women is more holy than it.

(7) The court of Israel is more holy than it.

(8) The court of the priests is more holy than it.

(9) The sanctuary is more holy than it.

(10) The Holy of Holies is more holy than it. (Kelim 1:6–9)

Jerusalem was constantly in the thoughts of Diaspora Jews. Their rabbis devised ways to keep the memory of Jerusalem's destruction alive, and to temper it with an intense yearning to see it rebuilt in preparation for the eschatological end of days. Excavations of ancient synagogues show that wall decorations were not uncommon and that the east wall, the wall indicating the direction of Jerusalem, was the most elaborately adorned.[3] At their moment of greatest joy in the wedding ceremony, the bride and groom broke a glass as a reminder of Jerusalem's destruction. In Polish weddings, ashes were placed on the groom's head and in Yemen the rabbi would rub the groom's forehead in dust as he recited Psalm 137, "If I forget you, O Jerusalem."[4] The *Amidah*, one of the fundamental prayers of Jewish liturgy, praised God as the builder of Jerusalem and asked that he rebuild it in our times. Similar sentiments were expressed in the prayers after meals. Among the songs sung at Passover was "Addir Hu," with its refrain asking God to rebuild Jerusalem "soon, in haste, in our own time, soon."[5]

Medieval Jews eagerly awaited the coming of the Messiah. Many believed his coming could be hastened by their positive acts, the most powerful of which were strict adherence to Halakhah and increasing Jewish presence in Palestine. Pilgrimage, and especially pilgrimage with the intent to remain in the Holy Land as settlers, was a strategic act that would hasten the redemption of the Jewish people. A similar phenomenon played itself out in contemporary Christianity with the belief that Christ's second coming would be hastened by establishing Christian communities in the Muslim-controlled lands of the east. The most prominent of these movements was the wave of armed, massed pilgrimages that we know as the Crusades, but before, after, and between these major initiatives, a steady stream of Christian pilgrims and would-be settlers made their way to Jerusalem. Medieval Jewish messianism tended to surge during the years just before dates that the sages calculated were particularly propitious for his arrival. The year 5000 on the Jewish calendar (e.g., 1240) was such a moment, as was 5200 and the start of each succeeding century.[6] During the thirty-year period beginning about 1210, for example, the so-called 300 rabbis, noted scholars from England, France, the Maghreb and Egypt, made their way to Jerusalem in pilgrimage, or aliyah. The Crusaders' capture of Jerusalem in 1229 displaced the survivors to Acre, and eventually many of their descendants returned to Europe. Similarly, the great social unrest in Europe in the late fourteenth and early fifteenth centuries, particularly in Spain, launched numerous pilgrim-aliyah groups in the years preceding 1440. The massive expulsion from Spain in 1492 triggered more arrivals. While many of these pilgrims headed to Jerusalem, others settled in Safed, which was beginning to emerge as the center for the study of Kabbalah. The Chmielnicki massacres of 1648 spurred another wave. Another grew out of the Hasidic messianic yearnings of the Ba'al Shem Tov and his followers beginning in 1740.

All through the Middle Ages, then, Jews infused with religious fervor made their way to Jerusalem. For pilgrims approaching Jerusalem from the north, from Damascus or Safed or Shechem, their first view of the walled city was from Mount Zophim. Pilgrims who had come by sea might ascend from the west via the Jaffa road. Pilgrims from Egypt, coming from the south by way of Hebron, saw the city walls first from the low hill now known as David's City.

The first view of the holy city of Jerusalem could overwhelm Jewish pilgrims. During a lifetime of yearning, years of planning, and months of dangerous, uncomfortable travel, their inner eyes were focused on this moment. "I thank God who has preserved and enabled me to witness this tremendous spectacle," wrote the Karaite Solomon ben Moses Sfaxi in a letter dated December 26, 1059.[7] Samuel ben Samson, on pilgrimage in 1210 in the company of Jonathan ha Cohen, reported that their initial sighting "was a moment of tenderest emotion, and we wept bitterly."[8]

Joy mixed with sorrow; elation tinged with bitterness. Unlike Christian pilgrims, for whom Jerusalem was the site of the triumphant resurrection of their savior and the portal to their personal salvation, medieval Jews saw Jerusalem as a place of ruin, of glories past, of a world now dominated by Christians and Muslims, in which Jews had been marginalized. Though the Temple ruins had been cleared, the Temple Mount had been Islamicized with the construction of the

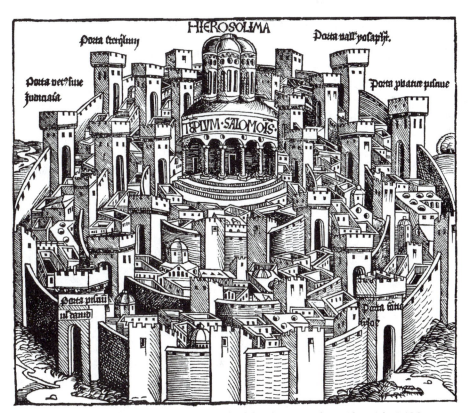

"Hierosolima" [Jerusalem]. Hartmann Schedel, *The Nuremberg Chronicle*, 1493.

Dome of the Rock and the Al-Aqsa Mosque. Jewish pilgrims to Jerusalem focused not on what is, but on what used to be. At the edge of Jerusalem, wrote Rabbi Jacob, the messenger of Jechiel of Paris, who made the pilgrimage from 1238 to 1244, "we go on one of the ruins and look at the Temple Mount and the wall of the Court of Women, and the Court of Israel, the site of the Altar, and the site of the Temple, and the Sanctuary."[9] "The site of, the site of," is repeated over and over in pilgrim accounts like a ritual stocktaking of ruin. In the thirteenth century, Nachmanides termed Jerusalem "more desolate than the rest of the country" and reported that Jews from many places "come to see the Temple site and mourn over it."[10] Estori Farhi wrote in 1312: "The roads of Zion are in mourning because the city has been so frequently destroyed and rebuilt on the same site."[11] In the fifteenth century, Obadiah Jaré da Bertinoro characterized Jerusalem as "desolate and in ruins."[12] In the sixteenth, the Casale pilgrim called it a "waste."[13]

The Bible and centuries of interpretations and commentaries had taught Jews that destruction was the result of God's wrath at the sinfulness of the Jewish people. The ruins of Jerusalem were a visible, tangible reminder of Jewish guilt, a prima facie case that God was punishing the Jews. Meshullam ben Menachem of Volterra in 1481 put it simply and directly: everything is in ruins "because of our sins."[14] The Casale pilgrim echoed his sentiment: Jerusalem "is waste through our sins. Nothing is left of the old construction" (41). The incessant repetition of the phrase "our sins" in this literature draws the reader in as an accomplice to communal guilt. It suggests that until all Jews adhere more faithfully to all the practices of Judaism, Jerusalem will remain in ruins. No wonder that for medieval Jewish pilgrims, lamentation became the principal rite of their visit to Jerusalem. The tone was probably set as early as the fifth century BCE by pilgrims returning from the Babylonian Diaspora, for the Babylonian Talmud prescribes the ritual for their pilgrimage in language that suggests that it was confirming a longstanding practice: "[On seeing] Jerusalem in its [state of] ruin, one recites: *'Our holy and our beautiful house, where our fathers praised Thee, is burned with fire and all our pleasant things are laid waste,'* [Isa. 64:10], and rends his garment" (BT Mo'ed Katan 26a). A document found in the Cairo Genizah describes the ritual lamentations in much more detail:

> If you are worthy to go up to Jerusalem, when you look at the city from Mount Scopus [you should observe the following procedure]. If you are riding on a donkey step down; if you are on foot, take off your sandals, then rending your garment say: "This [our] sanctuary was destroyed" . . . When you arrive in the city continue to rend your garments for the temple and the people and the house of Israel. Then pray saying: "May the Lord our God be exalted" and "Let us worship at his footstool . . . We give you thanks, O Lord our God, that you have given us life, brought us to this point, and made us worthy to enter your house" . . . Then return and circle all the gates of the city and go round all its corners, make a circuit and count its towers.[15]

For Jews living in or near Jerusalem, the ritual rending of garments could become both tiresome and expensive. A donkey driver named Simon of Kamtra asked in the early third century CE if—because he had to pass the temple ruins so often in the course of his work—he was still required to tear his garments every single time?[16]

But for the majority of first-time pilgrims to Jerusalem the emotions were personal and heartfelt, even though they were conditioned by the prescribed ritual. By expressing the emotions expected of them, they fulfilled a religious precept. Obadiah Jaré da Bertinoro in 1488 tore his garments on entering Jerusalem and again at seeing the Temple: "We beheld the famous city of our delight, and here we rent our garments, as was our duty" (234). In 1495, the Disciple of Bertinoro "rent my garment in two places as is required" (22). Moses Basola wrote of his arrival in 1521: "There I tore my clothes and wept for the destroyed and desolate unbuilt city."[17] Some pilgrims also fell to the ground as a sign of respect and mourning. Samuel ben Samson, for example, entered the city in 1210 through the gate next to David's Tower and prostrated himself there before going to the Temple area (103).

For medieval Jewish pilgrims, the holy city had three broad areas: the walled city, the walled Temple compound, and the city's environs. As a rule, we find that once the pilgrims neared Jerusalem, they—and their narratives—focused first on the city and from there ranged outward. Little was left of ancient Jerusalem and few of the important areas were accessible to Jews. Thus most of the medieval Jewish pilgrim chronicles found little to describe, with the exception of the walls with their towers and gates, the ruined Jewish remnants of the Temple Mount, and a few prime holy places in Jerusalem's immediate environs. Often their reports seem like mere compilations of sites. Jacob ha Cohen listed the Tower of David, the Gates of Mercy, Temple and Sanctuary, and the Western Wall.[18] Outside the city proper he mentioned the Monument of Absalom and the Mount of Olives. Samuel ben Samson in 1210 noted the Tower of David, Shechem Gate and then the Mount of Olives (103–104). Only a few pilgrims described things in detail: Isaac ibn Chelo devoted about 25 percent of his narrative to describing Jerusalem. But for others, Jerusalem's particulars did not merit much attention.

JERUSALEM'S CITY WALLS AND GATES

Jerusalem's walls could be entered through several gates. The walls delimited the city's sacred space and the gates were portals into that space. Since access to many of Judaism's holiest sites was denied to Jews, the gates in some way stood as surrogate for them. To walk reverently around the city and pray at its gates had become a regular part of pilgrim ritual as early as 1035, when Solomon ben Yehuda circumambulated the city and prayed at each of its gates.[19] The gates' importance can be judged by the fact that a large number of pilgrim chronicles both count and name them. There is some inconsistency in their reports, for either the number and names changed over time or the pilgrims found their Arabic labeling confusing. Isaac ibn Chelo (1334) and John Sanderson in 1601 found four city gates. Samuel ben Samson entered through the western gate (near the Tower of David) and mentioned only the Shechem Gate by name. The Italian Casale pilgrim counted six gates and added that they were locked nightly (81), but he seems to have confused city gates with Temple Mount gates. He mentioned that one of the three Mount Zion gates had a Jewish guard (81). Atypically, Meshullam ben Menachem didn't mention the gates. In fact, Jerusalem's fortifications didn't seem to impress him at all, for he wrote that "Jerusalem has no walls except a little on one side where I entered" (189).

THE TEMPLE MOUNT

Except for occasional references to the ruins of David's Tower and Solomon's Palace, medieval Jewish pilgrims' narratives pay scant attention to religious sites within the walled city. Instead, once having passed the city gates, pilgrims made their way through the city's narrow streets to the foot of the Temple Mount. There they confronted another set of gates. By the mid-eleventh century, the Muslim authorities were exacting a fee from the Jews to walk around the Temple Mount and pray at its gates.[20] Jewish pilgrims were not allowed to enter the Temple compound itself and could only contemplate it from afar.

In the early fourth century, the Christian pilgrim from Bordeaux reported that Jews would go to the "perforated stone" (i.e., the cleft rock now covered by the Dome of the Rock) where they mourned and tore their garments.[21] This practice was confirmed by St. Jerome, writing in Bethlehem in the fourth century. Jerome depicted the atmosphere of oppression and extortion that prevailed during these visits. The Jews were not permitted to enter Jerusalem, except for those times when they managed to bribe the Roman guards to allow them to lament the destruction of the Temple. Jerome described the Jewish pilgrims as crowds of decrepit women and old men in rags, which for him indicated the wrath of God. Jerome painted a picture of a miserable group of Jewish pilgrims, with the glowing

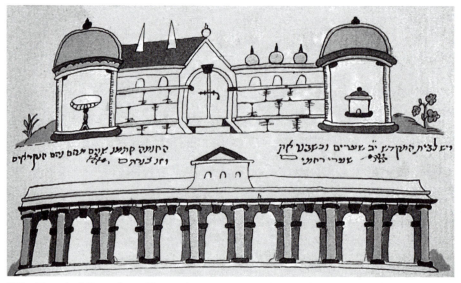

"The Temple." Jerusalem. Sixteenth century. In *The Casale Pilgrim*, trans. Cecil Roth (London: Soncino Press, 1929), 43.

cross and banners of Christianity in the background. They begged for bread and coins; they came on their knees with black and blue arms and loose hair; they ululated over the ashes at the site of the former sanctuary.[22] Rabbi Berakhiah, who was Jerome's contemporary, places his emphasis on the somber, almost furtive behavior of the Jews who visited the Temple ruins on the ninth of Av: "They come silently and they go silently, they come weeping and they go weeping, they come in the darkness of the night and they depart in darkness" (Midrash Rabbah Lamentations 1:17–19a). The practice all but ceased by the fifth century when Theodosius passed laws restricting the Jews, though it was revived briefly during the reign of the Empress Eudocia (438), when Christians would go and watch the Jews during the rites.[23]

In later periods, the Muslims and—during the Crusader period—Christians limited access to the Temple Mount. From time to time a few areas on the Temple's periphery attracted chroniclers' attention. Jacob ha Cohen mentioned a well in which the Temple priests used to wash themselves (98–99), and the Casale pilgrim took note of a conduit which used to drain the "blood of sacrifices" (46). Samuel ben Samson (1210) wrote that at the base of the Western Wall he could see "a kind of arch placed at the base of the Temple. It is by a subterranean passage that the priests reach the fount of Etam [Etham], the spot where the baths were" (103–104). Rabbi Jacob of Paris described "a declivity in front of the big building, surrounded by a thick wall like the wall of the Court of Israel, and from the south there is a descent like the steps that used to be in the south, and there are caves opening into the wall of the outer Court and leading under the Temple Mount, and it is said that you can penetrate them up to the [perforated stone]."[24]

Worshipers at the Western Wall. Postcard, circa 1910. Authors' collection.

By the late fifteenth century, however, one site was singled out: the segment of the retaining wall built by the Roman emperor Herod on the western side of the Temple Mount. In Roman and Byzantine times this was a commercial area. The early Mamelukes built a number of schools against Herod's wall, leaving only one small stretch open to view from the narrow street running along its side. Medieval Jewish pilgrims may have prayed there, or near there. Nachmanides, for example, wrote his son to greet his pupil Moses for him: "Tell him . . . that there, before the Holy Temple, I have read his verses, weeping bitterly over them" (227). Benjamin of Tudela reported that "the western wall . . . is one of the walls of the Holy of Holies. This is called the Gate of Mercy, and thither come all the Jews to pray before the wall of the court of the Temple."[25] Isaac ibn Chelo, in 1334, called the Western Wall one of the seven wonders of Jerusalem and related that Jews went there to say prayers.[26] In the 1520s the new Ottoman ruler, Suleyman, perhaps in order to attract more Jewish immigration to the city, designated the area a Jewish oratory, and had his architect build a parallel wall leaving a nine-foot-wide corridor that by imperial decree was to be a prayer place for the Jews.[27] Gradually the so-called Wailing Wall assumed prime importance, and began to figure in pilgrim accounts. The Casale pilgrim focused on the site's architecture: "Of the remaining Western Wall, only one section, forty or fifty cubits in length and halfway up, is from the days of Solomon, but not the entire western side" (79).

THE MOUNT OF OLIVES

East of Jerusalem rises the hill called the Mount of Olives, Jerusalem's second most important place for medieval Jewish pilgrims. It was popular in part because from there pilgrims had a spectacular view of the Temple Mount and the walled city of Jerusalem. It also had historic, ritual, and eschatological significance, and there pilgrims could fulfill several important halakhic requirements. There they could announce the new moon and the intercalation of the extra month in leap years, according to the Jewish calendar. There they could build their booths on Sukkot. There on the ninth of Av they could lament the succession of tragedies that had befallen the Jewish people.[28] As early as 1035 a pilgrim group was noted for going up to sing on the Mount of Olives.[29] Pilgrims were granted relatively unrestricted access to the Mount of Olives, although sporadically, as in the mid eleventh century, they had to pay a fee to ascend.[30] Medieval pilgrims often went to the Mount of Olives to pray, both individually and as part of a minyan. Samuel ben Samson (in 1210) went there at least twice to say prayers (104), as did Petachia of Ratisbon.

Samuel ben Samson mentioned a site on the mountain as the place where "in olden times the red heifer was burnt" (104). A hundred years later Rabbi Jacob of Paris confirmed the tradition: "we follow along the valley until we reach a platform which is on the Mount of Olives, where the red heifer was slain, and we go uphill to the platform which faces the Temple gate" (117). The English Protestant John Sanderson (1601) also noted the site on the Mount of Olives where one could see "the alter where they burnt the redd cowe."[31]

BETWEEN JERUSALEM AND THE TEMPLE MOUNT

On their way to and from the Mount of Olives, pilgrims could visit other Jewish holy sites on the east side of the city. Many were Greek or Roman tombs that by the Middle Ages had become associated with Jewish biblical personages. One of these was Absalom, whose tomb was visited by the twelfth-century pilgrim Jacob ha Cohen (98–99). In 1481 Meshullam ben Menachem termed this tomb "beautiful" and noted the custom of throwing stones at it because Absalom refused to obey his father. He wrote that the stones were removed annually (191–192). A nearby tomb was thought to hold the remains of King David. Moses Basola in 1521 observed that it had an iron door, the keys to which were kept by Muslims, and that no one was ever allowed to enter

Absalom's Tomb. Jerusalem. Photo, D. Gitlitz, 1967.

(74). Some pilgrims conflated David's tomb with the place where the Ark of the Covenant had been kept. Estori Farhi, in the fourteenth century, located the tent of the Ark in a vault south of Mt. Moriah. Two centuries later, the Casale pilgrim called the place "the palace of David the King, where the Ark was kept: some of it is still standing. There the kings of the house of David are buried" (45).[32]

Other sites in the vicinity of Jerusalem also drew the attention of Jewish pilgrims. Jacob ha Cohen in the twelfth century and Jacob the messenger of Jechiel of Paris in the thirteenth century visited the waters of Siloam (117). In the late fifteenth century Meshullam ben Menachem wrote that at the top of the hill behind the Mount of Olives was Hulda's "cave," with a tomb near it and a large building in ruins. A little down the hill was Haggai's grave and then Habakkuk's. But these were not the only attractions, he reported credulously: "All round Jerusalem there are many caves and in them are buried many pious and saintly people without number, but we do not know who they are except those marked; but it is a tradition amongst us from mouth to mouth from ancient times that there is no doubt as to their truth" (191–193). By the time Moses Basola visited Hulda's tomb in 1521, he found "a marble grave in a lovely pavilion." He had to give the Muslim caretaker four dirhams to enter and more money for the lamp oil (73).

Despite the ethos of lamentation that prevailed among medieval Jewish pilgrims to Jerusalem, the visitors were not blind to the city's more positive features, and their chronicles sometimes give us a glimpse of the joy they experienced as they roamed the city's streets. After all, in addition to being pilgrims, they were tourists.

Many recounted their impressions of Jerusalem's resident Jewish population. They felt the need to comment on the life of Jews there, sometimes cataloging their numbers and professions. Benjamin of Tudela (1173) noted that 200 Jews lived in Jerusalem near the Tower of David. Yet only fourteen years later, Petachia of Ratisbon found merely one Jew in Jerusalem, Rabbi Abraham, a dyer, who had to pay the authorities a fee to live there. Nachmanides (thirteenth century) counted two dyers (127). Isaac ibn Chelo (1334) found numerous residents, most of whom came from France (128). These French Jews followed various professions and apparently lived in tranquility. Obadiah Jaré da Bertinoro (1488) counted seventy families, most of them poor, and many widows as well. He noted that there were good relations between Muslims and Jews throughout the country (132).

We know a little about pilgrim lodgings in Jerusalem, beginning with the fact that they were scarce. In the early Arab period a Jewish pilgrim named Musa ben Barhun had asked a friend, Moses ben Jacob, to engage the house where he had lodged on a previous pilgrimage to Jerusalem. But it had already been rented, and Musa had to settle for less-desirable lodgings.[33] Meshullam ben Menachem, in the late fifteenth century, complained that the nice houses near Jerusalem's Gates of Mercy, where Jewish pilgrims were accustomed to lodge, had now been taken over by Muslims (191). Obadiah Jaré da Bertinoro engaged a room off a small courtyard with a blind man and five women as neighbors (243). On the other hand, some pilgrims clearly lucked out when it came to lodging. Moses Basola, in 1521, crowed about the house he had found, "No other house in Jerusalem boasts as good a view as this one" (79).

After worshiping, the pilgrims' principal focus was to chronicle the remnants, material and human, of Jewish culture in the city, and they were likely to jot down any picturesque detail that caught their eye. Isaac ibn Chelo, who came from Aragon, listed Jerusalem's seven wonders. They included the city gates; the Western Wall; the Tower of David (he said it was "solid"); Solomon's Palace, now converted into a market; Hulda's Tomb ("beautifully built"); the tombs of the Kings near the Cave of Ben Sirach ("beautiful"); and the Palace of the Queen Helena of Monobaz ("a fine building") (131–133). Obadiah Jaré da Bertinoro, in 1487, duly noted the city's destruction, but at the same time marveled at the secular sights it offered to visitors: "Jerusalem . . . contains four very beautiful, long bazaars, such as I have never before seen, at the foot of Zion. They have all dome-shaped roofs, and contain wares of every kind. They are divided into different departments, the merchant bazaar, the spice bazaar, the vegetable market, and one in which cooked food and bread are sold" (236–237). With similar wonder he took note of the trees and fruits that he had never seen in his native Italy.

Moses Basola (1521), too, noted the city's many springs and the "lovely gardens" (72). He also was struck by the city's four markets, including one he called a Jewish bazaar (78). The Casale pilgrim, too, seems to have enjoyed the markets. He found three of them, covered with domes. One sold silk and embroidered garments, one fruits and vegetables, and the third herbs and medical supplies (41, 47). But what really impressed him was the Muslim architecture covering the Jewish holy places on the Temple Mount: [It] "has two great domes covered with silver and gold. The greater is the Dome of the Courtyard, where was the place of the Holy of Holies: and therein is the Rock of Foundation. The smaller dome they call the House of Study of Solomon" (41). Meshullam ben Menachem (1481) admired the architecture as well. He wrote that "the buildings of Jerusalem are very fine and the stones are larger than in the buildings of the other places that I have seen" (194).

JEWISH SAINTS BE PRAISED!

About as far from Safed as one may walk on a Sabbath is the grave of
the Talmudic master Rabbi Judah bar Ilai. . . . On the grave is a handsome tomb at which candles are lit, and there I went and prostrated myself and lit candles to his memory. (Disciple of Bertinoro, 1495)[1]

These are the journeyings of the children of Israel . . . to prostrate themselves upon the sepulchers of the righteous: until they come with tears
and supplication to pray for the welfare of their brethren which are in
the diaspora. (Casale pilgrim, sixteenth century)[2]

While Jerusalem was the principal objective of pre-Diaspora Jewish
pilgrimage, the roads to and from the holy city were studded with
other shrines that drew the pilgrims' attention, sites important in the
development of Judaism. Among other sites, pilgrims visited Ramah, where
Rachel wept for her children (Jer. 31:15–17); Beersheba, where Abraham dug a
well and planted a tamarisk tree (Gen. 21:31–33); and Gilgal, where Joshua was
told to circumcise the Israelite males (Joshua 5:2).

After the early Diasporas and the definitive destruction of the Temple in 70 CE,
Jerusalem was still the main goal for Jewish pilgrims to the Holy Land. Like the pre-
Diaspora pilgrims, medieval Jewish pilgrims also visited sites en route to the holy
city. Yet, something fundamental had changed, for the shrines they sought out
were not the sites of key events. They were tombs. For these pilgrims, Jerusalem
lay in the center of a land made holy by graves. More than anything else, medieval
Jewish pilgrims wanted to see burial places. Early medieval pilgrim itineraries list
mostly tombs. Later medieval, personalized, pilgrim narratives and guidebooks
cite one tomb visit after another. For example, Abraham Zacuto reported in his
Book of Yohassin (circa 1504) that when Isaac ben Alfra visited the Holy Land in

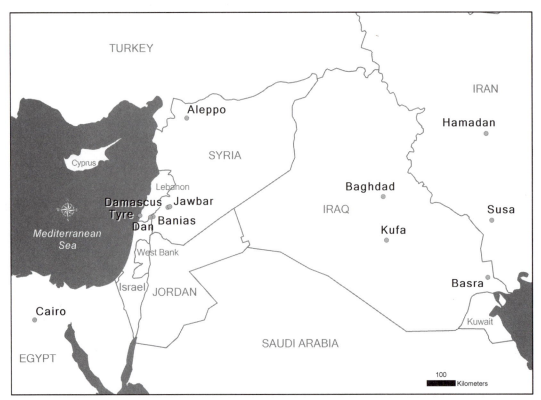

The Middle East

1441 he recorded more than two dozen separate holy grave sites; and Simon Duran, who visited two years later, listed ninety individual and many group graves. Additional scribal sources provided hundreds more holy grave sites.[3]

SAINTS

These grave sites contained the remains of revered Jewish ancestors, spiritual leaders, and renowned rabbis who held the status of saints. Even though Hebrew has no precise equivalent of the word *saint*, a concept which in the Western world is cast in the mold of Christianity, each of these holy individuals was believed to embody in some fashion the values and ideals of Judaism. Each was a model to be imitated. Each inspired reverence, usually through the study of their works (and sometimes, as is prevalent in Christianity, of their lives). Many were said to work miracles. Most were men, although occasionally some women also achieved revered status, usually as martyrs.

By Hellenistic times Jews in Palestine and the cities of the Greek world had began to venerate certain individuals who had been killed because of their Jewishness. The persecutions under Antiochus IV Epiphanes (215?–164 BCE) produced several martyrs. Their deaths were chronicled in the Second Book of Macabees and glossed in the Talmud and other rabbinical writings. The persecutions during the Roman period created many more. Jews adopted the Hellenistic belief that after a person died his or her soul remained near the place where the body was buried and was capable of hearing prayers and of influencing the gods to respond to requests. In addition to the prophets' graves that had been attracting pilgrims probably since before the Common Era, the graves of the martyrs soon drew pilgrims. These ideas spread widely through the Roman Empire.

It is likely that Judaism and Christianity influenced each other mutually as the grave cults evolved. As Christianity developed under Rome, the early Christians promoted martyrdom to the highest ideal of their new religion, beginning with the execution of Jesus, interpreted as the sacrificial act by which individual Christians would be redeemed. Given Roman antipathy to the new religion, Christians soon had legions of martyrs to venerate. Going on pilgrimage to a martyr's tomb was a way to express one's faith, and also an opportunity to beseech the soul of the saint to intercede with God on one's behalf.

The reports of medieval Jewish pilgrims differ from the reports of their Christian counterparts. Christian pilgrims to the Holy Land tended to focus their attention on their religion's single key figure, Jesus Christ. They went to Cana, where he performed a marriage, to Mount Tabor in the Galilee where he appeared to the apostles at Pentecost, and to the Sea of Galilee where he recruited some of his apostles. Insofar as they were able, pilgrims also wanted to imitate the New Testament events. They visited Bethlehem to play the part of the shepherds who gathered to worship the infant Jesus. Or they carried a cross along the Via Dolorosa in Jerusalem. To a great extent, the Christian pilgrim's eye was a camcorder narrating events that unfolded over time in a three-dimensional geographic space. The eye of the medieval Jewish pilgrim functioned instead as a still camera, taking snapshots of places where the revered figures were buried. Pilgrims visited the graves of the Patriarchs, the Matriarchs, other biblical figures like Ruth, Samson, Hulda, David, and the prophets, as well as historical rabbis like Hillel and Shim'on bar Yohai, who by then had achieved legendary proportions. They also prayed and lit candles at the graves of the many holy men, the *qadoshim* and *tzadiqim*, who had left their mark on Judaism as writers, heroes, martyrs, leaders, orators, jurists, and the creators of sectarian movements.

The practices derived from these beliefs struck some Jewish commentators as dangerously syncretic. As early as the tenth century, the Karaite Sahl ben Masliah, for example, complained:

> How can I keep silent while some Jews follow the customs of idolaters? They sit among graves of saintly persons and spend nights among tombstones, while they seek favors from dead men, saying, "Oh Jose the Galilean, grant me a cure!" or "Vouchsafe me a child!" They light lamps at the graves of saints and burn incense upon the brick altars before them and tie bowknots to the palm tree bearing the name of the saint as a charm for all kinds of diseases. They perform pilgrimage rites over the graves of these dead saints and make vows to them and appeal and pray to them to grant their requests.[4]

Although these beliefs were soundly rejected by the rabbis of the time, they persisted to a considerable extent among the Jewish masses. Judging from the numbers of references to tombs in medieval Jewish pilgrim itineraries and narratives, the pilgrims seemed obsessed with graves. Jacob ben Nathaniel ha Cohen even titled his twelfth-century narrative, "Account of the journeys to places in the Holy Land and the tombs there of the righteous."[5] Rabbi Jacob, the messenger of Jechiel of Paris (1238–1244), opened his narrative with this statement: "These are the journeyings of the children of Israel who wish to go to contemplate and pray at the graves of the Patriarchs, the righteous and the saints of the Holy Land, and to our holy and glorious Temple wherein our fathers prayed in Jerusalem."[6] This phrase was echoed nearly verbatim in the sixteenth-century Casale pilgrim's opening lines (33). Thus, while Jerusalem remained the pilgrims' presumed destination, it is clear that Jewish pilgrims also strove to visit as many tombs as possible. One might conclude that the graves became a goal in and of themselves. Jacob ben Nathaniel ha Cohen seems to have concentrated all his energy on visiting tombs: "God helped me to enter the Holy Land, and I saw the graves of our righteous Patriarchs in Hebron and the grave of Abner the son of Ner . . . and of Jonah ben Amittai, the prophet, in Kiriat Arba, which is in Hebron, and the grave of Hannah and the grave of Rachel at Ephrath, on the Jericho road on the way to Bethlehem" (92). At Shechem he noted the tombs of Joseph the Righteous, Zipporah, and Jonah, the son of Amittai. At Acre, the grave of Eliezer the Hasmonean. In Caesarea, that of the Jews martyred by the Romans. Moses Basola, like some other pilgrims, boasted of his zeal in visiting quantities of tombs. He wrote that on one Sunday in May 1522 he, along with a group of women and men, prayed at *all* the tzadiqs' tombs in Tiberias, "which are a mile or more apart."[7]

The holy graves and the enumeration of those graves in the pilgrims' chronicles served several purposes. For one thing, the graves functioned as cairns, claim stakes to assert Judaism's historical presence. As Samuel ben Samson phrased it in 1210, "these words deserve to be written in order that we might know the places of the graves of our forefathers by whose merits the world exists."[8] Chronicling the locations of the holy graves was both an act of reverence and an expression of yearning for possession of the land that had been once and forever promised to the Jews. For these writers, the tombs of the martyrs who gave up their lives for their faith, of the wise rabbis, and of the commentators and mystics who had inhabited these stony hills were tangible evidence that Judaism once flourished in this holy landscape. There was a subtext, unstated but always perceptible just below the surface: Judaism, these writers were saying, is eternal in part because the steadfast commitment of countless outstanding individual Jews has made it so.

Some pilgrims felt obliged to inform those back home of the precise location of the important graves. In the twelfth century, Petachia of Ratisbon augmented his account with snippets of geographical data designed to orient later pilgrims. Writing about the Upper Galilee, for example, Petachia noted, "There is Nithai, the Arebelite, buried at Arbel. Mount Gaash is very high, on it Obadiah, the prophet, is buried. The mountain is ascended by means of steps formed in the mountain. In the midst of the mountain Joshua, son of Nun, is buried; and by his side Kaleb, son of Jephunah."[9] Rabbi Jacob wrote in the same vein in the early 1240s: "From Jakuk one goes to Tiberias. At the top of the hill is a cave in which R. Akiba is buried, and below it is the burial ground of his pupils. Near it in the middle of the valley is the grave of R. Chiyya and his sons, and in that cave is buried R. Hunna of Babylon" (124).

The sheer number of cited tombs underscores their importance in the early itineraries, like the twelfth-century *Tombs of the Ancestors* (*Sefer Qabbalath Sadiqei Eretz Israel*), written perhaps by Joseph ben Isaac.[10] This 128-line rhymed itinerary starts its journey in Hebron and moves north, listing thirty-four holy tombs. The grave-visit tradition was still strong in the sixteenth century. About 1535 David dei Rossi wrote that his sister had returned from a pilgrimage to Jerusalem and Hebron and added, "She brings with her also a list of the tombs of all the Saints buried in the Holy Land. It has been handwritten for her by scribes in Jerusalem."[11] In 1537 a German Jew in Hebron compiled a list entitled *The Tombs of the Patriarchs*. By 1564 it had been printed in Safed, and soon after was reprinted in Europe with a Latin translation.[12] As an appendix to the narrative of his pilgrimage, Moses Basola listed the towns and the names of the holy persons buried in each. Similarly, Jews living near or caring for important graves understood the importance of preserving the knowledge of their locations. The Jewish community at Ezekiel's grave, near Baghdad, must have functioned like a kind of tourist bureau; Petachia reported that the Baghdad academy provided him with a list of 550 holy tombs of prophets and Amoraïm in the area (35).[13]

What did the graves look like? How were they cared for? What did pilgrims do during their grave visits? Most writers devoted little ink to describing the graves or the nature of the rites performed there. Generally speaking, the earliest itineraries and narratives left us only tantalizing snippets of concrete detail. It is not until the twelfth century that we begin to find particulars. Petachia of Ratisbon, for example, reported that in Mesopotamia "where there exists a congregation near the grave of a righteous man, they spread a costly cloth over the grave" (37).[14] Occasionally he gives even more information:

> Whoever has not seen the beautiful large structure over [Ezekiel's] grave has never seen a fine building. It is inside overlaid with gold. Over the grave is a mass of lime, as high as a man, and round the lime, and over it, is a structure of cedar wood, which is gilded. . . . There are windows in it, through which people pass their heads and pray. At the top is a large cupola of gold, and beautiful carpets cover the inside. There are also in it beautiful glass vases, and thirty lamps fed with olive oil. (29, 31)

The thirteenth-century French pilgrim Jacob noted that the grave of Jonathan ben Uzziel (on the road near Nabartein) was under "a fine big tree, finer than anyone ever saw in the world" (123). Samuel ben Samson was impressed with the burial areas around Meron. He mentioned that at Rabbi Eleazar's tomb there were two trees, making it an attractive place (108). Nearby, at the graves of Hillel and Shammai, he described the cupola: "Of a sort of white marble, the interior of which was adorned with reliefs representing branches of trees" (108).

The earliest itineraries do not say what took place at these graves, but later narratives give us glimpses of personal acts. In Meron, Samuel ben Samson tested the miraculous qualities of the well water near Hillel's grave: "We . . . threw out on to the ground a great quantity of their water, but there was no alteration in its amount." He and his fellow pilgrims must have tasted it as well: "This water is as sweet as honey" (108).

PILGRIM ROUTES IN THE HOLY LAND

"Seven roads start in the Holy City and go through all the land of Israel," wrote fourteenth-century pilgrim Isaac ibn Chelo, acknowledging the centrality of Jerusalem.[15] For pilgrims coming from abroad these same roads converged on Jerusalem. Most Jewish pilgrims reached the Holy Land by one of three routes. They came overland from the north by way of Syria, often from Damascus. They traveled from Egypt in the south, generally by the coastal road as far as Gaza or Jaffa (today Tel Aviv), from which they cut inland. Or they came by sea, as discussed in Chapter 5.

THE SOUTHERN HOLY LAND

Hebron, the Matriarchs and the Patriarchs

For most, the route of tombs began in Hebron. Perhaps the most important graves sought by Jewish pilgrims coming from the south were the tombs of Abraham and Sarah, Isaac and Rebecca, and Jacob and Leah in the Cave of Machpelah near Hebron.[16] Having been venerated since ancient times, Hebron never lost its importance. These tombs were also held sacred by Christians and Muslims, who honored the Matriarchs and Patriarchs as the progenitors of their religions as well. When the Christian pilgrim from Piacenza visited Hebron (circa 570), he reported that the day after Christ's birthday Christians held a celebration at Machpelah for the deposition of Jacob and Daniel, in which the Jews participated, using incense and candles and leaving presents at the tombs. He also noted that the sacred area at the tombs was divided down the middle by a screen, with Christians worshipping on one side and Jews on the other.[17]

The popularity of the Machpelah pilgrimage continued with the advent of Islam and the shrine was refurbished in the Muslim fashion. In 1047 Persian poet Naser-e Khosraw wrote a detailed description that included both measurements and sketches of the decorations. At Isaac and Rebecca's tombs both the walls and floor were covered with costly carpets. Abraham's and Sarah's tombs occupied two rooms in another building. Jewish pilgrims were not allowed to enter the chamber containing Abraham's tomb, but they could look through windows and see a well-made stone grave, with the walls and floors covered in rich materials, which may have been brocades. Silver lamps hung above his grave. Sarah's grave occupied another small chamber. The graves of Jacob and Leah were in other small chambers nearby.[18]

During much of the medieval period Jewish pilgrims were denied access to the caves themselves. However, this did not decrease their desire to visit them, to pray at them, and to approach the tomb chambers as closely as possible. The classic, most effective, and least dangerous strategy for opening the sanctuary doors was the bribe. It seems to have worked for Benjamin of Tudela, who visited Hebron (about 1270) while the Crusaders were in control and left us a description rich in detail:

[T]he old city stood on the mountain, but is now in ruins; and in the valley by the field of Machpelah lies the present city. Here there is the great church called St. Abram, and this was a Jewish place of worship at the time of the Mohammedan rule, but the Gentiles have erected there six tombs, respectively called those of Abraham and Sarah, Isaac and Rebekah, Jacob and Leah. The custodians tell the pilgrims that these are the tombs of the Patriarchs, for which information the pilgrims give them money. If a Jew comes, however, and gives a special reward, the custodian of the cave opens unto him a gate of iron, which was constructed by our forefathers, and then he is able to descend below by means of steps, holding a lighted candle in his hand. He then reaches a cave, in which nothing is to be found, and a cave beyond, which is likewise empty, but when he reaches the third cave behold there are six sepulchres, those of Abraham, Isaac and Jacob, respectively facing those of Sarah, Rebekah and Leah. And upon the graves are inscriptions cut in stone; upon the grave of Abraham is engraved "This is the grave of Abraham"; upon that of Isaac, "This is the grave of Isaac, the son of Abraham our Father. . . ." A lamp burns day and night upon the graves in the cave. One finds there many casks filled with the bones of Israelites, as the members of the house of Israel were wont to bring the bones of their fathers thither and to deposit them there to this day.[19]

Petachia of Ratisbon, who visited a few years later, was not quite as successful in gaining entry. He gave a gold coin to the caretaker of the shrine but was shown only the Christian image in the church over the tombs. With the donation of an additional gold coin he was permitted to descend fifteen steps to the cave, where he found that iron bars blocked his entry to the lower hollow in which the tombs were located. He prayed at the edge of the bars, but did manage to see enough to describe the cave and stones around the graves (63).

Some Jewish pilgrims employed stealth or disguised themselves as Christians or Muslims to gain access to the tombs. The writer of the Crusader-era Hebrew itinerary, *Tombs of the Ancestors*, was able to view the tombs "clandestinely through a window."[20] Jacob ha Cohen (circa 1187) disguised himself as a Gentile in order to get near (98). Samuel ben Samson (circa 1210) reported that he sneaked in (105).

The situation changed somewhat once Muslims were back in control. Meshullam ben Menachem (1481) reported that a mosque stood over the holy cave. Jews were permitted to go up to a small window in the cave wall to pray and to throw money and spices into it. But he also heard rumors that Jewish women could enter the mosque by dressing in Muslim fashion and covering their heads. Meshullam was impressed with the Muslim tradition of feeding the poor at the shrine and he detailed the daily menu: "thirteen thousand loaves . . . in honour of Abraham, Isaac and Jacob . . . ; and they put the bread in mustard and tender veal . . . and give venison and delicacies . . . and a mess of pottage."[21]

Obadiah Jaré da Bertinoro, who visited Hebron about the same time, said that no one, Muslim or Jew, could enter the area of the Patriarchs' tombs, and then tantalized his readers by adding—without detail—that he did manage to get into the cave where he prayed at the wall designated for Jews.[22] These conditions prevailed for at least the next 200 years. The Casale pilgrim (sixteenth century) noted that Jews prostrated themselves to pray at a small window near the door because they were not allowed to go inside (37). John Sanderson (1601) and his Jewish companions could not gain access either, but they were able to look through the small hole where they could just see a small lamp burning, and the Jewish pilgrims said their prayers there.[23]

Jewish pilgrims to Hebron might also be shown a house said to have belonged to Abraham. According to Benjamin of Tudela, "there is a well in front of the house, but out of reverence for the Patriarch Abraham no one is allowed to build in the neighbourhood" (42).

EPHROTH AND RACHEL'S TOMB

The second most important southern site was Rachel's Tomb, just north of Bethlehem. Like Machpelah, this shrine had been holy to Jews since ancient times. As one of Jacob's wives and mother of Joseph and Benjamin, Rachel was a founding mother of the three religions and her tomb was revered by Christians and Muslims as well. Christian pilgrims during the sixth and seventh centuries chronicled the deterioration of the shrine. The Piacenza Pilgrim noted that the water in the well at the shrine was sweet and that no matter how many people drank from it, the water level stayed the same. By 683, when Adomnan visited, the structures may have crumbled. He described the shrine as a poor, unadorned structure with a rail around it and names scribbled on it.[24]

By the twelfth century Rachel's Tomb seems to have undergone another transformation. Benjamin of Tudela described it this way: "the pillar of Rachel's grave . . . is made up of eleven stones, corresponding with the number of the sons of Jacob. Upon it is a cupola resting on four columns, and all the Jews that pass by carve their names upon the stones of the pillar" (40). Jacob ha Cohen also briefly described the eleven-stone monument, noting that it had four doors (98). In the thirteenth century, Jacob of Paris elaborated on how the monument came to have eleven stones: "tradition has it that ten of Jacob's sons sent the ten stones and Jacob, their father, gave the top stone; Benjamin did not give a stone as he was an infant . . . and Joseph did not give a stone because he was only about eight years old or because of his grief at having lost his mother" (120). Petachia of Ratisbon (also twelfth century) related a miracle story about Rachel's Tomb, noting that when Christian priests wanted to take away one of the tomb's stones for their own church, the stone kept returning to its original spot (59). By the late fifteenth century, according to Meshullam ben Menachen, Rachel's Tomb was marked by "a high monument of stones," over which the Muslims had erected an arch supported by four pillars (59).

Isaac ibn Chelo (fourteenth century) reported that "on the eve of the day of the great pardon [the Jews of Hebron] all resort to the tombs of *Rachel* and of *Nathan the Prophet* to perform their devotions there" (135; italics in original) and added at another point, "I have prayed for you and for myself on the sepulcher of our mother Rachel" (136). Was she merely another holy person or had some sort of Rachel cult, like that which flourishes in modern Israel, already begun to emerge?[25]

THE NORTHERN HOLY LAND

MERON

When the Romans banned Jews from Jerusalem in 135, so many scholars relocated to the Galilee that the area was soon peppered with the tombs of famous rabbis whose works were well known to educated pilgrims. Chronicles as early as the twelfth century reference visits to Jewish holy sites north of Jerusalem. Almost all Jewish pilgrims stopped at Meron, high on a mountain in the northern Galilee near Safed. Rabbis Hillel (circa 70 BCE–10 CE) and Shammai (circa 50 BCE–30 CE), both leaders of the Sanhedrin, were buried there in tombs that lay opposite each other. Rabbi Akiva and his son Rabbi Eleazar took refuge in the area during the purges of Jewish leaders following the Bar Kokhba rebellion in 135 CE, allegedly hiding in one of Meron's caves for thirteen years. Shim'on bar Yohai (flourished 135–170 CE), one of Akiva's disciples and in the latter Middle Ages widely believed to have written the basic Jewish mystical text, the *Zohar*, was buried there.[26] In 1495, the Disciple of Bertinoro noted that marking Shim'on bar Yohai's grave was "an extremely fine monument which can be seen as far as Safed" (21). Nearly three hundred years later, according to Joseph the Scribe of Beresteczko (1762), a domed structure still stood over the tombs. Joseph found it locked, and had to recruit the beadle from Safed to come and open the tombs for him in exchange for a good tip. Evidently local residents of all three religions regarded the tombs as holy, for Joseph's narration of the terrible earthquake that shook the area around Meron related that the resident Muslims and Christians ran to the domed building and called out, "Rabbi Simeon, Rabbi Simeon, you are a great and honored man . . . now show us as well your greatness and open your door to us!" At that, the door opened, and the people ran in and were saved.[27]

Meron was the reputed burial site of several other important rabbis, sages, and martyrs from the first and second centuries as well. Not all the tombs were revered. The Disciple of Bertinoro reported seeing a heap of stones on the grave of Judah the Punished (perhaps Jose of Yodkeret) "who caused the untimely death of his children" (20–21).

Because there are springs at Meron, the mountain's importance as a pilgrimage site probably antedates Jewish history. In the parched landscapes of the Middle East important springs were sites of worship and of divination in prehistoric times. Even though medieval Jewish pilgrims went to Meron to pray at the holy men's graves, they often commented on the miraculous waters found at Meron. Samuel ben Samson (1210) noted that Meron's wells contain sweet water whose level never seems to change no matter how much pilgrims dip out (108). The most detailed account of the miracle-working waters of Meron is Petachia of Ratisbon's in the late twelfth century:

> In Lower Galilea there is a cave which inside is spacious and high. On one side of the cave are buried Shamai and his disciples; and on the other Hillel and his disciples. In the middle of the cave there is a large stone, hollow like a cup, which is capable of containing more than forty *seah* [about 300 liters]. When

men of worth enter, the stone appears full of sweet water. One may then wash his hands and feet, and pray, imploring God for what one desires. The stone, however, is not hollow from below, for the water does not come from the bottom, as it only occurs in honour of a man of worth, since to an unworthy man the water does not appear. Though one should draw from the stone a thousand jars of water it would not be diminished, but would remain full as before. (57)

This sense of wonder at the miraculous nature of Meron's caves pervades many descriptions. Because the cave was a holy place, appropriate rules of ritual purity had to be followed, and this, too, might require supernatural intervention. Moses Basola reported that "if a large caravan of Jews comes, and each one lights lamps all around the interior of the cave and a menstruating woman enters, the lamps are immediately extinguished" (66). Rabbi Jacob (1238–1244) wrote: "There the Israelites meet on the second day of Passover and pray and say hymns and, when they find water in the cave, they all rejoice, for it is a sign that the year will be blessed, but many times they find no water, but when they pray the water comes in a twinkling" (122). Rabbi Isaac ben Latif, on pilgrimage to Israel in 1455, recounted how the miraculous water could also produce rain: "During years of draught [sic], men and women go to the tombs of Hillel and Shammai and pray in the cave. God hears and answers with water. At first stones that have a hollow within the cave fill up, and then the sky fills with clouds, and the rain falls, and the land gives its harvest."[28] Drought affected everyone, so it is no surprise to find Muslims joining with Jews in beseeching the magic waters of the Meron cave for rain. The cave's miracle-working waters had other uses as well. About the year 1285 Rabbi David Hanagid, a grandson of Maimonides, made a pilgrimage from Egypt to the cave to invoke the spring's power against enemies who wanted to oust him from office: "He would pray in the cave of Rabbi Hillel and Shammai, and cold water would issue. Then he excommunicated the slanderers. And on that day five hundred slanderers in Egypt died and two months later, their wives and sons were taken from this world."[29]

The Spanish refugees who converted Safed and its surroundings to a center of Jewish mysticism in the sixteenth century were little interested in water rituals related to the local agricultural cycle. They were much more interested in the graves of the famous tzadiqim. The *Zohar*'s doctrine of the soul, as expounded by Isaac Luria and other sixteenth-century Safed kabbalists, proposed that the *nefesh*, the physical soul, maintained an active presence at the grave site, and could be accessed by supplicants there. The wealthy and influential Avraham Galante, a member of this group, paid for a building to be erected over Shim'on bar Yohai's grave. Joseph Caro built a Sukkah over it. Isaac Luria used to lie prostrate on the tzadiq's grave, face to face, to better bind their souls together. From those days on, almost all accounts of pilgrimage activity at Meron focus on Rabbi Shim'on. Moses Basola found a minyan in the area "who made it a fixed practice to pray [there] each month" (90). When Basola went on the fourteenth of Iyar during the "Second Passover," "there were more than one thousand persons there: many came from Damascus with their wives and children, as well as most of the Safed community. And the entire community [went] to Buqai'a, the village where the cave that

R. Simeon bar Yochai and his son hid. . . . We spent two days and two nights there in joyous celebration" (91).[30] Joseph the Scribe (1762) wrote that pilgrims from far and wide visited Meron three times each year: in the month of Elul, before Nisan, and on Lag b'Omer, which they celebrated with feasts, music and "round-dances" (93).

SAFED

Pilgrims visited the graves of Jewish holy men in Safed in the mountains northwest of the Sea of Galilee even before the city became famous as the center of Jewish mysticism and the study of Kabbalah in the sixteenth century. Samuel ben Samson and his companions found Rabbi Haninah ben Hyrcanus's cave, which they walked around weeping. He noted that two Muslims were taking care of the site, including making sure there was enough oil to keep the lamps lit (107).[31] The Disciple of Bertinoro (1495) went there to see the caves in which Hosea ben Beeri and the distinguished second-century rabbi Judah bar Ilai were buried, and wrote that pious Jews prayed at both tombs and lit candles at Judah bar Ilai's (20). When Moses Basola visited the grave of Judah bar Ilai about twenty-five years later, he found "a handsome ornate house on [the grave] and a lamp burns there continuously, kept lit by donations from the travelers who come to prostrate themselves there" (64–65).

Both during the heyday of Lurianic Kabbalah in the late sixteenth century and up until today, Jewish pilgrims have visited Safed to pray in the synagogues founded by the masters of mysticism and to visit their graves. In 1602 the Ashkenazi pilgrim Solomon Shloemel was delighted to find that the city was a thriving, religiously intellectual place with 300 rabbis, eighteen Talmudic academies, and twenty-one synagogues. He also counted four *hederim* (schools for the instruction of small children), and noted that rich Constantinople Jews paid the salaries of their four teachers.[32] Joseph the Scribe of Beresteczko went to Safed to pray at Rabbi Luria's grave. He wrote that before visiting the grave itself he purified himself by bathing in Luria's *mikveh* (91). Evidently there was an earthquake and plague during those years and Joseph noted that Safed was being rebuilt with the full support of the Muslim governor (90).

TIBERIAS

Pilgrims to the north generally visited Tiberias, on the shore of the Sea of Galilee. The road from Safed was dangerous, reported Moses Basola in 1522, so that pilgrims had to travel in large groups and pay four dirhams to insure their protection (92). Tiberias's attraction was its many graves of famous holy men. Twelfth-century Jacob ben Nathaniel ha Cohen listed a few, but later writers went for larger numbers. Basola listed eleven important tombs of tzadiqim (more than he listed even for Meron), including some lesser-known rabbis (99). His contemporary, the Casale pilgrim, added the graves of Rabbis Johanan ben Zakkai; Hiyya and his sons, Meir, Jeremiah—who, he added, was "buried, upright"—, Huna, Nehorai, Ami, Asi, Judah; Maimonides and his son Moses and grandson David; Tarphon; and Samuel ibn Tibbon; as well as Rabbi Akiva, his wife, and 24,000 of his students (55). It seems likely that a regular circuit of grave visits had become a tradition, with groups of Jews walking to each one in turn to pray. This was clearly the case on May 18, 1522, when, wrote Basola, the entire "congregation" of Tiberias went to "pray at all the graves of the zaddikim there" (93).

Many of these graves were associated with miracles. Joseph the Scribe of Beresteczko (circa 1762) wrote how when Maimonides died in Egypt he had instructed his disciples to place his enshrouded body on a camel and to let the camel determine his burial site. When the camel reached Tiberias it would go no further, so Maimonides was buried there (92). Other graves were known for their power to effect cures. According to Jacob ha Cohen, who visited during Crusader times, people came to Rabbi Cahana's grave "from all places to light candles because the sick and barren are healed" (95). He narrated that when a Christian knight from Provence was told that Jews put lighted candles on a grave in Tiberias because that holy person healed the sick and helped the barren to conceive, the knight, unimpressed, removed a stone from the grave and threw it on the ground. At which point, according to the story, the man dropped dead (96).

Pilgrims to Tiberias also sought out the synagogues, or ruins of synagogues, associated with the tzadiqim. In the late twelfth century Petachia of Ratisbon visited a synagogue reputedly built by Joshua, son of Nun (55). Jacob ha Cohen found this synagogue in ruins, with only a few remaining architectural elements (95). In the sixteenth century the Casale pilgrim visited a synagogue of Shim'on bar Yohai, "to which men go up a stairway of hewn stones. Services are continually held there, and there are in it scrolls of the Law and lighted torches" (63).

Graves and synagogue ruins were not Tiberias's only attractions, of course. There was the lake and its tree-lined shore. There was an ample supply of tasty fresh fish. And there were hot springs, in which the pilgrim Joseph the Scribe of Beresteczko bathed before his stepdaughter's wedding (91).

SEPPHORIS

In the twelfth century Sepphoris (modern Tsippori), six kilometers from Nazareth, seems to have been a popular pilgrimage destination. Benjamin of Tudela noted several important Jewish tombs here: "Here are the graves of Rabbenu Hakkadosh, of Rabban Gamaliel, and of Rabbi Chiya, who came up from Babylon, also of Jonah the son of Amittai; they are all buried in the mountain. Many other Jewish graves are here" (44). Petachia of Ratisbon noted the tomb of a certain Yehoodah [Judah HaNasi], whom he identified as the compiler of the Mishnah. He recorded that a sweet aroma emanated from the grave (55). In the sixteenth century, the Casale pilgrim remarked that this grave site, which he identified as that of Judah the Patriarch (135–200), also contained his sons and disciples in a "beauteous sepulcher, closed by a door of stone" (65). Because Sepphoris was associated with Mary, it attracted medieval Christian pilgrims as well.

SHECHEM

Pilgrims visiting the northern holy places invariably stopped at Shechem (Nablus) to visit Jacob's well and the tomb of the Patriarch Joseph, which Rabbi Jacob ben

Nathaniel ha Cohen (twelfth century) described as being marked with two marble pillars (116). He noted Joseph the Righteous's cave, where candles were lit every evening. He went on to record another version the miracle story he had already associated with Rabbi Cahana's grave in Tiberias: that a Christian knight who took an ax to Joseph the Righteous's tomb was immediately struck dead (96–97). In 1250 a Muslim geographer reported that the Jews believed that Nimrod had thrown Abraham into the fire in Shechem, although the geographer deemed the site to be in Babylon. The traditional belief must have persisted, however, because in 1689, another Muslim to Shechem was shown a cellar in which Nimrod's grave lay.[33]

RAMAH

In Ramah, a village just north of Jerusalem, pilgrims could visit the tombs of Samuel, Elkanah, and Hannah and her sons (who were also reputed to be buried in Safed). In the sixteenth century the place was controlled by the Karaites, whose attempts to keep other Jews from worshiping there required Jerusalem's Muslim Kadi to intervene. Jerusalem court records note that Ramah's Muslims were offended by Jews' lighting candles at the graves, praying in loud voices, camping for several days, and letting their pack animals run loose in the town.[34] The Casale pilgrim observed that Samuel's grave had a beautiful construction on top of it, where "festal pilgrims pray" (51). Meshullam ben Menachem was suffering from ague when he went inside to pray for recovery in 1481. When Moses Basola visited in 1521, he had to pay six dirhams to the caretaker. He described Samuel's tomb as "a large palace with arches," noting that Jews were allowed to pray and light lamps at one end of the building (75). When John Sanderson accompanied some Jewish pilgrims there in 1601, he visited Samuel's house, which was also considered his burial place. He recorded that "uppon the top of the said house is the place wheare the Childerin of Isarell had thier haire cutt of, at which time they *made vowes* [and] gave great somms to the Sanctorum. At this day ther ar of the Jewes that wowe [vow] and performe, carie[i]ng their childerin to have their haire cutt there for devotion" (100).

THE COASTAL HOLY LAND

From Tyre in the north to Gaza in the south, the Mediterranean coast was dotted with sites that served pilgrims as ports of entry and departure and as supply centers. As a southern coastal city, Gaza figures in the pilgrimage narratives as a place of recuperation and refuge. Pilgrims arriving by ship or caravanning from Egypt stayed several days to rest and rent transportation. Meshullam ben Menachem detailed the foods and wine he found there and gave instructions about things to take from Gaza when heading inland (180–181). The sixteenth-century Casale pilgrim's journal's illustration of Gaza shows a neat city behind walls with an unrealistically large gate. He called it simply "the city of Samson: A fair place" (69). Gaza Jews told Obadiah da Bertinoro (1480s) that one of ruins in their city was all that remained of the building "that Samson had pulled down on the Philistines" (232).[35]

In Ashkelon the pilgrims could visit the remains of a well attributed to Abraham and see a miraculous spring in a cave. According to Jacob ben Nathaniel ha Cohen, in ancient times some priests in Jerusalem dropped a dish in the Pool of Siloam and the same dish turned up in Ashkelon's waters (93). Of the other cities along the northern coast route, little was noted by the pilgrims.

Pilgrims in Caesaria focused on the Roman persecution of Jews in that city. Jacob ha Cohen believed he saw the actual place of the execution of ten martyrs, then marked with a marble stone (97). A century and a half later Isaac ibn Chelo reported that he saw both the execution site and the burial site of one martyr (143).

In the twelfth century Benjamin of Tudela found many Jewish graves at the foot of Mount Carmel, near Haifa, but he did not seem to think any of them to be particularly important. However, on the mountain itself was "the cave of Elijah, where the Christians have erected a structure called St. Elias. On the top of the mountain can be recognized the overthrown altar which Elijah repaired, in the days of Ahab. The site of the altar is circular, about four cubits remain thereof . . ." (31).[36] Pilgrims who ascended the mountain knew that on the far side was the Kishon, where Elijah killed the prophets of Baal (Jacob 116).

Pilgrims disembarking at Acre found that the city made a good base for visiting nearby holy sites, like Kefar Hanan, Usha (Shiffrem), and Sepphoris (Tsippori). Rabbi Jacob mentioned several cemeteries near Acre and Haifa, including one containing "the grave of Deborah the Prophetess" (115). Other holy sites near the coast include a miraculous spring in Jabneh, noted by Petachia (57), and the burial sites of Gamaliel between Gath and Acre, and Jacob's son Benjamin at Caesaria.

MIDDLE EASTERN SITES BEYOND THE HOLY LAND

MESOPOTAMIA

Damascus and Baghdad were centers of Muslim political power, commerce, learning, and religious devotion. Mesopotamia held a special attraction for Jewish pilgrims from the western Diaspora. The Bible told them that during the Babylonian exile it was home to the first large Jewish community outside of the Holy Land. Later, the Babylonian Talmud had been compiled there, and academies of Jewish learning still flourished there. The Jewish population of the region was large and relatively prosperous. These reasons were sufficient to attract Jewish businessmen, tourists, and scholars from the western Diaspora. But Mesopotamia exerted an additional attraction to Jews: the graves of several major biblical prophets and other renowned Jewish sages who had served Judaism in exile. Thus many Jewish pilgrims en route to the Holy Land included a tour of Mesopotamia in their plans.

Pilgrims' narratives mention numerous important burial sites all along their routes through Mesopotamia, but with six exceptions (discussed individually below), they give scant information about them. Joseph the Scribe visited the cave of Noah and Shem (90), which he placed in Lebanon. The Casale pilgrim noted that Aaron the Priest was buried on Mount Hor, now called Jabal Haroun, "in a closed cave, upon which is a fair dome: and the Jews go thither to prostrate themselves and to pray on his grave, none saying them nay." He found that the Muslims also revered him (83).

ELIJAH'S TOMB

Elijah's tomb, together with the cave in which he took refuge, was one of the most important shrines visited by medieval Jewish and Muslim pilgrims. It was so popular, in fact, that several different locales claimed it. In the sixteenth century the Casale pilgrim reported that Elijah's cave was in Acre, near the graves of the prophet Elisha and his disciples (59). Then, without a trace of doubt or irony, he wrote that it was near Aleppo and then at Jawbar, not far from Damascus. Muhammad As'ad Talas, writing in the seventeenth century, said that the shrine of al-Khadir (the Muslim name for Elijah) was in a synagogue in Bahsita, adding that there the Jews "light candles and make votive offerings of oil to him."[37]

Of the Elijah tombs, Jawbar seems to have been the preferred site. The Karaite scribe Moses ben Samuel (fourteenth century) went there during a time of personal crisis to ask Elijah to intercede with God on his behalf: "My heart was sick and sad and I entered the synagogue of the prophet Elijah. I prayed before Him (God) in the cave of hiding. 'O my God, what will Thou give unto me.' . . . I

Elijah's Tomb. Sebil Kait-Bey, Palestine. Bonfils. Circa 1870. Collection of the University of Chicago, Middle East Department. Acquisition number 384-95. Used by permission.

placed the letter in the Ark and prayed before God as much as I could."[38] The Jawbar synagogue must have been splendid. The Casale pilgrim describes it as having "twelve columns, and the window through which the bird came to bring Elijah . . . bread and meat" (77). Moses Basola, his contemporary, was also impressed by the structure:

> There is a very handsome synagogue there, the like of which I have never seen. It is built in colonnades, with six columns on the right and seven on the left. Above the synagogue there is a beautiful cave in which, it is said, Elijah the Prophet—may his memory be blessed—hid. The synagogue is said to date from the time of Elisha. There is a stone upon which they say he anointed Hazael. At a later period, R. Eliazer ben Arakh renovated it. It is indeed an awesome place. According to what many people told me, no enemy has ever dominated it, and many miracles have been performed there. In times of distress, Jews always gather in it, and nobody harms them. (87–88)

EZEKIEL'S TOMB

Ezekiel's tomb was about a day's journey from Baghdad, in Kaphri, also known as Kufa (bordering An Najaf, Iraq). Petachia of Ratisbon was impressed by its size and its beauty, and how it was overlaid with gold and gilded cedar wood. Although the site was holy to both Jews and Muslims, Jews held the keys to this shrine. He wrote that the shrine complex was so large and attracted so many pilgrims that it employed 200 caretakers, supported by vows and offerings. While worshipers were not allowed into the grave chamber itself, they could put their heads through windows to see the grave. The chamber was decorated with carpets, glass vases, and "thirty lamps fed with olive oil" that burned day and night. The oil, too, was paid for by the pilgrims. While pilgrims came to Ezekiel's tomb year round, it drew the largest number around the feast of Sukkot.

According to Petachia, Ezekiel's shrine had several miraculous properties. In ancient times there had been a column of fire over the grave, but the presence of wicked people at the feast of Tabernacles had caused its disappearance (31). Even so, the divine was still manifest at the shrine in several ways. A large wall enclosed the shrine area, and its single opening was so low that pilgrims had to crawl on their hands and knees to enter. Petachia related that on Sukkot, when some 60,000 to 80,000 Jews gathered at the shrine to erect their booths in its courtyard, the entrance magically got larger so that people could enter, even on camels. Evidently the shrine was noted for enhancing fertility, for "whoever is barren, or whose cattle is barren, makes a vow, or prays over his grave" (27). Petachia cautioned that there were strong incentives for keeping these vows, relating the tale of a rich man who refused to fulfill his part of the transaction. His horse went through the magic gate into tomb precinct and could not be led out until finally the man had laid sufficient money on the holy man's grave (27). The tomb's reputation for punishing transgressors also meant that anything left at the shrine for safekeeping would be protected by Ezekiel's power, and anyone who stole something from the shrine would be punished. Muslims from the region deposited their valuables there before setting off on long or dangerous journeys (29).

Benjamin of Tudela's account differs somewhat. He found Ezekiel's tomb inside a large synagogue with sixty turrets, with a small synagogue—presumably a decorative replica—between each set of turrets. A large dome covered the tomb, beside which stood a lamp that had burned continually since time immemorial. Muslims and Jews both prayed there and the custodians of the site included both Muslims and Jews. Although Benjamin of Tudela termed it a "lesser" sanctuary, he also said that people came from afar away between Rosh Hashanah and the Day of Atonement to pray. Much like at a modern hillula (see Chapter 9), pilgrims set up a large camp at the site. There were all sorts of joyous festivities, including opportunities to shop at the commercial fair mounted by Arab merchants, who were attracted to the festival (67).

Petachia of Ratisbon also mentioned that "opposite to the grave of Ezekiel" pilgrims visited the graves of Hananiah, Mishael, and Azariah (33), Daniel's three companions who survived their afternoon in Nebuchadnezzar's fiery furnace (Dan. 3:19–27). Benjamin of Tudela found there the synagogue and grave of Isaac Napcha [Nappaha], the noted third-century rabbi (66).

THE TOMB OF EZRA

Ezra's tomb in Basra, in the south of what is now Iraq, was another popular destination. The Spanish pilgrim Judah Harizi (circa 1216) believed the grave had been discovered only 160 years prior to his visit.[39] According to Petachia of Ratisbon, in olden days the grave was in rotten condition when Ezra appeared to a shepherd one night and instructed him to have the Sultan tell the Jews to take Ezra's body to another place and build a sepulcher, or dire consequences would follow. When the Sultan balked, people died until the Sultan finally did what was requested (37). Both Jews and Muslims venerated Ezra's grave, and the Jewish community held the keys to the shrine. Benjamin of Tudela reported that a mosque and a synagogue stood near it. Petachia confirmed this, adding that Jewish pilgrims donated moneys to be spent for marriage portions to orphans, supporting disciples, and repairing the synagogues of the poor (37, 39).

The feature of Ezra's tomb that drew the attention of most medieval writers was the strange light that seemed to emanate from or descend upon the tomb during the night. Harizi's narrator explained, "On many a night that grave is washed with holy light—a godly light, men deem; and thither the nations stream. Moreover, by the holy prophet's side lie seven others, all Righteousness' brothers; and many a night, men tell, their sepulchers shine as well." When the narrator heard this story he went, saw, and believed (280–282). Petachia recorded similar information, although we do not know whether his account was eyewitness or hearsay: "Ezra, the scribe is buried on the boundary of the land of Babylon. When the pillar of fire is over his grave, the structure erected on it is not visible on account of the brightness" (51; see also 39). Evidently this pillar of light was visible each day at the eleventh hour and during the first hour of the night (39). As late as the seventeenth century the Muslim author Yasin al-Biqa'i (died 1684) claimed, "Many a time did I behold on Fridays and Mondays lights arising from the summit of . . . Mt. al-Rimthani up to the sky. It is said that lights do not rise except from prophets' tombs. . . . In the case of Ezra the light descends."[40]

DANIEL'S TOMB

The prophet Daniel's body was said to have been in Shushan (now Shush, in northwest Iran, near Khorramabad). Strangely, it was not buried in the ground, but instead was suspended in a casket from a bridge over the Tigris River. The river separated two villages that battled for control of the casket. Since neither could win, they agreed that each village would have the casket for a year. Benjamin of Tudela explained the rest of the story, variations of which appeared in other pilgrims' chronicles:

> When . . . Emperor Sinjar, king of Persia, saw that they took the coffin of Daniel from one side of the river to the other, and that . . . many people from the country were crossing the bridge he asked the meaning of this proceeding, and they told him these things. He said, "It is not meet to do this ignominy unto Daniel the prophet, but I command you to measure the bridge from both sides, and to take the coffin of Daniel and place it inside another coffin of crystal, so that the wooden coffin be within that of crystal, and to suspend this from the middle of the bridge by a chain of iron; at this spot you must build a synagogue for all comers, so that whoever wishes to pray there, be he Jew or Gentile, may do so." And to this very day the coffin is suspended from the bridge. And the king commanded that out of respect for Daniel no fisherman should catch fish within a mile above or a mile below. (52–53)

Petachia was captivated with the traditions surrounding this tomb, which he claimed was "made of polished copper conspicuous in the middle of the river ten cubits above the water. The Jews told him that any vessel passing underneath the

Daniel's Tomb suspended over the Euphrates River. "Babylon [Baghdad]." Sixteenth century. In *The Casale Pilgrim*, trans. Cecil Roth (London: Soncino Press, 1929), 75.

coffin will proceed in safety if those in it be pious, but will founder if this be not the case. He was further told that underneath the coffin there are fish with golden pendants in their ears" (39, 41). This casket was still in existence in the early six-teenth century, for the Casale pilgrim's work has a drawing of it suspended over the river (75). And the lion's den? Petachia found it in Babylon, where he was shown "a very deep lion's den, and also a furnace half filled with water. Whoever is attacked by fever bathes therein and is healed" (47).

Mordecai and Esther's Tombs

Benjamin of Tudela reported seeing these tombs on his visit to Hamadan (in Iran, north of Khorramabad), but he seemed more interested in the large number of Jews—he claimed 30,000—who lived in that city. As is the case with Elijah, several different places claim the tombs of these two Jewish heroes. Jacob of France, in the early thirteenth century, saw them in Hamadan, but reported as well that Queen Esther's tomb was near Kefar Bar'am, in the Galilee, close to where Obadiah the Prophet was allegedly buried (129, 123). The Casale pil-grim wrote that the tombs were in Persia and Medaea (71). Today the graves in Hamadan are located in a small domed building with a very low door that used to be closed by rolling a stone against it. The two tombs rest in an inner chamber. Al-though pilgrims may visit the tomb at any time during the year, the favored time is Purim, which celebrates Esther's intervention with the king to save the Jews from destruction. According to the Casale pilgrim, "Jews . . . gather there upon Purim and sing songs and praises with timbrels and dances, because it was there that the miracle took place" (71).

Tombs of the Jewish Sages at Hillah

The tomb of Rabbi Meir of the Mishnah, disciple of Rabbi Akiva, was located in Hillah near Babylon, in present-day central Iraq. Benjamin of Tudela was impressed with the large number of Jews and synagogues there: "[I]t is five parasangs to Hillah, where there are 10,000 Israelites and four Synagogues: that of R. Meir, who lies buried before it; the Synagogue of Mar Keshisha, who is buried in front of it; also the Synagogue of Rab Zeiri, the son of Chama; and the Synagogue of R. Mari; the Jews pray there every day" (66). Petachia of Ratisbon wrote that both Muslims and Jews worshiped at Rabbi Meir's grave, and gave this story as the reason why. Both Jews and Muslims had paid for the building of Meir's shrine, but a Sultan later removed one of the steps leading to it. That night Meir appeared to him in a dream, choking him and telling him to return the stone. This caused the Sultan to return the stone, carrying it on his own shoulders in front of everyone. Visitors to Meir's tomb would leave presents and make vows there (33, 35).[41]

Egypt

Jewish pilgrims to Egypt or passing through Egypt on their way to the Holy Land, took note of both saints' tombs and sites associated with the biblical stories of Joseph and of Moses and the Exodus. Benjamin of Tudela, for example, recorded seeing Joseph's storehouses "built of lime and stone, and . . . exceedingly strong" (102).

Two of the most important pilgrimage sites were near Fustat, now part of the city of Cairo. Fustat was the medieval capital of Egypt, the home of the Sultan and the place where Maimonides spent his final years. Nearby was the Ben Ezra synagogue, so called because Abraham ben Ezra supposedly bought the building from the Copts in 882. Maimonides worshiped there, and presumably witnessed the large pilgrimages to the synagogue at Sukkot and Passover. Some held the synagogue to be where the basket carrying the infant Moses came to rest and from which Moses negotiated the Israelites' release with the Pharaoh. An important competing tradition had Moses living at Dammuh, on the west side of the Nile not far from Fustat. One of the many miracle tales associated with Dammuh is that Moses stuck his staff in the ground there, and it quickly became a flowering tree. Pilgrims from afar visited Dammuh at any time of the year. Egyptian Jews tried to go on the seventh of Adar, traditionally the date of Moses's birth and death. They would fast and pray on the seventh, and then celebrate on the eighth with a feast, much like the modern North African hillulot. According to an eleventh-century document by Al-Maqrizi found in the Cairo Genizah, a pilgrimage to Dammuh was considered the equivalent of one to Jerusalem.[42] Joseph ben Isaac Sambari (1640–1703) wrote that the pilgrimage was a major event to the Jews of his time. The heads of the Jewish community in Cairo "would write eloquent letters in fine Arabic and send messengers from 25 Kislev throughout Egypt and all its towns: Rashid, Alexandria, Farask, Ur, Damietta and all the places of their dwellings, that on the seventh of Adar they are invited to fast and to pray in this synagogue of the town of Dammuh . . . and to have a joyous festival on the 8th. Men, women children and the heads of the thousands of Israel would assemble there."[43]

Judging from eleventh-century documents that criticized and attempted to prohibit certain behaviors at the Dammuh, the pilgrimage must have been a wild affair that was much like some of the Muslim Sufi saints' festivals of the time and some of the Christian practices at the many saints' tombs in the area. The Jewish community elders attempted to forbid brewing beer inside the synagogue precincts. They banned all jesting, puppet shows, gambling, playing chess, singing, and rhythmic dancing in the sacred space. They seem to have been particularly concerned about sexual excesses, for several statutes speak to keeping men and women strictly separate during the pilgrimage, and of forbidding unaccompanied women from attending—unless they were very old. The statutes also banned homosexual activity. Maimonides, in the *Mishneh Torah*, expressed similar concerns about the festivals and other places where men and women might evade the eyes of their community. He suggested that rabbinical authorities assign men to "patrol gardens, orchards, and rivers so that men and women would not assemble to eat and drink there and come to transgress."[44] The Dammuh pilgrimage waned under Mameluke rule and the synagogue was actually nailed shut in 1301 as part of a Mameluke campaign against minority religions. It was destroyed in the sultan's presence in 1498.

EUROPEAN JEWISH SAINTS' TOMBS

In Europe, the social unrest and rising anti-Semitism that motivated so many Jews in the later Middle Ages to take to the road on pilgrimage to the Holy Land also created local martyrs whose tombs likewise became places of veneration. One good example is the tomb of Rabbi Meir of Rothenburg. The German Emperor clapped Rabbi Meir in prison in 1286 for allegedly encouraging Jews to emigrate to Palestine, thus cutting into local profits from the *Judensteuer*, or Jew tax. When the rabbi died in prison in 1293, authorities would

Graves of Meir of Rothenberg and Alexander Salomon Wimpfen with kvitlach. Wörms, Germany. Photo, D. Gitlitz, 2004.

not release the body for burial until someone paid an exorbitant blackmail. In 1307, a local merchant, Alexander ben Salomon Wimpfen, produced the funds. Rabbi Meir was buried in the Jewish cemetery in Wörms and eventually Wimpfen was buried next to him. With few interruptions, pilgrims have come to pray and leave written requests (*kvitlach*) at their graves since the fourteenth century. Through the centuries numerous other important rabbis were buried at Wörms, and today at least five of them continue to attract pilgrims.[45]

THE CULT OF THE REBBE:
HASIDIC PILGRIMAGE

When I come to the *ohel*, I remember the days when I had personal audiences with the rebbe. It's a way for me to come to the rebbe, so he hears me and I hear him. (Yitzchok Hazan, on his visit to Reb Menachem Schneerson's grave, Brooklyn, New York, 1999)[1]

Then, we went walked down a long, dirt road towards the center of Mezibush [*sic*] and to a well bubbling up the legendary Ba'al Shem Tov water that has the power of healing. . . . Some of us . . . jumped into the well to take a Mikveh in the Ba'al Shem Tov water. Also, we collected some . . . water and carried it home. (Tzvi Meir Cohn, 2003)[2]

I went to Uman, Ukraine, for Rosh Hashana. Rebbi Nachman of Breslov is buried in Uman. I am a huge fan of his. . . . I had a huge spiritual experience there and am still riding the high of it today. I have every intention of going next year, and I encourage any Jew looking for a connection to go, you'll find it there. (John Berger, 2005)[3]

As we have seen in earlier chapters, veneration of holy men and women at their tombs has been common in Judaism for millennia. The pilgrimages to saints' tombs in the Holy Land were replicated in Diaspora lands at least as early as the twelfth century. In this chapter we will concentrate on northern Europe's reverence of holy men, both during their lifetimes and at their grave sites. Although Hasidic Jews themselves use the term *pilgrimage* sparingly, it is an appropriate label for these visits.

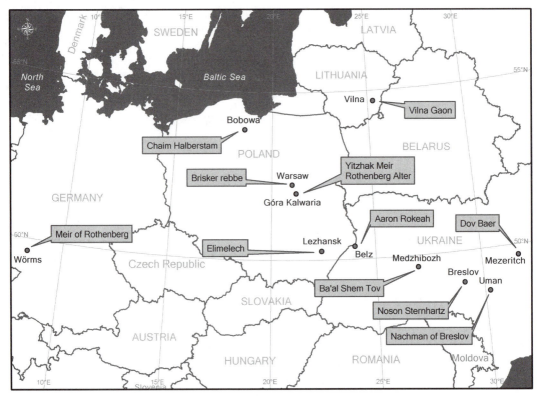

Hasidic Rebbes

HASIDISM: THE CONTEXT FOR PILGRIMAGE

By the early eighteenth century, the word *hasid* was becoming used in its modern sense of a charismatic, learned, and holy rabbi attracting a court of disciples who rely on him for mentorship. Often such men were known less for their encyclopedic learning than for their expression of devotion to the deity and their exemplification of the values and ideals of Judaism. They embodied a mode of life often called *hasidut*, the way of the Hasid. Such men were the Moroccan kabbalist Hayyim ibn Attar (1686–1743), whose followers gathered around him in Jerusalem, Rabbi Moshe Hayyim Luzzatto (1707–1746) in Italy, and the Vilna Gaon (1720–1790) in Lithuania.

Yet it is the development of a group of followers around Rabbi Israel ben Eliezar (1698–1760), known as the Ba'al Shem Tov (Master of the Good Name) and by his acronym Besht, that is generally considered to have established the paradigm for modern Hasidism. In his forties the Ba'al Shem Tov established himself in Medzhibozh, in the Ukraine, where he quickly attracted a following for his wisdom as a kabbalist, his satirical wit, and his ability to spin a parable that cut to the heart of a religious question. Jews also admired his skills as an herbalist and many believed that he had the power to cure the sick and to foretell the future. The Besht appealed to both traditional scholars and large numbers of people from the lower classes who had never acquired a deep knowledge of the Talmud nor could afford the time to devote themselves exclusively to its study. His approach drew much from the kabbalists' emphasis on both the outer revealed and inner hidden aspects of the Torah. The Besht preached that God is present in all of creation, and that therefore all things are in essence good, including human beings. Rejection of the pleasures associated with the world, as many of his contemporary ascetic Talmudists were teaching, was therefore wrong. Life was to be lived, enjoyed, loved. With regard to religious ceremony, enthusiasm of spirit was worth more than adherence to form. The Besht believed that constant focus on God and commitment to Torah could bring the joys of ecstatic spiritual worship to every Jew, regardless of his depth of knowledge of the Law. Though all humans sin, he preached, no one has sunk so low that he or she cannot raise himself or herself to God.

In general, the central tenets of Hasidism are simply put. God is omnipresent, inhabiting every detail of the created universe, so that human beings can be with him and serve him in every aspect of their lives. The potential for communion with God exists in every activity. The communication is constant and flows both ways. The most profound communion occurs in prayer, in those moments when humans are so intensely focused, so full of fervor and joy that the soul shakes loose its material bonds and enters into union with the divine. Prayer can be intensified through rhythmic movements of the body, shouting, singing, or wordless chanting.

The Hasidic movement began in the fragmented, tension-ridden society that emerged in Eastern Europe in the aftermath of the pogroms and false messiahs of the preceding century. It sprang from a reaction by Jews of a mystical bent against the prevailing culture of formalistic intellectual study of the Torah and against worship practices that many believed to be cold and devoid of emotion. During the preceding century, conflicts between the two main streams of European Jewish thought—rabbinic, Torah-centered, intellectual study versus emotional, Kabbalah-centered mysticism—had grown particularly acute. As the Ba'al Shem Tov's influence grew, his approach was bitterly opposed by the more traditional scholars for whom education was the only legitimate doorway to spiritual life. The split was geographic as well as cultural, with traditional rabbinic Judaism in northern Poland and Lithuania, and mystical approaches holding sway in southern Poland and the Ukraine.

After the Besht's death, his disciple Rabbi Dov Baer (Dovber) of Meziritch (Ukraine; 1710–1772), and then Dov Baer's disciples, worked tirelessly to promote Hasidism. Some of these rabbis possessed the knowledge and the charisma to attract their own courts of followers. They in turn collected others. Within only a few decades, Hasidism had become the dominant form of Judaism in much of Eastern Europe. The differences in the rebbes' interpretations of religious law and styles of worship led their circles to develop into distinct communities, or sects. Originally these were distinguished according to their geographic centers, and often they were differentiated by their mode of dress. Leadership of each group passed from father to son, so that the sects took on dynastic characteristics, including intense rivalry among dynasties or among splinter groups within a dynasty. Critics of Hasidism feared that the cult of the rebbe might well develop into a kind of false messianism.

Toward the end of the nineteenth century, when large numbers of Jews from Eastern Europe emigrated to the West, Hasidism became an important Jewish subculture in Western Europe and especially in the United States. Though initially strong, Hasidism gradually was moved off center stage by other developments in Judaism: the Enlightenment, the growth of other forms of Judaism like the Reform and Conservative movements, and the development of Zionism. When the Holocaust wiped out most European strongholds of Hasidism, Israel and the United States emerged as the principal centers of the movement. The two major Hasidic branches in America today are based in Brooklyn: the Lubavitch (sponsors of Chabad), in the Crown Heights area; and the Satmar, of Hungarian origin, clustered in Williamsburg. Several other Hasidic groups have settled in New York, such as the Belzer, Bobov, Breslov, Gor (or Gerer), Munkacz, and Viznitz Hasidim.

THE REBBE

The guiding authority in each Hasidic group is known as the rebbe, to elevate him above ordinary run-of-the-minyan rabbis. No less a figure than Maimonides (1135–1204) had given the cult of sages a semiofficial status when he wrote that "It is a positive precept to cleave to the sages and their disciples in order to learn from their ways."[4] At first the term rebbe was reserved for the leader of a sect of Hasidism, the charismatic spiritual guide and master for his circle of followers, but in time a Hasid's personal spiritual mentor also came to be honored with the title. The Hasidic rebbe might be ordained as a rabbi, but this is not required, nor is it always the case. He might be deeply learned in the Law, but this, too, is not essential. More important is the way he teaches through speaking and writing, and models righteous behavior by the example of his life. Beyond this, what characterizes the rebbe is his ability to "understand the various levels of the soul."[5] Rebbes are believed by their followers to have a special connection to God. Rabbi Elimelech of Lezhansk (1717–1787) wrote that the rebbe is a holy person, a tzadiq, who can mediate between the deity and the ordinary Jew and who, because of his holy deeds, has the power to tap into the flow of divine grace and thus to accomplish almost anything. Therefore, like the saints of Christianity or the *walis* of Islam, they are viewed as potential intercessors on behalf of the faithful. The tzadiq, in return for loyalty and material support from his followers, devotes his prayers and abilities to transmitting to them the divine blessings of life, livelihood, and children. In fact, a Hasid effectively attains the status of rebbe by agreeing to accept his followers' petitions. Any concern that such beliefs cross the line into alien practices is parried by the assertion that because God needs to be benevolent toward his creation, petitionary prayers enable him to fulfill his own purposes. The requests, therefore, are deemed to be for the sake of the Shechinah, not for the egoistic needs of the petitioner.[6]

In practice this special connection means that the words of the rebbe, whether commenting on a biblical passage or elucidating a halakhic point via an anecdote, have some of the force of revealed truth. A blessing from the rebbe is held by the believer to have almost talismanic power to protect against evil and to facilitate positive benefits. It is easy to see why the most renowned rebbes quickly became objects of pilgrimage. The physical presence of the rebbe enhances feelings of fellowship and renders prayer more powerful. This holds true whether the rebbe is alive and has gathered his followers around him for a session of shared study and commentary, or whether he has died and his followers are drawn together at his tomb. Rivka Gonen, a curator at the Israel Museum, put it succinctly: "We do have saints in Judaism. It's easier to talk to the tsadik, to go to these tombs and tell them your problems, because they're holier than most people. They're closer to God and can relay the message."[7]

THE REBBE'S FARBRENGEN

The Yiddish word *farbrengen* denotes a fellowship of men gathered informally around their rebbe to share a religious experience with one another. It has been described as "a Lubavitcher rock concert. The rabbi is the draw, but the feel of the crowd is just as important to the event—and to the crowd."[8] Its origin goes back to the Ba'al Shem Tov, whose disciples used to gather with him at his table for the third meal of the Sabbath and other occasions to talk, pray, sing, ask their rebbe questions about religious matters, and listen to him expound on sacred texts. In the farbrengen the Hasidic ethos is created, its patterns of thought and of worship transmitted to the community. For the ordinary Eastern European Hasid laboring all week as a tradesman or in his shtetl's fields, the farbrengen was an island of revitalization, a few hours when his spirit could be lifted from the mundane and he could share the joys of religious transport with his friends and his rebbe. Its role in modern times is similar. In describing the farbrengen hosted by the Bobover Rebbe Shlomo Halberstam in New Jersey, an Israeli journalist noted Halberstam's "warm, outgoing personality, a welcoming smile, a rare gift for storytelling and an inexhaustible fund of Chassidic tales that attracted people to his table or festive meals."[9]

The farbrengen is a multidimensional experience, with aspects of brotherhood, bonding, and warmth, of education and inspiration, of guidance, of self-discovery, and of transport beyond the self.[10] And of singing, often the wordless, melodic, spirit-focusing, mantra-like chant called a *nigun* that serves as a vehicle to mystic rapture. In all of this, the physical presence of the rebbe leverages up the intensity of the experience. For the rebbe's regular court of adherents, for travelers from near and far, the visit to the rebbe's farbrengen is a pilgrimage, a visit to a holy presence through which they may be transformed.

THE REBBE TAKES KVITLACH

On visiting their rebbe, many Hasidic Jews ask him to intercede on their behalf with God to answer their prayers or help them solve their problems. Similarly, they may make pilgrimage to a rebbe's grave, where his spirit is reputed to be strongly manifest, to request his intervention. Because they believe the rebbe's prayers enjoy a privileged status, the rebbe's followers value his blessing and his praying on their behalf. A written request of this nature is called a *kvittel* (plural, *kvitlach*). No one knows precisely where or how the custom originated, but it seems to have been common among Hasidim from the beginning of the movement.[11]

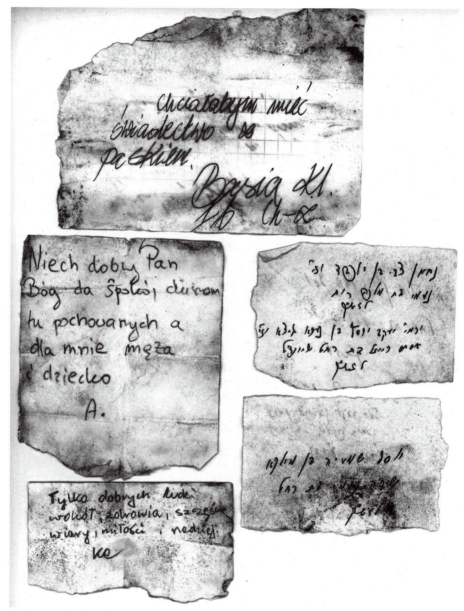

Kvitlach: "Basia asking for a school diploma, with distinction." "Dear Sir God, I am asking you for peace for everyone, and for me a husband and a child." "Only good people around me, health, happiness, faith, love, and hope." Hebrew kvitlach recording petitioners' names.

There is a formal procedure. The petitioner writes his or her name in the Hebrew fashion along with the name of his or her mother, and then briefly details the requested favor or the problem to be solved. When bringing the petition to a living rebbe, it is customary to accompany the request with a *pidyon* or *pidyon nefesh* (Hebrew, "redemption of the soul"), a cash donation for the rebbe's personal use or for some religious cause that he supports. Worshipers also leave kvitlach at tombs of important rebbes. In fact, leaving a kvittel is a fundamental component of the ritual that attends the visit of an orthodox Jew to the grave of a Hasidic master: "Here we *daven* and place '*kvitlach*.' We wash with a hand-driven pump and we turn away."[12]

The kvittel fulfills several needs, some psychological, some administrative, and some financial. It allows the petitioner to engage in a concrete act—formulating the request, writing it down, delivering it to the rebbe—that satisfies the longing to be proactive in seeking remedy for a particular problem. Kvitlach enable the rebbe to keep track of the many petitions he receives, to deliver them (i.e., pray them) systematically, and to make certain that none gets lost in the shuffle. And, of course, they can also provide a ready source of income for the rebbe or the institution that acts on his behalf.

Modern technology has introduced some changes. For example, at each of the dozens of rebbes' tombs that we visited in 2004, in addition to the mounded slips of traditionally handwritten kvitlach, we found multiple slips of paper with preprinted or photocopied prayers and petitions. Additionally, the Internet allows people to send their petitions by email, thus making a kind of virtual pilgrimage to the rebbe's grave site. One of the most popular e-kvittel sites is the grave of Rabbi Nachman of Breslov in the Ukraine. A number of other Hasidic groups and yeshivot also invite electronic petitions. Since the Shechinah is also believed to be accessible at Jerusalem's Western Wall, there is a brisk traffic in e-kvitlach there as well. The sponsoring groups promise to read the petitions aloud at the holy site, or to pray on behalf of the homebound pilgrim, to place the kvittel on the grave or in a chink of the Western Wall, and, after an appropriate interval, to dispose of the written petitions by burning them.[13]

PILGRIMAGE TO THE REBBE'S GRAVE

Among Hasidic Jews, the cult of pilgrimage to the rebbe's grave springs from a simple set of theological propositions: That after death eventually the body will be resurrected. That until that happens, the soul is never completely separated from the body's mortal remains. That some of the powers invested in the tzadiq in life are present in his remains. That in some fashion and to some extent, this power can be harnessed by the pilgrim at the tzadiq's tomb. Many Hasidim believe that a person's soul returns to the grave site on the anniversary of his death, at which time his communion with the deity is particularly strong. This *yahrzeit* or *hillula* tends to be the most propitious moment for visiting the Hasid's grave.[14] A second favored time is on certain holidays like Lag b'Omer, or each new moon when the deceased rebbe's presence is thought to be approachable. Thus, as the rebbe in life was held to be an able mediator between the individual Jew and God, so, too, the grave of the rebbe is a privileged place. It is a kind of portal, holy ground where the everyday touches the divine. Hasidim are clear to emphasize that praying *to* a deceased person is forbidden, since it denies the uniqueness of God and verges on idolatry, ancestor worship, and polytheism. On the other hand, they hold it perfectly licit to ask the spirit of a deceased rebbe to lobby the deity on one's behalf.

To judge from Rashi's discussion of the custom of gathering at the grave of an honored sage to honor him on the anniversary of his death, the practice was ancient.[15] So, too, was the parallel custom of visiting the graves of deceased relatives to request that they ask God to be merciful toward their surviving family (BT Ta'anith 16a). The graves of prominent ancestors were likewise powerful. Caleb, who went with Joshua's spies to reconnoiter the land of Canaan, stopped first in Hebron at the graves of the Patriarchs to request that they ask God to protect them on their mission (BT Sotah 34b). Three thousand years later, the Lubavitcher Rebbe Menachem Schneerson, whose grave has become the most important Jewish pilgrimage site in the Americas, was in the habit of going to his father's grave to seek counsel and to pass along his adherents' requests that his father ask God for mercy on their behalf.[16]

Hasidic Jews often honor an important rebbe by enclosing his grave in an *ohel* (Hebrew, "sheltering tent"). Generally this takes the form of a fence around his grave, but it may also be a small building that can serve as a prayer hall and a gathering place, allowing the rebbe's followers to spend a few moments at his grave in all sorts of weather. Guest houses, mikva'ot, yeshivot, and other support facilities may honor rebbes with especially large followings or exceptionally wealthy devotees.

From its outset in the eighteenth century, Hasidism's keynote has been the intensely emotional communion of the individual Hasid with God. For pilgrims finding themselves at the longed-for holy site after a lengthy, arduous journey, the intensity of feeling may well be a springboard to the sense of communion with the divine that is a common goal of pilgrimage. As Eitan Shuman put it, when he visited the graves of the Brisker rebbe and Rabbi Naftali Tzvi Berlin in Warsaw's Jewish cemetery in 2003, "it is an awesome feeling indeed to stand at the graves of our Gedolim and say a kippitel tehellim, a Kel Moleh Rachamim and leave a Kivettle. . . . This is the closest we will ever get to them . . . in this world at least."[17]

Some pilgrimages are, of course, life changing. They may radically alter a person's sense of religious commitment. For Hasidim, whose lifestyle already speaks to a commitment to a full Jewish life, the major aftereffects of pilgrimage may be a kind of

Grave of Moses Iserles. Kraków, Poland. Photo, D. Gitlitz, 2004.

glow that lingers to enrich the quality of their religious experience. Rabbi Yonas-san Gershom, long after his return from a pilgrimage to Nachman of Breslov's tomb in Uman, in the Ukraine, described the glow this way: "Now, as I make hisboddidus (private prayer) along the wooded Minnesota trails in the early morning light, I often find myself dancing and singing, 'Uman, Uman, Rosh Hashanah!'"[18]

With the exception of the Western Wall in Jerusalem, for Hasidic Jews the grave sites of their beloved rebbes are the most important places of pilgrimage. Some of the rebbes' tombs attract pilgrims mainly from the immediate locale, while others have a regional, national, or—like the sites discussed below—an international draw. The origin of many of these Hasidic rebbe cults is relatively modern, and it seems likely that as new rebbes attract major followings, some of their graves, too, will be hallowed by pilgrims. Here are some of the most representative Hasidic pilgrimage cults in Europe, the United States, and Israel.

ISRAEL BEN ELIEZAR, THE BA'AL SHEM TOV (MEDZHIBOZH, UKRAINE)

The old cemetery in Medzhibozh tops a hill north of the village. Next to it stands a guest facility with a mikveh and several large rooms, one of which functions as a synagogue. In the cemetery an ohel covers the Ba'al Shem Tov's gravestone. Pilgrim groups tend to define their own observances and bring the required ceremonial objects with them. Several hundred Jerusalem Hasidim, who gathered in Medzhibozh on the anniversary of the Ba'al Shem Tov's birthday in 2002, marched in solemn procession to the cemetery to deposit a new Torah scroll in its synagogue.[19] Tzvi Meir Cohn, the executive director of the Ba'al Shem Tov Foundation, described the traditional and not-quite-so-traditional ceremonial aspects of his visit in 2003:

> Inside the Ohel, we said the customary prayers and offered our request for blessings written on a piece of paper. Then we tore up the paper and threw the torn pieces onto the grave, as is the custom. Our Rabbi . . . delivered a sermon on Torah. Then, we sang 8 or 9 niggunim (songs without words) originated by each of the Rabbis leading to and including the seven Lubavitch Rebbes. Then, I sang my original composition, "The Baal Shem Tov Blues" accompanied by my guitar. This was a magical moment.[20]

Obligations thus fulfilled, his group could turn their attention to tourist activities. "Just outside the cemetery, there was a man selling Russian styled fur hats, a few fox skins and some other souvenirs. We purchased two hats and a fox skin." Near the grave site is a well known for the healing powers of its "Ba'al Shem Tov water." Cohen and his group hiked to the well and filled some bottles to take home with them.

The holiness of the graves of Hasidic rebbes makes them apt locales for religious events. The same way that Jerusalem's Western Wall attracts Jewish families from around the globe to celebrate their bar mitzvahs and weddings in the shadow of the Second Temple, the rebbes' graves attract their adherents to celebrate their joyous events in the rebbe's presence. In early October 2004, for example, twenty-one young Jews from five small Ukrainian towns made a pilgrimage to Medzhibozh to celebrate their bar mitzvahs in the court of the Ba'al Shem Tov. They were joined by a young couple from another town who had celebrated their wedding in Medzhibozh.[21]

Many of the pilgrims who come to Medzhibozh with organized groups also seek out the new Jewish cemetery inside the village. They may also go out into the fields near the river to visit a mass grave containing the remains of most of Medzhibozh's 4,600 Jews, who were murdered in 1942.

ELIMELECH OF LEZHANSK (LEZHANSK, POLAND)

In the late eighteenth century the tzadiq Elimelech Weissblum of Lezhansk (1717–1787) turned this tiny Polish brewery town into a major center of Hasidism. Elimelech was a disciple of Dovber of Mezherich, who had been a disciple of the Ba'al Shem Tov. He was the author of *Noam Elimelech*, a commentary on the Torah that defines the role of the tzadiq and the basic tenets of Hasidism. Unlike many great early Hasids, who emphasized the joys to be found in worshiping the God of creation, Reb Elimelech was an ascetic, who strove to distance himself from the material world. Among all the rabbis of his day, Reb Elimelech had the broadest fame as a worker of miracles. He reputedly had the ear of the deity and could therefore intercede effectively for those who requested God's help. He was known for his ability to heal the sick, to drive out demons, and to cure people of the vice of gambling. Among the faithful, his grave site in Lezhansk is believed to tap the same powers. Pilgrimage to his tomb remained constant until the beginning of World War II.

Reb Elimelech's grave is fenced with an ohel reputedly built in 1776, the only such monument in Poland to survive the Holocaust. In 1960 a group of American Hasidim financed the construction of a building to enclose it. The Hasidim who visited Lezhansk in the early 1980s found this building standing in an unkempt cemetery littered with trash. If they wanted to bathe, they availed themselves of the San River. For food they bought eggs and tomatoes from local residents. In 1986 the Nissenbaum Family Foundation restored the cemetery wall and gate. By the disintegration of Soviet-style Communism in 1989, Lezhansk had become a featured stop on Orthodox Jewish tours to Poland. Each year since then several thousand Hasidic pilgrims converge on Lezhansk to visit their rebbe's tomb. Pilgrims come not only from Israel and the western Diaspora, but also from the small surviving Jewish communities of Hungary, Belarus, and Lithuania. In 2002 more than twenty chartered planes brought pilgrims to the nearby airport of Rzeszów; in 2003 the number dropped somewhat because of unsettled conditions in the Middle East.[22]

Most pilgrims come to Lezhansk for the 21 Adar yahrzeit. They find the Jewish part of town plastered with posters in Yiddish giving them practical directions to the cemetery, the public telephone, the toilets, and the mikveh, constructed in 1990 on the site of the prewar mikveh. Fundraisers from Polish

Jewish charities and from Israeli and American yeshivot set up their tables along the streets. A temporary canteen provides thousands of pilgrims with kosher meals flown in from Israel and entertains them with Jewish music while they eat. An Israeli doctor is available. Uniformed Polish policemen with dogs guard the perimeter of the cemetery to prevent interference. A fire truck stands by if the candle lighting should get out of hand.

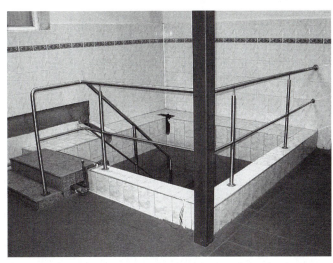

New mikveh. Pilgrim guest house. Lezhansk, Poland. Photo, D. Gitlitz, 2004.

During our visit to Lezhansk in July 2004, we were given a tour of the newest pilgrim-support facilities, located across the street from the cemetery in a two-story building funded and staffed under the aegis of the Hasidic community of Bnei Brak in Israel. The caretaker is not Jewish—Jews reside in Lezhansk—but he is very knowledgeable about the traditions he is helping to perpetuate. On the ground floor are two mikva'ot, a small kosher kitchen, toilets, and showers for the men. Upstairs in the facility is a large room reserved for prayer and study and another set of rooms with cots that can sleep forty-eight people. This is sufficient for most of the year, but for the yahrzeit celebration the Hasidim lodge with local people who welcome the opportunity to make a little money. The caretaker's own mother always takes in several. "But how do you cope when there are 3,000 pilgrims?" we asked him. "Ah. Then the people from Bnei Brak set up huge tents, with rugs and beds and everything. Plush as a hotel."

The most intense pilgrim activity is focused on the Rebbe's modern gravestone inside an iron cage, called an ohel, in a small, white, three-room structure. His original stone rests against the side wall, with an area in front of it for lighting candles. One lateral room is piled high with dog-eared prayer books in a hundred different editions. The other side room is reserved for women. On the anniversary of Reb Elimelech's death, thousands of Hasidim throng the cemetery and the open space in the road in front of a fence to spend the night in prayer and song. As at any highly visible event of such magnitude, the crowd may include notables like the chief rabbi of Israel, the mayor of Lezhansk, the governor of Poland's Podkarpacie Province, and the heads of Jewish foundations, as well as journalists—Polish, Israeli, American—eager to draw attention to Jewish activities in modern Poland. In 2002 Antoni Ledamski described the arrival at the Rebbe's ohel of the tzadiq Dawider, originally from Lelow, who now resides in the United States:

> Dawider solemnly carried a torah wrapped in an embroidered roll of black velvet, surrounded by a crowd of Hasidim. They moved quickly, nearly running.

Each minute one of the faithful comes up to him and kisses his hand. . . . The crowd gathered at the shrine parted to let Rabbi Dawider approach the iron fence that encloses the grave of Elimelech. Inside the enclosure there stood a crowd of men dressed in black. Heads in black hats moved rhythmically in a trance of prayer. The ohel resembled a buzzing beehive. It was somewhat empty only in the aisle, behind a curtain, where a few women who accompanied their husbands were praying.[23]

Many of the pilgrims to Lezhansk leave paper kvitlach on the Rebbe's grave with their own requests or those of people remaining at home. The folded papers fill the fenced area around the tomb to a depth of a meter or so. Some of the pilgrims light a candle for themselves or for a friend who was unable to make the journey. In 2000, Ledamski asked the ohel's caretaker about the candles: "Each of the pilgrims has 30 to 100 candles with them. Each candle has a card addressed to the zaddik attached to it. Around noon, I collected several sackfuls of trash: remains of 3,000–4,000 candles which had been lit on the evening of March 4."[24]

Grave and kvitlach. Elimelech of Lezhansk, Poland. Photo, D. Gitlitz, 2004.

As with most other towns in Polish Galicia that had a significant Jewish population before the Shoah, curious tourists and pilgrims can visit nearby sites once associated with the Jews. Lezhansk's former synagogue is now the Bank for the Protection of the Environment. The Jewish school near the cemetery operated for years as a restaurant. In 2004 we learned that it had recently been purchased by the Hasidim of Bnei Brak to serve as a kosher dining facility for pilgrims.

YITZHAK MEIR ROTHENBERG ALTER (GÓRA KALWARIA [GER], POLAND)

In 1859 the charismatic rebbe Yitzhak Meir Rothenberg Alter (1789–1866) settled in Góra Kalwaria, forty kilometers south of Warsaw. His approach to studying traditional texts was so popular that before long a narrow-gauge railroad was built to bring his followers from Warsaw to study with him. By the end of the century the town's 3,000 Jews comprised more than half its population and the Gerer Hasidim were the most important Jewish group in the kingdom of Poland. The Gerer tended to be extremists, devoted to Torah study, traditional in manner and dress. The successive rebbes of the town attracted pilgrims from all over Poland to pray and study with them. When the pilgrims arrived in Ger, they would purify themselves in body and spirit at the mikveh and then gather for hours in the synagogue and the courtyard of the Rebbe's house to share the splendor of the Rebbe's presence. This golden age of Gerer Hasidism lasted until World War II when almost all the community was wiped out.[25]

Rabbi Abraham Mordechai Alter (1866–1948) managed to slip away from the Nazis to Palestine in 1940, and from Jerusalem he rebuilt the Gerer movement. Before long, Gerer Hasidim had established important centers in Israel, the United States, and Belgium. In 1991 the Gerers financed covering Reb Yitzhak's grave with a sturdy brick prayer hall which also contains the grave of Reb Yitzhak's son, Yehuda Arie Leib Alter (1847–1905). It has become an important pilgrimage destination, especially on Reb Yitzhak's yahrzeit on 5 Shebat. It is also a common port of call for American United Synagogue Youth summer pilgrimage programs.

NACHMAN OF BRESLOV (UMAN, UKRAINE)

Rabbi Nachman of Breslov (1772–1810) came from a distinguished Hasidic dynasty.[26] His great-grandfather was the Ba'al Shem Tov. Both his grandfather and his father were important rabbis. His mother, thought to be gifted with powers of clairvoyance, was known as Feiga the Prophetess, and her two brothers were rabbis respected for their wisdom and their writings. Rabbi Nachman's teachings flowed from those of the Ba'al Shem Tov. He emphasized the possibility of each Jew's establishing a personal relationship with the deity through intense prayer and contemplation, either in Hebrew or in one's native language.

In 1798 Rabbi Nachman heeded a call from God to make a pilgrimage to Palestine to visit the Tiberias Hasidic community and to pray at the graves of holy men. Legends recall the novelesque episodes of the journey, during which Rabbi Nachman had to overcome a number of obstacles and was assisted by many miraculous events. Though he was moved when he disembarked in Haifa, his elation soon turned to depression and a desire to set sail immediately for home, since "[t]he moment I walked four steps in the Holy Land, I achieved my goal."[27] He then read out the names of all his followers and their prayers from the kvitlach they had given him back home, and directed his disciple Simeon ben Baer to prepare to leave. Simeon persuaded Nachman to continue, and the two of them visited Tiberias and Meron, where he prayed and sang for an entire night over Shim'on bar Yohai's grave. His trip home was horrendous: their ship was attacked by the French, they were imprisoned in their cabin, and in Rhodes had to be ransomed by the local Jewish community. In all, it took the two men a year to return to the Ukraine. Nevertheless, Nachman considered the pilgrimage a turning point in his religious life, even going so far as to have his previous writings deleted from the corpus of his work.[28]

Reb Nachman stressed joy in worship. He taught that sincere, intense commitment to the deity was the path to spiritual renewal. One technique for achieving this is through intense personal prayer while walking alone, immersed in the glories of creation. He taught that another is through the veneration of sages, particularly at Rosh Hashanah, when God is most attuned to human prayer and the tzadiq's spirit is most accessible at his burial place. Rabbi Nachman assured his followers that he would always act as their intermediary with the deity, but that he would be most attentive to prayers at his grave site. He told them: "If you come to me and say prayers over my grave, I will stretch myself this way and that way, and pull you out by your very earlocks from the gates of hell."[29] Reb Nachman's disciple Rabbi Noson Sternhartz interpreted this episode to mean that the rebbe intended his Hasidim to make pilgrimages to his grave. Another disciple, Rabbi Nathan of Nemirov, is credited with organizing the first great Rosh Hashanah pilgrimage to Reb Nachman's grave site.

Uman is a city of approximately 90,000 people 200 kilometers south of Kiev. When the Nazis occupied the area, they destroyed the Jewish cemetery. But a local Jew who survived the occupation kept track of the exact location of Reb Nachman's grave, and after the war he covered the grave site with an unmarked slab of stone. From the end of World War II until the disintegration of Soviet Communism in 1989, Jews found it difficult to secure permission to visit the grave, but a few foreigners, most of them Breslover Hasidim, managed to reach the city. By the 1980s, when restrictions were beginning to be relaxed, the slab marking the grave was covered with an embroidered cloth, and the cloth with a plastic sheet to keep it from being soiled by the hands of Jewish pilgrims anxious to touch the grave. For Rosh Hashanah in 1988, 250 Jews managed to assemble in Uman. By then the site had been roofed, and benches had been provided for the pilgrims to sit and pray.

With the fall of Communism and the Ukraine's independence, everything changed. In 1990 some 7,000 Jews made the pilgrimage, and the number has grown each year, with 10,000 attending in 2000 and some 14,000 from more than 50 different countries in 2003. Although the majority of the pilgrims are Breslover Hasidim, the pilgrimage also attracts other Hasidim and Sephardim who venerate Rabbi Nachman, and Israeli and western Jews of all persuasions. Some return every year and use the occasion to meet with Breslover friends and relatives residing in different countries. As with most Hasidic pilgrimages, the event is almost exclusively the purview of males.[30]

During the fifteen years following 1989, Breslovers—with the help of several wealthy philanthropists and the Ukraine government, which sees the pilgrimage as an important source of tourist revenue—have created an impressive physical infrastructure around the rebbe's grave. There is now a synagogue that accommodates 5,000 worshipers. An elegantly appointed Beit Midrash contains a library of holy texts and commentaries, and a second, reached by an elevated walkway, enables members of the Jewish priestly class to pray near the tomb without actually entering the cemetery. A nearby reception center offers worshipers nourishment at any hour of the day or night. A new mikveh provides several showers for cleansing and hot-water mikva'ot for ritual immersion. The building's second floor has dormitory rooms for seminary students who visit on group excursions. Wealthy pilgrims can stay at the brand new Shaarei Zion Hotel. Other pilgrims rent rooms from local residents, and those who cannot be accommodated sleep in tents. Prior to 1989, and in the first few years thereafter, many pilgrims brought their kosher food with them to Uman. Now a large dining facility and a kitchen capable of putting 4,000 hot meals on the table provide for the pilgrims' needs. During Rosh Hashanah the streets near the grave site are closed to traffic. Police, firefighters, and medical personnel are on hand. Market stalls hawk religious items, Ukrainian souvenirs, and other items of interest.

For a Breslover Hasid today, a visit to the rebbe's tomb in Uman is likely to be the highlight of the year's religious experience. Yonassan Gershom recalled years later the emotional impact of his arrival. It was near midnight when he got off the bus, but the tomb site bustled with activity. In 1997 he wrote:

> I wish that I could say I had the presence of mind to say "Shehechiyanu"—the prayer which thanks G–d for having "preserved us, kept us alive, and brought us safely to this time." But the only thing out of my mouth was, "I can't believe I'm really here!!!!" Which was indeed a prayer of thanks from the depths of my heart! I had finally made it to the "Rebbe's Zion."[31]

The Breslov Research Institute website, which advertises pilgrimage tours to Uman all during the year, targets a broad audience. There are tours for individuals, families, and groups; some are limited to "women and their special needs." An English-speaking taxi driver meets pilgrims at the Kiev airport. Ample security arrangements allow pilgrims to feel safe. And while they are in the region, religious pilgrims can visit a number of additional holy sites in the Ukraine and Poland, including the tombs of the Ba'al Shem Tov in Medzhibozh, the Magid of Mezritch in Anipoli, Reb Noson in Breslov, and Reb Elimelech in Lezhansk.[32]

Although pilgrims visit the tomb all year long, activity is greatest around the 18 Tishri anniversary of Rabbi Nachman's death and around Rosh Hashanah. The grave site itself is surrounded by masses of men praying the daily or festival liturgies, expressing their personal prayers in Hebrew or their native languages, and bringing their requests to their Rebbe. Anyone wishing to touch the grave, or even to glimpse it clearly, must push his way through the crowd. Worship groups form according to the prayer customs of the visitors: Breslovers, other Hasidic communities, Yemenites, Sephardim. In the main synagogue, distinguished Breslover rabbis take turns leading the service. On the second day of Rosh Hashanah, when Rabbi Nachman used to deliver his sermons or commentaries, Breslovers read portions of his teachings and expound on their meaning, thus creating a sense that their Rebbe's presence is still active among them.

For many Hasidim, the pilgrimage's emotional climax comes on the afternoon of the second day of Rosh Hashanah at the Tashlich service, in which one's sins are symbolically cast into a body of water. The pilgrims gather to pray at a reservoir, reputedly the site of a Nazi massacre of Jews, and then return to Uman's main synagogue in procession, joyfully singing and dancing.[33]

MENACHEM MENDEL SCHNEERSON (QUEENS, NEW YORK)

In modern times, the rebbe with the most far-reaching influence is without doubt Menachem Mendel Schneerson (1902–1994). Schneerson came from a long line of distinguished rabbis, including Shneur Zalman of Lyady, who in the 1770s in the Belarus town of Lubavich founded the Chabad movement. Chabad—an acronym for the Hebrew words for wisdom, understanding and knowledge—positioned itself on the conservative side of Hasidism, stressing the value of Torah study and of bringing the rhythms of everyday life into close harmony with traditional Jewish halakhic practices. Schneerson's classic education in Hasidic wisdom and his study at universities in both Berlin and Paris prepared him to reach beyond the traditional constituencies of Hasidism to Jews of diverse commitment and degrees of affiliation.

Schneerson's father-in-law Rabbi Joseph Yitzhak Schneersohn brought Chabad to the United States in the 1920s and began to reach out aggressively to America's increasingly secular Jewish community to persuade individual Jews to return to orthodoxy. Fleeing Nazi-occupied France, Reb Menachem joined him in 1941 and, when his father-in-law died, he became Lubavitcher Hasidism's seventh rebbe.

Though he rarely left his home in New York City's borough of Queens, Schneerson transformed Chabad into an extensive missionary movement. He sent out his *shluchim*—young, married, Chabad-trained rabbis—as emissaries to big-city Jewish neighborhoods and college campuses all over the world. As of 2000 there were nearly 4,000 of them in the field. Through highly visible public celebrations, workshops, pamphlets, web services, and streetcorner "Mitzvah Tanks," the Chabad movement has exerted great influence in modern Judaism.[34]

Schneerson attracted a large circle of followers during his lifetime. They gathered at his farbrengen to pray with him, to listen to his wisdom expressed in Torah commentaries, and to be guided by his advice and his gentle reproaches of their occasional missteps. He encouraged the habit of charity by giving his followers dollar bills that they were supposed to pass along to others less fortunate than they. But most people kept the bills, treasuring them as if they were holy relics. His reputation was enhanced by the friendship and respect shown to him by other important rabbis such as Yitzchak Kaduri, Israel Abuhatzeira (known as the Baba Sali), and Mordechai Eliyahu (former Chief Rabbi of Israel). Although the people who flocked to Rabbi Schneerson did not generally term themselves pilgrims, their journeys resembled other religions' pilgrimages to their holiest living figures, such as Catholicism's Pope, Buddhism's Dalai Lama, Hinduism's Meher Baba, and New Age gurus such as J. Z. Knight of Yelm, Washington, the Swami Maharishi Mahesh Yogi, and Baghwan Shree Rajneesh.

Schneerson's followers came to pray with him, but many also came so that he could pray for them. Their Rebbe accepted their kvitlach and offered prayers of intercession on their behalf. Some people interpreted the results to be miraculous: childlessness relieved, illnesses cured, disasters averted, or loved ones reconciled. When in the 1980s some of his followers began to speak of him as the Messiah, he did not actively discourage them.

Schneerson died in 1994, leaving no successor. He was buried in the Old Montefiore Cemetery in Queens' Cambria Heights. For many of his followers, he had not really gone, and as they had talked to him in life they felt they could continue to talk to his spirit, and thus the locus of the Reb Menachem's cult shifted to his grave site. Lubavitcher Hasidim, other Orthodox Jews, nonobservant Jews, and even people of other religions have turned the Rebbe's ohel into a major pilgrimage site. Fifty to 100 people visit the grave daily, with 500 or more on Sundays. Some Lubavitchers in the greater New York region return to the grave site repeatedly. American Jews whose origins are in North Africa, where there is a long tradition of visiting the tombs of tzadiqim, feel comfortable here. Israelis touring the United States are likely to stop by, since the cemetery in Queens is close enough to Kennedy Airport that pilgrims can visit the grave during a layover between flights. The largest crowds come on the 3 Tammuz yahrzeit. In 2001 more than 40,000 people lined up to be able to spend a minute or two praying at his grave.

Lubavitcher pilgrims rarely talk of visiting the grave site. Instead they speak of "going into the Rebbe," by which they indicate the state of communion with his spirit that they feel in the presence of his grave. There they can ask him questions, as they did in life. Should I study in this particular yeshiva? Should I make aliyah? Should we get married?[35] As Hayim Boruch Halberstam, who created the physical infrastructure near the grave site, observed, "Don't you go to visit the grave of your father? What does he know if you came? Why are you doing this? You know he's bones, but you keep talking to him. So that's why I keep talking to the Rebbe."[36] Many also come for life cycle events: a circumcision, a first haircut, a bar mitzvah.

Chabad has outfitted a nearby house as a center for pilgrims. There they can watch videos of the Rebbe's farbrengen or consult a library of publications and diverse materials about the Rebbe. They can wash their hands, as every Orthodox Jew must do as he leaves a cemetery. Other nearby houses provide lodging for pilgrims and for students who come from yeshivot around the United States to consult at the Rebbe's grave. There is a mikveh for pilgrims to cleanse themselves ritually before visiting the ohel. In a large enclosed tent in the yard, men can study the Torah, read other holy texts, pray, and write the kvitlach they will take to the Rebbe. A gas heater keeps the study center warm; coffee, tea, and cookies help the faithful keep to their tasks. As they go into the Rebbe, many don slippers (conveniently provided next to the path leading to the cemetery) so that they will not sully the holy soil with their shoes. Secular Jews may pick up a black skullcap from a box near the entrance. The grave itself is adjoined by a small granite prayer hall, open to the air. The low wall around the grave encloses an area that is filled with kvitlach.

Chabad actively encourages these cemetery visits. It sponsors websites in English, Spanish, and French with directions to the cemetery. It outlines the proper sequence of ceremonial behaviors. The website also advises pilgrims on proper decorum for their visit. They should dress appropriately and modestly with nonleather shoes. Men should wear a skullcap; married women should cover their hair. Men and women must enter through separate doors, and pray separately. When they have finished they should back away from the ohel to show their respect for the Rebbe. They should be prepared to light candles at his grave. The website also provides instructions about how to submit a kvittel to the Rebbe (in writing, by fax, or by email).

The Rebbe's prestige is such that political figures often find it advantageous to associate themselves or their policies with him. While he was alive, candidates for New York mayor and for Congress beat a path to his door. Zhalman Shazar, the former President of Israel, visited him, as did Prime Minister Menachem Begin. Prime Minister Benjamin Netanyahu came in 1996 and declared that the late Rebbe "had absolute conviction in the justice of our path."[37]

But the exalted visitors are far outnumbered by the crowds of ordinary Hasidim. Boys and men of all ages, prayer books in hand, their side curls swaying, rock back and forth in prayer. Teenage girls pray with zealous intensity. A young boy davens with fervor until he faints from a combination of heat and thirst and hunger. Women loop red ribbons around the shrine, ribbons that they will later cut into small pieces and parcel out to their friends as good luck charms.[38] For these worshipers, and countless others, the Rebbe is a source of hope and comfort, of stability and security. Debra Nussbaum Cohen, whose world, like those of so many New Yorkers, was rocked by the destruction of the World Trade Center in 2001, put it this way: "I find myself longing for a rebbe. I want to be able to turn for comfort to an all-seeing parental figure, someone who can assure me that everything will be all right. . . . I need a rebbe to say that the fog will lift, that he will carry my burden for me, that I can feel as secure as I did before 9/11."[39]

SHLOMO HALBERSTAM (SOUTH BRUNSWICK, NEW JERSEY)

The South Brunswick grave of Shlomo Halberstam (1908–2000) is a major pilgrimage center for the Bobov sect of Hasidism that he led for over fifty years. Halberstam descended from the dynasty's founder, Rabbi Chaim Halberstam (1794–1876), known as the Tzadiq from Nowy Sacz. Reb Chaim's grandson Shlomo Halberstam (1847–1906) moved the sect's center to the Galician Polish city of Bobowa toward the end of the nineteenth century. His son, Ben Tzion Halberstam, was murdered in 1941. It was Shlomo's grandson, also named Shlomo, who shifted the center of Bobover Hasidism to New York and through the strength of his personality rebuilt the decimated community. There are other important Bobover centers in Montreal, Toronto, London, Antwerp, and Jerusalem.

Until World War II, Reb Chaim's grave in Bobowa's Jewish cemetery was a popular pilgrimage site. As in most of Galicia, the Nazis murdered the town's Jews and tried to obliterate physical traces of their presence. In 1988 the Nissenbaum Foundation underwrote the cemetery's recovery. Since the disintegration of Communism it has again begun to attract Jewish pilgrims. A small, whitewashed ohel encloses the grave.

When Reb Shlomo died in New York in 2000, some 10,000 Hasidim visited his grave in Washington Cemetery. Since then, on the anniversary of his death more than 2,500 make the pilgrimage to the cemetery. Most of the pilgrims are Bobovers from Brooklyn and Lakewood, NJ.[40]

REB JOEL TEITELBAUM (KIRYAS JOEL, NEW YORK)

In 1929 Rabbi Joel Teitelbaum (1888–1979) was invited to assume the vacant post of Orthodox rabbi in the Hungarian city of Satmar. His charismatic leadership, his inspiring disquisitions on the Talmud, and the yeshiva that he founded in Satmar soon attracted a wide following. When the Nazis invaded Hungary, Rabbi Teitelbaum was among the minority of Jews who escaped. He fled first to Switzerland and then in 1946 to Palestine. The following year he made a fundraising trip to the United States and was so warmly welcomed by the Hungarian Jewish community in the Williamsburg neighborhood in Brooklyn that he decided to stay. Rabbi Teitelbaum's strident opposition to the founding of a Jewish state—an event he believed could only be brought about by the Messiah—brought him a hard-core following of like-minded Hasidim. Because he was the only major Orthodox rabbi to take such a stance, he also attracted vociferous enemies. His condemnation of Zionism persisted through the 1960s until a heart attack in 1968 took much of the fire out of his sermons. In the 1970s he devoted his remaining energies to building Kiryas Joel on land he had purchased near Monroe, just north of New York City.

Rabbi Teitelbaum was buried in the cemetery of Kiryas Joel. His funeral was the first of the now-annual pilgrimages to his grave site. On 26 Av, the anniversary of his death, more than 60,000 Orthodox Jews, the majority of them Hasidim, converge on his tomb in one of America's largest Jewish pilgrimages. As is the Hasidic custom at yahrzeit graveside celebrations, men and women worship separately. Most read or sing psalms, and many leave kvitlach or notes bearing the names of devotees who were unable to come. One distinctive feature of the pilgrimage to the Satmar Rebbe's grave is that it has become an occasion for an outpouring of charity, one of the virtues that he had stressed in his teaching. Fundraisers line the path leading to the tomb to ask the pilgrims for contributions for their favorite causes in honor of the "Grand Rebbe." In 1999, which marked the twentieth anniversary of his death, the pilgrimage drew some 90,000 people.[41]

AARON ROKEAH (BNEI BRAK, ISRAEL)

Aaron Rokeah (1880–1957), the Rebbe responsible for reviving Belz Hasidism in Israel after the Holocaust, is buried in Bnei Brak. His great-grandfather, the authoritative Talmudist Rabbi Shalom Rokeah (1779–1855), built the Talmudic academy in the Polish (now Ukrainian) city of Belz that soon became the center of a large Hasidic community, drawing thousands of Jews from all over Galicia to study with him. This dynasty's approach was among the most conservative: the Belz Hasids were strict constructionists, opposed to the Enlightenment with its liberalizing tendencies and resistant to any form of change. They were also radically opposed to Zionism. It was not until World War II, during which most of Reb Aaron's family were murdered and he himself experienced the confinement of the Jews in the ghettos of Viznitz, Kraków, and Budapest before eventually escaping to Israel, that the Belz movement endorsed efforts to create the Jewish state. Reb Aaron settled in Tel Aviv, where his home soon became the world center of the Belz movement. Reb Aaron's followers regularly visit his grave in Tel Aviv, particularly on 27 Elul, the anniversary of his death.[42]

The Belz community claims about 30,000 adherents, of whom half live in Israel. There are also large communities in New York, London, and Antwerp. Since Reb Aaron's death in 1957, leadership of the Belz sect passed to his nephew, Issachar Dov (1949–), a Rebbe whose charisma, organizational skill, and business acumen have attracted a following as strong as that of his uncle. Like so many rebbes before him, he engages his adherents both individually and in large groups. He takes the role of godfather at the circumcision of every Belz boy born in Israel. He tries to give a personal blessing to every Israeli Belz woman who is about to give birth. Belz pilgrims from Israel and around the globe come to see him before the High Holidays for two-minute appointments in which they give the rebbe their kvitlach and receive his blessing.

Reb Issachar Dov also built a house in Jerusalem's Kiryat Belz neighborhood with a reception hall that will accommodate 3,000 men after the Sabbath meal for singing, praying, discussing the Torah, and listening to the rebbe's sermons. Even more spectacular is the Belz World Center, constructed between 1985 and 2000, a 24,000 square-meter-building housing a great synagogue, a dozen smaller synagogues, a wedding hall, a kitchen capable of preparing 2,000 meals, and a bakery. Nearby is a Belz residential housing complex. There is also an apartment hotel so that overseas Belzers who want to be near their rebbe on the Sabbath or during the holidays will have a suitable place to stay. These are upscale examples of an infrastructure created to support pilgrimages to holy persons living or dead.

HASIDIC PILGRIMAGE TOURS

Pilgrimage is so strong in the Hasidic tradition, and there are so many important Hasidic graves scattered across Eastern Europe, that once Communism disintegrated in 1989, the tourist industry rapidly organized to promote religious tourism among Orthodox Jews. The national governments of Lithuania, Poland, Hungary, the Czech Republic, Belarus, and the Ukraine each launched marketing efforts to bolster the local economies. Three interest groups were targeted: Western and Israeli Jews wishing to visit the places of their family origins, Jews and others wishing to visit Holocaust-related sites, and Hasidic Jews wanting to visit the tombs of famous East European rabbis.

While tours designed for the first two markets often broaden their focus by including sites of general tourist interest, the Hasidim prefer tours of short duration that visit primarily cemeteries containing the graves of tzadiqim. En route they may stop briefly at Holocaust-related sites or at a few remaining or reconstructed synagogues and yeshivot. One typical trip, organized by Israel's Akiva Lachish Tours in 2002, focused on the anniversary of the death of Rabbi Elimelech of Lezhansk. Pilgrims flew to Poland on a chartered El Al flight. From Kraków they were sorted into groups that had elected tours of one to three days to various grave sites in Poland. The tour buses came together again in Lezhansk for Rabbi Elimelech's yahrzeit.[43]

PRAYING AT THE TZADIQ'S TOMB: SEPHARDIC PILGRIMAGE

My mother became paralyzed in her hands and legs. . . . They took her to the saint [the grave of Lalla Miryam Ha-Tzadiqah in Ntifa, Morocco]. They stayed there seven days. One night, the saint came along with a woman doctor to take my mother to a spring. There she asked her to rub her hands and legs. Next day she got better and stood up on both legs. She dreamt of Lalla Miryam in the form of a nurse. They used to visit her grave. (A Moroccan pilgrim, pre-1998)[1]

Once I took my son, who was seven months old, to cut his hair near the *Zaddik*. When we arrived we saw someone who had a child, and a bean had entered the child's ear. . . . When we were at the Zaddik we made a meal, and the man came and cried: 'Ho, Rabbi David u-Moshe, show me the cure for this child.' A Healer . . . called in the name of the *Zaddik*. He rubbed the child with the oil of the *Zaddik*. . . . He put forth his hand and pulled out the bean. . . . The people almost went mad. They began dancing and rejoicing because of the miracle that had been done to him. (A Moroccan pilgrim, pre-1981)[2]

It was unusual to go to the cemetery [in Fez] at night. . . . The lanterns lit the way to the tombs of the holy men and to those of family members. . . . Rabbis sat at tables that were set up at the gates of the cemetery, with bowls for donations for charity, and sellers of oil lamps and the poor lined the walls. As you go, with your lantern, you . . . gave a coin or two to each of the needy. . . . In the cemetery there were crowds, lights, darkness, dancing, singing. There is always a big crowd around the tombs, and fires around the tombs. Everyone who comes lights a candle at the tombs. (A Maryland woman born in Fez, circa 1980)[3]

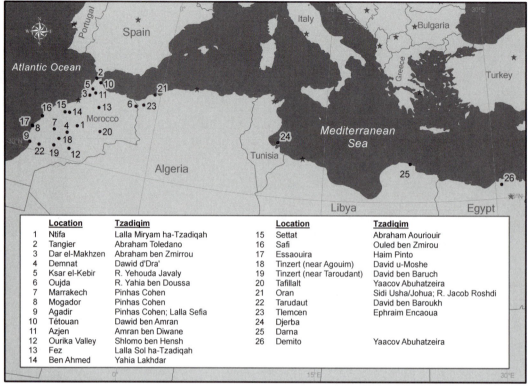

	Location	Tzadiqim		Location	Tzadiqim
1	Ntifa	Lalla Miryam ha-Tzadiqah	15	Settat	Abraham Aouriouir
2	Tangier	Abraham Toledano	16	Safi	Ouled ben Zmirou
3	Dar el-Makhzen	Abraham ben Zmirrou	17	Essaouira	Haim Pinto
4	Demnat	Dawid d'Dra'	18	Tinzert (near Agouim)	David u-Moshe
5	Ksar el-Kebir	R. Yehouda Javaly	19	Tinzert (near Taroudant)	David ben Baruch
6	Oujda	R. Yahia ben Doussa	20	Tafillalt	Yaacov Abuhatzeira
7	Marrakech	Pinhas Cohen	21	Oran	Sidi Usha/Johua; R. Jacob Roshdi
8	Mogador	Pinhas Cohen	22	Tarudaut	David ben Baroukh
9	Agadir	Pinhas Cohen; Lalla Sefia	23	Tlemcen	Ephraim Encaoua
10	Tétouan	Dawid ben Amran	24	Djerba	
11	Azjen	Amran ben Diwane	25	Darna	
12	Ourika Valley	Shlomo ben Hensh	26	Demito	Yaacov Abuhatzeira
13	Fez	Lalla Sol ha-Tzadiqah			
14	Ben Ahmed	Yahia Lakhdar			

Sephardic Tzadiqim

In modern usage, the label *Sephardim* designates both the descendants of medieval Spanish and Portuguese Jews as well as the Jews of North Africa and the Middle East, who share certain characteristics of language and ritual that contrast with those of the Ashkenazi Jews of Central Europe. As do the Ashkenazim, the Sephardim have long traditions of venerating holy persons. As with the rebbes of the Hasidic Jews, Sephardic tzadiqim are honored both while they are alive and at their graves. In the Sephardic tradition the most commonly encountered term for holy man, or in a few cases holy woman, is *tzadiq* (plural *tzadiqim*; feminine *tzadiqah*, plural *tzadiqot*). The label *qadosh* (holy; plural *qadoshim*) is sometimes used, occasionally in the phrase *ha-rav ha-qadosh* (the holy teacher or holy rabbi). A tzadiq whose reputation for wisdom is particularly notable may be called a *haham* (wise man). The term *hasid* is rarely applied by Sephardim to their holy figures.

In addition to pilgrimages to traditional Holy Land sites, Middle Eastern Sephardim made pilgrimages to the supposed graves of biblical prophets and Talmudic sages in places like Iraq and Iran, a practice that lasted until the recent emigration of most of those countries' Jewish population to Israel, Western Europe, and the United States. Such was the draw that in 1873, Rabbi Joseph Hayyim compiled a pilgrim manual for people wishing to visit three important graves near Baghdad. The grave of the Prophet Ezekiel, at Kefil, near Hillah, was contained within a mausoleum built by the Sassoon family in 1859. It attracted Jewish pilgrims on 6 Sivan during the festival of Sukkot. The tomb of Joshua the High Priest (often now called the Cohen Mausoleum), on the outskirts of Baghdad, tended to be visited each month on the new moon, especially by women praying to be able to conceive a child. The tomb of Ezra the Scribe, at el-'Ozir near Basra, was marked with a marble slab and covered by a wooden catafalque. In addition, the several alleged graves of the prophet Daniel attracted pilgrims, as did the tomb of Jonah at Nineveh (near Mosul, Iraq). The village of Alkosh not far from Mosul was believed to contain the tomb of the prophet Nahum. It attracted pilgrims during Sukkot to read from a manuscript that he is said to have written. A British archaeologist who visited Alkosh in the 1850s wrote:

> It is a place held in great reverence by Mohammedans and Christians, but especially by Jews, who keep the building in repair, and flock here in great numbers at certain seasons of the year. The tomb is a simple plaster box, covered with green cloth, and standing at the upper end of a large chamber. On the walls of the room are pasted slips of paper, upon which are written, in distorted Hebrew characters, religious exhortations, and the dates and particulars of the visits of various Jewish families.[4]

In Iran there is a tradition that the Abbasid mosque in Isfahan was built over the tomb of the prophet Isaiah. Pilgrims to Linjan, not far from Isfahan, venerated the tomb of Sarah, the daughter of Asher and granddaughter of Jacob.[5] Elijah is honored in Bar-Tanura, another village in the region of Mosul, where pilgrims visited a cave in which he is said to have taken refuge.[6] In Hamadan the alleged tombs of the fifth-century BCE heroes Mordechai and Esther attracted pilgrims from Iran and neighboring countries to read the Esther scroll at Purim. The two thirteenth-century tombs, draped with embroidered cloths, are enclosed within a shrine with a tall brick dome in the local Muslim style. Pilgrims are not deterred by the fact that scholars believe the tomb more likely contains the remains of Shushan-Dukt, a fifth-century CE queen, or the bodies of two thirteenth-century Jewish physicians.

Jewish visitors to the South Arabian sultanate of Oman might make a pilgrimage to Job's tomb at Jebel Izzin. Inside the small, dome-covered structure they would see the prophet's long, low burial mound shrouded with brightly colored cloths, and smell frankincense burning in a brazier against the wall.[7] In Jordan, Jewish pilgrims could visit the burial site of Aaron the High Priest, a two-hour mule ride from Petra in the mountains at Mount Hor.[8]

The main focus of Sephardic pilgrimage is tzadiqim who were historical figures, wise rabbis or leaders of the past two centuries. One popular Balkan sage's tomb was that of the Bosnian Rabbi Moshe Danon, circa 1819, hero of the episode when the leaders of the Sarajevo Sephardic community were imprisoned by the Muslim district governor, who threatened them with execution if they did not pay a massive fine. Danon is buried at Stolac, near Dubrovnik, where he died in 1830 on his way to Palestine. Until the Nazi destruction of Balkan Jewry, the tomb attracted substantial crowds, mostly women, at the late June or early July anniversary of his death.[9]

While in many ways similar to Ashkenazi reverence for holy figures during and after their lifetimes, Sephardic saint veneration has also been shaped by the practices of their Islamic and Christian neighbors. Prior to the destruction of Salonican Jewry in 1943, Greek Sephardic women were in the habit of making short periodic pilgrimages to Salonica's Jewish cemetery. The visits were called by the Arabic term *ziyara*, which denotes a ritual visit to a Muslim saint's tomb. In the gender-stratified Greek world of the time, these visits were one of the few occasions when women could gather in public. In the cemetery they cleaned family gravestones and gathered at the graves of noted sages to lament, pray, and ask the tzadiqim to intercede on their behalf with the deity. Men would visit the tombs during the "Great Visitations" that occurred prior to the major Jewish holidays, but most of the time the cemeteries were the province of women. Some graffiti, both petitions for help and ex-votos for help received, survived on fragments of stones after the Nazi desecration of the cemetery. They testify to the fervor with which the women sought their sages' help: Julia, the widow of Moise Kapuano: "For God's miracle that saved her from a serious operation. May this sage say a prayer for her health and for her sons' health and may God see fit to send them a blessing." Mazaltov, wife of Yohanan Avla: "For the miracle he bestowed on her ailing legs. May it be His will that the miracle be complete." Delisia Saltiel: "Done in accordance to an oath which she undertook asking for good health."[10]

The largest concentration of Sephardic holy men lies in the western Maghreb, particularly the southern mountainous regions of Morocco. These tzadiqim were almost always rabbis whose charisma and sometimes whose learning garnered them local followings during their lives. Many Islamic *marabouts* (from the Arabic *murabit*, indicating a man attached to God), particularly Sufis, were revered for their knowledge of the Qur'an. But while in Islam this was but one path to sainthood among many, in Judaism almost all of the male tzadiqim were profoundly dedicated to the study of the Torah. As is the case with the Ashkenazim, the leaders of prestigious Sephardic religious academies might be recognized as saints and their fame lies in their interpretations, both oral and written, of the Torah and the vast Jewish literature of commentary. Sometimes this took on miraculous overtones. For example, adherents of a number of Moroccan tzadiqim believe that the Prophet Elijah accompanied them in their study. Witnesses would describe a supernatural light emanating from the tzadiq or from Elijah. The tzadiq's deep knowledge of Torah, then, seemed both a product of human effort and a sign of divine favor.

While Hasidic sects tend to perpetuate themselves as dynasties, with leadership passing from father to son, tzadiq status tends not to be related to lineage but rather to righteous living. There are only a handful of Maghrebi Jewish families whose power is considered inheritable, that is, able to be melded with their ancestral merit. Among them are Morocco's Pinto, Cohen, and Abuhatzeira families and a few others.[11]

Living one's life in rigorous accordance with the prevailing notions of religious law is a key to revered status in both the Jewish and the Islamic traditions. For Jews, this includes strict adherence to religious law (Halakhah), moral behavior beyond reproach, and a commitment to charitable acts. The lifestyle of the tzadiq has a public dimension: his virtue is by definition exemplary. In the Moroccan

Jewish tradition tzadiqot, revered women, also, lived exemplary lives. But often their holy status resulted from a single act that demonstrated their idealized self-sacrifice. Legend holds that Lalla Sol Hatchouel, for example, preferred death to giving herself sexually to a Muslim. Bent El-Hmus gave her life to save some visitors from the Holy Land who were accused of selling wine to Muslims.[12] Lalla Bat-Khalifa was selfless in her devotion to Rabbi Yehudah Gadol Gil'ad, both during and after his death.

A certain number of the Jewish Maghrebi tzadiqim are legendary, and their grave sites became known only when they were revealed to one of the tzadiq's adherents in a dream. The most common foundation story is that the legendary tzadiq had been an emissary from Israel, collecting funds for some holy work there, and had died during his visit to the Maghreb. In other cases, the interest in Kabbalah that permeated many Maghrebi communities caused a number of these graves to be identified as the true burial site of Rabbi Shim'on bar Yohai, the reputed author of the *Zohar*.[13]

BARAKA

Pilgrims go to the Sephardic tzadiq because of his baraka. Both the tzadiqim and the marabouts of the Islamic tradition are believed to have powers to cure, to work miracles, to provide spiritual guidance, to protect against dangers, and to shelter their adherents with their all-encompassing blessing, called baraka. They possess an unlimited quantity of baraka that can be distributed at will among their devotees. If they are angered, their baraka can also do harm. Since Muslim marabouts tend to be recognized as such during their lifetimes, their baraka is transmitted by personal contact. They are presumed to be clairvoyant and may be consulted about future events. The relatively small number of Jews who achieved tzadiq status before their deaths, such as the Rabbis Yisrael Abuhatzeira and Ephraim Encaoua, were seldom asked to provide clairvoyance through their baraka, but instead were requested to mediate disputes based on their reputation for wisdom. Since most Sephardic tzadiqim achieve their venerated status only after their deaths, the most important source of their baraka tends to be their tombs.

Among both Sephardic Jews and Muslims, baraka is also conceived of at times as a physical substance, present at and removable from the holy site. The tzadiq's and marabout's baraka resides in everything that comes in contact with the holy place. In the case of a living saint, it may be found in something that he has touched, like his food, or a piece of clothing. It may adhere to dirt scraped from around his grave, or in water springing forth at the holy site. The Abuhatzeira tzadiqim would bless water that then assumed curative powers and could be drunk or rubbed on afflicted parts of the body. Pilgrims might place personal items on the tomb to absorb the saint's power. All such items may be taken home to be used as curatives or to provide tangible presence of the baraka of the tzadiq's tomb. In Morocco, the fervor for the miraculous and the supernatural emanates as well from the pre-Muslim Berber culture, which tends to minimize metaphysical preoccupations in favor of the immediacy of amulets, spells, and miracle-workers. Moroccan Jews prize tangible containers of baraka as amulets or talismans that can help effect cures or protect against evil influences. Jewish pilgrims to the tombs of tzadiqim may also emulate their Muslim neighbors in tying strings, scarves, or paper prayers to trees or other opportune places near the shrine. Since people believe that baraka is transmitted through contact, these tokens remind the tzadiq of their visit and their petitions, and stand as surrogates for the burdens they have left at the tomb.

Jewish tzadiqim only assume holy status when their baraka is strong enough to work miracles. Although some miracles are reported during the tzadiq's life (Yisrael Abuhatzeira's grandfather, Yaacov, for example, reputedly once walked on water), most occur only after death. The death itself is sometimes held to begin the process of miracle-working. The tzadiq's body may emanate light, or may suddenly sit up, or be too heavy to move. The bodies of many tzadiqim are reputed to be incorrupt. Still, all these are exceptions. The most common miracles are cures that occur after people have invoked the tzadiq's aid, preferably at the tomb. Some Jews and Muslims in the Maghreb believe that sleeping near a holy person's tomb (a practice often termed *incubatio*) encourages the saint to effect a cure, or to deliver the dreamer instructions that will lead to a cure. As is frequently the case with Muslim and Christian holy figures, many tzadiqim venerated by Sephardic Jews are believed to grant certain specialized categories of human requests, such as for health and fertility. Thus, for example, Dawid ben 'Amram (Tétouan, Morocco) is believed to be able to cure children of whooping cough. Lalla Sefia (Agadir, Morocco), who, during her lifetime, is reputed to have helped cure a Jewish girl of cholera, also protects against disease.[14] People with a particular need may make pilgrimage to several tzadiqim until their prayers are answered. One Moroccan couple in the 1930s visited the tombs of thirty tzadiqim before the wife finally conceived a child.[15]

Since the baraka radiating from Islamic holy figures is thought to benefit both the living and the dead, Muslims in many areas prize being buried in close proximity to the tomb of a favored marabout. The closest parallel among Jews is that, from medieval times onward, as we saw in Chapter 5, some devout Jews have yearned for burial on the Mount of Olives. However, because Judaism's pervasive sense that things associated with death are sources of pollution rather than of merit, Jews do not prize burying their dead close to their tzadiqim.

THE PHYSICAL SITES

The tomb shrines of Jewish and Muslim holy figures in Palestine tend to be vaulted, domed structures enclosing a grave marked with a simple horizontal stone. The tombs of Maghrebi marabouts, too, are generally enclosed by a *qobba*, a small, square, whitewashed building with a round dome. Often this is entered through a horseshoe shaped doorway. For more important marabouts, these *qobba* sometimes have a small mosque attached. In cases where marabouts have a major following, there may be outbuildings where pilgrims can lodge (and in former times their animals also), prepare food, and light candles.

In contrast, the tombs of most Maghrebi Jewish tzadiqim lie inside Jewish cemeteries adjacent to towns, and are open to the air. Sometimes the tzadiq's grave is marked with a pillar. When the tzadiq's tomb is covered, any decoration within the structure tends to be geometric or calligraphic, sometimes including a religious symbol like a menorah, as on the tomb of Rabbi Yehouda Javaly in the Moroccan city of Ksar el-Kebir.[16] Sephardic tombs that have become the focus of major hillulot in recent years have sometimes been enclosed within a modern structure that serves to shelter pilgrims and to host the ceremonies attendant on the tomb. There may also be a building where men can gather to study holy texts. The holiness of such places requires worshipers who approach them to be purified and to demonstrate the proper signs of respect. It requires worshipers to be ritually clean, not to have engaged in recent sexual activity, and, in the case of women, not to be menstruating.

In both Muslim and Sephardic traditions, some holy sites are found at prominent geographical features away from the cities or villages.[17] With the exception of a few caves reputed to have been the dwelling or burial places of tzadiqim in the period of the Roman persecutions, this predilection is not reflected in modern Jewish practices in Palestine. It is relatively common, however in the Maghreb, where some holy tombs are located not in mellah cemeteries but on distant mountainsides or by springs or notable trees. One is a mountainside cave near Sefrou, Morocco, where Jews went to light candles on the eve of the Sabbath, the new moon, and major holidays. On Lag b'Omer, Sefrou's entire Jewish community made a day-pilgrimage there as a surrogate for visiting Rabbi 'Amram ben Diwane's grave at Azjen, far to the north.[18]

PILGRIMAGES TO TOMBS

Pilgrimages to the tombs of holy figures have been characteristic of both the Jewish and the Muslim communities of the Maghreb since at least the sixteenth century. Among Jews it was largely a folk practice, operating outside the formal rabbinical establishment, but by the second half of the nineteenth century the rabbinical culture was beginning to bring the ancient folk practices into the ambit of rabbinical authority. Deshen relates a Moroccan example in which Rabbi Hayim Meshash, of Meknès, settled a marital dispute by recognizing a wife's right of pilgrimage: "And in the generation before us [the sages] added an obligation [on the husband] to take her on pilgrimage . . . to the graves of the pious ones (may their merit guard us), [even] in another city . . . and the rabbis of Fez and Sefrou disputed this. . . . But amongst us it is common practice to oblige the husband [to do so]."[19]

Prior to the second decade of the twentieth century, the catchment area for each Maghrebi Jewish tzadiq was for the most part limited to his or her village and its immediate environs. Moroccan Jews might visit the tombs of one of their local tzadiqim at any time during the year to request a favor, fulfill a vow, or seek the protection of the tzadiq's baraka. A few, like the Moroccan tzadiqim 'Amram ben Diwane, David u-Moshe, Haim Pinto, Yaacov Abuhatzeira, and David Dra Halevi transcended local importance to attain national or even international followings. Visits to the tombs of these tzadiqim were major undertakings and might involve journeys of several days. Pilgrims would likely stop to pray at the tombs of other tzadiqim along the route for fear that their spirits might be insulted if a visit were neglected. Some Moroccan Jews reserved a week or more to make an entire circuit of tombs of favored rabbis.[20]

SHARED HOLY FIGURES

Maghrebi tradition prohibited both Jews and Christians from entering the sanctuaries of Muslim holy men from fear that their presence might negatively affect the marabout's holiness and diminish the power of his baraka.[21] Despite these prohibitions, some marabouts attracted the devotion of both communities, and Moroccan Jews habitually made pilgrimage to the tombs of more than a dozen marabouts and female Muslim holy figures.[22] In the region around Oran, Algeria, for example, both Jews and Muslims prayed at the tombs of Sidi Usha (or Joshua), Sidi Nun, and Rabbi Jacob Roshdi.[23] In the 1920s in the Moroccan city of Demnat, Edward Westermark found that the Jews prayed and left offerings at the shrine of the Muslim marabout Sidi Brahim u-'Ali, who was entombed at the city gate, so long as there were no Muslims present. In Tangier, Jewish women who hoped to get pregnant would visit the tomb of the legendary Muslim female marabout Lalla Jemila. In Salé, Jews would bring offerings of candles and oil to the tomb of Sidi Bou Haha, near the wall of the mellah. Near the remote southern Moroccan village of Ouzguita, Jewish women would sometimes risk bathing in the sacred pool beside the tomb of Lalla Takerkouzt, despite the efforts of the tomb's Muslim caretaker to prevent them, or they might take home a bottle of the water to guard against disease.

Although some Muslim holy tombs attracted Jewish pilgrims, much more numerous were the tombs of Jewish tzadiqim venerated as well by the Muslim community. In the 1940s in Morocco more than thirty renowned Jewish tombs attracted dual devotion. In Tangier, Muslims would bring their children to the tomb of Abraham Toledano to protect them against diphtheria. They visited the alleged tomb of Abraham ben Zmirrou near Dar el-Makhzen, on the road to Marrakech, to pray for rain and for protection against illness. Curiously, sometimes the Muslim and the Jewish traditions would ascribe different occupants to a venerated tomb. For Moroccan Muslims, the tomb shrine on the city wall of Ksar el-Kebir holds the remains of a twelfth-century marabout; for Jews it is the shrine of Rabbi Yehouda Javaly. Muslims believe a tomb near Oujda to be that of Sidi Yahia ben Younes, who is said to have been a contemporary of Jesus and who predicted Muhammad's birth; for Jews it is the tomb of Rabbi Yahia ben Doussa, a refugee from the Spanish persecutions of 1391.[24]

HILLULOT

Like the yahrzeit commemorations at the tombs of Hasidic holy men and the Islamic ziyara tradition, the Sephardic world also fetes its saints on the anniversary of their deaths. In practice, though, there are significant differences, with the Sephardic practices more closely resembling those of their Muslim neighbors who celebrate ziyaras at the graves of their marabouts. Jews generally call these pilgrimage festivals *hillulot* (singular, *hillula*), an Aramaic term designating a wedding celebration. For legendary tzadiqim, or for those whose death dates are lost in antiquity, the festival generally takes place on Lag b'Omer.

Memorial candles at ohel. El Jadida, Morocco. Photo, D. Gitlitz, 2004.

Prior to the 1950s, families from the holy person's village and from the nearby region would gather at the tomb to request his baraka. In modern times, when so many villagers have migrated to cities, or even abroad, the annual festival is a time for homecoming and renewing ties of friendship and of clan. In the Muslim world the expenses of maintaining the tomb and of hosting the festival, including contracting musicians, are generally borne by the marabout's descendants, or by guilds or brotherhoods organized for that purpose. The support systems for the hillulot of tzadiqim are often less formal but just as effective. Everyone who attends is expected to bring a gift. These may include candles—always white—portions of the meat slaughtered in the saint's honor, or cash donations to the sponsors to help defray the festival's costs. Food and drink are plentiful and are often shared among the attendees. Sometimes the sponsors contract musicians or dancers to enliven the festivities.[25]

For Sephardic Jews, particularly those living in small and relatively remote villages like those of southern Morocco, pilgrimage to their tzadiq's tomb for the annual hillula might be the highpoint of a year's religious activities. Ben-Ami describes a process of emotional intensification similar to that observed in Christian pilgrimages. The pilgrim might prepare with several self-imposed purification rituals: fasting, cutting nails, immersion in the mikveh, or initiating a regimen of prayer. At the hillula itself an atmosphere of religious exhilaration predominates. The feasting, dancing, singing, and consumption of alcohol all heighten the spiritual intensity. Ben-Ami reminds us that "the reality inherent in each manifestation of the cult of tzadiq veneration is incomprehensible if viewed through the prism of normal, natural reality. The emotional dimension of these festivals embodies a reality of its own."[26] The tzadiq's adherents believe that miracles will occur, that he will literally appear among the pilgrims, or that his presence will be manifested through some sign.

Some Sephardic hillulot do not celebrate historical or legendary tzadiqim, but rather important Jewish cult objects. In Libya, for example, until modern times a hillula was held annually for a Torah scroll that was known familiarly as the "Little One" from the village of Darna. In popular speech in the region, as well, the Zghair Derna was often referred to as if it had been a living human being.[27]

PILGRIMAGE TO TZADIQIM IN MODERN TIMES

The custom of making pilgrimage to the tombs of tzadiqim or marabouts seems to have peaked during the two centuries from 1750 to 1950. Algeria came under French rule in 1830, Tunisia in 1881, and Morocco in 1912. Moreover, Algerian Jews were granted full French citizenship in 1870. This explains in some measure why Algerian Jews tended to be the most assimilated into modern Western (i.e., French) culture, and Moroccan Jews the least. All across the Maghreb, the late nineteenth and early twentieth centuries were periods of rapid change, and these transformations intensified during the 1920s and 1930s. Three of these changes had particularly important ramifications for Jewish pilgrimages. First was the increasing ease of travel. Improvements to the highway systems, especially in the 1940s, brought the tombs of tzadiqim in remote villages within reach of a much wider public. The relative ease and safety of travel, combined with the development of a tourist infrastructure, meant that what had formerly been largely a male activity could now be a family pilgrimage to a tzadiq's shrine. While the hillulot retained strong religious components, they came to take on the character of shared family holidays.

Ohel of Hanania Hacohen. Marrakech, Morocco. Photo, D. Gitlitz, 2004.

The second factor was the enthusiasm for particular tzadiqim generated among men of means in the years between World War I and II. Often migration from the ancestral village to the city had enabled these men to prosper, and they tended to ascribe their successes in part to the influence of their village tzadiq's baraka. In thanks, and to strut his success in his home village, the newly wealthy man took it upon himself to refurbish the tzadiq's tomb and to publicize the efficacy of his protection, perhaps even to pass on messages

Interior of ohel of Hanania Hacohen. Marrakech, Morocco. Photo, D. Gitlitz, 2004.

from the tzadiq that the patron had received through the medium of dreams. The patron might also sponsor the tzadiq's annual hillula.[28] Thus in the 1940s many tombs were embellished with impressive new structures: pavilions, crypts, guesthouses, slaughterhouses, synagogues, and rooms for study. The increased attention to the tzadiq and attendance at his hillula led to increased donations and profits from sales of candles and liquor, and this in turn led to the need for more sophisticated infrastructure and transparent administration of monies. Committees were organized to collect and administer the resources and to oversee publicity and annual events. The committees organized for the more important tzadiqim, which therefore handled larger sums of money, also funded charitable organizations benefiting the Jewish community. There were so many of these organizations, and of such diverse structures and uneven skills, that the colonial governments sponsored the establishment of oversight agencies such as La Commission des Sanctuaires et Pèlerinages Israélites du Maroc and

Ohel of Yacoub Slama. Nabeul, Tunisia. Postcard. Authors' collection.

La Commission de Contrôle des Sanctuaires et Pèlerinages Israélites du Maroc in 1947. It turned out, however, that these agencies had little effect over anarchic and contentious local practices. After Moroccan independence, the affairs of the entire Moroccan Jewish community were coordinated by a single agency, which in 1979 assumed responsibility for the country's hillulot as well, including publicizing them with brochures in Morocco and abroad.[29]

The third agent of change was the migration to the cities of large numbers of Jews who had formerly resided in the remote villages.[30] The festival now took on an element of homecoming. It became a chance to see old friends, now perhaps resident in different coastal cities, to introduce children to their grandparents who might still reside in the village, to speak the old dialect, listen to traditional tunes, and to share familiar regional dishes. The migration to the cities also led to a number of new holy places being created in the middle years of the twentieth century in the Atlantic coastal cities, particularly Casablanca, where by the 1950s more than a third of Morocco's Jews resided.

MAGHREBI TZADIQIM AND THEIR HILLULOT

So many tombs of Sephardic tzadiqim are venerated in the Maghreb that it is impossible to list them all here, let alone summarize their biographies or the miracles attributed to them, or to describe the pilgrimage customs associated with each. In his five years of fieldwork in the 1970s, Issachar Ben-Ami catalogued 571 Jewish holy figures, including 21 women, in Morocco alone.[31] A representative sample of some of the more important holy figures and their cults offers a glimpse of the rich North African Jewish culture of pilgrimage.

Lalla Sol ha-Tzadiqah in Fez (Morocco)

Sol Hatchouel (1817–1834) has fired the imagination of Moroccan Jews since her tragic death.[32] Her first name is often invoked in the Spanish diminutive form, Solica, or Suleika, and it is generally preceded by the Arabic honorific *Lalla*. There are two main versions of her story. Sol Hatchouel was a young Jewess born in Tangier. In the first version she fell in love with a handsome young Muslim boy and converted in order to marry him. When he died, she attempted to revert to Judaism, which so offended Muslim authorities that Tangier's governor sent her to the king in Fez, who ordered her execution. In the second version of the story, she was killed, because, when she was chosen to join the imperial harem, she refused to make that possible by converting to Islam. Other variants of the story, such as this one collected by Ben-Ami, are even more fanciful. "Lalla Solica once returned home, but instead of going into her father's house, she went into an Arab's house by mistake. The Muslim wanted her to be his daughter. She answered: 'God forbid.' . . . He kept trying to persuade her until he killed her. She herself gave him the knife so that he should kill her."[33]

Lalla Sol is buried in the Jewish cemetery of Fez next to the Jewish quarter (mellah) and the royal palace. The cemetery is so crowded that there is hardly any space to walk between the neat rows of hump-backed, whitewashed graves. The cemetery contains the tombs of several descendants of Maimonides and of many distinguished rabbis like Yehudah eben-'Attar and Abner and Vidal Haserfaty (or, Tserfati), who are venerated at their annual hillulot. Lalla Sol's tomb stands taller than most of the others in the cemetery and is the only one that is decorated with blue polka dots! On the side is an epigraph in French:

> *Ici repose Mlle Solica Hatchouel*
> *née à Tanger en 1817*
> *refusant de rentrer*
> *dans la religion is*
> *lamisme les Arabes*
> *l'ont assassinée à Fez*
> *en 1834 Arrachée de sa*
> *famille tout le monde*
> *regrette cette enfant*
> *sainte.*[34]

There are so many stories of Lalla Sol's miracles in matters of health that many pilgrims come to ask to be cured of illness or relieved of barrenness. Some hang scarves on the cupola of her tomb to absorb her baraka so that they can take it home with them. As is common with the important Moroccan Jewish graves, her sepulcher includes a large niche for the candles of those who come to venerate her. The candle cups we observed in 2004 included many made in Israel and in the United States.

Tomb of Lalla Sol ha-Tzadiqah. Fez, Morocco. Photo, D. Gitlitz, 2004.

Among the many novels and poems written about Lalla Sol, the most recent is Ruth Knafo Setton's *The Road to Fez*. A young woman named Brit, whose Moroccan mother has recently died, visits her mother's family in Fez to fulfill her mother's dying wish that she make a pilgrimage to the tomb of Suleika. Toward the end of the book, after several adventures and complex emotional crises, Brit visits the cemetery. The novel vividly communicates the magical flavor associated with Lalla Sol's intervention in cases of barrenness. Brit advises her uncle to take his wife to Lalla Sol, where she will see women with similar needs. The cemetery caretaker tells them, "Arabs and Jews. Especially women praying for a baby. They bring her couscous, money, flowers. Her baraka is still very powerful. At night her tomb glows. When you touch it, your fingers burn. If you see a double rainbow over her tomb, she will answer your prayer. If you and your wife want a baby, you've come to the right place."[35]

Portrait of Lalla Sol ha-Tzadiqah and her tresses. Museum of the Fez Jewish Cemetery, Morocco. Photo, D. Gitlitz, 2004.

'Amram ben Diwane in Azjen (Morocco)

One of the best known Maghrebi tzadiqim is Rabbi 'Amram ben Diwane (?–1782), whose tomb-shrine is adjacent to the village of Azjen, seven kilometers from Ouezzane (also spelled Wazzan), in northern Morocco. Legend recounts that Rabbi 'Amram was sent to the Maghreb in the late eighteenth century to collect money for the Palestinian Jewish community in Hebron.[36] Near the city of Fez, when his son took sick, Rabbi 'Amram offered his life instead, and the boy was saved.

Rabbi 'Amram is believed to have some of the most powerful baraka of any tzadiq in Morocco. He was so holy, in fact, that it is said that his grave sometimes radiates a halo-like light. People speak of his appearing at his hillula in the guise of a dove or a snake. One oft-told tale is that a mute boy tumbled into the tzadiq's bonfire during his hillula and, crying out to the rabbi to save him, had his voice restored. People talk of his having cured both paralysis and sterility. Women hoping to conceive or hoping for an easy delivery wrapped a cord around his tomb and then tied it around their waists.[37] Pilgrims would chant biblical verses over his grave, and would cover it with offerings of cloth, candles, and banknotes. Sometimes they would place a bottle of water, or oil, on his tomb to soak up baraka that they could take home with them and use for its curative powers.

Rabbi 'Amram is one of the few Moroccan tzadiqim to develop a true national following. Jews in Sefrou made annual pilgrimages to a cave on the mountain behind their village cemetery that served as a surrogate shrine for Rabbi 'Amram. Jews in Meknès venerated him at a cairn, a surrogate for his tomb. Although the Jewish community in Morocco has shrunk to a tiny number, Rabbi 'Amram's baraka and his hillula still exert a powerful draw among the remaining Jews and visitors of Moroccan origin from abroad, attracting more than 3,000 pilgrims in 2003. The May 16, 2003, bombing of the Cercle de l'Alliance social club and other Jewish-related targets in Casablanca, the Iraq war, and the increasingly high profile of terrorist acts in Europe, some involving Moroccans, caused the 2004 hillula to shrink to a tiny fraction of that number. We counted approximately 600 in attendance, including one large busload of Israelis. Four separate military checkpoints monitored the road from Ouezzane to Azjen, two trucks packed with soldiers stood guard from a grove of olive trees near the shrine compound's soccer field, and several military tents were pitched among the olive trees.

In recent years considerable resources have been spent to secure the grave site and to accommodate it to the needs of modern pilgrimage. The Jewish community even underwrote part of the expense of paving the

Entrance to ohel area of 'Amram ben Diwane. Azjen, Morocco. Photo, D. Gitlitz, 2004.

'Amram ben Diwane hillula. Azjen, Morocco. Photo, D. Gitlitz, 2004.

road to Azjen from Ouezzane, although now it is badly rutted. The two-hectare oval compound containing the Jewish cemetery is surrounded by a whitewashed stone wall, entered through a single gate with a barrier that can be raised and lowered. Cabins, sans plumbing, have been built for attendees. Some cabins are large enough to house a family and have a front porch where people can cook, eat, and socialize with their neighbors. Other cabins are single rooms with two cots and house mainly young people. An internal wall, with a gate memorializing its donors, surrounds a cemetery of neat, white, unmarked graves arrayed around several ancient olive trees. Within this area two tzadiqim's graves are surrounded by their own gated walls. The smaller, and less important, is the tomb of Rabbi David HaCohen. An old man who chanted blessings for tips explained that the rabbi was a great sage (*haham*), that, like all wise men, he lived near Azjen, and that he worked many miracles. The most immediate? The olive tree next to the grave has a large horizontal branch that gets in the pilgrims' way. A man tried to saw it off, and got 90 percent of the way through it when his arm was paralyzed. Although now only a thread of bark sustains the branch, it is just as strong as it was before. Next to the miracle tree in the center of the area, an oval heaped with rough stones serves for burning prayer candles and for amusing children who spend hours collecting, shaping, remelting the candle wax, and begging for more candles from their parents.

Rabbi 'Amram's area is much larger. The grave itself abuts a gigantic olive tree. The fire oval in front of the tree is five times the size of David HaCohen's. Blue benches for people to sit, pray, gossip, and snack surround the tomb. Behind the tree is a new synagogue, decorated with geometric tiles and hanging lamps, with a central bimah in the Sephardic fashion, and a women's area in back, near the door. The synagogue accommodates about 200 worshipers, and on the hillula Shabbat of 2004 it was packed to overflowing with pilgrims and family members of a bar mitzvah boy. Next to the synagogue is a large banquet hall. Enclosing the area is an arcade draped with the orange-colored cloth and green stars of the Moroccan flag, symbolically sheltering the tomb and the hillula within the Moroccan cultural context. Vendors use the arcade to offer candles, framed portraits of tzadiqim, both Moroccan and Israeli, skullcaps and tallith bags, charms, necklaces, and Moroccan-style caftans.

Pilgrims celebrate Rabbi 'Amram's hillula in four ways: they pray, they burn candles, they charge their souvenirs with baraka, and they socialize and eat. Except for the synagogue services, praying is a personal affair. With prayer books in hand, or speaking from the heart, pilgrims pray on the benches, on the steps of the synagogue, at the fire circles, and while strolling through the olive groves. One woman embraces the rabbi's grave and mouths silent prayers. On the whole, women pilgrims pray longer and more intently than the men.

Pilgrims do not actually light their candles, they burn them whole, tossing them one by one or pack by pack into the flickering fire oval. Thousands of candles are sold in packs of twelve, wrapped in purple paper. Most men just pause and fling. Many women perform elaborate ceremonies, touching the candles first to the rocks, gathering the smoke with their hands, and rubbing it on their faces. Some pilgrims dedicate each candle or pack to a loved one, speaking in Arabic, Spanish, French, Hebrew, or whatever language they find most comfortable. "For my mother." "For my daughter and her children." "For my sister in Madrid who could not come to the hillula this year." One smartly dressed woman rubs her candles against the tzadiq's grave stone before throwing them into the fire. A man with a cell phone pressed to his ear tosses candles onto the stones while relaying prayers from the person at the other end of the line.

Some pilgrims buy keepsake tzadiq portraits, embroidered skullcaps, or dresses from the vendors. But the preferred souvenirs are hillula items. Pilgrims place packages of candles or a bottle of water on a fire stone distant from the blaze itself, and then after a time, when it has absorbed an appropriate amount of the tzadiq's baraka, pack them up again to take some of the hillula holiness to their homes or to present as gifts.

The pilgrims seem to be always in mid-munch. Most Moroccan families bring trays of cookies, or dried figs, dates, and almonds, or homemade pastries, and, once they have completed their prayers, offer them as a gesture of hospitality and charity to everyone who is clustered around the grave. Pilgrims take one or two pieces from each elegantly arranged tray and offer a word of thanks. The Muslim workers—who have been hired to pick up candle wrappings, clean the toilets, and sweep the fire oval area—help themselves. Since sharing with friends and family and contributing to the less fortunate are both fundamental parts of the hillula tradition, everyone seems pleased as the platters are emptied. In mid-afternoon a full meal is set out in the banquet hall, but many pilgrims, believing that it is not kosher enough, or too impersonal for their family and friends, eat the food they have brought with them from home. Two large pilgrim groups under the olive trees roast skewers of lamb and lay out Moroccan salads and flat bread on rugs and blankets.

When all was said and done, when all have prayed and burned their candles, Rabbi 'Amram's hillula in 2004 was more about community than about religion. It congregated a significant portion of Morocco's small remnant population of Jews at an annual event that affirms their Jewishness and their sense of Moroccan Jewish identity. Many come every year; others come as often as they can. From Casablanca, from Fez, from Tangier, from Rabat, Jews greet old friends, break bread together, hug, kiss, gossip, dance, sing, and pray in the synagogue as a community. For the returning émigrés, the hillula reconnects them with their culture of origin. At the same time it is a gesture of solidarity with those few Jews who are trying to keep Moroccan Jewish culture alive on its home turf. The festival at Rabbi 'Amram ben Diwane's grave lets the returnees show their Israeli or French or Canadian or American children how once upon a time their grandparents used to celebrate hillulot as Jews in Morocco.

Meir Baal ha-Nes, Shim'on bar Yohai, and La Ghriba in Djerba (Tunisia)

Until the 1950s, when many Tunisian Jews emigrated, the island of Djerba, off Tunisia's southern coast, housed one of the most vibrant Sephardic communities of the Maghreb. Its many Talmudic academies, publishing houses, and synagogues were known all over North Africa. Today about 1,000 Jews—half of Tunisia's remaining Jewish population—live on Djerba, and the island still has eleven functioning synagogues. The largest annual Jewish pilgrimage in Tunisia, attracting Jews from all over the country as well as neighboring Libya, was on the 14th and the 18th of Iyar in honor of two second-century rabbis buried in Israel: Meir Baal ha-Nes and Shim'on bar Yohai. Some pilgrims come to one or the other of two festivals, but most stay for the entire period. The hillula still takes place in La Ghriba synagogue, said to have been named for a mysterious woman whose body remained intact when her house burned down. The synagogue is also venerated because it was the only one in the vicinity to possess real Torah scrolls.

The festival on the 14th of Iyar honors Rabbi Meir.[38] Pilgrims gather the day before to greet old friends and to shop in the festival market that attracts vendors from all over the region. In former times, the many pilgrims who traveled to the tzadiq's hillula from distant regions in Tunisia and Libya could spend the night in the large caravansaries outside the synagogue built specifically for that purpose. Although most of the returnees lodge in nearby hotels, a newly built caravansary serves as the focus of many of the festivities. At the evening service the men recite the Hebrew prayer for the dead and light candles for the two venerated rabbis. It is customary to bring gifts of nuts, raisins, and *boukha* (Tunisian fig liqueur) to the synagogue's rabbis. The rabbis take a portion for themselves and then return the rest for the pilgrims to take home to family members and friends who have been unable to make the trip. The next day pilgrims crowd into the synagogue's courtyard. Both men and women cover their heads. One by one they enter the synagogue's reception hall to deposit their donations to the synagogue and to get their receipts. From there they go into the synagogue proper and embrace the doors of the *heikhal* that holds the Torah scrolls.

The Lag b'Omer celebration on the 18th of Iyar honors Rabbi Shim'on bar Yohai. On the festival eve the prayer service features passages from the *Zohar*. In the morning, after prayers, the celebration moves to the courtyard of the caravansary. Some of the men pull out an automobile-sized three-wheel cart that supports a hexagonal-tiered construct of the festival's principal symbols, topped by a large candelabrum. One tier lists the twelve tribes of Israel with their icons. Another records the names of major Tunisian rabbis. Another, the names of Abraham, Isaac, Rachel, and Leah. Another, a dedicatory inscription in Hebrew: "This menorah is in honor of Rabbi Meir Baal ha-Nes and Rabbi Shim'on bar Yohai, may their merit protect us." Another portrays the mystical name *Shaddai* inscribed in a six-pointed star. Another, the tablets of the Law. The whole construction is referred to as "the Menorah."

After the festival menorah is displayed, dancing begins. An orchestra plays Tunisian music and, while the unmarried young people watch from the upstairs balcony, married men and women dance in the courtyard. After the dancing, a joyous ceremonial procession begins. The crowd follows the menorah cart, now covered with glowing candles and multicolored scarves and scented with perfume that the women have sprayed, to the nearby villages of Sghira and Hara Kebira that have—or had—active synagogues. Some pilgrims walk; others ride in cars with their horns honking wildly. In front of each synagogue or religious school, they stop to sing and chant prayers. Although the participants are mainly local Jews and visiting émigrés, local Muslims, who recognize the party's similarities to a ziyara, join in the festivities as well.

The synagogue itself has many interesting features. Among the many oil lamps hanging over the bimah, the three most ornate are dedicated to the tzadiqim and to La Ghriba. Pinned to the ark curtain are many silver memorial plaques, similar in shape to the ex-votos found at important shrines in the Christian world, that have been left by pilgrims who have asked the two rabbis to pray for their departed loved ones. Cut into the walls below the ark is a deep tunnel leading to a niche where legend has it that in ancient times the body of La Ghriba was found. This niche is the focus of activity for female pilgrims who have unmarried daughters. They crawl into the tunnel to place in the niche a lighted candle and a raw egg on which they have written the daughter's name. Later they return for the egg, which by then has been roasted by the heat of the candles. They take the egg home with them for the unmarried daughter to eat, thus ensuring her a speedy match.

The numbers of pilgrims coming to the La Ghriba hillula diminished greatly in 1948 when the State of Israel came into being and the Libyan government forbade Jews from traveling to the Tunisian festival. During Sukkot in 1985 a Tunisian policeman shot up the La Ghriba synagogue, leaving three dead and many wounded, leading to a hiatus in the pilgrimage of several years. In the 1990s, in an atmosphere in which the Tunisian government was projecting its commitment to religious tolerance and was also working hard to increase the country's tourist income, the hillula was reborn as a homecoming festival for émigrés. Attendance fluctuates with international political and local security concerns. In 2000 some 8,000 Jews, mostly émigrés, attended. In 2001, after the disruption of peace talks between Palestinians and Israelis, the number fell to 1,300. On April 11, 2002, the La Ghriba synagogue was bombed by a Tunisian Muslim suicide terrorist who resided in France, after which the number of foreign Jewish pilgrims fell to a few hundred. The government denounced the terrorist act and committed national funds to rebuild the synagogue.[39] Travel agencies in Paris and in Israel still market the pilgrimage aggressively to their local Tunisian Jewish populations. As with so many of the traditional pilgrimage festivals that now serve mainly foreign-based populations, the La Ghriba hillula combines elements of religious fervor and tourist activities in ways that reflect the modern conditions of life.[40]

Ephraim Encaoua in Tlemcen (Algeria), Paris (France), and Jerusalem (Israel)

According to legend, the physician Rabbi Ephraim Encaoua (1359–1442) came to the Algerian city of Tlemcen from Marrakech, to which he had fled from Spain in the wake of the 1391 riots that destroyed much of the Andalusian Jewish community. A number of miraculous events associated with his arrival in Tlemcen are directly relevant to his hillula.[41] He is said to have arrived mounted on a lion that was carrying a serpent in its mouth, and this is how he is often portrayed in the pictures sold to pilgrims. It is said that, thirsty from his travel and finding no water, he touched a large rock near Tlemcen and a spring bubbled forth. Pilgrims normally visit the spring as part of their hillula experience. Supposedly it was his cure of the Sultan's daughter that led to Jews being allowed to settle in Tlemcen, and the daughter's tomb is pointed out to pilgrims. Encaoua served as rabbi of Tlemcen until 1442.

האבן הזאת מצבת קבורת הרב הגדול מעוז ומגדול בעל הנסים

TLEMCEN
Tombeau du Rabbi Encaoua   mort en 1442 (Jud 5202 de l'ère hébraïque)

רבינו אפרים אלנקאוה זיע"א

Grave of tzadiq Encaoua. Tlemcen, Algeria. Early twentieth-century print. Museum of Fez Jewish Cemetery, Morocco. Photo, D. Gitlitz, 2004.

A commemorative plaque was placed in the synagogue in 1842 that said that community elders had dreamed that Rabbi Encaoua had died on 1 Kislev, a date that thenceforth serves for his hillula. A second pilgrimage to his tomb in the spring is generally labeled a ziyara.

The anthropologist Arnold van Gennep participated in the ziyara in 1914. He described how women accompanied their petitionary prayers with vows. Women would visit the grave three times: once to announce their intention, once to lodge their request and state their vow, and a third time to thank the tzadiq for interceding with God on their behalf. In each case, the petitioner would bathe the stone with anisette or water from the tzadiq's spring.[42] They would also leave a sugar-covered stone at the grave as a token.

Henriette Azen remembered in 1997 that when she was a little girl, and her father had safely survived his stint as a soldier in World War I, he took the entire family to Rabbi Encaoua's tomb in Tlemcen to fulfill a vow that he had made in battle. There he thanked the tzadiq in the accepted fashion: he squatted down in front of the whitewashed tomb, sucked on a piece of sugar that had been wet with water, and offered his prayer of gratitude. Having met their obligations, the family listened to the musicians who had been hired for the festival, danced, and picnicked with their friends. A number of Jewish merchants had set out their wares in the hillula market, and the family bought small blue medals, symbols of Rabbi Encaoua, and some small tissue sacks containing dirt from the cemetery near the tzadiq's grave. Later, Azen pinned the sack to her slip to bring her luck when she presented herself for her school examinations in Oran. In those days, she reported, Rabbi Encaoua's hillula excited more than just the Jewish population of Algeria. The Muslim mayor of Tlemcen, for example, hosted a formal ball for the pilgrims who had come from afar to the festival.[43] Newspaper accounts from the 1930s describe a multiday municipal celebration including balls and fireworks, gymnastic exercises, and a candlelit march from the synagogue.

Observance of his hillula came to a sudden halt in 1962 when Algeria gained its independence and the vast majority of its Jewish population emigrated to France and Israel. As with many expatriate Maghrebi Jewish communities, a version of his hillula was "transferred" to the new homeland, where the 2,000 Tlemcenian Jews in Paris hold his annual hillula in their synagogue. In 1976 Algeria permitted the expatriate community to renew the annual hillula in Tlemcen, and a few do make the journey. However, today most French Tunisians venerate Encaoua in Paris, where photographs of his Algerian tomb adorn the walls and an inscribed memorial plaque functions as his "replacement" grave.[44] Rabbi Encaoua has a "grave site" in Jerusalem as well. Some Maghrebi Jews credit Israel's success in the 1956 Sinai war on his intercession in response to their prayers.[45] Since the late 1980s, some French Tlemcenian Jews have traveled to Jerusalem to take part in Rabbi Encaoua's hillula there as well.

The old world, with its hundreds of tiny Jewish communities scattered across the rural hinterlands of the Muslim states of North Africa and the Middle East and living in relative harmony with their neighbors, is largely gone. The hundreds of tzadiqim who interacted on a daily basis with those communities, whose baraka comforted, assisted, and protected them against all manner of threats, are for the most part gone as well. The village mellahs, empty of Jews. The cemeteries, overgrown. The shrines, when they are tended at all, looked after by Muslim caretakers who receive a small salary from the Jewish communities that remain in the cities or who garner tips from expatriate Jews returning for a visit. The few annual hillulot that persist today are largely attended by pilgrims from the cities, expatriates from foreign lands, or tourists. Morocco's Jewish communities venerated more tzadiqim than anywhere in the Islamic world. Yet by the late 1990s, in addition to Rabbi 'Amram's hillula, only six other substantial hillulot were still being celebrated: Rabbi Yahia Lakhdar, near Ben Ahmed, on Lag b'Omer; Rabbi Abraham Aouriouir, near Settat, on Lag b'Omer; Ouled ben Zmirou, at Safi, also on Lag b'Omer; Rabbi Haim Pinto, in Essaouira, on 26 Elul; Rabbi David u-Moshe, at Tinzert, near Agouim, on 1 Heshvan; Rabbi David ben Baroukh, at Tinzert, near Taroudant, on 3 Tebet.[46] In 2003 this last hillula drew 1,300 pilgrims from the United States, Canada, France, and Spain, as well as from Morocco.[47]

ISRAEL AND THE REFOCUSING OF SEPHARDIC PILGRIMAGES

The two events that triggered the most radical changes in the Jewish cultures of the Islamic lands were the creation of the State of Israel in 1948, followed quickly by the independence of the former French protectorates. The long epoch of semi-harmonious coexistence between the religions changed rapidly to an atmosphere of distrust in which nationalities were redefined, loyalties were questioned, and local violence became a surrogate for the far-off conflicts of the Middle East. Jews emigrated from the Maghrebi countries en masse, with the largest portion of the émigrés going to Israel, and substantial groups to France (largely Paris) and Canada (mainly Montreal). A 1998 survey showed a Jewish population in Tunisia of 7,000 (down from 110,000 prior to 1948), and in Algeria 1,000 (down from 130,000). Morocco's Jewish population had declined from 265,000 in 1948 to 5,500 in 2003.[48] This exodus, pulled by educational, economic, or cultural opportunities and pushed by the often-justified paranoia of the shrinking remnant communities, has continued until the present. The figures from Morocco, which retained the largest numbers of Maghrebi Jews, are revealing. In 1971 Jews comprised roughly 3 percent of Morocco's population. Of Casablanca's 1,000,000 inhabitants, 100,000 were Jews (10 percent). Since then the country has grown and the Jewish population has shrunk. Today, Jews comprise less than .02 percent of Morocco's people.[49]

The Maghrebi and particularly the Moroccan Jews who streamed into Israel after 1954 were literally uprooted. Very few were Zionists, eager to shed their Diaspora past and mold themselves in the image of the pioneer. They were refugees, eager to hold on to as much of the culture of their country of origin as they could. The ideal of the Zionist melting pot and the secular orientation of their new homeland were largely products of a European Ashkenazi culture that in many ways seemed alien to the North Africans. The extreme economic difficulties associated with settling into a country that did not have in place the entire infrastructure to receive them properly, and for the most part segregated them in the new, half-built development towns, further marginalized the Maghrebi immigrants. Although several living sages made aliyah along with them, the immigrants found themselves cut off from their traditional village tzadiqim, whose mere presence in their cemeteries had legitimized their rootedness to those lands. In Israel the daily visits to the tzadiq's grave were impossible, as was the annual hillula that gathered friends and neighbors and émigrés at the traditional grave site in a festive commemoration of the power of their tzadiq.

Replacements were called for. In the early years, when Maghrebi village communities remained largely intact in the Israeli towns into which they had been placed, the tzadiq might be honored at the community's synagogue, and a modest hillula might be held in someone's home. But by the early 1970s the culture of tzadiq veneration gathered new strength among the Maghrebi communities and found new outlets for its expression. The Israeli anthropologist Yoram Bilu identified four ways in which this tended to happen: (1) by appropriating preexisting Israeli pilgrimage sites; (2) by creating new contemporary saints; (3) by transferring saints to Israel through dreams; and by (4) reinterring in Israel the remains of saints buried elsewhere.[50]

Sephardic immigrants quickly focused their tzadiq veneration on the Israeli grave sites of well-known rabbis like Shim'on bar Yohai in Meron and Meir Baal ha-Nes in Tiberias. This appropriation happened so rapidly that by the early 1960s the majority of pilgrims to the hillulot of Shim'on bar Yohai and of Meir Baal ha-Nes were Maghrebis. The same was true of celebrations at the cave of Elijah the Prophet on Mount Carmel and the tomb of Shimeon the Just in Jerusalem. Many Tunisian Jews visit the supposed tombs of Rabbis Eleazar Ben-Arakh and Eleazar Ben-Azariah, two ancient sages of the period of the Tannaim "rediscovered" near Moshav Alma. The tombs have now been improved, souvenir bottles of earth and oil are offered for sale, and there is an annual hillula at the site. Some Moroccans in the northern Jordan Valley make daily visits to the cave tomb in Hatzor Haglilit of Rabbi Honi HaMe'agel, a legendary first-century BCE Talmudic scholar known for working miracles. His hillula takes place on Israel Independence Day, a nonworking day in Israel, and draws upwards of 20,000 pilgrims from all over the country. So many attend that pilgrims may have to stand in line for hours to enter the tiny cave where they light white candles and chant the Psalms.[51]

Modern tzadiqim who had made aliyah along with the Sephardic immigrants also came to be venerated. The most important holy places of this sort are the grave sites of charismatic Maghrebi rabbis such as the Moroccan Yisrael Abuhatzeira, more commonly known as Baba Sali (died 1984) in Netivot, and the Tunisian Haim Houri (died 1957) in Beersheba. Each year their hillulot attract many thousands of pilgrims. The fact that these pilgrims include many Israelis from a broad range of religious traditions and national origins speaks to the way in which the North African culture of tzadiq veneration has firmly established itself in modern Israeli religious life.

Bilu and his colleagues documented numerous cases in which the tzadiq informed an adherent in a dream that his grave—or the baraka associated with his grave—is now to be found in a specific site in Israel instead of, or in addition to, the traditional North African grave site. The most successful example of this process was the transference of the baraka of the Moroccan legendary tzadiq David u-Moshe. This process was undoubtedly facilitated by the fact that in Morocco there had been a tradition of being able to appeal to a tzadiq at sites other than his actual burial place. Similarly, devotees of Rabbi David u-Moshe might light candles for him in the synagogue in Mogador that bore his name.[52]

While the relocation dream gives the new site an immediate, supernatural legitimization, in other cases the recreation of a tzadiq's holy place is a conscious act by the émigré community. Until the 1960s, the Tunisian hillula at the tomb of Rabbi Sayed el Maarabi attracted large numbers of Jewish pilgrims from Tunisia and Libya on the first of Tebet to the town of El-Hamma. Pilgrims often combined his hillula with several days of vacation at the El-Hamma hot springs.[53] A hillula now takes place in the Israeli city of Ramleh, where a stone from Rabbi Yosef Maarabi's grave was built into the foundations of the holy ark of the Tunisian synagogue, and at a synagogue named for the tzadiq in Paris. The French festival, initiated in the early 1980s, draws several hundred people each year on the first Sunday of Hanukah to light candles in the tzadiq's honor and to eat a Tunisian-style kosher dinner in the company of old friends.[54]

Despite the traditional Jewish prohibitions about disturbing a grave or reinterring the dead, there is an occasional instance of transferring bones to Israel, such as when Rabbi Haim Pinto buried in Ashdod the bones of several ancestral tzadiqim he had smuggled from Morocco.[55]

The most popular dates chosen for the new hillulot have been Lag b'Omer, Mimouna, and Israel Independence Day, which, as a public holiday, facilitates pilgrim travel to the shrine. Often the pilgrim customs at such sites replicate practices remembered from the immigrants' original homelands. Hillulot that are sponsored by a particular, close-knit immigrant community also serve in Israel as a surrogate pilgrimage in place of the one back home. During the hillula in Ramleh, Israel, for the eighteenth-century Tunisian Rabbi Hai Taieb, for example (which in the late 1960s drew some 1,500 immigrants from northern Tunisia), the walls of the Ramleh Tunisian synagogue were decorated with photographs of Jewish life in Tunis. Vendors hawked Tunisian sweets. Inside the synagogue old men nostalgically murmured, "Ah, ya ya ya, we lived with him [there], what a great one."[56]

SHIM'ON BAR YOHAI (MERON, ISRAEL)

The Lag b'Omer hillula for the second century Rabbi Shim'on bar Yohai is the largest in Israel, drawing over 150,000 adherents to his tomb near Meron, high in the hills of the Galilee. Shim'on bar Yohai had been a disciple of the renowned sage Rabbi Akiva, who during the Roman persecutions took refuge with his son Rabbi Eleazar in a cave near Meron for thirteen years. As in medieval times, this cave and Rabbi Shim'on's grave are the two major sites of pilgrimage activity at Meron. The grave itself is located inside a courtyard erected by Rabbi Abraham ben Mordechai Galante in the sixteenth century to shelter pilgrims. The tomb's interior is divided into men's and women's sections. The complex also contains a yeshiva. About 80 percent of the pilgrims to his hillula are Moroccan Sephardim; the second largest group is Eastern European Hasidim.

The date of the hillula is linked to events in the lives of Rabbis Akiva and Shim'on bar Yohai. Tradition holds that a plague slew many thousands of Rabbi Akiva's students before abating on Lag b'Omer, thirty-three days after the beginning of Passover (Hebrew *lag* means thirty-three). Observant Jews hold this thirty-three-day period to be a time of mourning during which no weddings, singing, or acts of personal beautification—like cutting hair—are permitted. On Lag b'Omer the prohibitions cease, pent-up demand for festivity is released, and celebrations can begin again. While the pilgrimage focuses on the virtues of Rabbi Shim'on, celebrants also kindle bonfires to acknowledge the light of Rabbi Akiva's teaching. As is common with Sephardic hillulot, families and friends socialize in picnics, dancing, and singing.

The earliest recorded pilgrimages to Meron were in the twelfth century, and pilgrims continued to visit the sites all through the Middle Ages and, in small numbers, up until modern times. However, its current resurgence, and the development of its hillula into a mass event involving many tens of thousands of people, came only with the Maghrebi aliyah in the 1950s and 1960s.

Pilgrims to Meron may visit the shrines of other tzadiqim en route. A Tel Aviv pilgrim of Tunisian origin wrote in 2004 that his family has gone on pilgrimage to Meron every year since 1957 in fulfillment of a vow that his father had made. Two days prior to start of the hillula they pack the family car for the drive north. They stop first at the cave of Elijah the Prophet on Mount Carmel to light candles, pray, and make a charitable donation. Then they go to Acre to lunch at a Tunisian sandwich shop. When the hillula is over, they drive home by way of Tiberias so they can visit the tombs of Rabbis Meir Baal ha-Nes and Maimonides.[57] Other pilgrims go by bus to Safed, and from there march in procession to the tzadiq's tomb.

Yoram Bilu has captured the chaotic, carnival-like atmosphere of the Meron hillula with a deft hand:

> Just before the main gates we met a congested muddle of pilgrims all moving slowly up the hill toward the sages' shrine. There were literally thousands of families forcing their way through a sea of tents, cars, and stands stocked with goods of every description. . . . [We] jostled our way through an improvised amusement park, lottery booths, pony rides, and exhibition tents, past a police recruitment stand on the hood of a jeep, the Lubavitch *"mitzva* tank," and a

stall with Druse ornaments that also sold extra-thin pita bread and local cheese. Nearer the shrine . . . there were candles, oil, and pictures of *tsaddiqim* heaped on stalls everywhere you looked.[58]

Edith Turner, an anthropologist, who with her husband Victor are the best known theorists of pilgrimage of the late twentieth century, attended the Meron hillula in 1984 in the company of Bilu and several other Israeli and American anthropologists. Turner recorded in her notebook a kaleidoscope of vivid details:

We crowd up . . . stopping . . . at some sideshow or gambling game, or Begin's election booth. . . . Then comes a group of non-Hasidic ultra-orthodox on the left side of the road, displaying long black-thonged arm bands, *tefillin*, which they urge men to come forward and be bound with; then a loving couple walking entwined. . . . Up through the crowd pushes a group of young people led by a singing woman and a young man with a drum. They clap and dance in a wide line, then pass on jovially. Now we proceed upward past an old Sephardi in a white jelabiya gown, selling blessings, and a couple of rascally beggars on the right, sitting comfortably on the ground with tin cans for money beside them. And at last we see in the crowd a group of young men in skull caps and ordinary clothes, toiling upward and singing. One of them bears in his arms a large object flowing with veils, topped with two crowned knobs. It is the Torah in Her silver case. . . . A party of Hasids scissor past through the crowd, touching no one. They wear beards and sidelocks, black coats and black wide-brimmed hats. . . . We press upward, now passing an incense seller on the left who displays on the ground incense grains heaped in different colors, with medicines too. . . . The zaddik's holy picture is in everyone's hands. He is depicted bearing the scroll of the *Zohar*. . . . Women are all around me . . . dancing Moroccan style. One woman turns out to be weeping; she tells us she is barren, and if only the zaddik would send her a son she would name the child Shimon.[59]

Again through Bilu's eyes, once the pilgrims manage to wedge themselves into the building enclosing the graves of Rabbi Shim'on, the scene is no less colorful or apparently chaotic:

Everyone was trying to touch the railings surrounding the pair of graves, which were buried under a mountain of candles, head-scarves, and currency thrown by the celebrants. The murmur of prayer, and the incessant sound of weeping permeated the site, and, from the corners of the chamber, women's voices steadily intoned the Maghrebi healing song, "Ha wa za idawina" ("Here he comes to heal us"), accompanying their supplication rhythmically on tambourines. Some managed to wade through the crowd with trays of food, offering the other pilgrims a taste of their thanksgiving offerings.

A Polish-American Jew who attended in the late 1970s was similarly overwhelmed by the sounds in the shrine:

A few men were saying prayers; occasionally someone would approach the grille and throw over it a box of the candles that were on sale outside.

Brueghel would have loved the scene. Aside from the tiny oasis of silence that surrounded the tomb, the room was a bedlam of noise that caromed off the walls and made the floor vibrate in sympathy. A group of people had gathered around a woman who had fainted; the men brought glasses of water; only other women touched the victim.[60]

For the older Sephardim, the Meron hillula recalls those they celebrated in Morocco. They gather in informal groups of family and friends, with people of all ages and men and women freely mixing. They bring tents, bedding, cooking utensils, and sometimes food with them and encamp on the hillsides around the shrine, often for several days. Although the emotional highpoint of the pilgrimage comes when they pay their respects and lodge their prayers at Rabbi Shim'on's tomb, much of their time is spent in their family groups: dancing, the women ululating and the men singing his praises, drinking alcohol, and feasting. Wealthier families may have brought a sheep or goat with them to be dedicated to the tzadiq and then slaughtered by a qualified shochet. They roast meat for the se'udat mitzva, the festive meal that is a routine part of a Moroccan hillula. The family strolls through the large commercial fair, buying food and mementos. And they give money or food to the many beggars who know that during the festival pious Jews will exercise the mitzvah of charity.

Some ultra-Orthodox Jews avoid the hillula altogether, put off by cautions that the central rabbinate in Jerusalem has broadcast: that the slaughtering is not up to kosher standards; that the mixing of the sexes in the crowd and the attendance of menstruating women renders the festival impure; and that the worship of the tzadiqim smacks of idolatry.[61] Many Hasidim who do attend are seminary students who have come with their rabbi just for the day of the hillula. Their black dress and their habit of clustering tightly around their rabbi separate them from the Moroccans. Although the two groups are in close proximity at the grave site itself, they rarely mingle and their traditions of observance are markedly different.[62] The Hasidim chant prayers in the sanctuary at the grave area, or ecstatically chain-dance—men only—on the shrine's roof.

In addition to the seminarians, some Hasidic family groups attend the hillula as well. In the Israeli Hasidic tradition, three-year-old boys are given their first haircut in the inner courtyard of the Meron sanctuary, in a ceremony called halaqa.[63] After his haircut the young man, dressed in his finest clothes, is danced through the company on his father's shoulders like a little king. The family hosts a party for their friends with plenty of food and liquor. When it is time for the evening bonfires to be lit, the cut hair is piled on a pillar on the shrine roof and burned, together with scarves, candles, and other items contributed to assure good luck.[64] Although the Moroccan Sephardim practice this custom as well, the rooftop world as Edith Turner described it belonged to the Hasidim:

There [were] two barrels, each with a fire, one on the Sephardi side of the roof and one on the Hasids'. . . . We ascended the stairs and penetrated through the crowd to the Hasids' barrel. This turned out to be a wide-rimmed, upright concrete cylinder, about twice the size of an oil drum, set on a wide concrete dish to catch burning debris. . . . It was surrounded by a group of Hasids who were mounting it up with fuel, candles mainly, and papers on which were written the name of the devotee, his or her mother's name . . . a request, and a prayer. The crowd of Hasids gradually thickened around the barrel. . . . Singing began, and circling dances. . . . They were all touching one another in ecstasy. A tiny rebbe with an ancient white splayed beard approached, which he was only enabled to do by dint of the elbow work of stalwart young Hasids who fought outward against their comrades to allow their elder to pass. Was he going to light the fire? A flash in the darkness—and a great shout as the first flames shot up. . . . They fed it candles and emptied into it bottles of holy oil. . . . The roof was one mass of black coats, hats, and pale faces; voices shouted "Bar Yohoi!" in harsh song—all the men moving and moving in a chain embrace until they were in a trance.[65]

For both groups of pilgrims, the Moroccan Sephardim and the European Hasidim, the few moments inside the shrine itself are likely to be the emotionally climactic experiences of their pilgrimage. So many pilgrims come to Meron on Lag b'Omer and the space around the tombs of Rabbi Shim'on is so limited that there is fierce competition to get as close to the graves as possible for as long a time as possible. Thus the ecstatic moments of presence are characterized by overheated, tightly packed bodies jostling and maneuvering for position. Since many of the pilgrims believe that baraka is best transmitted by physical contact, worshipers strain to touch the lattice surrounding the two tombs. They toss personal and cult items—candles, scarves, vials of oil, money—onto the tombs, both as gifts and the physical manifestation of their presence at the site. As in the Hindu concept of darshan, they see the holy figure and are seen by him; they make contact, but the essence of touch flows in both directions.

MEIR BAAL HA-NES (TIBERIAS, ISRAEL)

The tomb of Rabbi Meir Baal ha-Nes on the shore of the Sea of Galilee south of Tiberias is one of Israel's most popular Jewish holy sites. As such it attracts pilgrims year round, and is a regular stop on organized Jewish tours of the Galilee. Rabbi Meir's hillula on the 14th of Iyar, four days before Lag b'Omer, attracts substantial numbers of both Sephardim (see Chapter 7) and Ashkenazim. Ironically, no one knows which of the many Rabbis Meir is buried in the tomb. The eleventh-century Rabbis Meir ben Yitzhak or Meir Katsine? or Rabbi Meir ben Yaakov who came to Palestine in the thirteenth century with Rabbi Yehiel of Paris? The most popular candidate is Rabbi Meir the Tannaite scholar whose yeshiva prospered in Tiberias in the second century CE. Among the many legends surrounding Rabbi Meir Baal ha-Nes, one of the most widespread is that during his life he refused to lie down until the Messiah had come. He received his nickname ha-Nes (Hebrew, the miracle worker) because of his reputed fame as an advocate for the needs of the faithful, who opened their prayers with the phrase, "Meir's God, please answer me."

The large domed building containing the rabbi's tomb sits on a rocky plateau a little above the shoreline. Unlike most Jewish tomb shrines which have a single door, the high-volume of pilgrimage traffic here is channeled in one side of

Vendors, Meir Baal ha-Nes shrine. Tiberias, Israel. Photo, D. Gitlitz, 1995.

the building and out the other. A divider separates the women from the men. There are washing facilities and, in the surrounding courtyard, metal stands in which pilgrims can light candles. And there are always rabbis in attendance to answer questions, advise on the proper prayer, and offer blessings on the petitioners' behalf, for which services a generous tip is expected. This shrine also houses an educational facility and a major fundraising operation dedicated to assisting poor Orthodox Jews.

DAVID U-MOSHE (TINZERT, MOROCCO; SAFED AND ASHKELON, ISRAEL)

As we have seen, many tzadiq cults and their pilgrimages did not transfer spontaneously to Israel, but rather were rekindled in their new home by the efforts of individual devotees. Most often the new site now graced by the baraka of the tzadiq had been revealed in a dream. Ben-Ami, and Ben-Ari and Bilu detail the case of David u-Moshe, a Moroccan popular miracle-working tzadiq whose original grave site in Tinzert, near Agouim, also had been revealed to Jews of the High Atlas region in a dream. The fact that his name uses a Berber, not a Hebrew or Arabic, patronymic (*u* rather than *ben* or *ibn* for "son of") suggests that his cult is ancient. Nothing concrete is known about his life, though legends say he went from the Holy Land to Morocco to collect funds. Because people believe he offered his own life to save Jews and Muslims of Tinzert from a terrible plague, his tomb there was honored by both religions. Until the exodus of Moroccan Jews in the 1950s, his hillula would draw thousands of celebrants from Morocco and other Jewish communities of the Maghreb. At the tomb site they camped for up to a week, picnicked with their friends and family, lit candles to the tzadiq, and sang Judeo-Arabic hymns and drank glasses of wine or distilled liquor in the tzadiq's honor. They touched their hands to the marble slab covering his tomb and lodged their prayers of petition. Women placed rings on the tomb to absorb the tzadiq's baraka to take home with them.[66] Moroccan Jews unable to make the pilgrimage to Tinzert may have visited the tzadiq symbolically in the synagogue named for him in the city of Mogador.

Since the 1960s David u-Moshe has been honored at a hillula in Ashkelon in a synagogue named for him and held on the supposed day of his death. The site has been legitimized through the miracles the tzadiq's baraka has achieved there: a shaft of light illuminated the sanctuary at the end of the 1967 Six-Day War; a girl wounded in a terrorist attack was miraculously healed.[67]

One unusual event is the ritual slaughter of an ox that has been carefully tended at a nearby farm for the full year before the festival. The day before the hillula, the ox is brought to the synagogue in a truck, led inside where the chairs and benches have been removed, and slaughtered. When it has been examined and pronounced kosher, there is spontaneous cheering and singing. Men butcher the ox, a shochet dispatches many dozens of chickens, and women prepare the mountains of hillula food. In the evening, after solemn prayer, musicians sing and play and groups of women dance. While supper is served in the synagogue and the surrounding areas, an auctioneer sells candles and cups of arak to pay this year's hillula expenses and begin raising money for the next.

As might be expected, there are rival sites. If one hillula is good, two might be even better. In 1973 the Moroccan Israeli Abraham Ben-Haim dreamed that David u-Moshe told him that he was no longer in his tomb in Morocco and wanted instead to rest in the house in Safed (Shikun Canaan, Building 172) where Ben-Haim had lived since making aliyah in 1954. Ben-Haim thoroughly publicized these dream announcements to Israel's Moroccan community, at that time the largest postindependence immigrant group. Ben-Haim's ongoing program of printing the content of his dreams, announcing events concerning the tzadiq, and mailing this information to every Moroccan congregation in Israel helped established the importance of the holy site. He outfitted one room in his small apartment for Rabbi David u-Moshe. A marble tablet inscribed with the tzadiq's name and titles serves as David u-Moshe's surrogate grave-shrine. Ritual items (candles, tallitot, miniature Torah scrolls, prayer books), carpets, tapestries, and amulets differentiate the room from normal, non-ceremonial space.[68] By the late 1970s David u-Moshe's new home had become the most important Moroccan holy site in northern Israel.

His hillula on the new moon of the month of Hesvan is a major annual event, attracting 20,000 to 30,000 devotees, most of them Moroccans but also a smattering of Jews from other parts of the Maghreb. It requires substantial coordination of infrastructure services ranging from sanitary facilities to crowd control and security. On the evening of the hillula, crowds stream into the narrow alley leading up to Ben-Haim's house. As with most Maghrebi pilgrimages, two quite

different sets of activities take place: worship at the tzadiq's shrine and family festival. So many pilgrims press to view the shrine that organizers have attempted to
limit access to the room to brief visits by successive groups. Inside the shrine
room, women may kiss the tzadiq's marble "tomb." They pray and deposit their
offerings in the collection box. They may leave off bottles of water or oil to absorb
the tzadiq's baraka; these will be picked up later for ritual use or for curing. The
apartment itself is too small and flammable to permit the lighting of candles. Instead, pilgrims toss their lighted candles into a covered room on one side of the
apartment house's front yard that has been designated for the purpose.

After worship, the social aspects of the pilgrimage take over. Next to the apartment are small booths, staffed by Ben-Haim's female relatives and friends, who
distribute food and drink purchased with money from the previous year's contributions. In one booth, a shochet slaughters the lambs or goats brought by wealthier families. There is a fee for this, but meat slaughtered at the hillula is considered
more meritorious than meat that the pilgrims bring with them from home. Family groups set themselves up in alleys, yards, or along the street, to roast the meat
and share a meal among themselves and with friends who may stop by. In the evening bands play, singers praise Rabbi David u-Moshe, women whose vows were
granted through his intercession pass trays of candies and sweets to the throng,
while national political figures work the crowd for potential votes. Pilgrims also
browse the market stalls that have sprung up along the street leading to the apartment house to buy foodstuffs, sweets, portraits of tzadiqim, amulets, and a variety
of souvenirs. Beggars work the crowd for contributions, and sellers of blessings
ply their trade.

THE ABUHATZEIRA CLAN (TAFILLALT, MOROCCO; DEMITO, EGYPT; AND NETIVOT, ISRAEL)

Yaacov Abuhatzeira (1808–1880), a distinguished Moroccan rabbi from the
village of Tafillalt, was known as a tzadiq even during his lifetime. As is the case
with many tzadiqim, an abundant folk tradition connects him with miraculous
events. Among the many stories that speak to Rabbi Yaacov's uncommon merit as
a student of Torah is that the spirit of Elijah the Prophet often accompanied him
in his studies. When a neighbor who disobeyed an instruction not to look directly
at the divine light emanating from Rabbi Yaacov's study room was struck blind,
his sight could only be restored through Rabbi Yaacov's prayerful intercession. On
another occasion, a servant saw Rabbi Yaacov studying with three visitors, but
when she sent in four cups of coffee she found Rabbi Yaacov all alone. He is also
said to have once walked on water.[69]

Late in his life Rabbi Yaacov set off to make aliyah to the Holy Land. But he got
no further than the village of Demito, about fifty kilometers southeast of Alexandria, Egypt, where he died in 1880. It is said that the day he died the world was
enveloped in total darkness. Since his death an annual hillula has taken place at his
grave site in Demito.[70]

After Rabbi Yaacov Abuhatzeira left Morocco, his son Rabbi Massoud became
head of his Talmudic school in Tafillalt. When Rabbi Massoud died in 1909, his son
Rabbi Yisrael Abuhatzeira (1890–1984) took over his position, distinguishing

himself at an early age with his knowledge and with his charismatic power to transform people with his baraka. The effectiveness of his prayers of intercession soon earned him the nickname Baba Sali (Praying Father), the name by which he was known during the rest of his life. Rabbi Yisrael made aliyah to Israel in 1964, living for a brief time in Yavne before settling permanently in the development town of Netivot, just east of the Gaza Strip; he believed he could best serve his people by living among them. From there his influence radiated outward to the Moroccan and the broader Sephardic communities. His friendship with the Lubavitcher Rebbe Menachem Schneerson and Schneerson's many expressions of support for Rabbi Yisrael's work gained Baba Sali a following among Israel's Orthodox Ashkenazi community as well. On a daily basis, as individuals or in busloads, people came to see him to ask his advice or receive his blessing. It was a special privilege to be able to celebrate a bar mitzvah in his presence.

When Baba Sali died in 1984, over 50,000 mourners attended his funeral, and his grave site quickly became a place of pilgrimage.[71] Baba Sali blessed them when he was alive, and many believe his spirit blesses them in the same way. Between the Netivot synagogue and his grave site is a small building where pilgrims can sign up to receive Baba Sali's blessing and make an appropriate donation to continue the rabbi's work. Each year on 4 Shebat, the anniversary of his death, more than 100,000 Jews attend his hillula in Netivot, making it the second largest in Israel. For some devotees, who speak of "going to the Baba Sali," the hillula itself has been anthropomorphized.[72] A white-domed building covers the tomb, which is draped with velvet. As in Ashkenazi holy places, a divider keeps the men and the women apart. As per Sephardic custom, at the hillula praying, music, dancing, and feasting continue for several days. Many devotees throw the candles that they have lighted in the tzadiq's honor into an incinerator that has been placed in the tomb's courtyard. Some pilgrims touch lengths of red thread to Baba Sali's grave and take them home or distribute them among their friends as good luck amulets.

In death Baba Sali may be said to have become the single most important figure in the culture of tzadiq veneration that has so permeated modern Israeli culture. Streets and synagogues are named for him, and his portrait occupies a place of honor in many Israeli homes. In recognition of this role, in 1999 the Israeli government issued a postage stamp bearing his likeness.

Baba Sali's hillula may well have prospered strictly as a result of his reputation as a living tzadiq. But it has been helped along by the aggressive marketing by his son, Rabbi Baruch Abuhatzeira, who has consciously assumed his father's mantle of religious leadership, even adopting his style of dress and gesture.[73] It was Rabbi Baruch who managed the details of the funeral in Netivot; who promoted the construction of a spectacular Baba Sali synagogue in Netivot; who developed the land next to it as Kiryat Baba Sali, including a kindergarten, a Talmud torah, a yeshiva, a restaurant, picnic grounds, and shops; who has developed an ever-expanding line of Baba Sali merchandise, including photographs, postcards, posters, key chains, candles, wine cups, audio and videotapes, three-dimensional models of Kiryat Baba Sali, amulets, and carpets bearing Rabbi Yisrael's woven image.[74] Despite Rabbi Baruch's overt business activities, despite having been roundly criticized for an extramarital affair, and even despite five years in prison for corruption and fraud after a stint as Ashkelon's deputy mayor, he is still supported as a spiritual leader by the people who venerated his father. He is an active player in Israeli politics in the right wing Shas (Sephardi Torah Guardians) party, and as a result for many people attendance at his hillula has taken on political significance.[75]

TZADIQIM, POLITICS, AND PILGRIMAGE

Baruch Abuhatzeira is not the only tzadiq to use his power to exert influence in Israeli politics. David Kadourie, the leader of Israel's ultra-Orthodox Ahavat Yisrael party, distributed good luck amulets bearing the likeness of his revered grandfather Rabbi Yitzhak Kadourie until the Israel's Central Election Committee in 2003 banned the practice as a form of vote buying. Another is Rabbi Yaakov Ifargan (born 1966), a charismatic student of Kabbalah with a large following among the Sephardim who make up 60 percent of Israel's population. The Shas leadership quite calculatedly uses its association with mystic tzadiqim like Rabbi Ifargan to create an aura of religious legitimacy around their political agendas. Rabbi Ifargan also illustrates how the strong belief of many Sephardim in the power of their tzadiqim to persuade God to work miracles in their behalf has been carried over into their new lives in Israel. A 2000 *Time* magazine story about Rabbi Ifargan portrays one of his healing sessions in words that seem drawn from an American evangelical revival meeting:

> Gathered around the floodlit enclosure at midnight, they sing that he will make peace: ya'ase shalom. The words refer to God, but as 300 worshipers thump tambourines and clap hands in the warm night, they have someone else in mind. It is Rabbi Yaakov Ifargan, who shuffles through the crowd, small and bowed, the people touching him for his blessing. . . . "I will clean the people," he mutters and slings candles into a brazier until the flames rise six meters and wax sizzles onto the dusty ground. At 3 a.m., almost four hours into this ceremony, he turns to a row of handicapped followers sweating near the fire in their wheelchairs. "Are you a believer?" the rabbi asks [——], 22, who suffers from multiple sclerosis. People in the crowd raise [——] by his arms. The young man scuffs his feet through the dirt, then collapses into his wheelchair. "I do feel stronger," he says.[76]

YONATAN BEN UZIEL (AMUKA, ISRAEL): PILGRIMAGE AS MATCHMAKER

The pilgrimages we have been discussing are only a representative sample of the current Sephardic pilgrimage traditions in the Islamic world and in Israel. There are many others, some whose roots go back hundreds of years, and some of modern origin. One of the most interesting is the Tu b'Av pilgrimage to the grave of Rabbi Yonatan ben Uziel in the village of Amuka, near Safed.

Old problems in new settings may spark innovative solutions, and where there is an entrepreneurial will there is often a way. Pilgrimages in Israel have become big business. They suit the needs of the tourist industry, which has been quick to sponsor organized tours to major and minor sites. Religious fraternities associated with observant communities may also find pilgrimages to be a vehicle for reinforcing their particular traditional values. And then there are all those young, unmarried observant Israelis hoping to find an appropriate mate with whom they can settle down and raise a family. For over thirty years the religious fraternity Torah mi-Sinai, whose base lies in Jerusalem's Sephardic communities, has been sponsoring several day-long pilgrimages each year. Their driving force is the charismatic Aharon Cohen, who organizes, promotes, and leads the pilgrimage tours. One of the pilgrimages, the Tu b'Av excursion to Rabbi Yonatan ben Uziel, is targeted at single men and women who are shopping for a spouse.[77]

In ancient times Tu b'Av was a lovers' festival.[78] Rabbi Yonatan ben Uziel, a first century CE student of Rabbi Hillel the Elder, was a minor player in the Torah culture of that period, and his grave in Amuka seems to have attracted sporadic pilgrims from at least the sixteenth century. But by the twentieth century Rabbi Yonatan had somehow become known as the Sage of Good Marriages, and his grave became famous for helping people find appropriate mates. In the 1920s it took five hours to walk from Safed to Amuka, and parties of young people would make a full day's excursion to the grave. It is not surprising that along the path, laughing, teasing, and flirting, some romantic interests would be kindled, or that these would be attributed to the power of the saint.

Aharon Cohen's pilgrims board the bus early in the morning in Jerusalem for their trip north to Amuka. Along the way they visit other important grave sites in Tiberias, Safed, and Hatzor Haglilit. The pilgrims are observant Jews, so the men sit on one side and the women on the other. Still, the aisle between them is narrow, and in between the reading of texts, the singing of psalms, and listening to Cohen's religious and political commentaries on the sites they are visiting, there is plenty of opportunity for chatter, and the unmarrieds make the most of it. From the tour's leader there is a constant litany of reinforcement: "I hope you get married soon." "Don't ask the sage directly; ask him to ask God on your behalf to help you find a mate." And the pilgrims themselves tell stories of people they know who visited Amuka and were married shortly thereafter.

Cohen constantly reminds the participants that they are on a pilgrimage, not a social outing, and the group's choreographed activities support this view. Participants pray from Cohen's written compendium of the prayers, petitions, and blessings appropriate to each place. At the grave sites they light candles, sing, and leave kvitlach. Their processions are accompanied by the blowing of a shofar. There are newly-invented rituals, too, to reinforce the sacred, mystical power of the pilgrimage grave visits. At Rabbi Yonatan's grave the pilgrims circle the stone counterclockwise seven times, dedicating each circle to one of the Makers of the Covenant; candles—auctioned to the participants prior to beginning the ceremony—are lit in honor of each of the Makers (Abraham, Isaac, Jacob, etc.). At Rabbi Yonatan's grave some of the women wrap a red thread seven times around the tombstone, then cut pieces of the thread to wear on their wrists as a good luck charm. They may take lengths of thread home with them for unmarried friends who were unable to join them on the pilgrimage. At each site money for charity is collected, and Cohen reminds them repeatedly that if they get married within one year of their pilgrimage, it is traditional to contribute substantially to Torah mi-Sinai.

NEW WORLD HILLULOT

The culture of tzadiq veneration and of annual hillulot, taken to Israel in the 1950s largely by Moroccans, but also by immigrants from other North African countries, has taken root and has spread far beyond the Maghrebi Sephardim. Many Israelis of other origins participate in the hillulot, some of which are organized by travel agencies and even the national bus company. These celebrations continue to be part religious and part touristic, a chance to honor a tzadiq and secure his or her protection, but also an opportunity to spend a day or two with one's family in the countryside.

Commemorative hillulot for Sephardic tzadiqim are held from time to time in the United States as well. These are not the mass popular pilgrimages formerly common in the Arabic-speaking Jewish world, or in that world as recast in the State of Israel. Rather they resemble extended family gatherings, opportunities for clans to gather to honor one of their own. The hillula held in New York in 1999 celebrating Rabbi Hakham Yosef Hayyim's, originally of Baghdad, for example, drew members of the Hayyim family from Canada, Switzerland, Great Britain, and the United States, as well as a number of rabbis who had known, or whose fathers had known, the famous Iraqi Rabbi. A choir sang music composed for the occasion. A Baghdadi caterer provided ethnic dishes.[79] In Washington, D.C., the Magen David Sephardi, a congregation made of Jews from all over the North African and Middle Eastern Sephardic world, each year on Lag b'Omer celebrates a hillula for Shim'on bar Yohai. The event symbolically incorporates the individual congregants' favorite tzadiqim from a variety of countries and raises funds for the congregation by auctioning candles labeled with each tzadiq's name. As the Lebanese auctioneer one year remarked, "Before we start: This is a Moroccan custom, but here I see Iranians, Egyptians, Syrians, Turks, Moroccans, Libyans, Americans. *Am Yisrael khay!*"[80]

THE SHRINES OF THE HOLOCAUST

I was completely caught off guard when Bernard began weeping. I stopped and asked what the matter was. He responded "I had a little friend Moishele here in the *Krakov Cheder* and I still remember our *Rebbe*, with that '*kanshik*' [stick] in his hand." (Eitan Schuman, 1999)[1]

If I had been offered a free trip to see the camps, I would have turned it down. But I was in Poland for other reasons. . . . How could I not visit one of the Camps? So I went. I ended up going to five. Now, I must tell you: Go! See it with your own eyes. (Herschel Shanks, pre-1990)[2]

I wanted to go to Belzec because no one really does. I felt that as many as a million Jews died there in the space of nine months—and hardly anyone even knows about it. It was a pilgrimage to a holy site. (Shaul Rosenblatt, circa 2000)[3]

I wouldn't say I had a Jewish experience [at Auschwitz]. I would say I had a Nazi experience. (Mark Kurlansky, circa 1992)[4]

The Holocaust was in every sense of the Hebrew word a *hurban*, a destructive event of such magnitude that it changed the world. It was not a sacrificial offering in the religious sense, which is the Greek meaning of the word *holocaust*. It was murder, genocide, and most Jews prefer to refer to it with the Hebrew word for destruction, *shoah* (in this book we will use the terms *Shoah* and *Holocaust* interchangeably). The Shoah raised fundamental questions about the nature of humanity and about our place and purpose in the world. And it raised similar questions about God. The Shoah, like the atomic bomb, compels us to deal with it: emotionally, intellectually, and politically. Even avoidance of this issue is a kind of response.

Holocaust Sites

The 6,000,000 Jews who perished in the Shoah are gone. At best, each of the vanished Jews or all of them in the aggregate live on in the minds of the people who remember them. Human beings yearn for permanence, and memory, we believe, will hold back for a time the tide of oblivion. So we express our yearning through acts of memorialization: rites, ceremonies, venerating relics,[5] erecting monuments, and going on pilgrimages of memory. The places of the Shoah are memory sites. They require visiting, touching. It is not enough to read about them, to study them. Their physical presence and our physical presence at them slash through the gauze of abstraction with which we tend to drape historical events. They are liminal sites, places where for a time we leave our ordinary lives behind and cross over to the land of our collective past. Duty, curiosity, shock, nostalgia, personal loss—these are the vehicles that carry us across the ford.

Traditional holy religious sites are imbued with their special character by the presence of something or someone that has touched the divine. For believers, most religious holy sites function as portals to goodness: to healing, to prosperity, to peace of mind. Pilgrims journey to such places with the hope that the power of the site, the sincerity of their belief, and their offering of the time and resources devoted to their pilgrimage will increase the likelihood of their prayers being answered. The rituals they engage in at the holy places tend to be formally prescribed by their religious authorities, or at least sanctioned by repetition over eons. The

"Dor" (Generations). Part of Jewish barracks memorial. Buchenwald, Germany. Photo, D. Gitlitz, 2004.

objects they take away with them—a vial of holy water, a scraping of dirt, a scallop shell—extend the aura of the divine into their home environment.

The shrines of the Holocaust are not like that. They are made by man, not the divine. They are places of recollection, not portals to the miraculous. Historians like Peter Novick argue that the sacralization of Holocaust sites is part and parcel of the creation of a "secular religion" of memory, complete with its secular saints (the survivors) and its dogma (the obligation to memorialize).[6] They commemorate evil, not good; martyrdom, not divine intervention. They are shrines whose negative charge of energy draws people to them. And they offer only the repressive past. As Rabbi Abraham Palti recalled after visiting Auschwitz: "For me, to be in that place and walk on the ground where so many human beings were massacred . . . left an inextinguishable memory."[7] Once sufficient time has passed, pilgrims may ruminate on the meaning of their experience, but during their visit, the immediacy of the shrine's physical presence is overwheling. Treblinka: "The day was sunny, and I just couldn't believe that so many people had been murdered precisely there where I was standing" (Leonardo Simpser).[8] Majdanek: "The pain, the shouts, and the suffering of all those who died here, right precisely where I am now" (Paola Hamui).[9]

WHAT ARE THE HOLY PLACES OF THE SHOAH?

The shrines of the Holocaust, and of pilgrimage to them, are fundamentally of three types: places where the destruction occurred, monuments to the victims, and museums.

The sites dedicated to memorializing the Shoah have evolved continuously since the liberation of the camps. Survivors of Dachau, Bergen-Belsen, and Buchenwald constructed the first, informal memorials from the rubble of the camps. National or municipal memorials to the generic victims of Nazi or Fascist persecution were created during the next two decades: Warsaw (1948), Berlin (1952), Mauthausen (1957), Buchenwald (1958), and Dachau (1965).

At first the camps themselves were appropriated as memorials, although the question of memorials to exactly what was often contentious. Also appropriated were other physical sites closely related to Holocaust events, such as the ruins of the Warsaw Ghetto. In a second phase, new institutions were created to memorialize, educate, and archive information and artifacts. The first and most important of these was Jerusalem's Yad Vashem, planned in 1946 and finally opened in 1959. In subsequent decades these types of institutions were replicated in major cities of the survivors (New York, Los Angeles, Washington, Amsterdam, Brussels, Paris, Cape Town), and eventually of the perpetrators (Berlin, Warsaw). During the last twenty years Holocaust memorial-museums have proliferated at the local level, in synagogues and Jewish community centers around the globe.

The Holocaust engulfed victims from almost the whole of Europe, so that the places in which it is memorialized are found in nearly every country on that continent. In some areas survivor groups pushed for a shift in focus from memorializing the Shoah in its global dimensions to remembering the particulars of their own experiences. This, too, has led to a proliferation of sites. In Amsterdam alone there are individual monuments memorializing the martyrs of Dachau, Auschwitz, and Ravensbruck. Another monument commemorates Dutch-Jewish resistance. And in recognition of the fact that the Jews were not the Nazis' only victims, Amsterdammers also erected monuments to the murdered Gypsies and homosexuals, as well as a general monument to all Dutch citizens who were murdered by the Germans.

HOW DO HOLOCAUST SHRINES CONVEY THEIR MEANINGS?

On October 11, 1999, Alicja Bialecka, a staff member at the Museum and Memorial of Auschwitz-Birkenau, opened her remarks to a group of Polish high school educators with these words:

> Should the Museum and Memorial of Auschwitz-Birkenau educate and teach? Or should we only maintain the remains of the former camp, preserve it and make its terrain accessible to visitors? What should be done to commemorate those tragic events from the recent past? The site is an artifact and a document. However, it is also a recollection which reminds the visitor strongly of the Holocaust. But visitors also need proper explanation that will enable them to understand things that are incomprehensible and help them to comprehend things that are inconceivable.[10]

The shrines of the Holocaust are inherently problematic. The people who put together a Holocaust memorial—the lobbyists, the benefactors, the designers, the politicians—want their creation to convey meaning consistent with their particular agenda. The process of deciding what meaning or meanings are to be conveyed, and for what purpose(s), is likely to be very contentious, as each participant brings to the table individual experiences and expectations, political agendas, and dreams. Leon Wieseltier reminds us that memory itself is always a process of selection, of interpretation,[11] to which James Young adds that Holocaust memorials, whether they be monuments, museums, or the camps themselves, "juxtapose, narrate, and remember events according to the tastes of their curators, the political needs and interests of their community, the temper of their time."[12]

Bialecka, Wieseltier, and Young raise important issues about the meaning of Holocaust-related sites and the purposes they serve for the millions of pilgrims and tourists who visit them each year:

- Are the killing places to be preserved as fixed in time (1941? 1943? 1946?), or is their evolution during the Nazi period somehow relevant to comprehending their meaning?

- If the camps are artifacts, does their meaning reside in their physical remnants or in the culture that moved their makers to give them shape? Did the Holocaust happen at such places, or were the killing camps merely pustules whose eruption spoke to a widespread and pervasive infection?

- If the camps are documents, what is their text? Or more accurately, what are their texts? Who wrote them? Who reads them? Are they fixed or mutable? Do they speak to crowds or to individuals? If visitors need, in Bialecka's words, a "proper explanation" to comprehend them, who determines what is proper? Does "proper" change over time? Is it determined by local political or religious agendas?

- Can people be made to grasp the vastness of the Holocaust? Or is understanding impossible, as Bialecka's oxymorons suggest ("understand the incomprehensible, comprehend the inconceivable")? Does visiting the killing places contribute to peoples' comprehension?

- Is comprehension enough? Should pilgrimage to the camps transform people in some way? Should they impel the pilgrims to an action agenda of some sort?[13]

Memorials are always intended to support the political, social, and/or economic agendas of their creators. It is not surprising, then, that in the decades following World War II, nations have taken varied approaches to Holocaust memorials. In Germany, the monuments tend to exalt people victimized for their political resistance to Fascism. Until very recently, the main way of memorializing Jews there was to acknowledge the places in which they used to live. Memorials in Soviet-dominated postwar Poland mourned the Nazi rape of the nation. They considered Jews only insofar as they were a component of Polish citizenry and made no mention of Polish anti-Semitism or Polish complicity in the slaughter.[14] Only after Communism's collapse in 1989 have Polish memorials begun to acknowledge that Jews were never part and parcel of Polish identity, and to reassess the complex, often violent interrelations between Jews and Polish Catholics. Israeli monuments exalt Jewish heroes and martyrs and derive from the Shoah a justification both for the creation of the State of Israel and its obsession with military strength.[15] Non-Jewish victims are acknowledged, but more attention is given to the Gentiles who

Orthodox pilgrims from the United States. Auschwitz, Poland. Photo, D. Gitlitz, 2004.

took great risks to save Jews from being killed. Holocaust museums in the United States emphasize America's pride in its role in crushing the Nazis, liberating the camps, and welcoming diverse peoples as immigrants to a secular state.[16]

As the "writers" of memorials compose them according to their own agendas, so too the "readers" of those memorials, the pilgrims and students and tourists who come to visit them, interpret them in the light of their own experiences and concerns. Auschwitz, for example, may speak to Jews and to Gypsies of mass murder motivated by racial hatred. To Israeli Jews and Zionists, it may make patent the imperative that created the new nation. It may speak to Polish Catholics of national martyrdom. To Russian Communists, it may recall Fascism's attempts to annihilate the international leftist movement, some members of which happened to be Jews. It may speak to pilgrims from other lands and religions of the human capacity for evil, or of the horror, the tragedy, and the danger of genocide.[17]

Holocaust shrines speak to individual pilgrims according to each one's life experiences. "This is where you suffered for fourteen months in 1944–1945." "This is where your Lithuanian relatives went up in smoke." "This is like what happened to your Armenian uncles at the hands of the Turks." "This is what my grandfather helped create." "How could my grandmother say that she knew nothing about this when it took place only six kilometers from her house?" "This is why Israel must never yield." "This has no relation to the way we are treating our Palestinian neighbors, does it?" "This is the end result of what can happen if you let them call you 'nigger' without fighting back."

The sponsors of pilgrimages to Holocaust shrines tend to have specific agendas in mind. Parents, communities, and nations hope that pilgrimages to these shrines will help instill the proper values in their children. Governments may intend the shrines to serve as vehicles of understanding, or atonement for past actions, or justification of current agendas. Educators intend for them to educate. The guilt-ridden hope that supporting such visits will help purge their consciences. Ministries of Tourism want to boost local economies. But what the sponsors intend and what the pilgrims perceive are likely to be quite different.

PILGRIMS OR TOURISTS?

The yellow-arched sign, "McDonald's Welcomes You to Dachau," greeted the authors as we got off the train in the village of Dachau in summer 2004. Were we being greeted as tourists or as pilgrims? Millions of people visit the shrines of the Holocaust each year. Poles report that Auschwitz is their number one tourist-pilgrim attraction (actually it is number two, if you count the Catholic pilgrims to the Virgin of Czestochowa). Anne Frank's house in Amsterdam is close behind the Rijksmuseum and the Van Gogh Museum in numbers of visitors. In Germany, Dachau is a popular day trip from Munich, and downtown Weimar maintains a separate tourist office just for Buchenwald. Jerusalem's Yad Vashem memorial museum draws over a million visitors annually. In Los Angeles, Washington, and dozens of other American cities, Holocaust museums are an important attraction.

Crowds of tourists or throngs of pilgrims? Secular visitors whose experience is framed by an expectation of recreation? Or people looking to be moved, educated, or in some way spiritually affected? Open-air theme parks, or archives of relics? Yellow arches and Big Macs or yellow stars and arches of barbed wire?

Over two months we visited five concentration camps: Auschwitz-Birkenau, Buchenwald, Dachau, Majdanek, and Terezin. Adding to the dozens of Holocaust museums we had previously visited in Western Europe and the Americas, we went to several East European museums of Jewish culture, from Berlin's major new Jewish Museum to the three-room museum crammed into an annex of Munich's synagogue. We walked the streets and cemeteries of cities like Warsaw, Lublin, and Kraków that were the sites of major ghettos that fed the killing camps, and dozens of smaller towns and villages in which up to two-thirds of the pre-1939 population were Jews, and which are now Jew-empty.

Train station. Dachau, Germany. Photo, D. Gitlitz, 2004.

Central to the dichotomy of theme park-vs-shrine is the question of decorum. How visitors behave in a special place is related to their expectations and to the subtle signs that the places themselves convey. In this regard, the shrines of the Holocaust fall outside of familiar categories. The camps are indeed vast, open-air theme parks. They are artificial spaces twice designed, once by the original constructors for the purpose of killing, and once by their reconstructors for the purpose of recalling the killing through recontextualization. The ambiance is somber, as is the mood that it tends to elicit, a mood appropriate to standing in a holy place. No music, no glitz, no picnic areas, no oases of color and respite. Holocaust museums, which strive to evoke similar reactions in enclosed representative spaces, do not invite conversations about the aesthetic merits of the exhibits. Laughter, or any external sign of lightheartedness, would be a severe breach of decorum. In fact, most people seem to feel that these shrines commemorate evil and loss of such magnitude that to visit them with anything less than full reverent concentration is just plain wrong. Any intrusion of commercialism or tourism is thus by definition a travesty. As a German-Jewish pilgrim put it, "To visit Jewish historical sites of tragic significance is a kind of pilgrimage: a return to places that have been transformed into sacred sites that keep alive the remembrance of the Jewish past."[18]

Camp survivors feel this distinction acutely. For example, Boris Pahor, a Slovene Jew who survived fourteen months in German camps, in his stirring memoir of his return to the camps in 1967 vents his anger at the conversion of the shrines of the Holocaust into places of tourism. He decries the fact that today sightseers walk in the places where so many people suffered. To the tourists he contrasts the true pilgrims who come "to tread on truly holy ground, to pay homage to the ashes of fellow creatures who by their mute presence have raised, in our hearts, an immovable landmark of human history."[19]

During our visits, we found that a substantial portion of the people we talked with explained the motives for their visits in terms familiar to pilgrims. To remember and to honor their murdered relatives. To purge old ghosts. To reach clo-

Tourist wares. Terezin, Czech Republic. Photo, D. Gitlitz, 2004.

sure. To satisfy a compulsion. To strengthen a sense of identity. Because that is what Jews do. To probe the meaning of Jewishness. Or the existence of a benevolent intervening God. Or the nature and role of the State of Israel. Or the obligation to engage in responsible social action.

At the Munich museum we met a survivor who had spent her early youth in concentration and displaced person camps. She had come specifically to see the DP exhibit. As we talked, she made an expansive gesture with her arms at the photographs and posters and said, with tears in her eyes, in English, "This is my life!"

An American veteran, returning to Buchenwald for the first time since the day he accompanied Patton at the camp's liberation, compared the photos he had taken to those in the exhibit. "I must have been standing right next to their photographer. The same faces. . . . We pulled the bodies out of the car. . . . There were so many bodies piled up. . . . I will never forget all those bodies."

At Birkenau we interviewed a Spanish-speaking couple. He was a Mexican who lives in Houston, Texas, and said he felt compelled to visit Auschwitz-Birkenau ever since he had read an article about it in the *New York Times* a few years back. From his pocket he pulled out a tattered copy of the article to show us. She identified herself as French, but said that she had been born in Ceuta, in Spanish Morocco, to a Catholic mother and a Jewish father, from whom she felt completely estranged. Her son, who had just converted to Judaism, urged her to visit the camp as a part of her coming to grips with her family's heritage.

Most of the overt pilgrim activity we witnessed involved groups, mostly of young people. In the five camps that we visited, perhaps 80 percent of the visitors were teenagers. Of these, the vast majority were local, accompanied by a teacher who in German or Polish or Czech was trying to impart a sense of context for what they were viewing. These groups were clearly not pilgrims, for not once did we observe or hear reference to any sort of ritual activity or any motive other than education. The Jewish groups were different. Mostly they were American or Israeli. Mostly they were secular, with few *kipot* (Hebrew, small cap) in evidence. Many at some point in their visit stopped to light votive candles, recite a Hebrew prayer for the dead, or sing together.

The adult visitors were often in family groups, with the parents exploring with their children the meanings of the Holocaust and the camps. We saw many older couples. Their languages indicated that they were British, French, Dutch, Spanish, Mexican, Argentinian, Irish, or Israeli, and their comments to each other or to us suggested that a large majority was Jewish. In several of the Israeli couples one spouse spoke Polish. Those in their sixties, presumably the children of survivors, quizzed the camp docents on every detail of the displays. Those in their eighties for the most part walked silently from exhibit to exhibit, distant from their spouses, heedless of the guides, resistant to our attempts to engage them in conversation.

Wherever we went, we observed physical indications of pilgrim activity. Strings of folded Japanese paper cranes hung from the oven doors. The visitors' books at the Rashi museum in Worms, the Ghetto Museum in Terezin, the Jewish Museum in Berlin, and several of the camps are peppered with comments from pilgrim-visitors. Defiant phrases: "¡Nunca más!" (Never again!), "Am Israel Chai!" (The People of Israel Live!). Expressions of shock and dismay: "How could they be so savage?" "I don't want to be a member of a species who could do what was done here." And personal messages: "Vera K., daughter of Franz and Marta K., here 1941–1945. Emigrated to Colombia. Lived into their 90s." "Susan S., Philadelphia, granddaughter of a Czech deportee and Holocaust survivor."

Everywhere we saw the tin cans that had held votive candles. Their labels indicated that most were purchased in Israel or the United States. At the outline of the foundation of the Jewish barracks at Buchenwald, the labels were in French, English, Russian, and Hebrew. One bore a photograph of the assassinated Israeli prime minister Yitzhak Rabin. Another, in English, Hebrew, and Russian proclaimed, "Every person has a name." On top of the bunker at Mila 18 in Warsaw, the votive candles were arranged to form a six-pointed star. At Birkenau, despite the signs warning visitors not to venture into the ruins of the crematoria and gas chambers, every niche in the crumbling brick walls held a blue Israeli votive candle container.

Because the shrines of the Holocaust are cemeteries, or cemetery surrogates, we commonly found evidence of cemetery ritual. Pilgrims had placed memorial pebbles on every flat surface where Jews had died or were memorialized. Bouquets of flowers had been left beside the camp barracks, the prison cells, the execution grounds, the gas chambers and crematoria, and the ash pits. In some places kvitlach were slipped into the cracks of exhibit cases or stone monuments the way they would be at a tzadiq's or rebbe's tomb.

SURVIVORS RETURN AS PILGRIMS

As Boris Pahor makes clear, the survivors who return to the shrines of the Shoah are pilgrims, not tourists. They are moved not by idle curiosity, but by a need to come to terms in some fashion with their experiences. The trauma runs so deep in some survivors that they keep as much distance between themselves and their past as possible. Joseph Greenblum, who as a child was interned in Buchenwald, wrote that he wanted never again to visit Germany because "to travel there would evoke anger and painful memories." He contrasted his attitude with that of Rabbi Ismar Schorsch, chancellor of the Jewish Theological Seminary, who believed that such a trip would be "both painful and restorative."[20] Yankel Brandstein, unable to reconcile his bitterness at the destruction of his ancestral world, believed that "to go there and have pleasure is a sin." Peter Iszo Brandstein went back, intending to "eradicate certain places from my mind," but only succeeded in inducing a nervous breakdown.[21]

Painful. Restorative. Those two themes run through the memoirs of the survivors who have found the strength to make a pilgrimage their personal shrine of the Shoah. Sometimes the pain is loud and clear. But sometimes it sneaks up and clubs the pilgrim when he or she is least aware. Rose F., an Auschwitz survivor, visited the camp with her daughter in 1995:

> It was a devastating experience. I took my daughter with me. We went through the museum and I saw those windows filled with hair, and of course it brought back memories of when we were shaved [upon arrival]. And then the room

Confiscated suitcases. Auschwitz, Poland. Photo, D. Gitlitz, 2004.

filled with children's shoes. That was the hardest thing. I had been repressing something before I saw the children's shoes. . . . I saw children carried by Nazi soldiers to the Pit and dropping them into the Pit. Those were the children who had come with us on the transport. At the time, I didn't want to believe that was what I was seeing. I hid that in my memory until I saw the shoes.[22]

Daniel Singer's journey to southern France in 1939 for a sinus condition saved him from the fate suffered by the rest of his family. He described his return to Poland in 1999 as "a journey back into childhood and a pilgrimage from the Warsaw ghetto through Kraków's Kazimierz to Auschwitz in search of a vanished people." He was surprised to find that viewing the killing machinery of the extermination camps did not cause him deep distress, until one small detail penetrated his emotional armor:

I was less affected by such horrors. . . . But I was shattered when I looked at those terrible masterpieces of twentieth-century art, the showcases with the remnant possessions of the dead. Not the hair for textiles or the gold from teeth for ingots, but everyday human objects: brushes, spectacles, suitcases, shoes for kids and adults, and, to crown it all, because the victims believed or fooled themselves that they were being "resettled," a humanité morte, an extraordinary bric-a-brac of kitchen utensils, saucepans, washbowls. My eye was irresistibly drawn to a small child's chamber pot. . . .

In my mind, one child's chamber pot captured the horror . . .[23]

Survivor-pilgrims sometimes anesthetize themselves before returning to the sites of the Holocaust by preparing themselves to expect the worst. Sigmund Diamond, a child of Holocaust survivors, in his memoir of a pilgrimage to Poland in the late 1970s in search of his roots, describes in vivid detail almost everything he sees, and pours out onto the page his personal reactions to those sights and encounters. The exception? His visit to Auschwitz. At Auschwitz his lavish descriptions have turned to cold, brief enumeration. The turbulent emotions he must have felt there speak through the void they leave at the center of the narration.

The trauma felt by returning survivors is not easily shared. In the museum-barrack at Majdanek we met a Polish survivor who had emigrated to Israel in 1956 and had returned for the first time, accompanied by his wife and another couple. He answered our questions in two-word phrases as he leaned on his cane and look vainly for a place to sit down. His mouth was talking to us, but his eyes, and clearly his thoughts, were someplace he was not inviting us to go. On a rainy afternoon in Auschwitz we spoke for a time with Hana Greenfield, a survivor of Terezin, Auschwitz's family camp, and Bergen-Belzen (she was liberated there on April 15, 1945). Our conversation flowed smoothly until a chance question brought back a flood of difficult memories. "You ask is it hard to come back? Very hard. You don't know. I never wanted to come back to this cursed places. Never. It was always gray, muddy." We asked if she remembered how cold it was in the winter. "Cold?" A very long pause. "I don't know. I don't remember anything nice about his place."

Yet for returning survivors, sometimes the telling detail kindles a flicker of positive emotion. Hershel Shanks wrote of visiting Auschwitz in 1990 and of running into some elderly Israelis there. "Before one of the pictures, a small white-haired Israeli stopped short. There in one of the blown-up photos was his own face forty-four years earlier. He pointed, then reached in his wallet; he pulled out three pictures he always carried with him—death camp pictures. One was the same one we were all looking at. He was the only one in the picture who survived."[24]

Traditional Judaism gives a great deal of weight to remembering the dead. Jews observe the anniversary of a loved one's death as a special day. They visit family graves. In some traditions they light candles; in others, they place memorial pebbles on the gravestone to indicate—if not to the deceased, then to the community—that they are fulfilling their religious obligation to honor the departed. Yet the shrines of the Holocaust, and particularly the concentration and killing camps, are graveyards without graves, places of mass murder where the individual victims are subsumed by the enormity of the crime. For the surviving descendants, the anonymity of their vanished loved ones' deaths and graves can be painful. Stuart Schoffman, visiting Auschwitz in 2003 with a large ecumenical group, set aside a moment for a personal memorial. "I say Kaddish for my mother's grandparents by the marshy pond near Crematorium 5 where victims' ashes were dumped. It is the closest thing at Auschwitz to a grave."[25] The novelist André Schwarz-Bart poignantly reminded his readers that there is a much more ubiquitous memorial to the slaughter of the Jews: "The smoke that rises from crematoria obeys physical laws like any other: the particles come together and disperse according to the wind, which propels them. The only pilgrimage, dear reader, would be to look sadly at a stormy sky now and then."[26]

For the children and grandchildren of survivors, return to the places of destruction may bring a sense of closure to a long and painful process of coping with family history. Miriam Zakon, an American-born Israeli from Bnei Brak who visited Poland in 2001 with a party of Orthodox women of the N'shei Agudah movement, took solace in the contemplation room in Auschwitz's Jewish memorial barrack:

> I traveled to Auschwitz carrying three *yahrzeit* candles and a yellow pad. On its clear blue lines were lists of names, line after line of them. Thirty-four of my blood relatives were deported from Munkatz on one black day. . . . Including my husband's relatives, deported from Poland and killed in Auschwitz over the six-year-long span of the war, I brought over 80 names to this place of *kever avos*. As I sat alone in a darkened room, the only area in Auschwitz dedicated solely to Jewish remembrance, surrounded only by the light of flickering *yahrzeit* candles, I felt a tangle of mourning, pride, and connection to the past that I never will forget.[27]

POLITICAL FIGURES AS PILGRIMS

For the most part, heads of state do not visit Holocaust shrines from a sense of need or guilt. Their reasons are seldom personal. They may bill their visits as pilgrimages, but they go because they represent their nation and their visit to a Holocaust shrine positions them, and their nation, on the side of what is good and moral. In 1970 Germany's Chancellor Willy Brandt went to Warsaw's Ghetto Monument to apologize for his country's actions. Gerald Ford in 1975 became the first American president to visit Auschwitz, Pope John Paul II visited in 1979. U.S. President George H. W. Bush senior went in 1989.[28] England's Queen Elizabeth and German Chancellor Helmut Kohl each visited in 1995. President Jacques Chirac of France and Greek President Kostis Stephanopoulos went in 1996. Canadian Prime Minister Jean Chretien in 1999. U.S. President George W. Bush in 2003. Representatives at ceremonies on January 27, 2005, commemorating the sixtieth anniversary of the liberation of the camp included the presidents of France, Germany, Russia, Austria, the Ukraine, and Israel; Vice President Richard B. Cheney represented the United States.

Politicians visit Jewish holy places in Israel and sometimes in other countries (as when Moroccan officials take part in a hillula at a tzadiq's tomb) to project a bond of solidarity with the Jewish people. Those who make a pilgrimage to a Holocaust shrine—almost always Auschwitz, which has come to stand for the entire Nazi killing machine—go mainly to make a symbolic statement, to woo allies, or to curry votes at home. In June 2003 George W. Bush made his pilgrimage to Auschwitz. As he told TV Poland in a May 29 White House interview, "I think it's very important for the Polish people to understand how deeply Americans appreciate their sacrifice and their courage and their willingness to work with us in Iraq and in Afghanistan. I'm also going to Auschwitz to remind people that we must confront evil when we find it."[29]

ECUMENICAL GROUPS AS PILGRIMS

Many Jews make pilgrimage to the shrines of the Shoah with ecumenical groups pursuing a political or religious agenda. These agendas can be quite specific, as with the 2003 pilgrimage to Auschwitz, organized by Emile Shoufani, the Melkite Archbishop of Nazareth; his avowed goal was to create a rapprochement between leaders of the Jewish community in Israel and Europe and leaders of the Muslim and Christian Palestinian communities. Shoufani strove to promote a better understanding of the significance of the Shoah. How Israelis, citizens of the strongest state in the Middle East, because of their roots in the Holocaust feel themselves to be threatened and vulnerable. How their conflicts with Muslim Palestinians have nothing to do with race or religion, but center on territory and political autonomy. And how any overt comparisons of current events with the Shoah are, to say the least, inappropriate. Participating were 260 Israelis (135 Jews, 100 Muslims, 25 Christians), and 200 French citizens and Belgians (140 of whom were Arabs: 70 Christians and 70 Muslims), and 100 journalists.[30] Both Jewish and Muslim participants were criticized by their home constituencies for taking part. Jews feared that the uniqueness of the Jewish experience in the Shoah would be inappropriately compared to current conditions in Palestine. Muslims were accused of fraternizing with the enemy. But as the experience unfolded, the insights seemed to justify the risks. As an Arab journalist participant insisted, the Auschwitz pilgrimage was a "patriotic Arab deed. It was a demonstration of our humanity. Learning about Jewish suffering doesn't hurt our own identity and it doesn't make our own pain invalid. But it will make us more human."[31] Other Arab participants seem to find here an explanation for the Israeli behaviors that they find oppressive, and come to think of themselves as secondary victims of the Holocaust.[32]

Other ecumenical pilgrimages, organized predominantly by Christian groups, aim explicitly at furthering understanding between the two religions (and tacitly at

Pilgrims. Majdanek, Poland. Photo, D. Gitlitz, 2004.

assuaging a nagging Christian sense of guilt for not intervening more vigorously as the events of the Holocaust unfolded). Sometimes these ecumenical pilgrimages take on a decidedly New Age cast, replete with prayer circles, moments of meditation, personalized rites and ceremonies, and emotion-sharing marathons. Laura Carboni's journal report of her 2003 visit to Polish camps as a staff member of the Peacemaker Community's Bearing Witness Retreat captures the flavor of such pilgrimages."[33] Carboni's group of fifty people included survivors and children of survivors, Poles, Israelis, and Germans, some of them grandchildren of SS men. They toured various Jewish sites around Warsaw before visiting Auschwitz. Her reactions—and presumably of the group as a whole—to what she saw are almost entirely visceral rather than analytical. "We arrived at the Auschwitz I camp. We sat down and watched footage from the day they liberated the camps. I could only watch aghast. . . . The horror. The shock. The shock! . . . Beyond words, beyond imagination! . . . My tears turned to uncontrollable sobs . . . and not only despair, but also rage."[34] Carboni went to the camp primed to perceive evil, and the adjectives and adverbs she uses in her narration make clear that evil is what she found. "We passed through the wicked gates of Auschwitz with its cynical archway . . . hair brutally shaved . . . brutal laws of the camp."

The New Age religions' veneration of energy—emanating from the earth, from monuments and artifacts, from groups of people acting in harmony—surfaces at various points in Carboni's narration. "The energy of each of those prison walls, each barrack, each stone, watchtower and wire fence, permeated every fiber of my being, breaking through that layer of shock." "Can I find in Auschwitz, a place of immense suffering, mass murder and extermination, a healing energy? The answer is that I did find there a sacred energy. It is a sacredness born out of the thousands of people from all over the world who go there every year on a pilgrimage to bear witness to what happened there."

As is characteristic of Christian-Jewish ecumenical pilgrimages, participants pray together, often slotting Hebrew prayers into a matrix of worship that is familiar to the Christian members of the group. "It was in this place [the room where prisoners were stripped and shaved]," Carboni noted, "that we formed a circle and performed Kaddish. Ohad, a most sensitive and loving Rabbi, guided us through it. I was raw." Often they create their own rites and ceremonies. "Afterwards, we walked, most of us in silence, to an old torture barrack where we set up candles and again made a large circle."

Later the Peacemaker group shifted to Birkenau, where the members spent several days performing their own ceremonies. According to Carboni,

> After morning breakfast and small group councils, we made our way by foot or bus to the camp and set up meditation cushions and benches in the middle of the . . . selection railway platform[;] we set up our cushions and benches in a circle and placed an Altar in the center. Stones and wood radiating out like the rays of the sun held in its heart center an elaborate carved wooden box where, after we finished reading them, we placed the names of those who died there. Candles interspersed throughout the stones continued to burn throughout the day, keeping the flame of remembrance alive. We alternated between the reading of names and silent meditation.

New Age practices also emphasize personal rituals, idiosyncratic (within a common mold), and solitary (though rarely far from the group). These, too, have a part in the Peacemaker pilgrimage. Carboni reported: "I myself chose to spend a night in the camp. I spent some time walking through the darkness amongst the ruins of barracks, singing and talking with those who perished there. I set up a candle altar inside the children's barrack and performed my own service, allowing my voice to be carried to every nook and cranny, working into the darkness. I sat with the children. I meditated with them."

As is generally the case with New Age rituals, one important purpose is to achieve a sense of community, an idealized foretaste of the worldwide harmonic coexistence that is the ultimate goal. "That evening at the youth hostel our group met all together and the level of deep sharing was astounding," wrote Carboni. "When people ask me about the retreat these days, all I can say is that it was difficult and painful and entailed working through immense suffering and anger. It was also beautiful. It was healing and intensely moving to be with so many people all working through the darkness and reaching out to one another."

THE MARCH OF THE LIVING

Among Jews of the Diaspora, the largest and best-known pilgrimage program to Holocaust sites is the March of the Living. Founded in 1988, every second year it brings tens of thousands of Diaspora teenagers on pilgrimage to Poland and then to Israel. In recent years they have been joined by thousands of Israeli high school students making their own pilgrimage to Poland, as well as by students from NFTY (North American Federation of Temple Youth) and other Jewish youth organizations. The March of the Living experience is tightly structured to serve ends that are overtly Zionist, as its website makes clear:

> The March of the Living is an international, educational program that brings Jewish teens from all over the world to Poland on Yom Hashoah, Holocaust Memorial Day, to march from Auschwitz to Birkenau, the largest concentration camp complex built during World War II, and then to Israel to observe Yom HaZikaron, Israel Memorial Day, and Yom Ha'Atzmaut, Israel Independence Day. The goal of the March of the Living is for these young people to learn the lessons of the Holocaust and to lead the Jewish people into the future vowing *Never Again*.[35]

Advertising emanating from the hundreds of individual synagogues and Jewish communal organizations around the world frequently labels the experience a pilgrimage.[36] Moreover, both brochures of announcement and memoirs by participants make crystal clear that the Polish and Israeli components of the pilgrimage are inextricably linked. The Orloff Central Agency (Davie, Florida) for Jewish Education website, for example, announces the experience this way: "An extraordinarily powerful, intense pilgrimage including one week in Poland experiencing the tragedy of the destruction during the Holocaust, climaxing in a 'March of the Living' of 6,000 Jewish teenagers from around the world from the work camp to the death camp of Auschwitz; followed by an extraordinarily joyous week in Israel highlighted by participation in Israel Independence Day."[37]

The March of the Living experience begins long before the students board the airplane. As one participant put it, "the March begins the moment you make the decision to participate" (Silvio Bar Niv, Mexico).[38] Following that moment is an intense and often protracted orientation program with discussion of Nazism, the Holocaust, the Polish role, and the psychological stresses to which the participants will inevitably be subjected. This appears to have the trappings of an academic program, but this orientation is in fact the first ceremonial event in the pilgrimage to the death camps and the State of Israel. At the same time it builds the sense of shared experience, of communitas, that creates a bond of solidarity within the group.

The purpose of the Polish segment of the pilgrimage is to give the students the opportunity to experience viscerally the destruction of East European Jewry. If students look at all at modern Polish society during their visit, it is only to note bits of data that will confirm their prejudgment that the Poles participated in the Jews' destruction. They have been prepped to see evil, and their diaries reflect that preparation. "I didn't want to get to Poland. When the plane landed, I shivered. When I got off the plane, and for the first time saw that landscape—so cold, so dry, so gray—a sense of insecurity and discomfort took hold of me" (Leonardo Simpser, Mexico; 17). "[There was] a feeling I'd experienced the entire time we were there. Have you ever felt so unwelcome somewhere you could taste it in your mouth?" (Dara Horn, Short Hills, New Jersey).[39]

The Polish segment of the pilgrimage begins in Warsaw, where the students are taken along a "memorial route" from the Umschlagplaz where Jews were herded onto trains for Treblinka, to the area of the former ghetto, past the headquarters of the resistance at Mila 18, to the Rapoport monument dedicated to the ghetto fighters. At each site the students are instructed. They engage in some memorializing activity. They may pray together or individually. Taken as a group, these sites have a common narrative theme: Jews culled from normal life; herded together; transported to the camps; heroic resistance that ultimately failed.

Next, the student pilgrims board buses for the Kraków camps. One way in which the March of the Living engages participants' emotions is by shepherding them through a symbolic replication of the victims' experiences. Sometimes with a heavy hand, sometimes with a deft evocation of a telling detail, the March strives to instill in the students a bond of empathy with the victims, and some measure of appreciation for what they went through. The technique is not unique to Jewish pilgrimage. Christians who walk the Via Dolorosa in Jerusalem are symbolically replicating Jesus's journey to the place of crucifixion. Muslims on the hajj symbolically replicate Muhammad's movements in and around Mecca. Buddhist pilgrims to Bodh Gaya symbolically replicate the succession of activities that led Gautama to enlightenment. Black teenagers in the American South annually retrace the route of the Civil Rights March in Alabama from Selma to Montgomery. Replicate; self-identify; empathize. Sarah M. Brown (USA, 2001) became one with the victims in her poem about the March:

> I stepped into the boxcar, into the darkness
> Sixty years later, I stepped into that very same car.

Pilgrims. Buchenwald, Germany. Photo, D. Gitlitz, 2004.

Both times, I was with friends.
Both times, I peered at the world through a tiny hole in the wall.[40]

Most March of the Living participants are taken to three camps: Treblinka, Majdanek, and Auschwitz-Birkenau. There is some variance in the order in which the groups visit the camps, depending on the groups' dates of arrival and various logistic concerns. The pilgrimage is scheduled so that the culminating three-kilometer march from Auschwitz to Birkenau takes place on Yom HaShoah, Holocaust Remembrance Day. The students wear jackets of Israeli blue, with the emblems of each particular tour group emblazoned on the back. Israeli flags, supplied by the March's organizers, are everywhere, symbolically reclaiming the space both for Israel and the surviving Jewish people as a whole. Many students carry banners and placards, most of them bilingual in Hebrew and the language of the group's home country, identifying the group ("Marcha de la Vida—Mexico") and the March's unofficial motto: "¡Nunca más!" ("Never again!"). The groups form in alphabetical order by nation of origin, with the exception that the contingent from Israel marches first. The March to Birkenau, which is intended to be an emotional highpoint of the pilgrimage, is carefully orchestrated. Here is Dara Horn's description of the start of the 1992 March:

The March would begin at the sounding of the *shofar*. Everyone stopped talking, and the silence weighed heavily around us. Even the rain made no noise. I heard the sound of the *shofar* like the plaintive wailing of a tiny child. The March of the Living had begun. . . . We marched about 10 people across, and I could never see the beginning or the end of the line during the entire journey. For a moment, I wished I was 50 feet tall to be able to see all the people in our ocean of blue jackets, each with a unique face, and to laugh into the mouth of the crematory smokestacks for all their work had come to nothing. Our silence thundered our survival.

North American Federation of Temple Youth (NFTY) pilgrims on railroad tracks. Birkenau, Poland. Photo, D. Gitlitz, 2004.

From the moment the shofar is blown, ritual takes over. The lines of pilgrims, six across, form up behind eighteen representative students carrying flags of Israel and the particular year's dignitaries—distinguished rabbis and political and government representatives, who at times have included Poland's President and both Israel's President and the Chief Rabbi. Not a word is spoken, and the prevailing silence and the ordered line of march help create the sense of communal worship in a sacred space. The long line follows the railroad tracks leading to the Birkenau gate. As the young people enter the killing camp, representative marchers read out hundreds of names of victims. For the marchers, the names individualize the victims, but at the same time the long litany conveys a sense of the immensity of the slaughter. For Dara Horn, it was a moment of epiphany: "As I heard kids from Venezuela, India, South Africa, Mexico and dozens of other countries reading the names of family members who were killed, I began to understand that people everywhere were affected by what happened here . . . the people whose names were read had all met on the platform for a brief final moments in their lives and died right where we stood today." For seventeen-year-old Aviva Goldberg from Winnipeg, Canada, in 2002, the names created a sense of obligation: "to each of them I will give a name and a monument. To every man, to every woman, to every child."[41]

The March's destination is the crematorium ruins where the students remain standing for a long memorial ceremony consisting of speeches, prayers (Kaddish, "El Male Rahamim"), the lighting of candles, and the singing of the Israeli national anthem, "Ha-Tikvah."

The camp visits are intended to shock the students, to affect their emotions in a deep and lasting way. The camps themselves are banal; the details of what went on there are unspeakable. The shock tends to come at the moment the student pilgrims first comprehend that contradiction. Their awe at the moment when the familiar becomes alien is frequently highlighted in their diaries. "Auschwitz looks like a college campus. We went from bunker to bunker looking at the museum there. We stopped to look at this case of suitcases and I saw one with my name on it. Suddenly I could see myself in the camps and I knew I would have not made it. I broke down and had to leave the room in tears" (Sara Marks, Canada).[42] Julie Golick (Canada) had a similar reaction during her pilgrimage in 1999:

> I noticed before we entered that the complex was referred to as "Auschwitz Museum." It made me feel a little funny, as if this was all a joke and a form of denial. Anyway . . . we went upstairs then and turned left into a room. There I received my first shock. As I entered, and looked to my left, I felt a lump form in the pit of my stomach. I knew what it was: hair. An entire wall, as long as any classroom I've ever been in. . . . Piles and piles of it. It was all gray. Most of it was matted. I wished that it was all just a big mistake, that I wasn't really seeing what I was seeing. Then I saw a strand of braided hair. Just that, a braid. The lump got bigger.[43]

In the camps the Jewish victims who had been banished from everyday life in Germany and Eastern Europe were banished from life altogether. The student-pilgrims know this, and through their visits they come to feel it intensely. One way of dealing with the immensity of this loss of lives is to symbolically reclaim the camp spaces, to sacralize them for living Jews. The Israeli flags and the pilgrim marchers' blue jackets have this purpose. So, too, does the tableau of Jewish dignitaries conducting memorial ceremonies in front of the crematorium. A reclaiming activity on an individual scale occurs when the students are each given a small wooden plaque and told to inscribe it with the name of a family member or loved one or some other individual whom they have known or learned about who perished in the Holocaust and to place it in the camp in some spot meaningful to the student. Canadian Sarah Marks linked the living and the dead on hers:

> I dedicated mine to my great-grandparents who were lucky enough to be in America and to my mother who thinks she will never be able to make this trip. On the other side I wrote, "To the 6 million burned by the flames of hatred. Your voices and souls are in the voices and souls of the participants of the March of the Living 1994." . . . I sat on the railroad tracks and took everything in. I lit a few candles and placed my plaque right in the spot I sat in.

As the survivors' numbers dwindle with the passage of time, their communities increasingly prize them as a precious resource. Because they are witnesses who experienced the Nazi horrors firsthand, they speak with the voice of authenticity. One of the March's key features are these Holocaust survivors, from the students' home communities whenever possible, who accompany the groups. The survivors see the journey as an opportunity to transmit a portion of their experience on to the next generations of Jews. For some of them it is the first time they have returned to Poland. As witnesses with their firsthand accounts, the survivors help connect the high school students with the events of the 1940s, and help focus the March's ideological message, that stateless Jews were vulnerable, that Israel is the Jews' only hope for a prideful, safe existence. Inge Spitz accompanied the 2001 Canadian pilgrim group and saw her participation as a refutation of the Nazi agenda: "We are here. You did not succeed."[44] For Rena Schondorf, who survived Birkenau, the dominant note was pride: "This time we entered as proud Jews, not as beaten Jews." To Nathan Leipeiger, the bittersweet March tasted not of refutation but of hope for the future: "It was bitter because of my own memories of the death march with my father. . . . It was sweet because I was with thousands of young people—articulate, intelligent and committed—who are our future leaders."

Hana Greenfield was the survivor who accompanied the NFTY group that we tagged along with at Auschwitz-Birkenau in 2004.[45] Their closing act at the Birkenau crematorium resembled the March of the Living ceremony in almost every detail. About 200 teenagers sat in the amphitheater accompanied by their adult leaders and flanked by Israeli security men with bulging jackets. Six students took charge of leading the ceremony. One opened with a speech about how they started as tourists, but now saw themselves as pilgrims and witnesses to the survival of the Jewish people. Then another played the guitar while everyone sang "Am Yisrael Chai" ("The People of Israel Live"). Another student placed some small stones, which someone had brought from Israel, next to the wreaths of flowers by the crematorium. Next, they sang "El Male Rahamim," the hymn acknowledging God's mercy that is sung at every traditional Jewish funeral. When Greenfield was introduced, all other sound ceased. She spoke of the fear and anguish she felt as a sixteen-year-old being separated from her mother as they exited the transport train. As the details of her first few days in the camps emerged, the American teenagers seemed to be sharing her fright and bewilderment. When she finished her narration, there was complete silence. Then a student led the group, which had been welded by their shared experience into a congregation, in a recitation of the

NFTY pilgrims: ceremony at crematorium. Birkenau, Poland. Photo, D. Gitlitz, 2004.

Kaddish, the traditional prayer for the dead. They ended by singing "Ha-Tikvah," Israel's national anthem, starting low but swelling in volume as the song progressed. We, the security guards, and many of the casual onlookers joined in.

The March of the Living is built around a syllogism: We were defenseless against the forces of anti-Semitism because we had no state of our own, so that they were able to destroy 6,000,000 of us. This must not happen again. Therefore we must have our own state in order to be safe. This message, overtly and subliminally, pervades the March. And the high school students prove to be fertile ground for this idea. For them, Poland is oppressive. "How foggy and cold and dreary it was on that day as we all got off the plane. It is such a sad and solemn place. Nobody's friendly and, surely, nobody smiles" (Rachel Block, Phoenix, Arizona).[46] These student-pilgrims believed that they were passing through alien lands, and that any redeeming spark was to be found not among the native population, but among themselves.

The March of the Living pilgrimage visits several other Jewish sites in Poland, but almost always with a focus on the culture that was lost and on the trauma of its destruction. Warsaw's Jewish cemetery? "When I think of how many people are buried there, and their importance for the Jewish people, I realize how much was lost" (Leonardo Simpser, Mexico). The Warsaw synagogue? "We davened in the only shul left in Warsaw. It is a beautiful Orthodox synagogue that was kept during the war as horse stables. One of the 200 Polish Jews left in Warsaw opened the ark for us and sang a Jewish song that we sing every Shabbat" (Rachel Block, Phoenix, Arizona). The shtetl of Tykocin, near the Lithuanian border? "[It is] a town that used to have a Jewish majority (now there are no Jews living there—even those who survived the camps were chased out by their neighbors). . . . We leave Tykocin, making it once more 'Jew free'" (Dara Horn). Even the student dance at the close of the Sabbath is bittersweet. "I sat down for a minute next to a girl I had met earlier this week, whose mother had been hidden in Hungary as a child while the rest of her family was wiped out. We had both been dancing . . . I noticed that she was crying a little. When I asked her why, she said simply, 'Look, we're in Poland.' . . . I looked around again at everybody celebrating in Poland, our graveyard, and I did something I never did before: I laughed and cried at the same time. I cried because there was nothing to do but cry" (Dara Horn).

For the several thousand Jews who in recent decades have made their homes in Eastern Europe, the syllogistic Zionist story line can be an affront. As Rabbi Marna Sapsowitz, who spent December 2003 in the pulpit of Warsaw's liberal/ progressive congregation of Beit Warszawa, put it, "Polish Jews hate it. They perceive that what is conveyed to these kids is that Poland is one big Jewish cemetery and that there are no living Jews here. . . . Polish Jews want Jews from around the world to know that there are Jews in Poland! They report that their invitations to visiting groups of Jewish teenagers to join them in celebrating Shabbat are repeatedly declined. They wonder why the group organizers aren't interested in living Polish Jews, only dead ones."[47]

If there is anything positive to be found in Poland for these teenage pilgrims, it is a kind of in-your-face pride that the Jewish people survived. "I was at the front of the March, carrying the Israel flag. At one point, when we reached the top of the hill, I looked back and saw a sea of blue jackets following me. I've never felt more pride in being Jewish than at that moment" (Ilanna Besner, Montreal). "I felt even prouder when we finished the ceremony in Birkenau after the March, when all of us sang Hatikvah. It was the common language that unified us" (Janice Bacher, Montreal). "I thought about how big a number six million Jews must be. . . . And then I thought about how surprised and proud they would be at the same time, if they were to see what would follow, if they were to see this March" (Rachel Bernstein, Toronto).

For the high school students, Poland was oppressive, claustrophobic. "Israel. I urgently needed to get there. The closer we got, little by little I felt like a great weight was being lifted from me" (Leonardo Simpser, Mexico). "The March of the Living helped me to understand that as Jews we are vulnerable outside of Israel, that we are in danger" (Dov Mareyna, Mexico). The Israel component of their pilgrimage completes the religious and political paradigm, the journey from weakness to strength, from Diaspora to in-gathering, from being the "other" to defining the majority, from darkness to light. The students are so well prepared to receive this message that it is no surprise that their own words echo it back. "Leaving Poland for Israel is like passing from cold darkness to warm light" (Silvio Bar Niv, Mexico). "When I got off the airplane and stepped on Israeli soil, that cold I was telling you about went away, went away for ever, and became a Jewish warmth, happiness, pride, and resolve to fight" (Adrián G. Florens, Mexico). "This really was a journey from darkness to light. We had left Poland in the late evening shadows, and as we left the airport [in Israel] I could just see the orange sliver of the sun peering out from behind the Judean hills" (Dara Horn). "As I stood next to the Kotel with my hand upon its wall, I listened, absorbed, imagined, remembered, and prayed. Standing there, a flood of warmth and comfort filled my body. I was in Israel. I was safe" (Sarah Marlin, San Antonio, Texas).[48]

The success and popularity of the March of the Living pilgrimage led to the inauguration in 2003 of a similar program for adults.

PILGRIMAGES OF THE ISRAELI MINISTRY OF EDUCATION

For Israeli teenagers the pilgrimage to Holocaust sites in Poland has become almost routine. Since 1988 over 150,000 Israeli young people have participated in organized pilgrimages, more than a quarter of them with financial assistance from the Ministry of Education. Since the mid-1990s a pilgrimage tour has been built into the curriculum in Israeli high schools. The most visited sites are the Auschwitz-Birkenau and Majdanek camps and Warsaw with its monument to the ghetto resistance fighters. The tours also include visits to the physical vestiges of pre-Holocaust Jewish life in Poland, such as the reconstructed shtetl of Tykocin and the mass graves of the Jews slaughtered there, the remains of the ghettos in Warsaw, Kraków, and Lublin, and synagogues such as Warsaw's Nozyk Synagogue and Kraków's Ramah Synagogue (now a museum). Halakhically-observant Israelis often travel in separate buses, and their itineraries may include graves of noted rabbis like Rabbi Elimelech of Lezhansk, the great yeshiva of Lublin (now a medical school), or the yeshiva at Ger.

As with Diaspora teenagers who make the pilgrimage with the March of the Living, the encounter with the Holocaust on these tours is conditioned by orientation programs prior to departure and is then mediated by the students' teachers and the guides engaged to interpret the sites. The Ministry of Education in 1991 included among its aims for the program, to feel and comprehend the destruction, to understand "the need for a strong, autonomous Jewish state," to comprehend the heroism of those who resisted, and to increase participants' sense of "personal commitment to the continuity of Jewish life and the sovereign existence of the State of Israel."[49] There are minor but important differences between this agenda and that of the March of the Living. The March seeks to foster an appreciation for Israel as a safeguard of Jewish freedom for Jews living in the Diaspora. If it inspires some of the student pilgrims to make aliyah to Israel, so much the better. But aliyah is not its principal goal, and it must be careful not to de-legitimize their families' choice to live outside of Israel. Because participants are recruited through established Jewish organizations, the March delivers its message to students who have already expressed deep commitment to Jewish values.

The Israeli Ministry of Education's Polish pilgrimage program was piloted in 1966–1967. The first groups were young Israelis who felt compelled to visit the Polish sites and had the financial means to travel. The Ministry eventually broadened its ideological base by offering large-scale sponsored tours heavily underwritten by the government. For Israeli leaders, who fear that large numbers of young Israelis are disassociated from both their traditional Jewish roots and the Zionist ideals of their parents' generation, the program's principal rationale is to intensify and fuse the sense of Jewish and Israeli identity in a wide spectrum of the nation's young people. Early participants on the program were quoted widely as having said: "We left as Israelis and returned as Jews."[50]

As with the March of the Living, the Ministry's pilgrimage is shaped in accord with the Zionist foundation narrative, in which Diaspora, characterized by minority status, weakness, and destruction despite individual acts of courage and resistance, is followed by the establishment of Israel, the in-gathering, freedom, and safety through strength. The students leave their secure homes, they travel as a community of pilgrims to visit the anti-shrines of death and destruction, and they return transformed, ready to take their places in the adult world of home which, if the program's aims are realized, they now feel is the only place where they can live fully and safely as Jews.

As with the March, the message and its methods of delivery are tightly structured, with an emphasis on teaching through emotional engagement ("to feel and to try to comprehend"). The guides provide narrative background to what the students experience, but the impact is visceral, not intellectual. It is the product of a succession of ceremonies and rituals (mourning at Auschwitz, celebrating heroism at the Rapoport Monument), the prayers and songs, the display and invocation of symbolic objects such as the Israeli flag, and the shocking physical reality of the camps and the relics of destruction that have been preserved. Here are the places where it happened and the pieces left behind. A key component is the presence of Holocaust survivors who accompany every trip. From the emotional chasms of their memories, these aged Israelis, frequently relatives or neighbors of the young people they accompany, engage the students as witnesses of their witnessing. The emphasis on security arrangements for the pilgrims, as the Israeli anthropologist Jackie Feldman has noted, has important symbolic as well as strategic purposes. Students go everywhere in groups, usually in convoys of buses (alone = danger). They converse mainly with each other and the Israeli adults who accompany them (Poles = the enemy, anti-Semites). They travel with Israeli security agents (only Israel can protect them; and soon they will be Israeli soldiers protecting others).

The shift from pilgrimage to Poland by the self-selected few to mass pilgrimage of young people by status category (high school student, new soldier) has had at least one unfortunate side effect: it is seen to have trivialized the experience. Army officers traveling on a bus tour to Auschwitz in 1997 were observed playing cards. Israeli travel agents in advertised tours combined a pilgrimage to Auschwitz with a visit to a gambling casino. In 1999 a pilgrimage group from a kibbutz high school were caught entertaining strippers of both sexes in their hotel rooms. These incidents were treated by the Israeli press as national scandals, seen as presenting to the Central Europeans a dangerously ugly picture of young Israelis and pointing to deep-seated problems in the country's youth culture.

COMMERCIAL TOURS

It is not surprising that commercially organized tours to Holocaust sites are almost always billed as pilgrimages.[51] Advertising for Holocaust pilgrimage excursions must not only judiciously mingle memorializing and tourist activities, it must engage prospective pilgrims with what they already know, or think they know, about the sites they are going to visit. On the fourth day of one tour, pilgrims "drive to medieval Krakow, once the royal capital of Poland and home of Oscar Schindler."[52] *Medieval* suggests the pilgrim will see quaint old streets and buildings; *royal* suggests palaces; and *Schindler* recalls the 1993 movie *Schindler's List*, a Holocaust-related film with which most prospective customers are likely to be familiar. Tour advertising must walk a fine line between evoking the horror of the Holocaust and entertaining the tourist-pilgrim with glimpses of an idealized, picture postcard Europe. In practice, however, their jarring coupling of the banal stereotypical European picturesque with the brutal artifacts of genocide serves mainly to trivialize the Holocaust.

An American tour company's twelve-day "Jewish Heritage Tour to Poland, the Czech Republic, and Hungary" advertises, for example, that activities in Budapest include these stops: "the Jewish Museum [and] . . . the unique Weeping Willow Memorial, dedicated to Jews who perished during the Nazi reign of terror. Then, on to the Raoul Wallenberg monument, in honor of the Swedish diplomat who saved thousands of Jews during the Holocaust. Tonight, enjoy a boat cruise on the Danube River; see Budapest's most beautiful sights all aglow at night."[53] The lighthearted tourist activities in the early evening seem designed to relieve the tourist-pilgrim from the emotional stress of the day's visits. Toward the end of the visit, the tourist-pilgrim, who may have reached the limit of his or her ability to absorb the Holocaust-related activities, is offered a choice of visiting another concentration camp or having a free day.

HOLOCAUST MUSEUMS

Most Holocaust museums are conceived as storytellers and therefore are structured with a narrative sequence in mind. The U.S. Holocaust Memorial Museum in Washington, D.C., is a case in point, and the strategy repeats with some variation in Los Angeles and Jerusalem. In Washington, the visitor begins with the third floor's narration of Hitler's rise to power and the conditions—political, economic, religious—which made it possible. The second floor guides the visitor through the ghettos and the interment camps, and tours the mechanisms of destruction. The first floor narrates the liberation of the survivors.

Painting history with a broad brush, as these museums do, requires devising strategies to connect the visitors with the experience of individuals as well as with groups. A common approach is to selectively narrow the focus to a representative handful of people whose lives can be narrated in some detail. In Washington, as visitors enter they are given a "passport" with the name, picture, and some biographical information about "their" Holocaust victim. They are invited to project themselves on that person, to accompany him or her through the ghettos and camps, as if they themselves were there. The strategy is an ancient one, and many Jews will connect it with the familiar lines of the story of the Exodus narrated each year in the Passover service: "In every generation each individual is bound to regard himself as if he had gone personally forth from Egypt." A second approach is to salt the exhibit with photographs of individuals, and, whenever possible, to tell what happened to them. In the Washington museum this is accomplished by amassing in a "tower of faces" of 1,500 photographs of people from a single Polish shtetl, Ejszyski, and then narrating how on the two days of Rosh Hashanah in 1941, Nazi killing squads massacred all 4,000 Jewish residents of the shtetl. Likewise, many of the concentration camp museums strive to create a personal bond between the visitor and the victims with photographs or videos or narrated vignettes that link selected individuals in their normal lives before 1939 with their experiences and their deaths in the camps.

Whether visitors to Holocaust museums come as tourists or pilgrims, they are drawn into the experience through the metaphor of journey.[54] They journey through time, from the gathering storm clouds of the early 1930s, the conversion of anti-Semitism into state policy in the late 1930s and early 1940s, and the destruction of European Jewry in the East European concentration camps and killing machines, to the liberation of the few survivors and the founding of the State of Israel in the late 1940s. They also journey through a literal space within the museum. Unlike art museums that invite patrons to wander through the collections in whatever order they please, Holocaust museums channel their visitors through a conceptually sequenced environment.

One of the clearest sequences of simulated experience is described in the website advertising Richmond, Virginia's Museum of the Holocaust:

> As you enter the Museum, you are transported back in time. As you go through the exhibits, you will experience the atmosphere of Dachau Concentration Camp; you will feel as though you are actually on board the ship

"St. Louis." As you enter the city of Frankfurt, Germany, You [*sic*] will hear on the radio the announcement of "Kristallnacht" in a dining room.

You will enter a ghetto and stand in front of Sergeant Rauca, who sent 10,500 men, women and children to their death in one night at the 9th Fort. You will "escape" from the ghetto to a farm in Lithuania where you have the option to crawl through a tunnel to the "hiding place."

"Traveling" in a cattle car, you will enter the "Final Solution": a shower/gas chamber and walk through a crematory.

Afterwards, you will experience Liberation, walk in Displaced Persons (DP) Camps, Cypress [*sic*] and Palestine/Israel. You will also see the ship *Exodus 1947*. This is the ship that launched a nation, the nation known as Israel.

You will experience the very conditions that the millions that were transported to the concentration camps experienced. You may bring a votive candle or purchase one in the Museum Shop to light as a promise to *Never Forget*.[55]

The first task of museums organized in this fashion is to wrench the visiting pilgrims away from their comfortable, everyday existence, much as European Jews were physically and emotionally wrenched into the new, uncomfortable, menacing environment of the ghettos and camps. James Ingo Freed, the designer of the Washington museum, explained how visitors entering from Fourteenth Street encounter a monumental neoclassic screen, intended to deceive people into thinking they are crossing the threshold into a conventional monument. Instead, they find themselves in a shallow courtyard of brick and steel, hemmed in by walls slightly askew, in a threatening, landscape evoking some sort of industrial disassembly line. The museum gate is a lie, as were the monumental gates of many of the camps. "We wanted an evocation of the incomplete. Irresolution, imbalances are built in. . . . We disorient you, shifting and recentering you three times, to separate you emotionally as well as visually from Washington."[56] Architect Daniel Libeskind used this strategy, with an even more radical design, in the Jewish Museum in Berlin. This experience resembles that of every pilgrim who, in leaving home to set out on the road to the shrine, crosses a threshold into a new realm, with new rules, new companions, new concerns. Freed's design, like that of the Los Angeles Museum of the Holocaust and many other such museums, forces visitors into a journey of analogy, inviting them to sequence their experiences with those of the victims. In Freed's words, they progress from "alienation, separation from the body politic. Then there's transportation, then concentration. Then there is death."[57] The road through the museum is punctuated with displays of artifacts, reliquaries that house remnants of both the people who were destroyed and of the instruments of their destruction. The corridors are narrow. It is difficult to pause, impossible to turn back. The throngs of people pressing forward may awaken feelings of claustrophobia. Here there are no alternate routes, only a single channel fabricated to sluice masses of people toward an end predetermined but as yet uncertain. The chatter that filled the museum's early passageways has given way to silence. Clips of film are played over and over on the video monitors—jarring, disquieting, seductive—obliging the pilgrim-visitors to share the experiences of the victims, the perpetrators, and the liberators of the camps.

The road leads to a small wooden boxcar. Number 31599-G. Not a replica, but the real boxcar that transported thousands of real Jews to their deaths. It has four slatted windows and its doors bolt from the outside. Here the paradox of pilgrimage is most deeply felt. Sacredness, transcendence, the breath of the deity, the taproot of identity—whatever it is that pilgrims seek is always more strongly experienced when the pilgrim can establish physical contact with some aspect of the focus of his or her veneration. To touch a relic, some physical remnant of the past that brings its mystery to the present, is to touch the magic that gave it power. To replicate an event, in the place where it occurred, is to experience that event in a way that goes beyond the symbolic or the intellectual. Visitors to the Holocaust Memorial Museum will not travel in that boxcar to a Nazi killing camp—though it is quite possible that among them are one or two Holocaust survivors who did indeed ride in this boxcar, or one like it, to what should have been their death—but its stark, physical reality may transport the pilgrims for a moment into the darkest regions of 1944.

The boxcar is a text without words, in which each visiting pilgrim can read many meanings. It is half of a dialog, with the other half supplied by each pilgrim's own life experiences. It may shout or whisper. Its overtones, like those of the artifacts in all of the Holocaust memorials and museums and tourist-friendly concentration camps, include despair, hope, grief, solitude, solidarity, guilt, horror, and even irony. The Washington museum pilgrims have a choice: they can follow the road into the boxcar, or they can circle around it. That was a choice not available to East European Jews in 1944.

Organizers intend that their museums and monuments convey meanings both textually and symbolically. They hope to shape the responses of their pilgrim-visitors, knowing that complete control will always elude them. Helen Fagin, who in 1984 joined a six-year effort to put together the Holocaust Memorial in Miami, Florida, described, both explicitly and through her choice of adjectives, the intended effect of its symbolism on visitors. Their first impression is to be of contrasting elements, "luminous Jerusalem stone" and "somber black granite." Inscribed on the granite panels is a

> short but concise history of the event, from 1933 through 1945 [followed by] a chronological pictorial depiction of Holocaust events and experiences, accompanied by textual explanations and maps. Interrupting this pilgrimage is an Eternal Light and an enclosed shrine-like space leading to a narrow passage. The decreasing ceiling height of the tunnel creates the feeling of a diminished self, while the names of the most infamous death camps stare out of the two narrowing walls at the visitor.[58]

The pilgrims then encounter a forty-foot-high bronze sculpture that "depicts close to one hundred figures in different family groupings. They cry out with anguish, they tell of pain, of despair, of life and of death in a man-made hell. Topping the sculpture is a hand evolving from an arm bearing the ultimate mark of man's dehumanization, a number which became man's identification, canceling his real human identity." They come next to a wall inscribed with names, a "sort of surrogate gravestone," and then to a quiet reflecting pool. "At the end, one leaves having experienced an unusual epiphany. . . ."[59] Washington's Holocaust Memorial Museum conducts its pilgrim-visitors into a similar space: a six-sided, stone, completely empty Hall of Remembrance, whose tiers of steps invite quiet contemplation. Yad Vashem, the Jewish Museum in Berlin, the Jewish Memorial at Auschwitz, and many others conduct the pilgrim-visitor toward the end of the symbolic journey into similar contemplative spaces.

The Simon Wiesenthal Center's Beit Hashoah–Museum of Tolerance in Los Angeles is much more aggressive in channeling its visitor-pilgrims through experiences that hammer home the consequences of intolerance. The museum's first half deals with stereotyping. As they go in, visitors have to choose whether to enter through a door marked "Prejudiced" or a door marked "Unprejudiced." The museum's prevailing theme is unsubtle: the second door cannot be opened. Subsequent rooms bombard the visitors with technologically-sophisticated hands-on exhibits that explore the pathologies of prejudice and require the participant to make moral choices. Most topics are drawn from local culture: the Los Angeles Riots, racial epithets and graffiti, American hate groups. The Holocaust half of the Los Angeles museum requires pilgrim-visitors to travel as a group. Each carries a "photo passport" identifying him as some particular European Jew from the 1930s. The road takes them past a series of dioramas depicting the events leading to the Holocaust. Just beyond the section detailing the roundups, the concentration of the Jews in ghettos and the deportations, the road surface changes from carpet to concrete, and visitors are led through a gate into an environment of a killing camp. Again there are two doors ("Children and Others," and "Able-bodied"). This time both open but they lead to the same place, an enclosed area that feels like a gas chamber. At the end of the pilgrims' Holocaust journey, they emerge into a "Global Situation Room" that flashes up-to-date information about incidences of stereotyping, persecution, and genocide, thus bringing together the museum's two halves.[60]

Anne Frank's house in Amsterdam (Netherlands) is both a place of destruction and a memorial museum. In the four-story house and shop at 236 Prinsengracht Canal, Anne's family and four other Jews took refuge on July 9, 1942, and hid for three years before they were caught and sent to the camps. Anne Frank died in Bergen-Belsen and the diary she left behind has become the main portal through which hundreds of thousands of young readers enter the world of the Holocaust. This tiny museum-memorial, with more than 600,000 visitors per year, is Amsterdam's third-most visited tourist site. It serves simultaneously as a place of pilgrimage for people who feel deeply about the brutality of totalitarian states toward children, for survivors and their descendants who had to wall themselves up out of sight to escape the killing machines, and for Jews in general.[61] Like the other museums we have mentioned, it is configured as a narrative. Visitors first view a film about the Holocaust that ends with bulldozers clearing bodies at Bergen-Belsen, and then pass through the house's false wall that disassociates visitors from their here/now and leads them into the intimate, alien time and spaces of the Frank family's hideout. The rooms are small, the visitors many. The atmosphere of claustrophobia is palpable. One by one the visitors, now pilgrims, pass through the bedrooms with their tightly shuttered windows and walls decorated with Anne's photographs and drawings, then the toilet and the nook that served as a kitchen. It is not hard to imagine how the Frank family must have felt being constrained inside these very walls for so long. Finally, the pilgrim-visitors descend to an exhibition space displaying Anne's diary translated into more than fifty languages. Now the visitors are back on familiar territory. They know books, they know the diary, and they can exit into the street with the feeling—familiar to pilgrims whose journeys symbolically replicate those of the holy persons whom they venerate—that they have somehow shared Anne's experiences.

More than any other Holocaust museum, Jerusalem's Yad Vashem Holocaust Martyrs' and Heroes' Remembrance Museum, established by an act of the Knesset in 1953, calls on the tourist to become a pilgrim. Over 1,250,000 people visit the complex each year. Paying respects to Holocaust victims at Yad Vashem has become an obligatory act for foreign dignitaries making their first visit to Israel. If a Diaspora Jew visits only two sites in Jerusalem, they will be the Temple's Western Wall and Yad Vashem.

As with the other museums we have discussed, in its narrative sections Yad Vashem allows visitor-pilgrims to progress along a chronological path from the rise of Nazism to the founding of Israel. From pre-Holocaust Germany, visitors pass through a narrow tunnel, intended to evoke the sewer pipes used as highways by Warsaw's ghetto fighters, to photographs and realia that chronicle the Shoah itself. The path ends in the Hall of Remembrance, a contemplative space covered with a tent-like roof. On the floor are large stones inscribed with the names of the six Nazi killing camps, various concentration camps, and other European sites where large numbers of Jews were murdered. It is in this deliberately shrine-like space that visiting dignitaries attend memorial ceremonies. Pilgrims may also visit the Sanctuary of Names to search out the names of their murdered friends and relatives and what is known about the circumstances of their deaths.

However, unlike the major museums built since the 1980s, Yad Vashem's extensive grounds and multiple exhibition, conference, and study spaces allow the visitor to wander at will. One of the complex's most moving features is a Children's Memorial where visitors can light candles in memory of the 1,500,000 Jewish children killed during the Shoah. Yad Vashem also contains a museum of artworks related to the Holocaust, an immense library, an archive of documents related to the Holocaust, a school, and a conference center. In an outdoor Valley of the Communities the names of more than 5,000 destroyed Jewish communities are listed. There is also an Avenue of the Righteous Among the Nations, in which trees have been dedicated to notable non-Jews who took great risks to save Jews during the Nazi period.

One of the principal purposes of Holocaust museums is to evoke a strong emotional response from visitors, be they Jews or not. An American Catholic on a 2002 parish-sponsored pilgrimage to the Holy Land described her response to her visit to Yad Vashem as "one of the most moving experiences of my life." She and the rest of her pilgrim group wept as they emerged from the Children's Memorial. The mosaic in the museum's Hall of Remembrance "brought home to me just how vast a number six million is."[62] The creators of these museums intend for the emotional jolt to permanently affect the perspective of the visitor, and that in the best of cases it will translate into an action agenda of some sort. Presumably the outcome of the experience for the American Catholic pilgrims is a greater sympathy for the victimized Jews, an understanding of Israel's sense of isolation and precariousness, and her preoccupation with security issues. Other outcomes might be more active political or financial support for Israel, or efforts to stop genocide in other parts of the world.

On March 15, 2005, the new Holocaust History Museum opened at Yad Vashem. Whereas the original museum focused on the collective destruction of European Judaism during the Shoah, the renovated museum emphasizes dozens of individual, intimate stories of people who were herded into ghettos and camps and eventually consigned to slaughter. Recreated home environments, poems, artifacts, and diaries help give human depth to the faces and names of victims recorded in the Museum's archives. As did its predecessor, the new Holocaust History Museum buttresses the Zionist vision of Israel as homeland and refuge as it exits visitors onto a cantilevered balcony with a panoramic view of Jerusalem. As Prime Minister Ariel Sharon remarked at the museum's opening, "When you leave this museum, you see the sky of Jerusalem. I know how a Jew feels when he emerges from these depths and breathes the air of Jerusalem. He feels at home. He feels protected. He feels the terrible difference between living in one's own country, in one's homeland, in a country which can provide protection, and standing alone, utterly defenseless, confronting a beast in human form."[63]

TOO MUCH OF A GOOD THING?

One of the most ironic objections to the European camp memorials and the proliferation of Holocaust museums is that they do their jobs too well. They heighten the general public's awareness of Jews and of things Jewish, but they do so only in terms of the destruction of the major part of European Jewry.[64] Many Jews find several aspects of this upsetting.

The first is that restricting historical focus to a single tragic ten-year period necessarily glosses over the rich artistic, philosophical, and theological contributions of countless individuals. Young bitterly observed that the fact "that a murdered people remains known in Holocaust museums anywhere by their scattered belongings, and not by their spiritual works, that their lives should be recalled primarily through the images of their death, may be the ultimate travesty."[65] Modern secular Jews, the argument goes, find it too easy to anchor their sense of Jewish identity to the Shoah. At its memorials the Holocaust is accessible, largely through the emotions, to the majority of modern Jews who do not have the theological or linguistic training, the time or the will to delve deeply into pre-Holocaust European culture. A pilgrimage to a Holocaust shrine lets Jews off too easily; it releases them from the obligation to appreciate the world of their ancestors. Not to mention the fact that people from the cultures of the perpetrators may find a visit to a Holocaust shrine a comfortably easy way to expiate their nations' guilt.[66]

A second concern, particularly among ardent Zionists, is that the Shoah should never be memorialized in and of itself, but only as the prelude to the founding of the Jewish national homeland in Israel. For Rabbi Stewart Weiss, for example, who protested the cancellation of the Israeli half of the March of the Living program in 2002 because of security concerns, the March is meaningless if it does not have both its yin and its yang: "By removing Israel—the centerpiece of this entire phenomenon—from the equation, the entire raison d'être of the March has evaporated. There is simply no point in making a pilgrimage to Poland if Auschwitz remains the final stop on the journey. It is only in the ascent to Israel—and subsequent celebration of Yom Ha'Atzmaut on Jewish soil—that the transition from darkness to light and from degradation to glory is effected."[67]

A third concern is that the cult of Holocaust memory fosters an ideology of victimhood. This is the flip side of the idea that only the State of Israel can insure that something like the Holocaust can never again happen to the Jews. Too much focus on the Shoah does not create a confident, healthy sense of identity based on pride of achievement, but rather an identity steeped in precariousness and paranoia—unfortunately never altogether unjustified. The hyper-attention given to the Holocaust, manifest in ceremonies and monuments and pilgrimages to the shrines of the Shoah, tends to stereotype the prewar European Jewry as passive. These attitudes have far-reaching psychological consequences, particularly for the ways that Israel deals with her neighbors: The non-Jewish world is our enemy, if not today, then potentially tomorrow. We can trust no one, only ourselves. Any posture except vigorous militancy is a sign of weakness, and invites a repetition of the tragic events of the Shoah.

THE SHRINES OF NATIONHOOD

I left one spring morning in the year 1909 . . . on a tour to Palestine, a journey which was to me, as to so many others, a dream of delight. . . .

Soon we shall stand upon the land of the Patriarchs, Prophets and Kings, walk amid the ruins of fortresses, temples and homes of our glorious ancestors, wander through the ancient wonder-fields and cities of the Bible, . . . and travel through the plains, mountains and valleys that were conquered and defended by the heroes of our history and are the sole surviving witness of Israel's national life in times gone by. (Benjamin Lee Gordon, 1919)[1]

Holy places and pilgrimages to them are often bound up with concepts of territoriality. A major shrine is an *axis mundi*, the earthly terminus of the conduit that connects people with their god, and a locus for the power that molds their religious and ethical behaviors. It can also give focus to a territorial identity, serving as a cairn that indicates to a people and to their neighbors that this is their land given to them by their god. Lesser shrines—the tombs of saints and places where miraculous events occurred—extend the range of presumed ownership. During the centuries of exile, Palestine's holy places drew pilgrims from the far reaches of the Galut and were the focus of the Jewish people's yearning for permanent return to their homeland. The shrines exerted two types of magnetism. Theologically, the Holy Land, and particularly Jerusalem, were the places where God's presence, his Shechinah, was most strongly felt. Historically, it was the locus of familiar Bible stories.

Jerusalem and the Holy Land's other shrines were predominantly religious in nature. During the long dispersion Jews made the arduous journey to visit them primarily for reasons of spirit. For the most part, those who attempted to remain in Palestine did so to hasten the coming of the Messiah. Some yearned to die in Jerusalem and be buried on the Mount of Olives to insure their speedy resurrection at the end of time. Others came to Jerusalem, Safed, or Tiberias to study Torah with renowned rabbis. Very few thought practicably about building a new Jewish nation in the land once ruled by David and Solomon.

ZIONISM, PILGRIMAGE, AND ALIYAH

For the late-nineteenth-century and early-twentieth-century Zionists who dreamed of re-establishing a Jewish nation in the ancestral homeland of Palestine, the medieval Jewish pilgrimage culture offered both opportunities and difficulties. Earlier pilgrimage to Judaism's holy places had stemmed from a deep religious faith. Many early Zionists, on the other hand, were ardent secularists, some of whom considered organized religion as contributing to, not alleviating, the Jews' ills. Their personal convictions inclined them to distance themselves from religious pilgrimage and to undercut the principles on which it was founded. For them, God was not punishing Jews with exile because of their communal sins; rather, Jews were the victims of historical anti-Semitism. If Jews in the Diaspora had been landless, here they must have land. If they had been urban merchants, here they must be pioneer farmers. If they had been weak and fragmented, here they must be united and strong. If their Jewish identity had been tied mainly to their beliefs and religious practices, here it must be grounded in nationhood. If in the Galut they had waited endlessly for the Messiah to lead them back to the Holy Land, now they must take their fate into their own hands and marshal their physical and financial resources, their political acumen, and their will to forge a new society. By 1880 some 40,000 Jews lived in Palestine, many of them in new settlements constructed with the help of Sir Moses Montefiori.

Theodor Herzl, considered the founder of modern Zionism, would have established a Jewish state in Africa or South America or wherever in the world land and political support could be found. But at the First Zionist Congress in Basel in 1897, he soon learned that the majority of the Eastern European Jews attending had no interest in a Jewish homeland anywhere else but in Palestine. Even in their modernism, their dreams of a territorial homeland were inextricably linked with the traditional religious aspirations of their communities, many of whose members had visited the Holy Land on pilgrimage. The term they often applied to their journey was *aliyah*, in its ancient sense of "going up" to the Temple in Jerusalem. The term was ripe for appropriation by the early Zionists, who adeptly redefined aliyah in political and territorial terms. Beginning in the early 1880s, a substantial number of Eastern European Jews were already migrating to Palestine in a movement now termed the First Aliyah. With the financial support of England's Baron Rothschild, they had established seven additional agricultural settlements by 1884. The Second Aliyah (1904–1914), spurred by the Russian Revolution, brought waves of idealistic young Jewish socialists to dedicate their manual labor to the building of communal agricultural settlements, *kibbutzim* and *moshavim*, wherever land could be purchased. Successive aliyot—there were six in all prior to 1948—brought more immigrants.

The early Zionists knew that they could build on the ancient pilgrimage tradition by couching their main goals—such as immigration to Palestine and the construction of a strong, land-based Jewish nation—in familiar language. The immigration movement during the pre-independence decades was almost entirely secular, but it was given a quasi-holy cachet by the terminology in which it was couched. The immigrants were labeled by the collective noun *'olim*, or "those who have ascended," another term originally applied to pilgrims. Likewise, *'olim* who subsequently abandoned Palestine for Europe or the Americas were termed *yordim*, "those who have descended."

As the new nation was being created, leaders recognized the need to bring a sense of national unity and pride to the *'olim* who were flooding into Israel from the most diverse cultural traditions and circumstances. One of the factors that united this diversity was their rootedness in historical Judaism as narrated in the Bible. The traditions of the Temple, the three annual harvest pilgrimages, the holy tombs of the Matriarchs and Patriarchs, and the places hallowed by battle and martyrdom were part of a shared culture. Zionist planners knew how reverence for these holy places and the annual pilgrimages to them had helped weld the twelve independent tribes into a unified nation. Their new land needed something similar if it was to gel as a nation. Thus, from the late 1800s through the present day, a large portion of Jewish Zionist leadership has strived to create a secular national religion. Charles Liebman and Eliezer Don-Yehiya have defined this civil religion as "the ceremonials, myths, and creeds which legitimate the social order, unite the population, and mobilize the society's members in pursuit of its dominant political goals. Civil religion is that which is most holy and sacred in the political culture. It forges its adherents into a moral community."[2]

In practical terms, this often meant that the lines between religious and secular goals, strategies, and rituals were deliberately blurred. One way was by drawing connections between Israel's new national holidays and traditional religious practices. The sequence of these festivals, the official ceremonies devised to draw people together to celebrate them, and the physical sites where the commemorations take place, all tie into the Zionist Israeli foundation story as well, instructing the participant, as Jackie Feldman has put it, "that the only alternative to chaos, nihilism and death of the Shoah is the order of the Israeli nation-state."[3] Independence Day (Yom Ha'Atzmaut) was a *hag* (pilgrimage festival), a *yom tov* (holiday), or a *shabbaton* (special Sabbath). After Pesach came Holocaust Remembrance Day (Yom HaShoah) and the Memorial Day for Israel's war dead (Yom HaZikaron). The process worked in the other direction as well, with Hanukah being transformed into a national holiday of independence and triumph over the enemies of the state, publicly celebrated with bonfires, speeches, torch-lighting ceremonies, and athletic contests.

In addition to these holidays, the Zionist movement and, after 1948, the State of Israel have promoted a number of specific places as nationalist shrines. Some of these have roots in ancient religious traditions, which have been co-opted and fused with the ideology of nationalism to foster a sense of national identity and commitment to Israel's prevailing official ideology. Others commemorate relatively current events, but do so in a way that echoes ancient practice. In the remainder of this chapter we will consider five representative shrines of nationhood—Tel Hai, Masada,

Mount Herzl National Cemetery, Yitzhak Rabin's Grave, and Jerusalem's Western Wall—and how the cultic practices associated with them have helped shape and sustain Israel's national identity.

PIONEER MARTYRS, TEL HAI, AND THE SHRINES OF ZIONISM

In 1920 Joseph Trumpeldor and several of his colleagues were killed defending Tel Hai—one of the kibbutzim established to delineate Israel's northern border—from an attack by local Arabs. Trumpeldor had already had a distinguished military career. He had immigrated to Palestine in 1912 after losing an arm in service in the Czar's army in the Russo-Japanese War. In 1914 the Turks exiled him to Egypt, where he organized a Jewish brigade to assist the British in their war against the Ottomans, who were allied with Germany.

Because of his high profile and the story that his last words had been "It is good to die for your land," Trumpeldor was promoted as a hero-martyr by the militant groups that were struggling to increase their foothold on the land. Zionist groups portrayed him as a brave pioneer who made the ultimate sacrifice to defend the home he had wrested from the barren land. Ze'ev Jabotinsky's Union of Zionist Revisionists honored him as a fallen warrior. They founded a youth movement in his honor called Brit Yosef Trumpeldor, or Betar, which was not uncoincidentally the name of the place where Bar Kokhba's troops had made their last stand against the Romans nearly eighteen centuries earlier. Betar and other Zionist youth organizations sponsored periodic youth pilgrimages to Tel Hai, with the largest number gathering for the anniversary of Trumpeldor's death on 11 Adar Beth.

Jewish schoolbooks of the 1920s and 1930s linked Trumpeldor to biblical heroes whose courage and sacrifice in the face of overwhelming odds helped preserve

Norwegian pilgrims at Tel Hai, 2004. Photo, Norwegian Israel Center Against anti-Semitism, Tomter, Norway (www.norskisraelsenter.no). Used by permission.

the Jewish people in their nation.[4] In 1934 a monument in the shape of a roaring lion was erected over Trumpeldor's grave in nearby Kefar Giladi. For more than eighty years the grave has been one of Israel's principal shrines of nationhood, visited regularly by veterans of HaShomer (The Watchman) Association, Betar, and other youth groups who commemorate his sacrifice with ceremonial rites and special memorial prayers. In the 1980s it took on new significance when the religious-nationalist cause that was staking out territorial claims by filling the West Bank and Gaza with new settlements seized upon another statement attributed to one of Tel Hai's fallen defenders: "No settlement is to be deserted, nothing built is to be relinquished." While it still stands as a potent symbol for the Israeli right, in recent years Tel Hai mainly attracts Israeli school groups and American students visiting Israel on summer pilgrimage programs.

MASADA AND "NEVER AGAIN!"

According to the Roman historian Flavius Josephus, after the Jewish revolt against the Romans had broken out in 66 CE, a group of Sicarii (whom he characterized as a violent, religiously motivated group of assassins and thieves) captured Herod's mountain fortress-palace on Masada, overlooking the Red Sea. From there they staged raids against the Romans in Jerusalem and Jewish settlements like that at Ein Gedi. In 73, after the Temple's destruction, 967 men, women, and children barricaded themselves on the mesa top. They resisted a Roman siege for the better part of a year, but when it appeared likely that Roman soldiers were about to overrun their camp, their leader Elazar Ben-Yair persuaded the men to kill their women and children and then each other, until only ten were left. By lot they chose one man to kill the other nine and then commit suicide. The Romans learned the details from two women and five children who had hidden themselves to survive. The fact that Jewish historians and philosophers largely ignored the story for the next eighteen centuries indicates that the episode was generally regarded as cautionary of foolhardy misjudgment.

In the late nineteenth century, however, Zionists revived the story, and by 1920 excursions to Masada had become part of their educational agenda of knowing the land. A Hebrew translation of Josephus's works appeared in 1923. Despite the remoteness of the site and the verticality of the mesa walls—or perhaps because of them—young kibbutzniks began to trek to Masada as an adventure, a right of passage that tested their strength and courage. It was also "a commemorative ritual that re-enacted the spirit of active heroism and love of the country . . . ; the pilgrims' route became a symbolic reenactment of a struggle for survival."[5] As at Tel Hai, by the 1930s the Zionist Revisionist Movement was bringing pilgrimages of young people to Masada to strengthen their resolve with the example of its defenders' suicidal heroism. On the mesa top they would read the stirring words of Yitzhak Lamdon's 1927 Hebrew poem *Masada*: "Masada shall not fall again." A few years later a scout for the Palmach, the strike force of the militant Haganah movement, wrote, "in Masada we saw a war of liberation, a war of heroism, a war of the few against the many, a war of loyalty to the Land, a war of loyalty to the nation."[6] In the 1940s, youth groups hiked to the top on

Passover and conducted ceremonies memorializing their brethren who were perishing in Europe.

At the end of the 1948 War of Independence, Masada was within the borders of Israel, facilitating youth pilgrimages that continued all through the 1950s. The preferred time was shifted to the Hanukah season, with the pilgrimages culminating in rituals that featured the lighting of torches and speeches affirming the age-old commitment of Jews to independence, freedom, and national rebirth. Yigal Yadin's excavations in the early 1960s, the 1961–1962 Adolf Eichmann trial, and the growing importance of the Shoah in the foundation story of the Israeli state heightened Masada's significance as an emblem of the "never again" ideology. From the 1960 until 1986, every new Israeli soldier swore his oath of allegiance and received his first rifle in a torchlit ceremony on the rocky mesa overlooking the Dead Sea.

With the passing of the founding generation and the growth of radical religious nationalists whose aggressive settlements on the West Bank and Gaza were provoking upward cycles of violence, Israeli intellectuals began to rethink the meaning of Josephus's story. Were the defenders of Masada heroic freedom fighters, or were they religious fanatics?[7] Was the mass suicide an act of heroism, as per the vision of the right-wing Likud party, or, as David Ben-Gurion put it, "the inevitable culmination of senseless decisions by a reluctant Jewish settlement compelled by religious terrorists to launch a suicidal rebellion?"[8] The polarized interpretation reflected similar divisions in modern Israeli politics and contributed to diminishing the value of Masada as an unambiguous shrine of nationhood.

Today Masada continues to draw enormous numbers of pilgrims and tourists. It is the second most frequented tourist destination in Israel after Jerusalem. Although collective mass bar mitzvahs continue to be held there, as are a number of commemoration ceremonies throughout the year, ease of access—via the "Snake Path" and recently the cable car—coupled with tourist accommodations along the shore of the Dead Sea has led to a commodification and trivialization of the site, its symbols, and the nationalist pilgrimages that were such an important part of early state history.

MOUNT HERZL: ISRAEL'S NATIONAL CEMETERY

In its location, topography, contents, and presentation, together with the ritual purposes to which they are put, Jerusalem's Mount Herzl cemetery has become one of Israel's most important secular shrines. As did Tel Hai and to a certain extent Masada, it grew out of the Zionist urge to glorify military strength and martyrdom in defense of the homeland. Journeys to the graves of national heroes, particularly on ritual occasions, became a way of linking with the ancient Jewish pilgrimage tradition of visiting the graves of holy figures. Just as the ancient and medieval holy graves helped to sacralize the territory of the Jewish homeland, so too did the grave sites of new martyrs cast their sacred aura over the emerging State of Israel.

Since in the years immediately following independence, neither the Western Wall nor Judaism's traditional holy cemetery on the Mount of Olives was accessible to Jews, a new site had to be chosen for a national cemetery. As Maoz Azaryahu has pointed out, the creation of the Mount Herzl National Cemetery and its investiture with sacred meaning took place in three phases.[9] The first was the decision right after the 1948–1949 Independence War to reinter the body of Theodor Herzl in Jerusalem. As the return of Joseph's body from Egypt provided a tangible symbolic focus for the ending of a period of exile and the beginning of a settlement in a reclaimed homeland, to the Zionist theorists the transfer of Herzl's bones symbolized the end of the Galut and the rebirth of the Jewish state. The site they chose was a barren hillside just west of Jerusalem, at 834 meters the highest hill in the region, which they renamed Mount Herzl. On September 18, 1949, representatives of cities and kibbutzim from all over Israel gathered for the ceremony, which included pouring small bags of earth from each of the settlements into Herzl's grave. Almost immediately the grave became a pilgrimage destination for organized children's and military groups and for individuals from Israel and abroad. Before long the desert hillside had been transformed into a park, and a museum celebrating Herzl's life and accomplishments had been added.

Over the next few years the government promoted a number of ritual events to build up Mount Herzl's significance as one of the new state's central secular shrines. It was the focal point of national Hanukah celebrations, one aspect of which was for runners to bring torches from other sites of heroism and martyrdom across the nation to kindle the national menorah there. It was the place where national protests against certain United Nations decisions were staged, where the annual yahrzeit of Herzl's death was commemorated, and where, at least in the early years, Israel's Independence Day was celebrated. In 1964 the bones of Ze'ev Jabotinsky, the driving force behind revisionist Zionism, were brought from New York and buried near Herzl's bones. His grave, too, was sprinkled with dirt from the graves of other prominent Jews like Trumpeldor and various members of the underground military resistance fighters of the Irgun, who had lost their lives during the struggles to establish the state.

The second phase in the sacralization of Mount Herzl was the construction there of the national military cemetery in 1949. Plantings separated the military graves from those of Herzl and Jabotinsky, and eventually the park-like cemetery was terraced so that the soldiers fallen in each of Israel's wars were memorialized in separate adjoining areas called the Mount Herzl Military Cemetery. A walk through them is a walk through Israeli history. Since the country is small, and almost everyone personally knows someone who was killed in military action, a pilgrimage to the cemetery is both an expression of personal grief and of national identity. The stream of visitors is unending. As with Herzl's tomb, the Military Cemetery is the scene of national public rituals, such as the celebration of Yom HaZikaron. Since 1969 this ceremony has opened at the Western Wall and then proceeded to Mount Herzl, thus symbolically linking Israel's prime religious-national site with its most important secular-national site.

The third phase was the broadening of the Mount Herzl Cemetery to include a pantheon of the graves of Israel's greatest political leaders, called the "Greats of the Nation." This section lies between the Military Cemetery and the graves of the early Zionists. In 1952 Eliezer Kaplan, the finance minister who was key to Israel's survival during the founding period, was buried there at the insistence of David Ben-Gurion, who felt that the project would help fuse pre-state Zionist history (Herzl, Jabotinsky) with the history of the state created as the realization of their dreams. Though not all the great early leaders are buried there (Chaim Weizmann,

Menachem Begin, and Ben-Gurion[10] himself are among the absent), the "Greats of the Nation" section of Mount Herzl now includes the graves of leaders such as Prime Ministers Golda Meir and Levi Eshkol and President Chaim Herzog.[11]

YITZHAK RABIN, A SPONTANEOUS NATIONAL CULT

Prime Minister Yitzhak Rabin was assassinated on November 4, 1995, as he left a pro-peace rally that had turned out 100,000 supporters in Tel Aviv. Rabin, a hero of the Independence War, chief of staff of the Israeli Defense Forces (IDF) in 1964, and, with Moshe Dayan, architect of the Israeli victory in the Six-Day War in 1967, had superb military credentials. He used them during his two terms as Prime Minister to marshal support for efforts to negotiate peace with Israel's neighbors, including the Palestinians. During his first term (1974–1977), he negotiated the peace treaty that returned the Sinai to Egypt. During his second, from 1992–1995, he worked with Yasser Arafat to open the way for a Palestinian state on the West Bank and Gaza. The policy of giving up captured land for the promise of peace split Israeli society down the middle. The pro-peace faction lionized Rabin, while the religious-nationalist right demonized him for his efforts. The assassination had cataclysmic aftereffects that Israel is still struggling to cope with.

U.S. President Bill Clinton attended Rabin's funeral in the Mount Herzl cemetery and saluted him with the phrase "Shalom, Haver" ("Goodbye, friend"). Almost instantly the phrase was plastered on bumper stickers all over Israel and among Jewish communities abroad. Rabin's tomb became an instant pilgrimage site. Authorities calculate that in the next few weeks more than a million and a half visitors made a pilgrimage to his grave site. There they left candles, memorial pebbles, and written messages and kvitlach, just as they would at the tomb of a sainted tzadiq or rebbe or at the Western Wall itself. The grave became an obligatory stop for visiting dignitaries like U. S. Secretary of State Madeline Albright, who visited in 1997 with Rabin's widow; French Prime Minister Lionel Jospin, The E. U. Commissioner for External Relations Chris Patten, and Chinese President Jiang Zeman, who visited in 2000; Canadian Minister of Foreign Affairs John Manley in 2001; President Yowerri Museveni of Uganda in 2003; Prime Minister Meles Zenawi of Etholiopa in 2004; and many others. Rabin's grave continues to draw pilgrims ten years after his death.

The Rabin cult may have sprung up spontaneously, but it is being carefully nurtured by the keepers of Israel's symbolic landscape. While the other tombstones in Mount Herzl's "Greats of the Nation" section are identical, plain, horizontal stone slabs, Rabin's gravestone juts up above the others. Each year on the anniversary of his assassination elaborate ceremonies focus attention on the grave. As with many such events, the government attempts to use them to bring together disparate elements of Israeli society. The ceremonies—now entering the realm of tradition—include a lowering of the national flag to half staff, commemorative events in several government venues, and a memorial ceremony at the tomb itself.

The site outside City Hall in Tel Aviv where Rabin was shot also became an instant memorial, with candles, flowers, and written messages appearing every day.

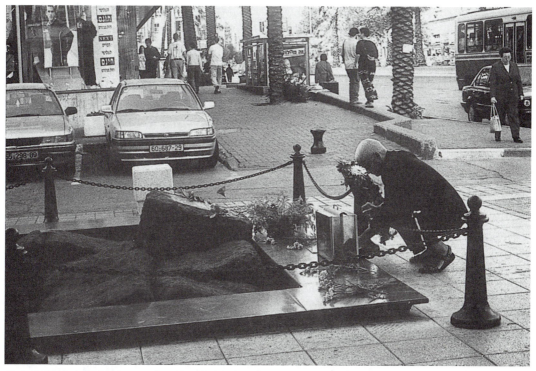

Site of Yitzhak Rabin's assassination. Tel Aviv. Photo, D. Gitlitz, 1997.

Yitzhak Rabin's Tomb. Mount Herzl cemetery. Photo, D. Gitlitz, 1997.

It, too, continues to attract pilgrims. As with Rabin's grave site, spontaneity and official sanction are combined. The place where Rabin fell is now marked by a black memorial stone set into the pavement. As a visiting American high school student wrote in 2003, the place exudes symbolic power, for foreign visitors and some Israeli nationals alike:

> Our whole group assembled into a large circle to hold an emotional memorial service for Rabin, which concluded with the singing of Hatikvah. As we began to sing, two young men who were walking by, both shirtless and in cut off shorts, abruptly stopped and joined our circle. Another lady, who was strolling with her friend down the street, also heard Hatikvah and without a word of explanation hurried from her friend to join us. At the end of their anthems the Israelis walked off as it nothing had happened.[12]

Rabin's anointment by his followers as a martyr for peace also makes his assassination site an ideal stage for political demonstrations, such as the November 3, 2003, gathering of more than 100,000 people to demand that the government abandon the settlements, end the occupation of the West Bank and Gaza, and negotiate peace.[13] The two shrines and the events connected with them also attract noisy dissent from those who disagree with the thrust of Rabin's peace initiatives. During the commemorative season, both sites have to be guarded around the clock to discourage graffiti and vandalism. Although they are widely hallowed as shrines of nationhood, they are not yet shrines to national unity.

PROLIFERATION OF SHRINES

Sometimes it seems that the tomb of everyone whose service to the Israeli nation is particularly valued has come to function as a shrine of nationhood.

The grave of the poetess, pioneer, and agronomy teacher Rachel Bluwstein, whose devotees refer to her merely as Rachel, has attracted a continuous small stream of pilgrims since her death from tuberculosis in 1931. They come to her resting place at Kibbutz Deganya, on the shore of Lake Kinneret, to read her poetry aloud from a book chained to her gravestone, to resonate with her love of the Israeli landscape, and to celebrate her contributions to forging a bond between the Jewish immigrants and the land on which they struggled to live. Because Deganya played such an important role in the development of the kibbutz movement and the creation of the privatized cooperative agricultural moshavim, the entire cemetery is important to the civil national religion, and is known unofficially as the "Pantheon of the Labor Party."[14]

In the cemetery of Nahalal, in the Jezreel Valley, the grave of Colonel Ilan Ramon, the Israeli astronaut who lost his life in the Columbia space shuttle explosion, has been a pilgrimage site since his burial there on February 11, 2003. Pilgrims take pictures of the space shuttle emblem on his grave stone, they place written messages to him in a metal box, and sometimes in groups or as individuals they pray. Interviews with pilgrims the year following his death suggested that they came because he was a good man who "symbolized everything that one could say is positive about this country."[15] As is often the case in Israel, the spontaneous and popular is quickly incorporated into the official national mythology. Information about Colonel Ramon is now part of the material given to licensed tour guides, and the Israeli Defense Force (IDF) has made available a booklet of his letters. Young people with guitars and candles have given way to organized tours. And while they are at the cemetery, many of the tourist-pilgrims also visit the grave of Moshe Dayan.

On the slopes of Mount Gilboa, not far from the cave where Gideon's men mustered before attacking the Midianites (Judges 7:1), is another shrine of nationhood, the grave of Yehoshua Hankin, known as the "Redeemer of the Valley" for his work in the 1920s acquiring 60,000 hectares of land in the Jezreel Valley and accommodating it to agriculture. Just as important is the grave of his wife, Olga, who served the region as a midwife. Though she was secular in her convictions and never bore children, her grave has become a religious as well as a national shrine: childless women from all over Israel come to pray for her intercession in helping them conceive.[16]

Dozens of sites of key events in the War of Independence function as shrines of nationhood. Among them are Yad Mordechai and Nitzanim, kibbutzim that mounted a heroic six-day resistance to attacks before finally falling to the Egyptians.[17] There is Machon Ayalon, a small kibbutz near Rehovot set up for the clandestine manufacture of ammunition for Israeli soldiers. Many pilgrims make their way to Latrun, overlooking the road from Tel Aviv to Jerusalem, which was the site of three battles during the Independence War, and now houses the Israel Tank Corps Museum.

THE KOTEL AS A NATIONAL SHRINE

Since 1967 the Western Wall (*Kotel* in Hebrew) in Jerusalem has attracted an unending stream of Jewish tourists and pilgrims. It may be the one holy site in Judaism that meets all needs: it is a place to pray, to firm up one's personal sense of Jewish identity, to feel the continuity of Jewish history, to engage in some ritual right of passage and to feel at one with the modern State of Israel. On June 7, 1967, when Israeli troops swept into Jerusalem's Old City, they sprinted through the streets dodging sniper fire to get to the Western Wall. There, in full battle gear, they wept and cheered. If they were religious, they prayed. If they were not, they exulted. Barely an hour passed between the soldiers reaching the Wall and General Rabbi Shlomo Goren's blowing the shofar there. A week later, at the start of the pilgrimage festival of Sukkot, 250,000 Jews from all over Israel made their way to the Kotel in what must have been the largest mass pilgrimage to the site since the Romans destroyed the Temple in 70 CE. In addition to its many meanings, the Kotel was now, unambiguously, the emblem of Jerusalem reunited as part of the Jewish State of Israel.

While the Kotel functions as both a secular and a religious shrine in modern Israel, the question of which meaning is predominant often has practical consequences. For example, after the 1967 War a number of ramshackle houses in Jerusalem's Moroccan quarter were bulldozed to create the large ceremonial plaza to the west of the Kotel. If the plaza were a religious shrine, it would pertain to the Ministry of Religious Affairs as an open-air synagogue, with emphasis on decorum, prayer, and strict adherence to halakhic requirements. If it were a secular shrine, it might fall under the auspices of the Ministry of Education and Culture, which could develop its tourist potential and with the Department of Antiquities authorize and supervise further archaeological explorations. The solution? Each ministry would control a subsection of the plaza, thus insuring its sanctity for the tefillin purveyors and Torah stands, and making possible some unobtrusive digging, with everyone collaborating on issues of crowd control, access and egress, and security.[18]

It is impossible to disentangle the mixture of purposes that bring pilgrims, tourists, and worshipers to the Wall. Observant Jews, following presumably ancient practices in acts of worship, are also demonstrating in a political way their insistence that the modern Israeli state be grounded exclusively in halakhic observance. Secular Jews and tourists don cardboard head coverings in acknowledgment of the Wall's ancient and current religious significance. The largest crowds congregate on the three traditional pilgrimage festivals of Passover, Sukkot, and Shavu'ot, conducting a mélange of private and collective rituals that mix prayer, festive communion with family and friends, and celebration of national identity. On Tisha b'Av vast crowds representing every segment of Israeli society, the observant and the secular, Ashkenazim and Sephardim, urban sophisticates and kibbutzniks, the solemn and the festive, Lubavitchers and clutches of dating teenagers, and members of every ethnic group, come together to sing, pray, read from Psalms and Lamentations, and hang out with family and friends, in a "unique . . . foodless picnic," a "meeting of messianic aspiration and national sentiment."[19]

Some of the symbolic rituals of statehood, which were played out elsewhere before 1967, were transposed to the Kotel after the reunification of Jerusalem. The IDF, for example, which formerly swore in new soldiers in a ceremony on Masada, shifted the oath taking to the plaza in front of the Kotel. The overtly nationalist festivals—Independence Day, Holocaust Day, Jerusalem Day—have also come to feature emotionally intense ceremonies at the Wall. All these events commingle religious and nationalistic themes. Just by being present, almost everyone who comes to the Wall—pilgrims, tourists, and the local observant community—is demonstrating a commitment to the fusion of historical, religious, and political currents that flow together there. As Danielle Storper-Perez and Harvey E. Goldberg have noted, even "in the energetic Friday evening dance to the Kotel from the Jewish Quarter on the part of young male yeshiva students, it is difficult to untangle the political overtones from the religious commitment."[20]

ISRAEL AS A SHRINE FOR THE DIASPORA

I am always awed by walking in ancient Jerusalem, and especially when standing and praying next to those ancient stones of the wall my ancestors built millennia ago. . . . These stones which my forefathers walked past on their pilgrimages to the Temple—who knows, perhaps some of my ancestors were even priests in the Temple, or market vendors selling pottery and livestock to the pilgrims. (Leiah Elbaum, 2000)[1]

I was never a pilgrim, but I was a Jew, going to Israel. Do you see what I'm saying? How can you go to Israel as a Jew and be just a tourist? ("Iris," 1998)[2]

I know I've romanticized this country to some sort of ridiculousness, but then that's part of the purpose of Israel, to give us a place to feel so sentimental about that nothing makes sense and sense doesn't matter. . . . As a Jew, I know Israel is the only place in the world that really is my holy land if there is such a thing as holy land. I think there is, but then, I'm not very holy. When the recent violence started up again I felt ashamed that I had not make [sic] my first pilgrimage to Israel. ("Rossi," 2004)[3]

One of the men in our group said to him, "If you go to Israel, what do you do there?" He answered, "Do? You don't do anything. You walk around Jerusalem, you sit in a cafe and you figure out who you are." (Stuart Berman, 1997)[4]

Pilgrimages to the shrines of nationhood support Israelis' sense of national identity and commitment. In an analogous but much broader way, pilgrimage to the State of Israel serves the Diaspora as a touchstone of their Jewishness. For religious Jews in the Diaspora Israel has always been The Holy Land. The

Temple Mount radiates holiness out from Israel's center, and the holy places that dot its hills and plains have attracted religious pilgrims continuously for three millennia.

In the last 150 years many Jews have come to ground their feelings of Jewish identity less on their religious convictions or observances than on their sense of cultural and tribal inheritance. They may even consider themselves agnostic or atheist, yet see no conflict between their lack of religious faith and their personal commitment to Judaism. Large numbers of these secular Jews from the Diaspora visit the State of Israel each year. They go on trips sponsored by the Israeli government, by their individual synagogues, by regional Jewish federations, and by national and international organizations of Jewish teenagers. Some make the journey by themselves or accompanied only by their immediate family. Something in Israel draws them, even though they are likely to find it difficult to put into words precisely what that something is. Some frame their visit as a learning experience and structure their time to include museums, archaeological sites, or the kibbutzim, battlegrounds, cemeteries, and civic monuments that are the scenography of modern Israeli history. Some go to look up distant relatives. Some plant trees, or weep at Yad Vashem. Some bask on the beaches, or shop on Dizengoff Street, or slather their bodies with mud from the Dead Sea. Many declare that they go to Israel because they feel guilty if they have not yet been there.

To these decidedly secular pilgrims we can add the many thousands of Jewish visitors to Israel each year who consider themselves religiously observant to a degree but who are not Orthodox. These are Jews who in the Anglophone West may term themselves Reform or Conservative or Reconstructionist and in much of the rest of the world are just Jews who, without sectarian labeling, are not strictly observant of Halakhah or comfortable with the theological certainties of the Orthodox. In Israel these idiosyncratically observant Jews visit the same wide variety of sites as the secular Jews. But they are also likely to include religiously charged sites on their tour, or to celebrate key family life-cycle events like bar or bat mitzvahs in the Jewish state.

What characterizes such visits to Israel, and particularly most first-time visits, is the extent to which they build on the traditional paradigms of Jewish religious pilgrimage. They involve long-distance travel to a privileged place. They tend to be identity-affirming, ethnicity-reinforcing, and, sometimes life-changing. They often target sites that have been traditionally imbued with religious significance. They engage in behaviors that seem like ritual and are often derived from or are similar to time-hallowed rituals of Jewish pilgrimage. While the visitors themselves characterize their journeys with an array of labels—tourism, study, expressions of solidarity, family reunions, celebration, commemoration, even vacation—the flag under which they travel most frequently is that of pilgrimage.

While modern Jews make pilgrimage to a wide variety of special places (saints' tombs, Holocaust memorials, family homesteads, and sites of Jewish historical significance), Israel is the apex of pilgrimage destinations for both observant and secular Jews. Israel is the gazetteer of biblical events, the time-honored homeland, the refuge from anti-Semitism, the prideful and pride-inducing Jewish state. Israel is holy in a secular way because it was traditionally holy in the religious sense. As Israel's mystical power once lay in its being the principal physical Jewish portal between the mundane and the divine, Israel now functions as a connector between the diffuse Jewish Diaspora, with its infinite gradations of ways of being Jewish, and the historic core of Jewish identity. The thrice-annual pilgrimage to the Temple in biblical Jerusalem helped unite the Hebrew tribes and foster a unified pan-tribal Israelite identity.[5] To a considerable extent, the modern State of Israel serves a similar function for Diaspora Jews today.

Jewish advocates of all stripes view pilgrimage to Israel as a catalyst for fostering their agendas. These run the gamut from secular to religious, from political to moral: To increase the degree of religious observance; to loosen the purse strings of philanthropy for Jewish causes; to increase commitment to Jewish institutions in the Diaspora; to boost immigration; to solidify political support for Israel as the eternal homeland of the Jews and as a refuge in a recurrently anti-Semitic world; and to help Diaspora Jews resist assimilation.

Machpelah; Ruth Gitlitz at Leah's Tomb. Hebron. Photo, James B. Gitlitz, 1976.

ISRAEL AS A CATALYST OF JEWISH IDENTITY

The most common reason why Diaspora Jews make pilgrimage to Israel is to bolster their sense of Jewish identity. The postmodern, increasingly secular world in which most western Jews find themselves has fostered a sense of disconnectedness, of rootlessness, particularly among Jews who are not fully observant. Their Jewish education is likely to be minimal. Increasingly, they are likely to be members of a family in which only one parent is Jewish. They are unlikely to be fluent in Hebrew, so that they have little access to traditional Jewish learning. They rarely know the languages of their immigrant ancestors, so that Yiddishkeit or Ladino, Judeo-Arabic, or Persian literature are similarly closed to them. The Jewish component of their sense of self is likely to center on doing Jewish things in the company of other Jews. For nonaffiliated, nonreligious Jews, their vestigial Jewish identity may be little more than a sense of being part of a continuous tradition. Israel—the ancient homeland and the modern state—connects them to this tradition. For Diaspora Jews, a pilgrimage to Israel provides an opportunity to reexamine and perhaps reshape the ways in which they are Jewish, to experience what the sociologist David Mittelberg calls a process of "reethnification."[6]

This fact is not lost on the Israeli government nor on the myriad of organizations committed to serving the world's Jewish communities, all of which strive to increase Jews' identification with their cultural or religious heritage. A Houston synagogue, for example, promoted its June 2004 "Congregation Beth Yeshurun Pilgrimage to Israel" in this way: "This is an exciting opportunity for you, your family and friends to visit (or revisit) Israel, to walk along the ancient streets of Jerusalem, to stand on the shores of the beautiful Sea of Galilee, to shop along the busy streets of Tel Aviv, and to reaffirm one's Jewish roots in the land where the Jewish People began."[7] An Oakland California Conservative synagogue sponsored "A Historical, Political and Personal Pilgrimage for People of All Ages" in February 2005.[8] A nearby Reform congregation's Pilgrimage in July 2005 offered the opportunity to "walk in the footsteps of our ancestors and witness the modern miracle [of] Israel. . . . Best of all, we will grow as Jews and as a Jewish community."[9]

While most of the synagogue tours—as well as those organized by local Jewish Federations, the United Jewish Appeal, and other broad-based Jewish organizations—are avowedly secular in purpose, they function in many ways that are analogous to religious pilgrimages. The participants tend to bring with them an expectation that what they are going to experience on the trip will affect the ways in which they interpret or practice their Judaism.[10] The tours are mediated by a trained guide or bus driver providing a knowledgeable, authoritative, legitimizing interpretation of what the group is seeing or experiencing. The participants eat, socialize, travel, and pray together, and soon weld themselves into a company of pilgrims whose whole is both greater than and supportive of its individual parts. The group leaders frame a number of ritual experiences that go beyond what the participants are accustomed to at home, and these rituals sacralize the overall experience for the group members. It may be a simple grace after meals, or the wearing of knitted kipot, or the fact that they are eating only kosher food. The pilgrims celebrate Shabbat or other Jewish holidays as a group, with the group members taking roles in the ritual, and the observances are portrayed as special because they are taking place in the Holy Land. They learn a few words of modern Hebrew and are surrounded by Israelis speaking Hebrew, which creates an auditory link between the here-now and the biblical past. They visit historic sites that hammer home the

Pilgrim certificate, 1976. Authors' collection.

seamless continuity of Jewish tradition. The Exodus story is replayed, symbolically, in sites that memorialize the victims of the Shoah and the redemption offered by the creation of the modern Zionist homeland. The martyrs of Masada are linked to the heroes who fell in the War of Independence and subsequent conflicts. The pilgrims may plant a tree in a ceremony that both memorializes departed loved ones and links the pilgrims symbolically to the development of the land. They may visit a kibbutz to see how the urban ghettos of Europe have been replaced by the idealized agricultural world of the Israeli pioneers. The tours are scheduled so that certain key experiences—Friday evening at the Kotel, sunrise at Masada, a wreath-laying at Yad Vashem—will stand in memory as highlights.

LIFE-CYCLE PILGRIMAGES TO ISRAEL

For many Jews, a family pilgrimage to Israel for a life-cycle event has become an identity-affirming ritual. The most popular venue for such an event, particularly for Jewish families from the United States, is the bar mitzvah tour. For religious Jews, the preferred site for celebrating one's bar mitzvah is the Western Wall. They are scheduled with government assistance each Monday and Thursday morning. By Orthodox custom, men and women at the Western Wall are separated by a partition; conservative dress is required; and the young men put on tefillin. Bar mitzvah boys read from the Torah; at bat mitzvahs, male family members read the Torah portion in the young girl's honor.

For families who are having difficulty scheduling at the Western Wall or who are looking for something a little different for their son or daughter, other options are available. The Western Wall Tunnels, located near the precinct of the Holy Temple, were excavated in the 1970s and have become a favored Orthodox venue. For those who prefer a less crowded or less Orthodox environment, other popular

Pilgrims at the Kotel. Kvitlach. Jerusalem. Photo, D. Gitlitz, 1995.

sites in Jerusalem are the South Wall Excavation Area, David's Tower, the Hurva Synagogue, and Mount Scopus. Outside of Jerusalem prime sites are Masada, Ein Gedi, and Neot Kedumim, a privately-run nature preserve ten minutes from the Ben-Gurion Airport that purports to "embody the panorama and power of the landscapes that helped shape the values of the Bible."[11]

The large market for bar/bat mitzvah pilgrimages is a niche recognized by the tourist industry. Tourist companies promote them primarily as a significant religious experience, a way to "celebrate a child's religious entry into adulthood . . . in a more meaningful way than a religious service and a big party back home."[12] No matter what their particulars, in the last analysis all these bar/bat mitzvah tours are designed to strengthen young peoples' identification with Judaism and with the State of Israel. For "Jewish boys and girls reaching bar/bat mitzvah age," as one tour operator puts it, this is "the time for them to get in touch with their Jewish roots and origins in the Land of Israel." The experience will be "enriching, horizon-expanding," and lead to an "internalization of values."[13] It will provide "a young man or woman with an unbreakable link with what it means to be Jewish," as it intensifies "attachment to their Jewish heritage . . ." and helps the family "experience together the phenomenal renaissance of their ancient homeland."[14] In the words of another, the goal is to "make the important connections between the bar/bat mitzvah child, the Land and the Torah."[15]

The religious experience of the bar/bat mitzvah is generally promoted as one component in a pilgrimage package designed to appeal to a broader array of tastes and motivations. The bar/bat mitzvah party is offered opportunities to participate in mini-seminars on historical and religious subjects, to view educational films, to tour archaeological sites, to visit a kibbutz and interact with kibbutzniks in the dining hall, to trek in the desert and meet Bedouins, to spend time with Israeli teenagers, to bob in the Dead Sea or go kayaking on the Jordan River, or to plant a tree. For more religiously-inclined Jews, the bar/bat mitzvah tour may include visits to synagogues, a mikveh, and various saints' tombs. A broadly-focused tour in 2001 assured potential pilgrims that "Bar and Bat Mitzvah opportunities will be available," and also informed them that they will "visit the wonderful eating places that abound in Israel and the holy places and services of Shabbat will allow participants to sample Jerusalem's many wonderful religious communities."[16] Pilgrimage as smorgasbord, not committed to any one main dish but to sample, with bar/bat mitzvah as one of the menu options.

While Jews of any stripe can be bar or bat mitzvah in Israel, marriage is a different matter. Under Israeli law, only the certifiably Orthodox can be married with a religious ceremony in Israel, and civil marriage is not permitted. Thus for Orthodox Jews living in the Diaspora, pilgrimage to Israel to be married at one or another of its holy sites exerts a strong attraction. While bar/bat mitzvah in Israel is intended to be an identity-enhancing experience for teenagers and their friends and family, people who write about their wedding pilgrimages tend to stress the emotional intensity and "the great spiritual benefit of being married in the Holy Land."[17] "My sister made it clear that . . . to be able to get married in Jerusalem on the holiest day of two people's lives would be the greatest gift," wrote Yechiel Fuchs in January 2005. On such an occasion, even the most trivial aspects of the celebration take on a special cast: "The smorgasbord, . . . chupah, dinner and dancing were all beautiful and simply so extraordinary because we were in Jerusalem overwhelmed by the kedusha, the holiness, of Eretz Yisroel."[18] As with bar/bat mitzvahs, there is a variety of holy venues to choose from, with the most popular being Rachel's Tomb, Masada, and almost anywhere in Jerusalem.

DIASPORA YOUTH PILGRIMAGES

Both scholars and activists have long recognized that the most opportune time to affect identity is while it is in the process of forming. Data collected for the 1990 National Jewish Population Survey and from Project Otzma (a year-long community and education program in Israel under the auspices of the Council of Jewish Federations) are remarkably consistent in suggesting that young Jews between their late teens and their mid-twenties are the ones most likely to be meaningfully affected by visiting Israel. The optimal moments appear to be right after high school, the junior year in college, and between college and graduate school. While the experience may affect any aspect of Jewish identity or practice, it consistently correlates positively with increased formal affiliation with Jewish institutions, heightened observance of Jewish religious practices, and enhanced self-esteem in matters relating to Jewish identity, as well as with a decreased rate of marriage with non-Jews.[19] The outcome of this research has been a concentration of efforts to get Diaspora teenagers to visit Israel in the company of other Jews. The American Conservative movement's United Synagogue Youth (USY), the Reform North American Federation of Temple Youth (NFTY), and the Reconstructionist No'ar Hadash, all sponsor youth pilgrimages to Israel, as do Young Judaea, Hadassah, Toujours Israel, Habonim Dror, and numerous other Jewish organizations in the United States, Western Europe, Latin America, and Australia.

The Birthright program, underwritten by a combination of private philanthropy, the Israeli government, and Jewish communities in the Diaspora, is one of the most ambitious efforts to bring western Jewish students on pilgrimage to Israel. Between its inception in 1999 and 2003, it has sponsored ten-day visits to Israel by over 48,000 students from twenty-five different countries. Birthright is open to any Jewish college-age student who has not previously visited Israel on a sponsored group program. The program's purpose, according to its co-founder, Michael Steinhardt, is to "attract students who were not too in touch with their Judaism," in order to intensify their connection with their Jewish heritage so as to "reawaken a renaissance in North American Jewish Culture."[20] Charles Bronfman, one of the principal financial backers of Birthright, is similarly forthright about the program's intent to serve as a catalyst of identity:

> We are saying to young adults—particularly those for whom the idea of being Jewish is at least ambivalent, if not downright negative—that it's decision time in your life. You have to make some fundamental decisions and one of them is who you are. So, why don't you come here, meet some other people and meet your peers in Israel and find out something about how all this happened and what the roots are. Then, you have some information. If you want

to go further, you go further, and if you don't want to go further, you don't go further. But, armed with some knowledge, some sort of beginning, you'll make a better decision.[21]

The directors of Birthright trips and similar pilgrimage programs consistently echo these sentiments. Talia Liebler-Gabay, who led a youth pilgrimage to Israel from Contra Costa, CA, in Summer 2004, reported that students say that it "helps strengthen their Jewish identity."[22] Simone Weichselbaum, who accompanied an American University student pilgrimage to Israel in 2001, told reporters that "the point of the trip is for people to learn about themselves," to which Rabbi Toby Manewith, of the AU Hillel, added that "this trip is not geared to make anyone more religious, but only to allow participants to find their place in their religion."[23] Participants tend to echo these themes.

Do such programs work? A 1990 study of youth pilgrimages to Israel concluded, "Israeli society serves as a 'collective ego' that can help add more meaning to life."[24] A 1997 evaluation of Birthright and similar programs also answered with a resounding yes, as did a follow-up study in 2004. The authors found that these programs have a beneficial impact on students' attitudes toward their Judaism, the Jewish people, Israel, and the relation of all three to their personal sense of Jewish identity.[25] Queens College student Max Sivan, who had no real interest in Judaism prior to the Birthright pilgrimage, wrote that "People came home from this trip and felt things they hadn't felt before. . . . This trip gave them the opportunity to find something they didn't even know they were looking for." Sivan is now an outreach worker for Hillel's Foundation for Jewish Campus Life.[26]

PILGRIMAGE TO DEMONSTRATE SOLIDARITY

World War II, the Shoah, and the traumatic experiences of Jewish communities in many Islamic lands following the creation of the State of Israel have all reinforced commitment to the premise that for Jews Israel is the world's only trustworthy bastion of strength and refuge against the forces of anti-Semitism. The Zionist movement and the government of Israel are grounded on this principle and have promoted it among the communities of the Diaspora. It is a fundamental part of the ideology that fosters aliyah and external financial support for Israel. However, most Jews living in North America, Western Europe, and countries in other parts of the globe with secular governments and universal enfranchisement do not view Israel as a place of potentially imminent asylum for themselves and their families. Nonetheless, they tend to endorse the need to support Israel so that it can be a place of refuge for those Jews who need a safe haven. Western Jews do make aliyah, of course, but most Diaspora Jews do not feel compelled to make Israel their actual homeland. Rather, it serves as an insurance policy whose symbolic value and potential are to be cherished. They tend to believe that for Israel to fulfill its role, it must be helped to remain strong: material help, in the form of contributions; political help, in the form of lobbying governments to support Israel's actions; symbolic help, in the form of expressions of solidarity.

Since Israel's founding, pilgrimages have become a favored vehicle for express-ing solidarity. In 1991, for example, just before the first Persian Gulf War, groups of students from New York's Yeshiva University went to Israel on pilgrimages as "an effort to show solidarity with Israelis on the brink of a Middle East war." Other Yeshiva University students journeyed to Israel on solidarity pilgrimages in 2002, in the midst of the Palestinian Intifada and in March 2003, as violence was escalating once again.[27] That summer, as the Intifada raged and suicide bombers blasted their way onto the evening news, the Jewish Community Federation of San Francisco organized a number of congregation-based solidarity pilgrimages to Israel. Beth Jacob's pilgrimage, called "Meet Israel's Leaders," featured discus-sions with Israeli political, social, and religious leaders. Kol Emeth's pilgrims met with both Israeli and Palestinian victims of the violence. Saratoga's Beth David and Foster City's Peninsula Sinai's pilgrims, called "Torah and Zion," combined Shavu'ot celebrations with visits to important Zionist historic sites.[28] In late July and August 2004, the North American Reform movement sent more than 200 leaders to Israel on a "Spiritual Pilgrimage" intended to "demonstrate the Ameri-can movement's unconditional support of the State of Israel and the Israeli peo-ple."[29] Israel's Ministry of Tourism actively promotes these kinds of pilgrimages. In 2005 its GoIsrael website, for example, invited potential pilgrims to "Start your search here to find a mission, to enable you to show your solidarity with the State of Israel. It's time to make a difference. It's time to say: 'Israel. I care. And I'm going.'"[30]

PILGRIMAGE TO GENERATE POLITICAL SUPPORT

Activists with more focused political agendas related to Israel often use pil-grimages as a way of generating support for their causes. Pilgrimage to express opposition to the monopolistic influence of Israel's Orthodox community on re-ligious life? In 1997 the Union of American Hebrew Congregations urged its members to demonstrate support for religious pluralism in Israel by joining "a sacred pilgrimage to Israel in June, 1998 to meet with government leaders, to make our voice heard by the Israeli public and to worship openly in any sites holy to our people." In 1998, 175 U.S. Reform rabbis joined Rabbi Eric H. Yoffie, the head of the Board of the Union of Hebrew Congregations, to do pre-cisely that.[31]

Pilgrimage to appeal to Jewish voters back home? When Governor James Hunt of North Carolina, running against incumbent Jesse Helms for a senatorial seat, accused the Senator of having the worst anti-Israel record in the Senate, and Helms won the election by the narrowest of margins, Helms began actively to court the Jewish vote. He quickly joined a group of his Jewish supporters on a pil-grimage to Israel, where he posed for pictures—a yarmulke on his head—at the Western Wall.[32] Or to enlist the support of elected officials for Israel? In 1995 the Italian-American mayor of New Haven, Connecticut, accompanied 180 Con-necticut Jews on a pilgrimage to Israel to cement relationships with New Haven's sister cities of Afula-Gilboa in the Galilee. A private grant channeled through the Jewish Federation picked up the mayor's expenses.[33]

While a graduate student in 1967, author Gitlitz inquired at the Israeli consulate in Boston about opportunities for him and his former wife to study Hebrew in Israel. The consul steered them to a generously subsidized five-month Ulpan program for *'olim hadashim*, new immigrants to Israel.

"But my wife is not Jewish," Gitlitz told him, "and we have no intention of settling permanently in Israel."

"It does not matter," the consul replied, "It's a good investment for us. If we get you to Israel for five months, we've got you forever."

That journey was not a pilgrimage, but an extended visit whose purpose was ostensibly to study Hebrew. Still, the consul recognized its potential importance for the nation as well as for the graduate student. A life-cycle event, strengthening the author's sense of identity. An expression of solidarity. An investment in future political support.

Who is to say whether this book, about to go to press thirty-eight years later, is the fruit of the consul's investment?

ROOTS PILGRIMAGE

We had planned to go to Beirut, where [my father] was born. . . . I imagined, in some childlike way, reversing the path of my father, traveling back in time and history with him. Just thinking of it left me a little dizzy with excitement. (Herbert Hadad, 1988)[1]

Ellis Island . . . has assumed for me a kind of mythic status in my family's beginnings in this country. The first American soil on which they set their feet, it has the status of a kind of Jewish holy place. (David Margolis, 1993)[2]

Saturday morning, my daughter and I arrived at the Shaar Ha-Shamayim synagogue [in Cairo] "The Gate of Heaven" commonly called Temple Ismaliah, where I had my Bar-Mitzvah. . . . I expected it to be in decay after more than 30 years. To my surprise it was as beautiful and resplendent a building as at the time when I had left Egypt in 1950. . . . I entered with great emotion, since this was the place where my father used to take me, and, I remembered very clearly the beautiful singing of Cantor Chichchek. (Victor D. Sanua, 1983)[3]

The central fact of modern Jewish demographic history is migration. In today's world the percentage of Jews who still live where their great grandparents did is miniscule. From the 1880s to World War I, East European Ashkenazi Jewry went west to France, England, and the Americas, and in World War II the majority of those who did not emigrate were annihilated. Of the survivors, many went to Israel or the Americas. After the breakup of the Ottoman Empire in 1918, many eastern Mediterranean Jews also migrated to the West. Since the 1950s, most Jews have left Muslim lands. With the disintegration of Communism in 1989, much of the remnant Jewish population of the former Soviet Union has also taken to the road.

The Jewish migratory experience of the past 125 years mirrors those of many other ethnic groups, but with two key differences. Émigré Italians, Greeks, Poles, Chinese, Indians, and others left clearly defined nation-states in which they were the majority and which continue to thrive in some form as nations today. Smallish numbers left; larger numbers remained behind, so the émigrés could maintain connections with a homeland still peopled by their friends and relations. But the relationship of Jewish émigrés to their former "homelands" was different. In most of those lands Jews had been the "other." Their families may have lived there for 1,000 years, but only by the sufferance of a majority population of whose culture they could never become part. When Jews emigrated, particularly those who departed during the last seventy-five years, they left few people behind. There is no sizeable remnant Jewish population in North Africa or Eastern Europe to perpetuate the ancestors' culture. In the "home" that never truly was home, Jewish culture today has all but vanished.

In large measure Jewish identity is forged through acts of remembering shared experiences. The stories that fill the pages of the Bible, the holidays like Sukkot, Hanukah, Purim, Pesach, and Tisha b'Av commemorate ancient significant events, as do the modern Yom HaShoah (Holocaust Remembrance Day) and Yom Ha'Atzmaut (Israel Independence Day). Contemporary Jews, particularly those who are not strictly observant of Halakhah and who live in societies that encourage rather than impede the assimilation of minority cultures into the national mainstream, sometimes look to shore up their sense of self by delving into their family's past. This urge is not unique to Jews, of course, but is common in modern societies with large immigrant populations. The immigrants struggle to survive; their children strive to assimilate; and their grandchildren, if they are connected at all, yearn to remember.

Every generation tries to understand the world of their parents and grandparents. This was easier when the generations all lived in the same household, and the grandchildren could prompt the old-timers to tell them tales of what it was like when they were young. The physical environment in which those stories unfolded was familiar to both the tellers and the audience. There was a continuity of life-cycle experiences. But for the grandchildren of the migrants from distant lands, the task of connecting with the vanished culture of another age and place is much harder. It requires a conscientious narration of the story, the creation of word pictures that convey the feel of place. Inevitably it condenses experience; it simplifies motives and processes and events into packages that are easy to remember and able to be shared. Eventually anecdote gravitates toward myth, places that were complex and specific become generic, and the ancestral world is remembered not as it was but as it must or should have been. The conveying of this world and its values to the next generation becomes an act of ritual retelling, something Jews are well accustomed to: "Because we were slaves unto Pharaoh in Egypt. . . ."

In 1976 Alex Haley published *Roots*, a chronicle of the efforts of a Black American to define himself by coming to understand his family's African origins and the horrors of their experiences as forced immigrants and slaves.[4] The book was a smashing success, not only among African Americans, but among all the American immigrant populations. The following year the television miniseries based on the saga reached an even wider audience. The times were ripe for this message. The mass mobilizations of World War II, the migration of Americans from the farms to the cities, the rapid change in women's roles in the economy, and the replacement of the multigenerational extended family by the small nuclear or single-parent family had contributed to a national malaise of rootlessness. Haley's book resonated far beyond the United States as the developed nations of the West underwent similar rapid changes and enjoyed an unprecedented prosperity that made it possible to devote time and material resources to exploring family history. But its impact appears to have been strongest among those encapsulated ethnic groups that were still negotiating their place in the broader cultures of their homelands: in the United States these included Blacks, Native Americans, and Jews.

In recent years substantial numbers of Americans have gone searching for their families' past. The roots pilgrims plunge into genealogical research, they collect old photographs and letters, and they scour libraries and archives for information about their ancestral origins. They quiz their elders for anecdotes and rummage through their attics for mementos. Their heads know that the old world is gone, but in their hearts they feel that the compost of family history will nurture their personal sense of rootedness.

Many believe that a physical journey to the scenarios of their family history will deepen their understanding and self-awareness, that their presence in a physical landscape will be more meaningful than the abstractions of the oral or printed word. Enabled by discretionary money and coddled by the ease of modern tourism, the roots-detectives set off for their ancestors' homelands. In one sense they are tourists, lured by the sights portrayed in glossy brochures. But they are also pilgrims who hope that by walking the walk, tasting the taste, and gossiping with the people—or the descendants of the people—whom their ancestors left behind, they will come to understand themselves better.

The roots pilgrim is a double person, a doppelganger. One persona physically travels the world as it is today, as it has evolved from the reality of the ancestors' world. They other persona walks in the mythic, remembered world, the world as it must have been the day his or her ancestors left. Sometimes the physical journey prevails, with its unavoidable minutiae of transportation, lodging, food, and souvenirs. Sometimes the mental journey takes over, superimposing its interior landscapes onto the hard edges of the real now. Roots pilgrims are selective observers who hone in on those aspects of the environment that confirm their expectations and fit into the paradigm of meaning that they have brought with them. As Lisa Grant put it, as they seek "to connect or re-discover with some aspect of the past, [they] are their own heritage producers."[5]

Roots pilgrims are seekers. Unlike other pilgrims, their principal goal is not renewed faith or access to miraculous intervention by the divine, but an intensified sense of self, of connectedness to past personal history. The specific focus and the intensity vary by generation. The immigrants recall their personal experiences, idealized or stigmatized by their selective memory, and hope that their visit will show them the world they recollect and the people they once knew. The second generation lacks the personal experience with the homeland, but is likely shaped by the vivid recollections of their parents. They expect concrete evidence to validate their inherited memory. The family stories are detailed enough for them to have acquired a visceral expectation of what the homeland must have been like. They hope to find their street, their synagogue, their parents' house, close to the way their parents have described them. Their shrine may be a community building, a mikveh, a legendary restaurant, or a school. By the third generation the pictures are fading; they evoke at best a generic impression of the world that the roots pilgrims are going to visit. They know that their grandparents' specific environment is gone, but they hope to feel a connection through places and experiences that they can accept as approximations of that world. This is what makes the Polish village of Tykocin, on the Lithuanian border, so popular. With its 1642 synagogue and its picturesque wooden houses, all restored in the 1970s, it is a stand-in for villages now vanished or so changed by the forces of modernity that they no longer evoke the atmosphere of what the ancestors' shtetl must have been like. Like Barcelona's Pueblo Español, Indiana's Connor Prairie, or New Brunswick's Acadian Historic Village, Tykocin is structured to cater to nostalgia and to project authenticity.

Roots pilgrims may find it difficult to put their specific need into words, but they feel certain that it is tied up with their sense of self. As Sigmund Diamond wrote in the late 1970s,

> My journey to the East was also a journey into my past, an obligation to myself, undertaken in the hope that I might ease my restlessness if I could "return" to parts of the world I had never seen but in which I had "lived" for many years. . . . I was not sure about why I felt as I did about Jewishness; I certainly did not feel that way about Judaism, if by that one means a matter of conviction as to a right way of life. My attachment was to a people of history rather than to a set of beliefs. At least I had always thought so, but perhaps on this, as on other matters, I had begun to change. I was not sure: perhaps the journey would tell me.[6]

Roots pilgrims tend to begin their journeys with a churning mix of enthusiasm and nervousness, self-confidence and doubt. They cannot circumvent the fact that the world they yearn to experience has long since disappeared. No matter how much data they amass, they can never connect all the dots or fill in all the colors.

While Jewish roots pilgrimages are as varied as the people who undertake them, they tend to target three kinds of memory shrines. One is the land where substantial remnants of Jewish culture still exist and in which some elements of their families still remain. The second is lands where Jewish culture was violently eradicated, either murdered or expelled. The lands of the Shoah are the principal example, although the parts of the Islamic world that today are all but empty of Jews belong to this category. Third are places that served as way stations on the path to resettlement and cultural assimilation: Lisbon and the Spanish Pyrenees for Jews fleeing the Holocaust, Ellis Island and New York's Lower East Side for Jews immigrating to the United States.

PILGRIMAGE TO PRESERVE THE HYPHEN

In ethnic communities in the modern Western world it has become fashionable for people to think of themselves as having a hyphenated identity: Italian-Americans, Dutch-Indonesians, Lebanese-Mexicans, Yemeni-Israelis. Jews whose families come from Fez may think of themselves as Moroccan-Israelis, or Israelis of Moroccan descent, or Jewish-Moroccans living in Israel (or Israeli-Moroccan Jews living in Montreal). As families integrate into their new homeland's culture, the hyphen evolves and may even disappear. A wry family observation recalls that our grandparents were Jews who lived in America, our parents were American-Jews, our generation is Jewish-American; and our children . . . ?

Diaspora Jews often find that roots pilgrimages are a useful way of helping to preserve the sense of "the hyphen" for themselves and a strategy for transmitting that sense to the next generation. Such pilgrimages begin with the notion that there are enough practitioners of the old culture left that visiting them will be a positive, bonding experience. Such was the case for Joelle Bahloul, for example, who, in the early 1990s, sought out the home in Setif, Algeria, from which her Jewish grandparents had emigrated during the French-Algerian war. When Bahloul identified herself to some local women, "they started to chant, to kiss my hands, to ululate and recite Koranic verses. Then they led me on a tour of the house that resembled a journey through the past." They regaled her with anecdotes about her relatives, and enthusiastically inquired about their lives.[7] Leon Wahba, who revisited Cairo in 2001 after a forty-two year absence, connected with the physical scenarios of his childhood, such as the Cicurel Department Store on King Fouad Street: "My maternal grandfather, my mother, her sister and her husband had all worked there at one time or the other. It was our favorite shopping store." And the Adly Street Synagogue: "Memories of weddings and bar mitzvahs flooded my mind as we walked as reverently as we could through this magnificent structure where my grandparents, parents, and each of my many uncles and aunts were married."[8]

In Fez (Morocco) in May 2004, we had the pleasure of spending a few hours with a Moroccan Jew now living in London. Her family had lived in Sefrou, a city near Meknes, which once boasted a large and thriving Jewish community—at one time Jews were in the majority in Sefrou—but now holds only memories and the graves in the large Jewish cemetery on the western edge of the city. She is typical of the first generation Maghrebi Diaspora Jews, most of whom left North Africa in the late 1950s to resettle in Israel, Paris, London, Montreal, or the United States. Now in their sixties, some go back to reconnect with the scenes of their young adulthood, sometimes with their younger family members in tow. This British-Moroccan-Jewish woman's agenda included catching up with old friends, eating her fill of Moroccan-Jewish delicacies, visiting Sefrou to light candles on some of her ancestors' graves, doing the same at other family graves in the cemetery in Fez. It was there in the small Jewish museum adjacent to the cemetery that we met her and a friend who still lives in Fez. Here are notes jotted down that evening about the shared hours in the museum:

> The museum in the old synagogue is a tribute to the obsessive hunting and gathering skills of Egmont, the cemetery's caretaker. It is the communal attic of the Fez Jewish community, four rooms of mounded artifacts, organized like a curio cabinet that ascribes to the Victorian aesthetic of Too Much is not Enough. School books. Sewing machines. Torah covers. Elijah chairs. Kosher butcher signs in Hebrew and Arabic. Engraved pictures of famous rabbis, historical and legendary. A wedding dress. Somebody's mineral collection. Silver

Searching for the past. Museum of the Fez Jewish Cemetery, Morocco. Photo,
D. Gitlitz, 2004.

spice boxes and Esther scroll covers and mezuzah cases. Fountain pens. Chess
sets. Amulets. Crocheted children's clothes. Lalla Sol ha Tzadiqah's two
golden tresses. A stamp collection. Everything piled floor to ceiling, nothing
cataloged, most of it dusty. An adjoining room full of photos in which two
women are oohing and aahing and flinging French expressions of rapture
into the air. One is a Fezli from Sefrou and the other from London (though
also born in Sefrou). The Londoner hadn't been back in years, and she was
going through old books of photos picking out family members and friends
and suddenly she burbled: "My God!, there are my wedding pictures! Look,
there is my fiancé. Oh, yes! We had the reception in. . . ."

A nachas of shared joy, of the discovery of a past made concrete, preserved, waiting for her, and someday, perhaps, for her children and great-great-grandchildren
to connect with as they make their own roots pilgrimage to Morocco.

ROOTS PILGRIMS AND THE SHOAH

After World War II, Jewish roots pilgrims to Germany and Eastern Europe
have faced much greater physical and mental challenges than those to other parts
of the Jewish world. Most shtetls are gone. The once Jewish neighborhoods are
not as they were. The legendary scenarios of their family's history—the Jewish

districts of Weimar, Lublin, Warsaw, Minsk, and Vilnius, the townscapes of Bobowa, Lezhansk, and Kazimier Dolny, the shtetls in Galicia, Lithuania, Poland and Belarus—have been bombed and bulldozed, and many have been rebuilt with Soviet-style apartment blocks. In some instances even the names of villages, provinces, and countries have changed. Their relatives are gone, probably murdered, most likely with the knowledge or even the complicity of the parents and grandparents of their village's current residents. The concentration camps and museums are filled with detritus stolen from murdered Jews. The gravestones of pre-Shoah ancestors were taken to pave streets. The 6 million who perished in the Shoah are commemorated not in individual graves, but in communal ash pits or the places where they were slaughtered. Instead of joyful communion, the Shoah roots pilgrim tends to experience the anguish of loss.

Yet even so, pilgrims hope to find some positive, identity-enhancing sense of connection with the world their ancestors no longer inhabit. "There was a tremendous sense of anticipation . . . [of] excitement for the impending discovery of our Eastern European heritage," wrote Eitan Schuman, who accompanied a group of Hasidic twelfth graders to Poland in 2003. But this ebullient optimism was tempered with her very next phrase, with "the anxiety of seeing the aftermath of the utter annihilation."[9] For roots pilgrims to the lands of the Shoah, this conflicted mindset tinges everything they see or think. Jeffrey Dekro captured this eloquently in the account of his pilgrimage to Poland in 1987. He wrote that the instant his plane crossed the Polish border, "I sense ghosts, and tears come to my eyes." The ghosts were of his lost family members, but also of their world from which he was forever excluded. "I feel sad as I recall all I've never known and can never know: grandparents, German, Yiddish, culture, prayers." As he traveled, his eyes selected only those bits of landscape that fit the template of meaning he had

School flags left at the Old Synagogue. Kazimierz, Kraków, Poland. Photo, D. Gitlitz, 2004.

brought with him. "The Warsaw runway is beneath us . . . smoke rises over the trees—whose? Why? I see my first railroad tracks." But at the same time, he recorded details that allowed him to project himself into his ancestral world: "cobblestones, stone walls, concrete, centuries of history and legends. . . . The sense of familiarity is overwhelming—homecoming to my history."

Roots pilgrims visiting the Holocaust lands approach the site of the old homestead with conflicting expectations, even as they yearn to discover some tangible link with the family past. As he approached his mother's village of Ostroleka, in a moment that he characterized as coming to the end of a pilgrimage, Sigmund Diamond later recalled, "I was sure that nothing from my mother's time had escaped destruction, but the truth is that I was hoping that I would spy some vagrant graffiti, overlooked by the destroyers, that would reveal this place as the place where my mother had been born."[10] But there was nothing.

The pilgrims' nervousness increases at the moment of approaching their goal. Will the old home square with their mental picture? Who is living there now? Will they welcome the visitor? Will they impugn the pilgrim's motives? Will they turn a cold shoulder, or react violently to the returnee who they fear may harbor claims to usurped property? Will they ignore the returning roots pilgrims, or treat them like ordinary tourists to be marketed to but not engaged with?

The roots pilgrims who visit Holocaust-related sites are in for emotional rough sledding. This is true whether they are survivors, the relatives or descendants of survivors, or merely Jews who feel a tribal connection to the destroyed 6 million. Despite pilgrims' attempts to frame these experiences as an intellectual exercise, for example as a study tour to learn more about Eastern Europe and the Shoah, they cannot help but become emotionally involved. Maxim Biller, who was raised in Germany by Russian-Jewish parents, struggled with this mixture of motives and emotions during his visit to Poland in the early 1990s with a group of German-Jewish young adults. "We've come here to get a handle on what happened; we want to learn something about ourselves and about anti-Semitism. We are struggling, without realizing it, to achieve a crystal-clear Jewish self-definition. So we are visiting, between Breslau and Lublin, the sites in this part of the world where Jews lived and bit the dust. Concentration camps and cemeteries, ghettos and shtetls." Along the way they found themselves giddy with insights, walloped by horrors, and drained by the catharsis of reciting Kaddish in the killing camps. Eventually they cut their group visits short, exhausted by the "psychological maelstroms." Yet many of them, still unfulfilled, set off on individual quests to find their relatives' villages. "They were in search of something, a missing piece of their fractured Jewish identity. But they found nothing, only Poles . . . living in formerly Jewish houses."[11]

The houses sought out by the roots pilgrims are not in any sense their homes. Homes are characterized by the presence of family. They are made meaningful by person-to-person relationships. The returnee expects to be welcomed, integrated, or at least acknowledged. If there is no family, no connection, no sharing, then the visitor is an interloper. Sad tales outnumber the happy. When Alan Scher Zagier visited his ancestral Belarus village of Lida, most of whose Jews were murdered in the Shoah, he met a man who was almost certainly related to him. "We share a last name—maybe more—but it's clear Mikhail Zager is in no mood for a possible long-lost family reunion with an American searching for his family's roots. He just wants us out of his apartment. Right away. 'Ne govorite im nichego,' shouts Zager, a former Red Army soldier. 'Don't tell them anything.' "[12] Andrea Simon, visiting her relatives' Belarus town of Volchin, cringed at her reception. She asked one local woman her feelings about how Volchin's Jews had been slaughtered. "With others around her nodding approval, she responded that when the villagers saw the hunger and suffering in the ghetto, when they heard the screaming and the shooting, when they learned about the terrible humiliation of undressing and how babies were lifted by their legs or arms [and shot], they thought that the Jews couldn't have had a god. To which another woman added: 'It's a sure sign that not only don't you have a god, but you killed Jesus and this is why you got this terrible punishment.' "[13]

Some pilgrims have better luck. A girl name Rina, part of Maxim Biller's group, met a farmer in her ancestral shtetl who dragged from his barn a fragment of a gravestone bearing her family name in Hebrew letters. She purchased it and took it back to Germany with her, happy that "she had got her hands on a piece of the past,"[14] something to sustain—at least for the moment—her sense of Jewish identity. But such experiences are rare.

Eventually Jeffrey Dekro reached a sort of epiphany in which he felt that he melded with his ancestors and entered their Polish world. The moment of fusion occurred as he entered the old Jewish cemetery behind the Moses Isserles Synagogue in Kraków. "I lunge forward, pulling my father and his parents—my grandparents. I walk, feeling strong and alone, for about ten to twenty steps, and I begin crying." The next day, reflecting on his experience, he wrote: "Last night I was transported from 1987 to earlier times: before the war and even back to the eighteenth and nineteenth centuries. In that way I have become a part of Polish Hasidic life, and I also enter the world of my grandparents Dora and Joseph."[15] The emotional punch of sudden communion with vanished relatives in these

Cemetery. Tarnow, Poland. Photo, D. Gitlitz, 2004.

circumstances is common, as is the way its intensity catches roots pilgrims by surprise. Howard Jacobson described his reaction to the ruined cemetery in the family's town of Serhai:

> I am upset in a way I never expected to be by the modesty of these memorials. . . . Anonymous yet uniting. And it becomes necessary for me to separate from my companions for a little while, . . . so that I can say something to the stones in private. Not much. Just . . . that I am here, and that it is ironic that it should be me of all people, the least familial, the least loyal, the least nostalgic of Jews, who has come.[16]

SURROGATE HOMELANDS

Roots pilgrimages are not always to the distant homelands of one's ancestors. The destinations can be events like the annual ethnic festivals held in various regions of the United States. They can be food fairs, folk concerts, or museum exhibits. They can be rallies that honor an important foreign visitor. Way stations, too, can be targets of roots pilgrimages. So many Jewish and other immigrants to the United States entered through Ellis Island that it has become one of the major goals of roots pilgrimage in the American Northeast. Since large numbers of Jewish immigrants settled first on Manhattan's Lower East Side, it, too, has come to be perceived as a secondary homeland by those Jews and their descendants who eventually migrated to the suburbs or other parts of the United States. Gitlitz remembers his father James Gitlitz's fascination with visiting the Clinton Street area of the Lower East Side where his own father Louis had lived briefly around 1899. He was not looking for any particular building or person, but took pleasure just from being there and showing the place to his sons. For other Jews who have all but disassociated themselves from active Jewish life and are ignorant of its scope and richness, the Lower East Side exudes authenticity as a reminder of a lifestyle, values and traditions now vanished. Jonathan Boyarin recounts the reactions of the rabbi of a Lower East Side synagogue when a Long Island Jewish family brought their thirteen-year-old there for his bar mitzvah: "These people come to the East Side the one time when they want a little *Yiddishkayt*. . . . They don't know there are tens of thousands of Orthodox Jews in Flatbush, in Williamsburg, in Boro Park . . . they think this is it, this is the last remnant of *Yiddishkayt* in America."[17]

The Lower East Side, as Hasia Diner has argued, is a "mythic place," similar to Eastern Europe "as a point of memory, replete with an instantly recognizable set of images of people and places, described with a sensual trope built around sounds, smells, and tastes." It came to be seen as a "metaphoric middle ground where Jews dwelled among themselves while waiting for permission to enter the real America."[18] By the 1920s it had already become a place of pilgrimage for Jews who by then had moved away, and who returned periodically to revel in the sights and smells and food, to shop, and to impress their former neighbors with how well they had done economically. In the 1930s, the best-known cafes and restaurants—like Greenbergs for the Rumanian community, or the Russian Bear or Russian Kretchmas for the Russian Jews, or Katz's Delicatessen for everyone—were attracting former Lower East Siders back for nostalgic evenings of food and hamish ambience. Some establishments, like the Café Royal, offered theater and ethnic music.[19]

Today the Lower East Side is still a focus of Jewish roots tourism, with visits sponsored by formal Jewish organizations or tour companies. The tours commonly include synagogues like the Eldridge Street Synagogue, the Romaniote congregation of Kehila Kedosha Janina, the Bialystoker Synagogue, the former synagogue that now houses the Angel Orensanz Foundation, and the one-room shuls along East Broadway from Clinton to Montgomery. The Lower East Side Tenement Museum is an obligatory stop. Culinary excursions to the Lower East Side continue to be so popular that Alan Dershowitz has termed them "noshtalgia tours."[20] Tour companies even offer niches within the niches, such as the "radical walking tour" that "focuses on the massive Jewish immigration of the turn of the century and includes Julius and Ethel Rosenberg, Abraham Cahan and the *Jewish Daily Forward*, Sidney Hillman and the Amalgamated Clothing Workers of America, Socialist and Communist Party activist Rose Pastor Stokes, and more."[21]

The Lower East Side and Ellis Island are major destinations for Jewish roots pilgrims. But actually any place of Jewish memory or a Jewish-oriented event can become the focus of Jewish roots pilgrimage. Marion Jacobson has written about how a Klezmer Club has become a pilgrimage event for the seniors and unmarried young professionals who flock to it twice a month in suburban Washington, D.C., to eat, schmooze, feel a sense of community, and re-imagine the world of their mothers and fathers or of their childhood. As they dance and sing along with the musicians, it does not matter that many of the tunes were composed in America, not Europe, and are a pastiche of show tunes, summer camp songs, disco-rock, and traditional melodies.[22] What is important, as Tevye the Anatevka milkman knew well, is that the experience leaves the audience with a roots-enhancing feeling of "Tradition!"

The physical spaces associated with the *Landsmanshaft* that supported the immigrant generation also serve as a pilgrimage destination for the émigrés or their descendants. This is the case, for example, for Jewish communities with roots in Maramarosh, a Hungarian-speaking town now in Romanian Transcarpathian Transylvania. Between the end of World War II and 1989 the ancestral grave sites were accessible only with difficulty. Instead, in New York, Maramarosh Jews make pilgrimage to the cemetery in Queens owned and maintained by the Maramarosh Landsmanshaft. In Tel Aviv, Marmoros House, a synagogue and Holocaust memorial maintained by the small resident Maramarosh community, is a pilgrimage destination for Maramarosh Jews from all over the world who are visiting Israel. These two sites function as surrogates for the Transylvanian homeland.[23]

We have already seen how several Maghrebi Sephardic pilgrimages to saints' tombs have been replicated in Israel. These visits continue the North African tradition of saint veneration, but they are also roots-affirming exercises for the pilgrim participants. The Ethiopian Sigd pilgrimage on the 29th of Hesvan celebrates the giving of the Law. In Ethiopia Jews would observe a half-day fast and climb in pilgrimage to the top of the highest mountain near their homes to recite Psalms, read from the Torah and the book of Nehemiah, and express their longing to return to Jerusalem. Now living in Israel, some 35,000 Ethiopian Jews gather each year since the mid-1990s either at the Western Wall or at the Talpiot platform, overlooking the holy sites of the Old City. There they recite the traditional prayers and songs and give thanks for having finally reached their goal. Along with the religious component is the pilgrimage's role in Sigd community building. As one teenage participant remarked in 2004, "[The children] need to see it for themselves. It's something that really strengthens them, to see the whole community gathered here today."[24]

ROOTS PILGRIMAGE AND TOURISM

In today's affluent, mobile world, tourism is big business and thematic tourism is profitable: art and theater tours, ecotourism, archaeological circuits, culinary adventures, tours that trace the footsteps of Saint Paul or Martin Luther. Roots tourism is a similar niche that is marketed by companies with names like Jewish Heritage Tours and Routes to Roots.[25] Roots pilgrims often need professional help in navigating the intricacies of genealogical research. They may require knowledgeable, multilingual guides. More than that, they need a storyteller, a docent, someone who can represent the voice of their family history, who can provide context and help them fill in the voids in ways that are meaningful to their personal quest for identity.

Individually tailored roots pilgrimage tours are expensive. This and the fact that many people begin with little specific knowledge of their particular family lead roots pilgrims to seek generic tours. The most common package is the broadly focused tradition tour designed to create a sense of solidarity with the old-world Jewish cultures that are the ancestors of Western or Israeli Judaism. They seek out synagogues and cemeteries, and claim that "Jews cannot help but feel the power of such sacred sites" (Heritage). They connect pilgrims with their family history by analogy: this is the kind of village in which; this is the type of synagogue where; this is the concentration camp where your ancestors may have. The providers carefully distance themselves from superficial tourism: "[We offer] far more than sightseeing. Together, we will delve deeper into Jewish roots, tradition, and history—both ancient and modern—in such a way that you will leave with an infusion of strength and pride in your heritage" (National). Nevertheless, they also entice their prospective clients by combining Jewish sites with other tourist highpoints. These three themes—ancestor Jews then; pilgrim Jews now, and glossy popular culture—weave through almost every advertisement for Jewish roots tours. Here is an Internet description of the Budapest component of a 2004 Elderhostel trip to Jewish sites in Eastern Europe:

> Lectures focus on the history and contemporary life of the Hungarian Jewish community. We take field trips to the former Jewish ghetto—alive with Kosher restaurants, butchers and bakers, a Jewish hospital, cultural center, bath, schools, a rabbinical seminary—and the Jewish Cemetery in Óbuda. We have excursions to the Castle District with its medieval synagogue, Heroes' Square, and Chain Bridge; attend a Sabbath dinner; and learn Hora dancing.[26]

Hora dancing has nothing to do with Hungary, of course, but the insertion of an element of modern Israeli folk culture reminds the participants of Israel's role as the successor to East European Judaism.

The tourist industries in the lands with former large Jewish communities are eager to facilitate roots pilgrimages. The payoff comes both in hard currency and in projecting an image of ecumenical tolerance. During our own unguided visit to Kraków in Summer, 2004, we were struck by the effectiveness of the Polish tourist industry's packaging of Jewish heritage themes. We coincided with the fourteenth annual Festival of Jewish Culture, whose sponsors include several private foundations and Kraków's Centre for International Culture Cooperation. The festival is a several day multimedia extravaganza of tours, lectures, films, and klezmer concerts held in Kraków's former Jewish district of Kazimierz. The seven synagogues that survived World War II have been retrofitted as museums. All were open and thronged with tourists scuttling behind government-sponsored guides who narrated Kazimierz's Jewish past in Polish, German, English, French, Russian, or Hebrew. Multi-language posters announcing Jewish-themed events covered every flat surface. Restaurants offered "Jewish style" cuisine. Signs pointed out locales where Steven Spielberg had filmed scenes of *Schindler's List*. The Polish tourist office handed out brochures and maps detailing sites of Jewish interest. Local

Souvenirs. Kazimierz, Kraków, Poland. Photo, D. Gitlitz, 2004.

Jewish Festival posters. Kazimierz, Kraków, Poland. Photo, D. Gitlitz, 2004.

tour companies advertised day-trips to nearby Auschwitz and Plaszow and longer excursions to the former Jewish shtetls of Polish Galicia.

East Europeans are not the only promoters of Jewish roots pilgrimage. The national, regional, and municipal tourist offices of Austria, Belgium, Egypt, France, Germany, Holland, India, Italy, Morocco, Spain, and Tunisia crank out similar incentives to Jewish tourists. Former Jewish neighborhoods, like Seville's *judería*, the *cal* of Girona, the *ghetto* of Venice, the *juiverie* of Strasbourg, the *mellahs* of Fez and Sfax, the "Jew Street" of Cochin, and dozen of other cities, small and large, are promoted as places where émigré Jews can reconnect with their cultural roots. Advertisements for foreign travel to synagogues, cemeteries, and monuments beckon to potential roots pilgrims from seemingly every Jewish community newspaper and magazine.

In the Muslim world, Morocco, which bills itself as a welcoming society, has been especially successful in attracting roots pilgrimages. André Levy documented how, between 1980 and 1995, some 2,000 Israeli-born Jews of Moroccan heritage returned to Morocco on organized pilgrimage and roots tours.[27] These visits serve the interests of the small remnant Jewish community in Morocco, of Jews in the Moroccan Diaspora, and of the Moroccan government. They are likely to be sponsored by any of these sectors and by commercial tour companies as well. The promotional material tantalizes potential visitors with the scenic wonders of Morocco. The specific targets are Moroccan émigré Jews and their descendants: "If your origins are Moroccan or if your parents or grandparents lived in Morocco . . . these events will reintroduce you to, or acquaint you with, the Rif and the Atlas [mountains], the imperial cities rich with history, ancient and modern Morocco where for nearly two thousand years our community has existed and produced many eminent rabbis."

Tours such as these fuse at least three kinds of experiences: religious pilgrimages, roots pilgrimages, and tourism. Saint veneration is such a fundamental part of Maghrebi culture, both Muslim and Jewish, that for Jews of Moroccan heritage it is an essential component of their ethnic identity and provides a convenient focus for their roots pilgrimage. As Oren Kosansky has argued, and as we have seen earlier, for these roots pilgrims the hillula itself is viewed less as a religious event than as "a nostalgic attraction." The tour of which it is a part "permits a temporary, selective, and controlled evocation of a transcended past that, while arousing nostalgic emotions, has been willfully left behind."[28] These perspectives hold both for the foreign émigré communities and for the two-thirds of Morocco's remaining Jews who live in urban Casablanca, but whose roots lie in tiny communities, now devoid of Jews, scattered all over the Moroccan landscape.

Diaspora Moroccans participate on these tours for many reasons. Some go back to honor their parents' graves and to visit old friends who have stayed behind. Some return because they have vowed to do so. Some go to satisfy a craving to see the place that was so important to

Jewish Festival guide. Kazimierz, Kraków, Poland. Photo, D. Gitlitz, 2004.

their mother or grandfather. Some have a family connection with a particular tzadiq whose grave they want to visit. Some return so that their children can experience first hand the landscapes in which their parents grew up. Typically, roots pilgrims like these will walk the streets of their old towns, pop into the stores, nosh on recalled delicacies, seek out the ancestral house, and try to connect with neighbors who might remember them or their family members from years past.

As with other sectors of the tourist industry, roots pilgrimage thrives and wanes according to the political vagaries of the times. Until the death of the Spanish dictator General Franco in 1974, many Jewish tourists refused to visit Spain. Until the collapse of Communism in 1989, it was very difficult for people to visit many Jewish heritage sites in Eastern Europe. While Morocco and Tunisia have aggressively sought Jewish tourism, and Jordan, Iran, and Egypt have sporadically welcomed Jewish visitors, entry to some other Islamic countries has been more problematic. A 2003 report on patterns of Israeli tourism suggests that largely for reasons of security, Israeli "travel to Jordan and mainland Egypt has all but disappeared, as have 'heritage' tours to Morocco."[29] Our own research in Morocco in April and May, 2004, confirmed that the number of visitors from Israel has declined precipitously.

CONNECT; DISCONNECT

By the 1920s many of the Jews who had left Eastern Europe in the waves of immigration at the turn of the century were pulling themselves from poverty into the middle classes. They were helped by their Landsmanshaften, the fraternal organizations of immigrants from a particular region or town that gave them material assistance and advice, and mediated their absorption into the new society. As the immigrant generation matured, the Landsmanshaften now assumed the role of maintaining meaningful ties between the immigrants and their European origins. During the period between the World Wars the Landsmanshaften dispatched emissaries from the West to inquire into conditions in the old homelands. They also helped channel the charitable contributions that the immigrants were sending back to the old country. It is not surprising that they soon found themselves operating as travel agents and tour organizers, appealing to their clients' desire to revisit their hometowns, to spend time with their European relatives, and to participate for a time in the culture they had left behind. A typical tour docked in Le Havre, followed by visits to Paris, Berlin, and Warsaw, before depositing the tourist-pilgrim for a week or a month in the heart of the Pale, in big cities like Bialystock, Lvov, or Minsk, or in their home shtetls in the neighboring countryside.

Entrepreneurs got into the act as well. Gustave Eisner, a Polish-American journalist and travel agent, marketed his services to middle-class New York Jews. His advertisements in Yiddish periodicals and on the radio touted the pleasures of reunion with the people and places left behind. In promoting a trip to the Polish city of Lodz in 1934, he wrote that the joy experienced by meeting with landsmen in the fraternal hall in New York "cannot compare with the joy that you could have if you were to take a trip to your old home, where your cradle stood and where your relatives and childhood friends still live." The pilgrims themselves seem to have felt the same way. As Z. Tygiel wrote for the New York journal *Farband* before embarking for Poland, "a deliciously sweet feeling envelops you when you make a trip home. . . . Even the sour, the bitter, aspects of your youth are concocted into a sweet dish. Every little place, for another the worst, the ugliest, is dear to you, because it is connected to your youth."[30]

These purple expectations were fulfilled for some roots pilgrims. Others found mainly disillusionment. In the 1930s James Gitlitz and his two brothers funded the visit of their parents, Louis Gitlitz and Jennie Shulman, to the villages they had left as teenagers forty years before. Family legend holds that Louis and Jennie found no pleasure in what they saw in White Russia. The villages were dirty; life there was uncomfortable. They did not like the food. After the first few hours, they had little to talk about with their European relatives. So they cut short their visit and sailed back to the United States. They were typical of the immigrant Jews who no longer found meaning on both sides of "the hyphen." The writings of the New York Yiddish journalist Chune Gottesfeld, who visited his ancestral village in Galicia in 1937, chronicle a similar disillusion. He did not immediately recognize old friends. The town's streets were muddy and, at night, unlit. He felt awkward and increasingly estranged. As Daniel Soyer has pointed out, the disconnect between émigrés and their birth lands during the period between the World Wars is evident in the photographs of Jewish roots pilgrims in their old country environments. The well-dressed Westerners are surrounded by relatives in traditional clothing, often in a state of disrepair. The smiles on the Westerners' faces seem forced, while the old-world relatives seem mystified, depressed, distanced. The photos tend to underscore differences, not similarities.[31]

The émigrés bring different expectations to their roots pilgrimages. Their preconceptions are colored by family recollections and idealizations filtered through songs, folktales, novels, plays, and films. Their Polish shtetl is likely to be Anatevka, their North African mellah a set from *The Arabian Nights*. The process of selective memory has set them up for disappointment. Their experiences mirror those of many modern "ethnic tourists," people who feel themselves trapped in a frenetic, complex, demanding, urban, impersonal, rootless society, and who think that visiting a simpler, less-developed, bucolically-rural or folksy-urban culture will help them achieve a greater sense of authenticity. Surely—they hope beyond all logic—the homeland will not have changed significantly since their ancestors left.

Roots pilgrims set out expecting to strengthen their connections to their ethnic heritage, believing that this will help them achieve a clearer sense of self. Paradoxically, they generally find that the old country is a foreign land. Third- and fourth-generation descendants of émigrés rarely speak the old country language. They do not understand local mores. Neither the idealized culture of ancestral memories nor the conditions that drove their ancestors to leave exist any longer. The ironic result is that their roots-pilgrimage often strengthens not their old country identity but their sense of belonging to their new homeland. Their ancestors may have been Tunisian or Polish or Ukrainian or Iranian Jews, but they themselves are now Americans or Mexicans, French or Israelis, whose diverse roots have been blended in their new homeland's cultural melting pot.

SHRINE WARS

It belongs to me, I've had it for a long time;
There's nothing like it in this world,
    It's mine.
I know you want it and I really can't blame you.
You'd like to touch it, but if you do,
    I'll maim you . . .
I saw it first! It's mine!
I had it last! It's mine!
Oh, can't you see it's made for me?
    It's mine, it's mine, it's mine!
      (Keith Grimwood and Ezra Idlet, 1993)[1]

For the 1,878 years between the Roman destruction of the Temple in 70 CE and the proclamation of the State of Israel in 1948, Jews did not have to manage the holy sites to which they directed their pilgrimages. Control of access, maintenance of order, collection of pilgrim fees, administration of shrine finances, construction and repair of the holy sites' physical structures— all these were in the hands of the prevailing governments. Jewish pilgrims to Jerusalem, Hebron, or the Galilee traveled at the sufferance of others. During those nineteen centuries Jews were spared having to deal with the moral, political, military, and pragmatic issues involved with shrine control. The primary concern of Jewish pilgrims during the long Diaspora was how to get to Jerusalem and back home safe and solvent. Or, for a few pilgrims, how to get to the Holy Land and make a new life for themselves there.

With the exception of the period of the Crusades, when Christian and Muslim armies focused their havoc-wrecking energies primarily on controlling the holy places that they both claimed by divine right, most of the armed conflicts in the

Holy Land were the by-products of the clashes of great empires whose capitals were far away, or else were local squabbles over land or economic issues. Even so, shrine control is almost always used as a tool for political dominance. To occupy the shrine, to defile it, and to superimpose the altar of the victor's god over the holy place of the vanquished people are to say that the victor's god is stronger, and that the conquered people should accept dominance gracefully, since they can no longer look to their god for assistance. The tool is often flawed, however, for defeat can be rationalized. It is not that the gods are weak, but that the people have sinned and need to be punished by rendering them powerless until their sins have been purged, a new version of the old order can be restored, and the holy sites can reconnect the people with their deity.

With modern Israel's emergence as a political entity, administration of the holy sites moved to the front burner. From 1948 to the summer of 1967, Israel controlled the holy sites in the Galilee, the south, the coastal plain, and the corridor leading from the coast to Jerusalem. The Old City of Jerusalem, locus of the majority of the most important holy sites for Jews, Muslims, and Christians, as well as the hill country of what is most often termed the West Bank, was part of Jordan. After the Six-Day War in June 1967, Israel held everything west of the Jordan River.

In the mid-1990s, with the strengthening of a separate sense of Palestinian identity among the people of Gaza and the West Bank and the emergence of the Palestinian Authority as a governing entity, Israel has gradually, partially, and somewhat intermittently ceded sovereignty over much of the West Bank to the Palestinian Authority. As this book goes to press, the Israeli government is moving to withdraw from Gaza and to dismantle some of the West Bank settlements.

The proposed withdrawal is tearing Israel apart politically. During much of the last two decades of the twentieth century, the large Israeli political parties, in order to muster a ruling majority, have been forced to ally themselves with ultra-Orthodox nationalist groups that believe in a greater Israel defined by the Bible. For them Israel's borders extend from Dan to Beersheba and from the Jordan to the Mediterranean. It is holy in its entirety by biblical promise, by the individual holy sites that it contains, and by the ancient and continuous tradition of Jewish pilgrimage to those holy sites. They also believe that on these issues there is no room for compromise. For Israel, then, the war has two fronts: externally between Israelis and Palestinians; and internally between an accommodationist center and a religiously motivated, inflexible, extreme right.

This same landscape is the locus of many sites held holy by Palestinian Muslims, and, in the cases of a few sites—like the Dome of the Rock and the Al-Aqsa Mosque in Jerusalem, and the Tomb of the Patriarchs in Hebron—by the larger Muslim world. For many devout Muslims, these sites also define a holy geography that can never be ceded. Radical Palestinian nationalists understand the depths of these feelings and use them to muster popular support for their political agenda. Tearing the fabric on both sides, then, are the as-yet irreconcilable tensions between religious extremists, for whom the deity requires exclusivity and prohibits compromise, and political pragmatists who believe that any permanent peace requires a degree of sharing, and that the imperatives of religion and security must be balanced by a respect for human rights.

Palestinian Christians in these contested areas and Christian communities the world over also regard this land as holy. But they are not currently major players in the battles for control. Some Christian groups, acutely aware of historical precedent and fearing for their own long-term access to the shrines, push for the internationalization of Jerusalem. From time to time the Vatican has proposed administering the contested holy sites for all religions in a non-partisan fashion. But neither Jews nor Muslims seem eager to allow that particular camel's nose back into the Middle Eastern tent.

In choosing material for this chapter we faced an unfortunate embarrassment of riches, since so many holy places are in conflict. We have selected five popular Jewish pilgrimage sites that we believe illustrate the major points at issue and the frustrations of trying to deal with them. For Jews, Joseph's Tomb in Shechem (Nablus) is a holy outpost in hostile territory, which requires Israel to continually weigh the value and costs of assuring Jewish access. We will also see how the battle over this Tomb has taken place in the halls of government and the media as well as in the streets. Rachel's Tomb, on the outskirts of Bethlehem, forces the issue of where to draw the geographic border between Israel and Palestine. The pilgrimage to Yaacov Abuhatzeira's shrine near Alexandria, in Egypt, shows how the conflict between Israel and Palestine spills over into the Islamic world at large. The Cave of Machpelah in Hebron has a long history of shared access that may offer some useful keys to the resolution of conflicts over pilgrimages and shrines. Finally, recent battles at the Western Wall and the Haram al-Sharif illustrate the limits of progress when two religions each claim exclusive sovereignty over the holiest places.

JOSEPH'S TOMB: THE POLITICS OF OCCUPATION

Medieval pilgrimage traffic to Joseph's Tomb in Shechem (Nablus) included visits by the Christians Eusebius of Caesarea and the Bordeaux pilgrim in the fourth century, the Jewish traveler Benjamin of Tudela and the Muslim Ali al-Kharet in the twelfth century. Nevertheless, until modern times the small domed shrine was of relatively minor importance. For one thing, there is no universal agreement about who is buried there. The biblical Joseph tradition is based on Joshua 24:32, which says that after Joseph died in Egypt, his bones were brought to Shechem for burial on land purchased by his father, which then became the inheritance of Joseph's children. Most Muslims believe that even if that were so, the biblical Joseph's bones were moved centuries ago to the Cave of the Patriarchs in Hebron, and the shrine in Nablus contains instead the remains of a local sheikh named Yossef or Yusuf, perhaps the nineteenth-century Sheikh Yusuf Dukat. The Samaritan Jewish community, living for centuries on nearby Mount Gerizim, opts for the biblical Joseph. The shrine attracted little attention from archaeologists or academic historians who, in the current charged political atmosphere, prefer not to venture on-the-record opinions regarding the site's authenticity. After all, as Elhanan Reiner of Hebrew University has remarked, "What is important is what people think. Where is Joseph really buried? Who can tell you?"[2]

The unfortunate answer to Reiner's seemingly rhetorical question is: anyone with a political ax to grind.

From 1948 until June 1967, while Jordan administered the West Bank, Jews were denied access to all holy sites there. Stung by this experience, and not wanting to risk the ire of the many religious communities that consider various parts of Palestine to be holy, within a month after Israel took control of the West Bank in 1967, it passed the Protection of Holy Places Law that optimistically guaranteed, "The Holy Places shall be protected from desecration and any other violation and from anything likely to violate the freedom of access of the members of the different religions to the places sacred to them. . . ."[3] But optimism soon clashed with pragmatic reality. Although Orthodox Jewish pilgrims were now regularly visiting Joseph's Tomb, the shrine was in the middle of one of the most densely populated Palestinian areas, near refugee camps that seethed with Palestinian resentment against the Israelis whom they viewed as occupiers. The Israelis sensed that visits to the tomb by non-Muslim pilgrims could provoke violence, so they believed it expedient to exercise a measure of control over pilgrim access, even if this did not fulfill the letter of the 1967 law. Samaritan pilgrimage fell off sharply. In 2000 one Samaritan recalled that period: "Before the occupation we used to go there and pray, to celebrate, if we had a baby. But when the Israelis came, they forbade us to go there without a special permit. And during the [1987] Intifada there were too many problems, and we stopped going altogether."[4]

In 1985 the Israeli government permitted a group of Breslover Hasidim to establish Yeshivat Od Yosef Chai ("Joseph Still Lives") at the Tomb. It soon attracted a small following of Breslovers from Jerusalem and from the newly-established Jewish settlements in the West Bank. Fear for their safety prompted the Israel Defense Force (IDF) to post a small garrison at the site and that, in turn, focused the attention of Palestinian militants on the Tomb.

Before long both sides viewed the Jewish presence at Joseph's Tomb less as an expression of religion than as an assertion of territorial rights. Religious nationalists were now speaking of Joseph's Tomb as the third most important Jewish holy site in Israel.[5] It became an explicit agenda item during the talks that led up to the signing of the Oslo Accords in 1993. It was agreed that all religious groups would have access to the site, that joint patrols would guarantee that access, and that, while the Palestinian Authority (PA) had ultimate authority in the area, Israel retained the right to station guards within the Tomb compound.

In 1996, with the intensification of hostilities between Israel and Palestinians resentful of Israeli occupation, the potential flash point burst into flames. In September, in a pitched battle outside the Tomb, six Israeli soldiers and one Palestinian were killed. For the next two years the Tomb was off-limits to Jewish pilgrims, who were halted in their attempts to reach it by PA soldiers or by the IDF, each fearing that provocation would lead to a resumption and escalation of violence. In August 1998 two students from the yeshiva were murdered. The IDF and the PA security forces agreed to tighter scrutiny of the area, to limit Jewish visits, and to try to reduce Palestinian violence. On October 2, 2000, open fighting erupted again. Six Palestinians were killed, as well as an Israeli border policeman who was critically wounded and eventually bled to death because IDF forces felt that they were unable to evacuate him without making the situation worse. Five days later Israeli Prime Minister Ehud Barak ordered the IDF to pull out their forces.

Shortly after the withdrawal, a mob of jubilant Palestinians overran and pillaged the site with the tacit permission—some say the assistance—of the PA security forces that had promised to protect the tomb. The next day Rabbi Hillel Lieberman, one of the yeshiva's founders and guiding teachers during its eighteen-year history, was found murdered in a nearby cave. Nablus's mayor promised that the destroyed Tomb would be restored to its pre-1967 appearance. When it was finished, the dome was painted bright Islamic green.

For the next two years the IDF all but shut off Jewish access to Joseph's Tomb. Then, in response to pressure from religious leaders and nationalist politicians, it began escorting small groups of worshipers to the site. Early in 2003 Palestinians destroyed the large stone that marked Joseph's reputed grave. Again the IDF withdrew in response to a desire from both Israel and the PA to decrease violence at the site. Militant Jewish groups picketed Prime Minister Ariel Sharon's office, decrying the "national disgrace" of the army's withdrawal of troops from the Tomb.

Palestinian youths in Joseph's Tomb after its destruction, October 7, 2000. AP photo, Lefteris Pitarakis. Used by permission.

Rabbi Menachem Felix, long associated with the yeshiva at the Tomb, lamented the withdrawal by evoking history, sacrifice, and—seemingly as an afterthought—modern negotiated agreements: "[W]hat's the purpose of leaving, when we have all the reasons and justification to stay, the merit of thousand of years, of Joseph's bones that are buried there, of the blood that was spilled there—and even, for those who want, the Oslo Agreements give us the right to be there!" At the same time, fearing further escalation and bloodshed, several prominent rabbis forbade pilgrim travel to the Tomb without the army's permission.[6] The off-again-on-again policies of the Israeli government infuriated extremists on both sides. In late September several groups of Jews without the army's permission made their way to the shrine to pray. They were attacked, as were the Israeli paratroopers who subsequently went to protect them. Opposition members in the Knesset protested that the pilgrimages could be provocative, and the defense minister again shut them down. Nevertheless, on October 17, 2003, hundreds of worshipers, with IDF protection, made a Sukkot pilgrimage to the Tomb. As soon as they had departed, Palestinians set fire to it.

For Israeli religious nationalists, possession of a shrine like Joseph's Tomb is justified by the precedents of history. It confirms the nation's relationship with the deity and pragmatically stakes the claim for continued possession. Israelis who see the Jewish settlements in the occupied territories as counterproductive, or who think that the saint and tomb cults popular among the ultra-Orthodox are little better than paganism, are apt to consider the attention given to shrines like Joseph's Tomb as part of a government sponsored land grab.[7] This view flies in the face of the argument that Jacob had legitimately purchased the land on which Joseph was buried, and that from Midrashic times until the present a steady stream of Jewish pilgrims has demonstrated Jewish continuity at the site.[8] Holders of such views fear a domino effect, since for the purposes of staking claim to territory, each individual holy place is part of a web: "Israel shows that it does not know how to accept such a precious a gift as this, to keep it, to understand its value and greatness—that of this holy site, of all Eretz Yisrael."[9]

The Internet buzzes with similar arguments to support Palestinian claims. Joseph is the "hero of Bible and Koran stories. . . . The locals have venerated it, [as well] as numerous other shrines and tombs that adorn the hilltops and cross-roads of Palestine. The shrines have deep roots in the Palestinian soul; they pre-date all modern faiths, survived all religious reforms."[10] As a *Washington Post* reporter acutely observed after the riots in 2000, the Palestinians burned "every shred of [Israel's] sovereignty over this place."[11]

Moderates and extremists on both sides feel that the dispute over control of Joseph's Tomb can be won only by marshaling the weight of world opinion. They present the main components of their case with a debater's logic:

1. *History*: Our claim is endorsed by the deity and stretches back for centuries.

2. *Commitment*: Unlike the shallowly-motivated people of competing religions, we and the distant pilgrims who come to Joseph's Tomb revere it deeply. "On any given day, Palestinian peasant women . . . can be seen paying their respects at the tomb of the chaste lover, whose long eyelashes reduced the fortress of Zuleika's heart."[12] And, from the Israeli side, Joseph "is a Jewish figure, of marginal import to Muslims and Christians. . . . [The Muslims are] just here by accident. Their connection to this place is superficial, and a big part of it is a desire to counter the Jews."[13] "The Israeli government . . . didn't think [Joseph's Tomb] was worth fighting over to hold on to. Jewish holy sites, our connection to our past, and to our Land, didn't matter. And that gets to the heart of the problem. Whose land is it? Whose Holy Sites are they? Who cares more?"[14]

3. *Demons vs. angels*: Terminology matters, and the spin doctors often administer a demagogue's rhetoric. Our enemies are monsters; we are not. A contributor to the *Jerusalem Post*, exemplifying the extremist rhetoric in his essay on the destruction of Joseph's Tomb, noted the "painful scenes of mayhem and destruction" as the structure was torn apart, "brick by brick, in a frenzy of hate and defilement" by "a crazed horde of Palestinian rioters" who demonstrated a shocking "lack of respect for Judaism and its sacred places."[15] Another reporter hyperbolized attackers

"engaged in a pogrom reminiscent of scenes from Kristallnacht."[16] Rhetoric on the other side portrays young, innocent, Palestinian Davids, armed only with stones, confronting a mighty Israeli Goliath. Here the Tomb's attackers are simply "the people of Nablus," while their opponents are "well-armed Israeli Soldiers" including one "mercenary." The Yeshiva at the Tomb is an "enclave of hatred in the heart of Nablus."[17]

4. *Biased press*: Each hyperbole elicits a counter, beginning with the assertion that our side is systematically demonized in the world press. That's why the *New York Times* propagates "the blood libel of 'Arabs despoiling a Jewish holy place.'"[18] Each side professes outrage at the double standard. As Israeli Cabinet Minister Nathan Sharansky put it in 2000, "[i]f we would have razed the gravesite of one of the founders of Islam, billions of Muslims would have taken to the streets. . . . It's inconceivable that the world should not know about this travesty."[19]

5. *You can't trust them*: The opposing side is accused of breaking commitments, as when the PA promised to protect the Tomb site once the IDF had pulled out but then seemingly collaborated in its destruction. Or as when the Israeli government promised to restrict Jewish pilgrim access to the Tomb but then escorted groups of pilgrims to build their sukkahs there.

6. *You can trust us*: Each side insists that only it can guarantee the tomb's security and protect free access by pilgrims. Shimon Peres, speaking in 2000 as the Regional Cooperation Minister, assured the world: "When Israel controlled the sites, there was free and safe access for Jews, Christians, and Muslims." The Israeli Prime Minister, speaking on television, broadened this message: "If the Palestinians cannot keep their promises regarding the holy sites, how can they be given control of other things?" The Palestinians retort that at Joseph's tomb they "fought the army base, not the holy place. The holy places of Jerusalem, Bethlehem, Hebron would be safe in Palestinian hands, as they have been for uncounted generations."[20]

RACHEL'S TOMB: WHERE TO DRAW THE LINE?

Rachel's Tomb, which Palestinian Muslims call the Bilal Bin Rabah Mosque, is often considered Judaism's third holiest site.[21] It sits on the northern outskirts of Bethlehem on the road to Jerusalem. While a steady stream of Jewish pilgrims has visited it since at least early medieval times, its popularity has increased in recent decades as the women's movement claimed Rachel as the unofficial spiritual mother of Jewish womanhood. As with most holy sites located on the West Bank, Jews were afforded little access to Rachel's Tomb during the nineteen years following the 1948 War of Independence. In discussions following the Six-Day War in June, 1967, the Tomb's status became an issue for political cartographers and geography-sensitive politicians. Should Rachel's Tomb be part of Jerusalem, part of Bethlehem, or part of the then rural area between the two cities?

Right after the war Israeli Prime Minister Levi Eshkol gave what he thought were clear instructions to draw the Jerusalem map to include Rachel's Tomb within the new municipal boundary of the city. Jerusalem was to be forever

קבר רחל אמנו

Rachel's Tomb. Photo, James B. Gitlitz, 1976.

Israeli, and inclusion of Rachel's Tomb would insure perpetual access for Jewish pilgrims. Defense Minister Moshe Dayan and Interior Minister Haim Shapiro disagreed for reasons of security: Jerusalem had enough headaches with the holy places already within its borders. The Minister of Religious Affairs, Zerah Wahrhaftig, wanted Jerusalem's map to include Rachel's Tomb and also Bethlehem's Church of the Nativity, arguing that it would be useful for Christians to rely on Israel to protect their access to Christianity's holiest places. In the end, and without ever reporting back to Eshkol, the mapmakers left Rachel's Tomb five hundred meters outside of Jerusalem's southern border.[22]

Although the 1993 Oslo Accords put most of the West Bank under Palestinian control, at the same time they guaranteed Jews free access to their traditional holy sites. Negotiations about the permanent arrangements in the West Bank were to follow. The jurisdictional status of Rachel's Tomb emerged as a symbolic wedge-driving issue. By 1995 the Rabin government was engaged in full-fledged internal discussions—perhaps better described as pitched ideological battles—about the concept of relinquishing occupied land in exchange for a Palestinian commitment to peace. Parties on the left lobbied that the chance of ending the bitter armed conflict was worth the price of redrawing the maps. Religious parties on the extreme right considered relinquishing any hectare of Jewish-held land to be an act of treason against God's covenant with Israel. Moderate Palestinians wanted the negotiations to proceed; nationalists insisted that everything from the Dead Sea to the Mediterranean must be Palestinian.

Israel's ultra-Orthodox nationalists formed a coalition called The Jerusalem Committee for Rachel's Tomb. Member of Knesset (MK) Hanan Porat went to lobby Prime Minister Rabin and there he was joined by MK Rabbi Menahem Porush. Porat made his case and then Porush threw his arms around Rabin and sobbed, "It is Mama Ruhi. How can you give away her grave?" Rabin tried to calm him, and the rabbi responded, "How can I calm down? . . . The Jewish People will never forgive you if you abandon Mama's tomb."[23] Emotional appeals at the top levels of government were backed up by activities on the ground. When they learned that the map of Jerusalem's boundaries was under discussion, members of the coalition moved to create a constant Jewish religious presence at the site. The Yeshiva of Rachel's Tomb was established. Woman's groups conducted classes there. Porat organized a daily study group for married men to study religious texts; another met to recite Psalms. They prayed and studied aloud in the shrine's courtyard to insure, as the Committee for Rachel's Tomb website boasted, that "the sounds of Torah learning filled the air of Bethlehem."[24] Orthodox Jews worldwide were encouraged to write letters to pressure the government.

It was action calculated to incite official intervention. Bethlehem's Muslim community found the activities at the Tomb offensive. Students from the nearby Aida and Deheishe refugee camps gathered to throw rocks at the Tomb complex. There were sniper incidents. The Israeli government, believing that the worshipers could no longer be adequately protected by the Tomb's existing physical structure, began to fortify the site. In September 1995, a brouhaha involving an archaeological tunnel at the Temple Mount in Jerusalem sparked Palestinian rioting both at Joseph's Tomb and Rachel's Tomb. In the aftermath, access to Rachel's Tomb was temporarily halted. When it resumed, Jewish religious groups stepped up their activity. A major effort was mounted to celebrate the 11 Hesvan Yahrzeit of Mother Rachel there. By July 1997 the former simple domed Tomb and prayer hall resembled a military garrison surrounding a complex of worship and study spaces.

By late 2000 there were almost-daily shooting incidents at Rachel's Tomb. After a particularly violent spate on Rosh Hashanah, access was again closed. Nevertheless, small groups of women from Hebron defied the ban and made their way through Bethlehem to pray there. IDF soldiers were called, and they ordered the women to leave. Again, Palestinian protestors threw rocks. Again, the worshipers demanded protection, which the army provided. Again, pressure on the government mounted until eventually the Israeli general in charge of the area approved yahrzeit ceremonies at the Tomb. Religious nationalists applauded. As the Jerusalem Committee for Rachel's Tomb put it, "the Jews who visit the Tomb force the government to take firm action to protect the grave of Rachel. If we continue to demand and actually go to visit our 3rd most important holy place we will make sure that it will remain in our hands rather than be given away as a gift to Arafat."[25] In May 2001 a committee member e-mailed her troops: "It is very important for us to come . . . tomorrow, Tuesday, May 8th and show the army and the world that we will not abandon Kever Rachel. To be on the safe side, pack an extra sandwich."[26] No wonder that Palestinian polemicists interpreted the increased religious activity at Rachel's Tomb as a cynical mask for a land-grab.

Tension spiraled upward. The women's group Yesh Sachar Lifulatech, dedicated to permanent Israeli control of the Tomb, pressured Israel's national bus company to begin regular service there from Jerusalem's Central Bus Station. The IDF provided armored buses to ferry pilgrims the last few hundred meters. From the other side, buses brought scores of young Palestinians from the Deheishe refugee camp, a distance of about 1.5 kilometers, to harass Jewish worshipers. The air around the holy site buzzed with shouts, prayers, stones, gasoline-filled bottles, hand grenades, and bullets.[27] In early October 2001 shooting around the Tomb and in the Gilo district of southern Jerusalem moved the IDF to ring

Interior, Rachel's Tomb. Photo, L. Davidson, 1997.

Bethlehem and take control of the Aida refugee camp. The flow of Jewish pilgrims increased, peaking for Rachel's yahrzeit festival and again for Hanukah celebrations at the Tomb. The pilgrimages were widely advertised and thousands answered the call.

On June 5, 2002, the Israeli government announced its plans for a security fence separating the Palestinian West Bank from Israel. On Jerusalem's southern flank it would follow the Green Line that marked the armistice agreement of 1948. As in 1967, there was little consensus with regard to Rachel's Tomb, which still lay 200 meters outside the planned fence. Jerusalem's mayor Ehud Olmert demanded the fence line be redrawn on the grounds that thousands of Jewish pilgrims regularly pray at the tomb, and they must be protected; the tomb was already under Israeli jurisdiction; and, the fence was likely to establish a permanent de facto border for Israel, and it would be unconscionable to exclude Mother Rachel's grave. The army reiterated the 1967 arguments that annexing Rachel's Tomb had negative implications for security. Politicians on the Left felt that it would have even graver negative consequences for world opinion. The religious Right hued and cried.

Again, the keep-the-shrine coalition won the day. On September 12, newspapers announced that the Israeli Security Cabinet had approved a "Jerusalem Envelope Plan" that put Rachel's Tomb inside the proposed security fence. Palestinians were furious. A week later, the Palestinian newspaper the *Jerusalem Times* quoted Jerusalem's Mufti, Sheikh Ikrima Sabri: "the Israeli decision to annex the Bilal Bin Rabah Mosque, known as Rachel's Tomb, in Bethlehem, to the Jewish Municipality of West Jerusalem is a dangerous escalation in the already volatile situation as the site belongs to the Muslim Wakf."[28] Bethlehem's mayor agreed and lambasted the Israeli plan to expropriate thirty to forty Palestinian-owned homes in the process of securing the shrine. As always, religious and territorial claims were inextricably joined. The Israeli religious Right hoped, and the Palestinian nationalists feared, that the "temporary" security fence would turn out to establish permanent borders.

Work on the fence began, and the battle over the boundary moved to the courts. Palestinian groups in Jerusalem's northern and eastern suburbs and the Municipality of Bethlehem petitioned Israel's High Court of Justice to stop the work or to force rerouting the fence so as to minimize its negative impact on Palestinian neighborhoods. In June 2004, justices ruled that despite the paramount nature of Israel's need for security, it must balance those needs with humanitarian considerations and the concern for human rights.[29] Even so, on February 3, 2005, the Court turned down the Bethlehem petition that the route be changed, asserting that the route allows Jews to pray freely at the site and "does not impede Palestinian residents' freedom of movement and business concerns."[30]

YAACOV ABUHATZEIRA IN EGYPT: THE POLITICS OF PROTEST

Although Israel is one thing and Judaism is another, unfortunately the two are often equated, either through ignorance or design. This has often led sympathizers with Palestinian aspirations of statehood to vent their anger at Israel by targeting Jewish religious sites abroad. Since the current conflicts began, synagogues or Jewish centers have been attacked in France, Argentina, Morocco, and Turkey, among other countries. Tunisia's pilgrimage shrine of La Ghriba was attacked in 2002. While a popular Jewish shrine in Demito (near Alexandria, Egypt) has not suffered this kind of violence, its pilgrimage has fallen victim to the conflicts in Palestine.

The tomb-shrine, which caps a ten-meter hill, is reputed to contain the remains of the Sephardic tzadiq Yaacov Abuhatzeira, who died there in 1880 on his way to the Holy Land from Morocco (see Chapter 9). (Others believe that it is really the grave of a second Moroccan kabbalist and tzadiq, Yaakov Aharon Elbaz, and say that, because Elbaz was traveling on a flying carpet or reed mat, he is revered under the name Abu Hazira [Arabic *hazira* means mat].) Abuhatzeira's traditional hillula was similar to those of other North African Sephardic saints. It began on the supposed anniversary of the tzadiq's death in the middle of January and continued for about a week. Families gathered at the tomb to pray, picnic, feast, and drink alcohol, and to leave on the tzadiq's tomb written notes of thanks or petitions for help.

Throughout most of the twentieth century the tomb of Abuhatzeira drew many Jewish pilgrims from Egypt, Tunisia, and Morocco. During the quarter-century between the 1979 signing of the Camp David Accords between Israel and Egypt and the beginning of the Second Intifada in 2000, numerous Israeli pilgrims visited the shrine as well.

This pilgrimage—like others to Christian, Muslim, and Jewish holy sites in Egypt—was promoted by the Egyptian Ministry of Tourism as a development activity. Despite the economic benefits of pilgrimage tourism, some local Muslims objected to the annual influx of Jews. The consumption of alcoholic beverages and sometimes pilgrim clothing violated Islamic customs. The Jews' mere presence was seen as an affront to Muslims. The heavy security was both inconvenient and insulting.[31]

With the Second Intifada, however, the situation changed radically. Feelings of resentment against Israelis and powerlessness with regard to being able to help the Palestinians combined with a widespread conviction that Egypt's central government was not taking the legitimate concerns of its own people to heart. The Egyptian press, the Arab-language television networks, and numerous imams voiced a constant series of stories detailing and condemning alleged Israeli atrocities. They highlighted any controversy involving the Temple Mount, the Dome of the Rock, or the Al-Aqsa Mosque. In the Egyptian press the terms *Israeli*, *Zionist*, and *Jew* tended to be used interchangeably, thus both blurring and amplifying the target of animosity. (Ironically, the Israeli press and Jewish media in the Diaspora, while outraged by this semantic confusion, are themselves guilty of referring to Palestinians as Arabs and of presupposing that all Palestinians are Muslims.) As a result, in 2000 the Egyptian government denied visas to Israeli pilgrims who wanted to visit the tomb. The few Israelis, Moroccans, Tunisians, and French Maghrebis who managed to go were allowed to celebrate the hillula, but with a heavy Egyptian army guard. When interviewed by a reporter at that time, Ahmed Sami, a young farmer in Demito, symbolically linked his village and far-off Jerusalem, complaining to an *Al-Ahram Weekly* reporter: "Jews should be prevented from coming to our land in the same way they are preventing Palestinians from going to Al-Aqsa." For Mustafa Rasslan, another outspoken villager, the tzadiq's presence was an outrage and a blasphemy, as well as a constant reminder that poor, suffering, Muslim Arabs were more deserving of victim status than the triumphant Jews: "I'm sick and tired of Abu Hassira's shrine that Jews use as a wailing wall. . . . I'm offended and I don't want my children to see this mulid" [Arabic, holy man]. Rasslan wanted the tzadiq's bones dug up and removed from Demito altogether.[32]

Subsequently the Egyptian Ministry of Tourism classified Abuhatzeira's tomb as a tourist site, worthy of preservation and promotion, as were many Christian, Coptic, and Muslim holy sites. Rasslan petitioned an Egyptian administrative court to overturn the ruling, and it did. On September 8 a state-run newspaper reported that the tomb was removed from the official list of tourist sites. The rationale marginalized Jews completely from Egyptian culture. "Jews had no effect on the ancient Egyptian civilization. . . . The Jews were not a settled people. . . . For a monument to be connected to a people it has to be related to their beliefs and their religion. It has not been proved that the Jews had practiced this in any stage of Egyptian history." The judge also linked his decision more directly to current events, arguing that the pilgrimage offended Egyptian Muslims and Christians who saw their holy places being desecrated by Jewish soldiers.[33]

The anchor of a popular Egyptian news program demanded that the Israelis remove Abuhatzeira's bones to Israel. A Parliament member warned of the harmful psychological effects the festival would have on Egyptian morale, pointing out that in the current atmosphere the festival would be more political than religious in nature.[34] In January 2001 the government prohibited the hillula from being held at the tomb. Journalists were denied access to the village. Jewish pilgrimage traffic to the site all but dried up. Egyptian moderates protested on the grounds that putting Abuhatzeira's tomb off-limits was un-Muslim in nature, had negative economic effects, and projected an unfortunate image to the world about Egyptian intolerance.

By the spring of 2001 the government sought a middle ground by reclassifying the tomb and its mound as an archaeological site. Jews could now visit as paying tourists but would be prohibited from conducting ceremonies there. When Egypt denied visas to several potential pilgrims, the seventy rabbis who had planned to attend canceled their flights.[35] As always, such measures rarely placate the extremists. Demito's Rasslan argued that this would only mean that Jews would come to his village year round, rather than just for the hillula. Then, in an attempt to undercut Jewish claims to the site, Rasslan said that he possessed documents proving that Abuhatzeira was Muslim, a descendant of Tarek ibn Ziad, the illustrious eighth-century conqueror of Spanish Andalusia.[36] Perhaps with this in mind, in January 2004, Egypt's Supreme Administrative Court upheld the festival ban. Yet a year later the American ambassador to Egypt reported that Jews once again had official permission to make their pilgrimage to the tomb.[37]

CAVE OF MACHPELAH: THE POLITICS OF SHARING

As nearly always, exclusivity of ownership is a key issue. Hebron's Cave of Machpelah is the traditional site of the tombs of Abraham and Sarah, Isaac and Rebecca, and Jacob and Leah. Some Jews even believe that Adam and Eve are buried there among the Patriarchs and Matriarchs. The unbroken tradition of Jewish pilgrimage to the Machpelah graves stretches back to biblical times. For Orthodox Jews, then, the shrine is Jewish *a priori*. On the other hand, because Ishmael, Abraham's son with Hagar, is held to be the founder of Islam, Muslims, too, venerate the site as holy. Some Muslims would have it exclusively so. As Yasser Arafat put it in 1996, "Abraham was neither Jewish nor a Hebrew, but was simply an Iraqi. The Jews have no right to claim part of the Tomb of the Patriarchs in Hebron, Abraham's resting place, as a synagogue. Rather, the whole building should be a mosque."[38] While there are several other Jewish holy sites in Hebron and its immediate vicinity (e.g., the tombs of Ruth and Jesse near the cemetery; the Terebinths or Oaks of Mamre; King David's Pool, also known as the Sultan's Pool; the tomb of Abner, who served Saul and David as military commander), none of these has attracted as many pilgrims or as much political attention as the Cave of Machpelah. As a result, none has been a flash point for conflict in the same way.

The modern history of violent struggle to control the Cave of Machpelah began in the years following the World War I, when the West Bank became part of the League of Nations' British Mandate for Palestine. Tensions in Hebron between the Islamic majority and the Jewish minority ran high, and in the rioting that swept Palestine in 1929 sixty-seven Hebron Jews were killed, their synagogues destroyed, and the survivors driven out of the city. A small Jewish community reestablished itself in 1931, but it was decimated again in the violence that erupted in 1936. The British evacuated all the Jewish survivors with the exception of one individual, who hung on until 1947. After the 1948 War of Independence Hebron became part of Jordan and, from then until 1967, Jews were barred from the city or the Tomb, despite the fact that the armistice agreement stipulated there would be Jewish access.

Jewish resettlement of Hebron after the 1967 war was problematical. The local Arab population objected to the influx, while the IDF feared that resettlement would create an untenable security commitment. In 1968 a group of ten ultra-Orthodox families was authorized to hold a Passover seder in a hotel in the city. When the holiday ended, they refused to leave. Supporters rallied to their cause; the army was reluctant to remove them by force; David Ben-Gurion spoke out in favor of resettlement. In 1970 the Israeli government began to construct a Jewish settlement, called Kiryat Arba (the biblical name of Hebron prior to its conquest by Caleb [Joshua 14:15]), on the vacant summit of a hill 750 meters east of the Cave of Machpelah. Today it houses more than 7,000 Jews, while several dozen others have taken up residence in Hebron itself. Defending them from Arab harassment, defending Hebron's Arabs from Jewish harassment, and preventing minor incidents from growing into full-fledged violence keep both the IDF and the PA security forces on edge.

By far the most egregious incident of violence at the Cave of Machpelah occurred in February 1994, when Baruch Goldstein, an American-born ultra-Orthodox

Machpelah; Mosque over the Tombs of the Matriarchs and Patriarchs. Hebron. Photo, D. Gitlitz, 1967.

resident of Kiryat Arba, opened fire during a Muslim prayer service inside the mosque over the Tomb, killing 29 and wounding 125 worshipers before he himself was beaten to death by the crowd. In June, an Israeli government commission concluded that Goldstein acted alone. But while his actions were loudly condemned by the mainline press in Israel, the Arab world, and elsewhere, he is revered as a hero and a martyr by a segment of the ultra-Orthodox community. Goldstein was buried in Kiryat Arba, and his tomb became a shrine and place of pilgrimage to those who sympathize with his politics. There was a bench for worshipers, an altar for burning candles, and a large headstone whose inscription included the words "holy" and "martyr." The Goldstein shrine and its pilgrimage cult so incensed majority Israeli public opinion and significant segments of the government that in June 1998 the Knesset passed a "Law Prohibiting the Erection of Memorials to Terrorists." The IDF ordered the two words removed. Goldstein's family petitioned the court to prevent it, and the Supreme Court issued a temporary injunction to halt the excision. Though the shrine was eventually destroyed, the grave site continues to attract right-wing pilgrims who are convinced that Goldstein acted to thwart a planned Palestinian attack on their settlement.

The 1994 Goldstein massacre has had long-ranging consequences. Responsible Israeli and Palestinian authorities recognize that the Cave of the Patriarchs is holy to both Islam and Judaism. They also appreciate Hebron's political and demographic constraints: large numbers of Orthodox Jews from all over Israel are determined to make regular pilgrimages to the shrine, the Jewish residents of Hebron and its environs are a small drop in a big bucket, and both sides are armed. These realities have compelled cool heads on both sides of the conflict to seek ways to compromise. For example, by the terms of the Interim Agreement of September 1995, security in 80 percent of Hebron would fall under PA control while the IDF would maintain security in the other 20 percent to protect the Jewish enclaves around the Cave of Machpelah. The PA would exercise civil powers in both areas.

Several incidents of violence, as well as the Israeli elections, delayed the implementation of this agreement. It was not until a new protocol was negotiated in 1997 that redeployment began. Under this new accord, the two sides would jointly patrol the most sensitive areas. Each side's religious traditions at the Cave would be respected, Muslim and Jewish worshipers would be scheduled and positioned so as to avoid contact with one another, and annually each side would have ten days of exclusive access to the tombs. Any new construction or physical modification of the site must be approved by both parties. Both sides agreed to manage traffic in the city and to and from the shrine so as not to inconvenience either pilgrim access or the everyday activities of Hebron.

Have these attempts at compromise and collaboration had an effect? Some, although extremists on neither side are happy. Some Jewish worshipers bitterly object at being restricted to the cave's Abraham and Jacob areas while the Isaac chamber, the largest, is reserved for Muslims.[39] While it is impossible to measure the numbers of incidents that have *not* occurred because of these procedures, since Goldstein's action there have been no further massacres inside the shrine. Outside, violent confrontations are still common.[40] In many cases, such as riots during Sukkot 2001 and clashes in early 2005, the immediate spark that kindled the violence was Jewish pilgrimage activity.

The intermediate-term strategy is clear. Collaborate on administrative and logistical details. Emphasize the rhetoric of sharing, and dampen the claims of exclusive ownership. Try to keep the extremist hotheads apart. Yet even assuming the best of intentions—which are by no means a given—as this book goes to press, no one can say that peaceful coexistence at the Cave of Machpelah has been achieved.

THE TEMPLE MOUNT/HARAM AL-SHARIF;
THE WESTERN/BURAQ WALL

The question of who rightfully controls Jerusalem's holy sites has ancient roots. For more than 3,000 years rival claims have been watered with blood, pruned with sharp swords or their modern equivalents, and ground into the soil by pilgrims' feet. To this day rival claims continue to bear bitter fruit. The most casual glance at the historical record notes four continuous trends: the rival claims go back nearly forever; they are asserted in times of stress in order to advance current political agendas; religious extremists, the ones who march under the banner of exclusive possession, always seem to outflank the political pragmatists who, in the din of clashing claims, advocate the need to share; the never-ending pressure of pilgrims keep the issues perpetually in the foreground.

By the early years of the twentieth century, rivalry over the Temple Mount increasingly mixed religious tradition with nationalism. Christians were largely marginal to the conflicts that were escalating on a daily basis among Muslims and Jews. To Jewish fundamentalists, God gave Jerusalem to the Jews, while the Muslims were the descendants of the Amalekites, whom the Bible instructed the Jews to destroy (1 Sam. 15:3). The site is holier for Jews than for others. The Muslims have Mecca; the Christians Rome; and the Jews Jerusalem. For Muslim extremists, the Jews were foreigners, non-natives, who under Joshua's leadership had usurped land belonging to Palestine's native populace, and now were doing it again. In 1919 there were riots. Jews wanted to blow the shofar at the Wall. They were forbidden by a ruling from the British Mandate, which agreed that it was an insult to Islam. Benches so that the old men could pray? Another insult. A small cloth screen to separate men and women? Ditto, since to Palestinian Muslims these clearly constituted first steps in a Jewish campaign to seize the mosques on the Haram. Though the narrow alley next to the Kotel had for centuries been a cul de sac, Jerusalem's Arabs cut a second opening so as to turn it into a through street, and began to drive cattle along it during the Jews' prayer times. The Jews protested to the Mandate, which ruled that the Western Wall is the place where Muhammad had tied Al-Buraq, and that moreover it fell within the Muslim religious endowment (*waqf*) which now devolved to the Palestinians. In 1931 the British "Shaw Commission" ruled on ownership and access: "To the Moslems belong the sole ownership of, and the sole proprietary right to, the Western Wall, seeing that it forms an integral part of the Haram al-Sharif area, which is a Waqf property. . . . The Jews shall have free access to the Western Wall for the purpose of devotions at all times. . . ."[41] Free access except that they could not blow the shofar, or pray loudly, or leave the cabinet with the Torahs at the wall overnight, or bring out the Torah on weekdays, or put up any kind of a cloth divider, and so forth. Compliance was monitored by the British authorities.

From 1948 to 1967, under Jordanian rule, Israeli Jews were denied any access to the site. After the Six-Day War the headaches began.

1967   The Old City fell to Israel on June 7. There is no question that recovery of the holy sites was a first priority, more for their symbolic than their military value. The IDF took the Temple area and euphoric soldiers prayed and danced at the Wall. Within an hour General Rabbi Shlomo Goren raced to the wall with Yitzhak Rabin and Defense Minister Moshe Dayan. Goren blew the shofar, the heavily armed soldiers cried, prayed, and danced. Dayan noticed that someone had hoisted an Israeli flag over the Dome of the Rock. Acutely aware of provoking an overtly religious war, Dayan ordered it taken down. A paratroop company was deploying on the Haram; Dayan ordered them out. A few days later, Dayan agreed to return control of the Haram to the Muslim waqf, insisting only that Jews be given the right to visit the site provided that they did not pray there. Goren was incensed, and a few weeks later on Tisha b'Av led a prayer service, with shofar and Torah, on the Haram. The army ordered them out. Goren fired off a letter to the Ministerial Committee for the Safeguarding of the Holy Places, expressing dismay that the only place in the world where Jews, as Jews, were expressly forbidden to pray was Judaism's holiest site. Dayan realized that to Islamic extremists, any hint of Israeli appropriation of the Haram and its mosques could provoke an explosion. Jewish religious extremists, on the other hand, wanted to throw the Muslim defilers off of the Holy Mount and rededicate the site to Judaism by erecting a new temple there, citing the precedent of the Macabees.

1969   Political pragmatists clashed rhetorically with strict adherents of Halakhah and with Christian fundamentalists, who believed that Christ would not return until the Third Temple rose on the Temple Mount. In August, one member of this latter group, an Australian Protestant named Rohan, set fire to the Al-Aqsa mosque. Across the Arab world, Israel was blamed.

1971   Amid the escalating violence, the Vatican offered to administer Jerusalem as a neutral city in order to guarantee universal access. Prime Minister Golda Meir termed the offer hypocritical: "Why is it permissible for Christian holy places to be under the regime of a Muslim state, but it is considered to be a defect for those places to be under the regime of a Jewish state?"

1982   Alan Goodman, an Israeli citizen with a U.S. passport, shot up the Dome of the Rock, killing one and wounding three. Since then, several other plots to wreck havoc on the Haram have been thwarted by Israeli security forces. For the most part, Amos Alon argues persuasively, the deeply religious plotters and schemers are "the terrorist fringe of an informal worldwide movement that encompasses fundamentalist Jews and fundamentalist Christians united in a belief that the End of Days is near."[42]

1990   Rumors circulated that Jewish extremists were plotting to blow up the Temple Mount's mosques. In the following riot a dozen Palestinians were killed.

1996   Israel carried out archaeological explorations near the Temple Mount compound. Palestinians accused Israel of trying to undermine the foundations of Al-Aqsa. According to the official website of the Palestinian Authority, "The tunnel is designed to tighten the grip of the Israeli occupation forces on the sacred compound, protect Jews who visit it and Judaize the Old City."[43] The UN Palestinian observer petitioned the Security Council to bring pressure to halt it. The tunnel, connecting the Western Wall Plaza and the Via Dolorosa, opened to tourists. In the ensuing riots, eighty people were killed.

1998   Old gall in new barrels. On May 22, the Mufti of Jerusalem, Sheikh Ikrima Sabri, stated that "the Western Wall . . . belongs to Moslems, and was given to the Jews as a place of prayer only because the British asked and the Moslems agreed out of the goodness of their hearts. The Western Wall is just a fence belonging to a Moslem holy site. . . . Why should we allow the Jews to share places which are holy to us and to Islam?"[44]

1999   Muslim archaeologists used bulldozers to scrape dirt from the entrance to an underground chamber in the southeast corner of the Haram, claiming it is a seventh-century mosque. Some Jews protested that it could be part of the Second Temple. Christians ascribed it to the Crusaders. Lawsuits failed to stop the work. Right-wing Israelis burned Palestinian flags in the streets near the Haram.[45]

2000   On September 28 Ariel Sharon, at that moment leader of the opposition Likud party, visited the Temple Mount with several supporters, some armed, to symbolically underscore Israel's claims to the site. This provoked widespread rioting in Jerusalem, followed by the ratcheting up of systematic violence known as the Second Intifada. The waqf banned non-Muslims from visiting the Temple Mount.

2003   In May, without fanfare, the Temple Mount was reopened to non-Muslim visitors. Waqf officials later protested that the mosques are for Muslim worshipers, not a museum for non-Muslim tourists.

2004   Responding to news that Israel planned to extend the archaeological tunnel under the Al-Aqsa mosque, Sheikh Ikrima Sabri warned that violence would surely follow, since the mosque and the platform on which it stands are inalienable Muslim possessions. Hundreds of Palestinians threw rocks from the Haram platform onto Jewish worshipers at the Western Wall below. When the Israeli police responded with stun grenades and rubber bullets, 1,000 or more Muslims barricaded themselves in Al-Aqsa.

2005   On Fridays, incendiary anti-Israeli sermons at Al-Aqsa. On Saturdays, protests by Jewish extremists for control of the entire Temple Mount. Israeli and Palestinian policemen nervously scan visitors to the Haram plaza, prohibiting Jews from entering with prayer books, and hoping that the metal detectors that all have to pass through will prevent weapons from being brought into the mosques.

And tomorrow. . . .

LOOKING BACK TOWARD THE FUTURE

With regard to holy places and the pilgrimages to them, it is feasible that some of what is at issue can be resolved by negotiation. The conditions of access can be hammered out. The safety of pilgrims can be guaranteed. Overt mocking of another religion's beliefs or practices can be penalized. Over time, working together can become a habit. Competent authorities can pave streets, provide electricity and clean water, pipe away sewage, and sweep up the detritus that pilgrims leave behind.

Success in these kinds of activities works to buttress the moderate political center, to broaden support for cooperation and compromise as a means of survival. It is much harder to contain the extremists who believe that compromise is treason, harder to prevent the inevitable acts of violence from undermining the commitment to peace, harder to keep a cork in the bottle of revenge. The media, even the writers who are not in thrall to their political convictions, frequently do more harm than good. Everyone knows the sales value of bad news, the dramatic impact of photographs of a surging crowd, a massive explosion, a dead child. Peace is boring, while few things are as riveting as a good fight.

What cannot be negotiated satisfactorily are competing claims for divinely conferred sovereignty. When a people affirm that their God gave this holy place to them and to them alone, when they assert that God has chosen them and only them to administer this shrine for the good of all humankind, when people shout that their God interprets anyone else's control of this place as an outrageous insult and will punish them for permitting it to happen, there is no room for negotiation. Under these conditions, pilgrims do not promote understanding, they provoke conflict. On these issues, the practical logic of realpolitik and the unshakeable certainty of religious faith speak different languages. Since God is immortal, there is no statute of limitations on the deity's demands. When it comes to memories of ancient religious insults, the evil that men do lives after them, and the embers of outrage never grow cold.

The timetable for redress of wrongs stretches beyond the horizon. When it comes to regaining sovereignty, today is the best time, tomorrow is good. But, the extremists believe, if we fail this week, in a thousand years we may succeed.

Under these conditions, the only achievable peace is a protracted ceasefire.

APPENDIX: HEBREW MONTH EQUIVALENTS

Tishri	September–October
Hesvan	October–November
Kislev	November–December
Tebet	December–January
Shebat	January–February
Adar	February–March
Adar sheni	February–March in a leap year
Nisan	March–April
Iyar	April–May
Sivan	May–June
Tammuz	June–July
Av	July–August
Elul	August–September

NOTES

Chapter 1. Jewish Pilgrims?

1. Robert Silverberg, *Kingdoms of the Wall* (New York: Bantam, 1992); Gao Xingjian, *Soul Mountain*, trans. Mabel Lee (New York: HarperCollins, 2000); Ruth Knafo Setton, *The Road to Fez* (Washington, DC: Counterpoint, 2001).

2. This definition comes from the introduction on pilgrimage from our *Pilgrimage: From the Ganges to Graceland: An Encyclopedia* (Santa Barbara: ABC-CLIO, 2002), xvii.

3. Richard Niebuhr, "Pilgrims and Pioneers," *Parabola* 9, no. 3 (1984): 7.

4. Nelson H. Graburn, "Tourism: The Sacred Journey," in *Hosts and Guests: The Anthropology of Tourism*, ed. Valene Smith (Philadelphia: University of Pennsylvania Press, 1977), 17–31.

5. Erik Cohen, "Pilgrimage Centers: Concentric and Excentric," in "Pilgrimage and Tourism: The Quest in Guest," ed. Valene Smith, special issue, *Annals of Tourism Research* 19, no. 1 (1992): 49.

6. For example: Emanuel Marx, "Communal and Individual Pilgrimage: The Region of Saints' Tombs in South Sinai," in *Regional Cults*, ed. Richard P. Werbner (London: Academic Press, 1977), 29–51. Also, E. Wolf, "The Virgin of Guadalupe: A Mexican National Symbol," *Journal of American Folklore* 71, no. 1 (1958): 34–39.

7. Victor Turner, "The Center Out There: Pilgrim's Goal," *History of Religions* 12, no. 3 (February 1973): 191–230. Victor Turner and Edith Turner, *Image and Pilgrimage in Christian Culture. Anthropological Perspectives* (New York: Columbia University Press, 1978). The Turners' work builds on Arnold van Gennep's earlier analysis of rites of passage (*The Rites of Passage* [Chicago: University of Chicago Press, 1961]). The theoretical literature on pilgrimage is vast and will not be summarized here.

Chapter 2. Beginnings: Converging on Jerusalem

1. *Epic of Gilgamesh*, trans. N. K. Sanders (Baltimore: Penguin, 1960), 110.

2. Mircea Eliade, *The Sacred and the Profane: The Nature of Religion*, trans. Willard R. Trask (New York: Harcourt, Brace, 1959), 11–12.

3. To cite just one example: The Sumerian god *On*, who ruled the heavens, was incorporated into the Babylonian pantheon whose capitol city was considered the portal of access to him (in the ancient Semitic tongues *Bab* = gate, *El* = god, *On* or *Onu* = of the heavens). These concepts seem to have been referenced by Jacob when he termed the place of his dream "the house of God, and this is the gate of heaven" (Gen. 28:17) (See Nozrem ha Brit, "Jews and the Hajj Pilgrimage," http://www.jews-for-allah.org/Jews-and-Muslims-Agree/jews_and_the_hajj_pilgrimage.htm [accessed January 25, 2004]). Hans-Joachim Kraus goes so far as to state that every ancient Israelite cultic practice was connected to the Canaanite world (Hans-Joachim Kraus, *Worship in Israel: A Cultic History of the Old Testament* [Richmond: John Knox Press, 1965], 36). Seth Ward, following Victor Turner's typology of pilgrimages, considers the early Israelite pilgrimages that "emerge from earlier religious beliefs and symbols [which have been] transformed to fit into the new religious framework" to be archaic pilgrimages (Seth Ward, *God's Place in the World* [London: Cassel, 1998], 66).

4. Enoch Zundel ben Joseph, *Ets Yosef* (originally published in 1829). Cited by Shlomo Riskin in his *parasha* for Shabbat R'eh 25 Av 5760/August 26, 2000, http://www.ohrtorahstone.org.il/parsha/5760/ekev60.htm (accessed June 18, 2003).

5. A contrary view is offered by Roland de Vaux who, from external evidence and close textual analysis, concludes that "the stories claiming that the patriarchs founded these sanctuaries really mean that the patriarchs adopted them and that the patriarchal god of the father, the private god of the nomadic group, was assimilated to the god of the settled people with whom the nomads came into contact" (*The Early History of Israel*, trans. David Smith [Philadelphia: Westminster Press, 1978], 281).

6. In addition to archaeological evidence, child sacrifice is mentioned in 1 Kings 16:34, 2 Kings 3:27, 23:10, and Jud. 11.

7. The attribution of Abraham's altar to Jerusalem is problematical: Jerusalem is not three day's distant from Beersheba; the area is forested, so there would be no need to carry wood there. Nahum Sarna, *The Jewish Publication Society Torah Commentary: Genesis* (Philadelphia: Jewish Publication Society, 1989), 392.

8. Ronald S. Hendel, "Sacrifice as a Cultural System: The Ritual Symbolism of Exodus 24:3–8," *Zeitschrift für die alttestamentliche Wissenschaft* 101(1989): 374–376.

9. Christian exegesis recognizes a fourth paradigm as well: one reading of the book of Hebrews considers the Exodus to be a foreshadowing of a soul's pilgrimage from birth through death to heaven. See William G. Johnsson, "The Pilgrimage Motif in the Book of Hebrews," *Journal of Biblical Literature* 97, no. 2 (June 1978): 239–251.

10. Vaux, *Early History*, 376–388, 426–439.

11. Rainer Albertz, *A History of Israelite Religion in the Old Testament Period*, trans. John Bowden, 2 vols. (Louisville: Westminster/John Knox Press, 1994), 1:7.

12. Roland de Vaux, *Ancient Israel: Its Life and Institutions*, trans. John McHugh (London: Darton, Longham & Todd, 1965), 278. Babylonian art frequently depicts worshipers kneeling before trees (W.O.E. Oesterley and Theodore H. Robinson, *Hebrew Religion: Its Origin and Development*, 2nd ed. [New York: Macmillan, 1937], 24). See also Susan Ackerman, *Under Every Green Tree: Popular Religion in Sixth-*

Century Judah (Atlanta: Scholars Press, 1992); Mark S. Smith, *The Early History of God: Yahweh and the Other Deities in Ancient Israel* (San Francisco: Harper and Row, 1990).

13. The oak's name, *Moreh* (teacher), suggests that it may have been a well-known place of oracle.

14. H. H. Rowley cautions that "all these stories which bring the patriarchs into association with trees and springs and stones were intended to legitimate [pre-existing] shrines" (H. H. Rowley, *Worship in Ancient Israel: Its Form and Meaning* [Philadelphia: Fortress Press; London: SPCK, 1967], 22–23).

15. The two terms, interchangeably, seem to have signified "big tree" (Vaux, *Ancient Israel*, 279).

16. Vaux, *Ancient Israel*, 289.

17. Kraus, *Worship in Israel*, 140.

18. Menahem Haran notes that with the exception of the shrines at Dan, Ophrah, and perhaps—judging from archaeological evidence—Arad, all the others are arrayed in the Canaanite hill country between Shiloh in the north and Hebron in the south (Menahem Haran, *Temples and Temple-Service in Ancient Israel: An Inquiry into the Character of Cult Phenomena and the Historical Setting of the Priestly School* [Oxford: Clarendon, 1978], 41). Beersheba is another exception.

19. The name that Abraham invoked, *El-'Olam* (the God of Eternity), may well refer to a Philistine or Canaanite god called by that name (Vaux, *Ancient Israel*, 293).

20. James A. Montgomery, *A Critical and Exegetical Commentary on the Books of Kings* (Edinburgh: T. & T. Clark, 1967), 300.

21. Vaux, *Early History*, 604. The Hebrew word *gilgal* indicates circularity.

22. Sandra Scham, "The Lost Goddess of Israel," *Archaeology* 58, no. 2 (March/April 2005): 39.

23. Toorn finds that it was common for Israelite women of this time to lodge intercessory prayer petitions at local shrines and to swear vows to provide the shrine with certain resources if the prayer was favorably answered, noting that Num. 30 is dedicated in its entirety to this subject (Karel vander Toorn, *From Her Cradle to Her Grave: The Role of Religion in the Life of the Israelite and Babylonian Woman*, trans. Sara J. Denning-Bolle [Sheffield: Journal for the Study of the Old Testament, 1994], 96).

24. "[Hannah] took . . . a three-year-old bull, an ephah of flour, and a skin of wine" (1 Sam. 1:24). Other food offerings were brought as a shrine fee or for incorporation into the rites. For example, Jeroboam's wife brought Ahijah the prophet at Shiloh "ten loaves, some cakes, and a jar of honey" (1 Kings 14:3).

25. For Kraus, the dancing was an assimilation of local custom, echoing contemporary Canaanite nature worship (*Worship in Israel*, 174).

Chapter 3. Jerusalem, the State Cult, and the Three Harvest Pilgrimages

1. Philo Judaeus, "The Special Laws," in *Philo*, trans. F. H. Colson, 10 vols. (London: William Heinemann, Ltd.; Cambridge: Harvard University Press, 1929–1962), 1.69; vol. 7:139.

2. Margaret Barker, *The Gate of Heaven: The History and Symbolism of the Temple in Jerusalem* (London: SPCK, 1991), 19. *The Babylonian Talmud*, ed. I. Epstein (London: Soncino Press, 1961). Further references will be indicated BT.

3. Another tradition sites the dream at Bethel (see below).

4. Joseph Dan, "Jerusalem in Jewish Spirituality," in *City of the Great King: Jerusalem from David to the Present*, ed. Nitza Rosovsky (Cambridge: Harvard University Press, 1996), 60–61.

5. In the second-century-BCE Essene text of Jubilees (Little Genesis) 8:19, Mount Zion is explicitly termed the center of the navel of the earth. Cited in W. D. Davies, *The Territorial Dimension of Judaism* (Berkeley: University of California Press, 1982), 2.

6. Midrash Tanhuma Pekudei: "You also find that there is a Jerusalem above, corresponding to the Jerusalem below. For sheer love of the earthly Jerusalem, God made himself one above." Cited in J. Zwi Werblowsky, "The Meaning of Jerusalem to Jews, Christians, and Muslims," in *Jerusalem in the Mind of the Western World, 1800–1948. With Eyes Toward Zion*, ed. Yehoshua Ben-Arieh and Moshe Davis (Westport: Praeger, 1997), 16.

7. Rainer Albertz, *A History of Israelite Religion in the Old Testament Period*, trans. John Bowden, 2 vols. (Louisville: Westminster/John Knox Press, 1994), 1:129–130.

8. The Deuteronomist's assertion that Solomon did this to appease his many foreign wives (1 Kings 11:1–4) does not disguise the political motivation of this policy.

9. Some scholars hold that these calves were not idols, but decorations enriching the base of a throne meant for the one unseen God. See Hans-Joachim Kraus, *Worship in Israel: A Cultic History of the Old Testament* (Richmond: John Knox Press, 1965), 149. Menahem Haran believes them to be external court symbols indicative of Dan's status as a royal temple (Amos 7:13) (Menahem Haran, *Temples and Temple-Service in Ancient Israel. An Inquiry into the Character of Cult Phenomena and the Historical Setting of the Priestly School* [Oxford: Clarendon, 1978], 28–29).

10. Kraus, *Worship in Israel*, 46. H. H. Rowley cites early-twentieth-century examples from the Arabian Peninsula (H. H. Rowley, *Worship in Ancient Israel: Its Form and Meaning* [London: SPCK, 1967], 117).

11. W.O.E. Oesterley and Theodore H. Robinson, *Hebrew Religion: Its Origin and Development*, 2nd ed. (New York: Macmillan, 1937), 180–181.

12. Rowley, *Worship in Ancient Israel*, 89.

13. Kraus stresses that it is impossible to wrest a coherent picture from the copious flecks of data in Psalms without oversimplifying, conflating different periods, or relying on false analogies, and that the best we can do is "take separate points of detail from the tradition and try to co-ordinate them" (Kraus, *Worship in Israel*, 208).

14. Shlomo Riskin argues that the Hebrew verb *ye'ra'eh* should more accurately be translated "shall be seen," suggesting that an important part of the essence of the pilgrimage experience was to be seen by the deity in the holy place. "Parshat Re'eh, Shabbat R'eh 25 Av 5760, August 26, 2000," http://www.ohrtorahstone.org.il/parsha/5760/ekev60.htm (accessed June 18, 2003). This simultaneous viewing and being viewed is similar to the Hindu concept of *darshan*.

15. Exempted were "a deaf man, an imbecile and a minor, a person of unknown sex, a hermaphrodite, women, unfreed salves, the lame, the blind, the sick, the aged, and one who is unable to go up on foot." BT Hagigah 2a and Mishnah Hagigah 1:1.

16. Shemuel Safrai, "The Temple," in *The Jewish People in the First Century*, ed. Shemuel Safrai and Menahem Stern, 2 vols. (Philadelphia: Fortress Press, 1976), 2:865.

17. Shemuel Safrai, "Pilgrimage to Jerusalem at the End of the Second Temple Period," in *Studies on the Jewish Background of the New Testament*, ed. O. Michel et al. (Assen [Netherlands]: Van Gorcum, 1969), 15, 19.

18. Flavius Josephus, *The Jewish War*, in *Josephus [Works]*, trans. H. St. J. Thackeray et al., 10 vols. (London: William Heinemann, Ltd.; Cambridge: Harvard University Press, 1976), Book 2.515; vol. 2:523.

19. Some foreign proselytes journeyed to Jerusalem during the pilgrimage festivals to appear before a Jerusalem *Bet Din* and to seal their process of conversion with a ritual sacrifice (Shemuel Safrai, "Relations between the Diaspora and the Land of Israel," in *The Jewish People in the First Century*, 1:199–200).

20. Philo Judaeus, "On the Embassy to Gaius," in *Philo*, trans. F. H. Colson, 10 vols. (London: William Heinemann, Ltd.; Cambridge: Harvard University Press, 1929–1962), 281–282; vol. 10:143.

21. Safrai, "Temple," 2:878. Binder attributes this practice to the fact that sacrificial worship was common among contemporary religions of the eastern Mediterranean region, including those of the Greeks, Romans, Egyptians, Scythians, and Parthians, who might presumably sacrifice to their own gods in the most appropriate temple at hand (Donald D. Binder, *Into the Temple Courts: The Place of the Synagogues in the Second Temple Period* [Atlanta: Society of Biblical Literature, 1999], 31).

22. Jackie Feldman, "La circulation de la Tora: les pèlerinages au second Temple," in *La société juive à travers l'histoire*, ed. S. Trigano, trans. John-Christoph Ettias, 4 vols. (Paris: Fayard, 1992–1993), 4:164. He cites Tosefta, Shekalim 1.1, as his source.

23. Goodman points out that Jerusalem's religious status was Herod's only economic asset (Martin Goodman, "The Pilgrimage Economy of Jerusalem in the Second Temple Period," in *Jerusalem: Its Sanctity and Centrality to Judaism, Christianity, and Islam*, ed. Lee I. Levine [New York: Continuum, 1999], 72).

24. A guesthouse was excavated on Mount Ophel in 1914. David Bivin, "Synagogue Guest House for First-Century Pilgrims," *Jerusalem Perspective Online*, http://www.jerusalemperspective.com (accessed January 20, 2005). The guest house's inscription reads, "Theodotos, son of Vettenus, priest and synagogue head, son of a synagogue head, grandson of a synagogue head, built this synagogue—whose foundations were laid by his ancestors, the elders and Simonides—for the reading of Torah and for instruction in the commandments, and the guest house with its rooms and water installations as lodging for needy [pilgrims] from the Diaspora."

25. Flavius Josephus, *Antiquities*, in *Josephus [Works]*, trans. H. St. J. Thackeray et al., 10 vols. (London: William Heinemann, Ltd.; Cambridge: Harvard University Press, 1976), Book 17.217.

26. Ibid., 11.110; vol. 4:205.

27. Norman Kotker, *The Earthly Jerusalem* (New York: Charles Scribner's Sons, 1969), 97.

28. Feldman, "Circulation," 171.

29. Ibid., 172.

30. Safrai, "Relations between the Diaspora," 1:190. The annual half-shekel tax may have evolved from the mandated one-time tax for males over the age of nineteen when they took part in the census (Ex. 30:11–16). By the time of 2 Kings and 2 Chronicles, it seems to have become an annual tax for the repair of the Temple, and, by the fifth century BCE, an annual tax for Temple activities (Neh. 10:32–34).

31. Aristeas, *Aristeas to Philocrates (Letter of Aristeas)*, trans. and ed. Moses Hadas (New York: Harper & Brothers, 1951), 135.

32. Josephus, *Antiquities*, 12.145–146.

33. We follow the detailed reconstruction found in Kraus, *Worship in Israel*, 210–224.

Kraus believes that during the pilgrimage festivals at this time the Ark itself was taken out to the gathering place, from which it was carried in procession back to the Temple.

34. Sources in the contemporary Jewish literature for these practices are listed in Safrai, "Temple," 2:865, 2:903.

35. Safrai, "Pilgrimage to Jerusalem," 21. Safrai notes that some pilgrims who came to study with a particular sage—his main example is Saul of Tarsus who came from Cilicia to study Torah under Rabbi Gamaliel the Elder—stayed in Jerusalem beyond the festival itself. Some remained long enough to be considered immigrants rather than pilgrims. See also Safrai's "Relations between the Diaspora," 1:193–194.

36. Safrai, "Pilgrimage to Jerusalem," 15.

37. "Historia de Legis Divinae Translatione 5," in Extracts from Aristeas Hecataeus and Origin and Other Early Writers, trans. Aubrey Stewart (London: 1895). Cited in Karen Armstrong, Jerusalem: One City, Three Faiths (London: HarperCollins, 1996), 120.

38. Barker, Gate of Heaven, 39. See also Joachim Jeremias, Jerusalem in the Time of Jesus. An Investigation into Economic and Social Conditions During the New Testament Period, trans. F. H. and C. H. Cave (Philadelphia: Fortress Press, 1962), 101.

39. The temptation of handling cash was diminished by using a voucher system: "He who wanted [to purchase] drink offerings goes over to Yohanan, who is appointed to be in charge of the seals. He pays him a fee and receives a seal from him. He goes over to Ahiah who is appointed to be in charge of the drink offerings. He hands over the seal to him and receives the drink offerings from him. Then in the evening the two come together, and Ahiah brings out the seals and receives money for them. If there was [sic] an excess [of funds over seals], the excess belongs to the sanctuary. And if there was too little money, Yohanan paid out of his own pocket" (Mishnah Shekalim 5:4).

40. Safrai, "Temple," 2:866. It was so named because women were not allowed to pass beyond it into the inner courtyards of the Temple.

41. Victor Turner, "Liminality and Communitas," in The Ritual Process: Structure and Anti Structure (Chicago: Aldine Press, 1974), 94–130.

42. We follow the analysis by Mark S. Smith, "The Psalms as a Book for Pilgrims," Interpretation 46 (1992): 156–166. Additional insights from Philip E. Satterhwaite, "Zion in the Songs of Ascents," in Zion: City of Our God, ed. Richard S. Hiss and Gordon J. Wenham (Grand Rapids, MI: Eerdmans, 1995), 105–128; and Loren D. Crow, The Songs of Ascents (Psalms 120–134): Their Place in Israelite History and Religion (Atlanta: Scholars Press, 1996), 23–25.

43. Philo, "Special Laws," 1.70; vol. 7:141.

44. Sandra Scham, "The Lost Goddess of Israel," Archaeology 58, no. 2 (March/April 2005): 36–40. See also William H. Dever, Did God Have a Wife?: Archaeology and Folk Religion in Ancient Israel (Grand Rapids, MI: Eerdmans Press, 2005).

45. Kraus, Worship in Israel, 225–229. See Jud. 20:23, 21:2; 1 Sam. 7:5; 1 Kings 8:33–35; Isa. 15:2, 22:12, 29:4, 32:11, 58:5; Hos. 7:14; Ps. 44:25; Mic. 1:8–16, 4:14; Jer. 4:8, 6:26, 14:12, 36:6–9; Joel 1:5–14, 2:1–16; Neh. 9:1.

46. Kraus, Worship in Israel, 226–227, notes the many close parallels between these ceremonies and those performed at the ruins of the sanctuary at Ur.

Chapter 4. Pilgrimage in the Early Diasporas

1. Jeremiah 41:5 suggests that the few Jews who remained behind in Palestine may have built a temporary altar at the site of the Temple ruins.

2. See also Jewish Encyclopedia Online, s.v. "Pilgrimage" (by Gerhard Deutsch et al.),

citing Heinrich Grätz, *Geschichte der Juden*, 3rd ed., iii. 157, 668, http://www.jewishen-cyclopedia.com (accessed January 15, 2005).

3. The history of the development of the synagogue lacks consensus. One's view depends in great measure on one's definition of synagogue. Erich Gruen's definition reflects the views of the broadest constructionists: "A structure in which or an institution through which Jews could engage in communal activity that helped to define or express a collective identity" (Erich S. Gruen, *Diaspora: Jews Amidst Greeks and Romans* [Cambridge: Harvard University Press, 2002], 105). The Babylonian Talmud, Meg. 29a, written much after the fact, writes that the Shechinah went with the Jews into exile and inhabited the synagogues they built there in Nehardea and Hutsal. Most historians, however, believe that synagogues did not develop until later. Several have been found in Egypt in the third and second centuries BCE with inscriptions that indicate they served as places of study. By the second century BCE, during the Hasmonean period, several were constructed in Palestine based on models probably developed in the Diaspora. In the Galilee there were a few by the first century BCE, and they were common by the third CE (Dan Urman and Paul V. M. Flesher, *Ancient Synagogues: Historical Analysis and Archaeological Discovery*, 2 vols. [Leiden: Brill, 1995] 1:xx–xxv). See also Lee I. Levine, ed., *Ancient Synagogues Revealed* (Jerusalem: Israel Exploration Society; Detroit: Wayne State University Press, 1982). Donald Binder believes these early "synagogues should not be viewed as being in opposition to the Temple, but rather as extensions of it," and that both in the Diaspora and in Palestine they "served as subsidiary sacred precincts that extended spatially the sacrality of the temple shrine and allowed Jews everywhere participation within the central cult" (Donald D. Binder, *Into the Temple Courts: The Place of the Synagogues in the Second Temple Period* [Atlanta: Society of Biblical Literature, 1999], 32).

4. Hans-Joachim Kraus, *Worship in Israel: A Cultic History of the Old Testament* (Richmond: John Knox Press, 1965), 230.

5. Yehezkel Kaufmann, *History of the Religion of Israel, from the Babylonian Captivity to the End of Prophecy*, trans. Clarence Efroymsen (New York: Ktav, 1976), 4:32.

6. Jeffrey L. Rubenstein, *The History of Sukkot in the Second Temple and Rabbinical Periods* (Atlanta: Scholars Press, 1995), 99–100.

7. Jacob Martin Myers, *The World of the Restoration* (Englewood Cliffs, NJ: Prentice-Hall, 1968), 9.

8. Shemuel Safrai, "The Temple," in *The Jewish People in the First Century*, ed. Shemuel Safrai and Menaham Stern 2 vols. (Philadelphia: Fortress Press, 1976), 2:865.

9. Jonathan J. Price argues that the so-called Diaspora communities were so varied that "all generalities about 'Diaspora Judaism' should be banned until each Jewish community is understood in its immediate context" (Jonathan J. Price, "The Jewish Diaspora of the Graeco-Roman Period," *Scripta Classica Israelica* 13 [1994]: 179). Nonetheless, we believe that certain broad tendencies can be acknowledged without undue risk.

10. Isaiah M. Gafni, *Land, Center and Diaspora: Jewish Constructs in Late Antiquity* (Sheffield: Sheffield Academic Press, 1997), 30.

11. Flavius Josephus, *Antiquities*, in *Josephus* [*Works*], trans. H. St. J. Thackeray et al., 10 vols. (London: William Heinemann, Ltd.; Cambridge: Harvard University Press, 1926–1965), 4:116; vol. 4:533.

12. Philo Judaeus, "Moses," in *Philo*, trans. F. H. Colson, 10 vols. (London: William Heinemann, Ltd.; Cambridge: Harvard University Press, 1929–1962), 2.232; vol. 6:565.

13. This position finds ample support in both the Torah (e.g., Lev. 26:33; Deut. 4:26–28, 28:63–65) and the Prophets (Jer. 5:19, 9:15; Dan 9:4–7). Yet the fact remains that during Hellenic and Roman times the vast majority of Jews lived outside of Palestine and, as Gruen reminds us, "to assume that they repeatedly lamented their fate and pinned their hopes on recovery of the homeland is quite preposterous" (Gruen, *Diaspora*, 233).

14. Midrash Shekalim, Chapter 8, deemed the annual half-shekel tax obsolete with the destruction of the Temple. See Gruen, *Diaspora*, 246; Martin Goodman, "Nerva, the *Fiscus Judaicus* and Jewish Identity," *Journal of Roman Studies* 79 (1989): 40–44.

15. Midrash Rabbah Genesis 32, 19 (296); 81, 4 (974). Cited by Michael Avi-Yonah, *The Jews of Palestine: A Political History from the Bar Kokhba War to the Arab Conquest* (New York: Schocken, 1976), 80.

16. Teddy Kollek and Moshe Pearlman, *Pilgrims to the Holy Land* (New York: Harper, 1970), 24, 29.

17. Mark Friedman, "Jewish Pilgrimage after the Destruction of the Second Temple," in *City of the Great King: Jerusalem from David to the Present*, ed. Nitza Rosovsky (Cambridge: Harvard University Press, 1996), 137. See also Kollek and Pearlman, *Pilgrims to the Holy Land*, 30.

18. *The Lives of the Prophets*, trans. Charles Cutler Torrey (Philadelphia: Society of Biblical Literature and Exegesis, 1946). Torrey translated an early Greek version of the work. Page numbers are indicated in the text.

Chapter 5. Life on the Pilgrimage Road

1. Issac ben Joseph ibn Chelo, "The Roads from Jerusalem," in *Jewish Travellers in the Middle Ages*, ed. Elkan Nathan Adler (1930; rpt. New York: Dover, 1987), 136. Subsequent references to this work are cited by page number in the text.

2. Samuel Jemsel, "Samuel Jemsel the Karaite," in *Jewish Travellers in the Middle Ages*, ed. Elkan Nathan Adler (1930; rpt. New York: Dover, 1987), 329.

3. Meshullam ben Menachem of Volterra, "Meshullam ben Menachem," in *Jewish Travellers in the Middle Ages*, ed. Elkan Nathan Adler (1930; rpt. New York: Dover, 1987), 163. Subsequent references to this work are cited by page number in the text.

4. Amnon Cohen, *Jewish Life Under Islam: Jerusalem in the Sixteenth Century* (Cambridge: Harvard University Press, 1984), 67.

5. Elijah of Pesaro, "On the Way," in *Roads to Zion: Four Centuries of Travelers' Reports*, ed. Kurt Wilhelm, trans. I. M. Lask (New York: Schocken, 1948), 44. Subsequent references to this work are cited by page number in the text.

6. *Genizah*, a Hebrew word, means "hiding." The Cairo Genizah, discovered in Fustat, a town near Cairo, in the early twentieth century, is a trove of medieval Jewish manuscripts, containing religious and secular writings.

7. Jacob ben Rabbi Nathaniel ha Cohen, "Jacob ha Cohen," in *Jewish Travellers in the Middle Ages*, ed. Elkan Nathan Adler (1930; rpt. New York: Dover, 1987), 92. Subsequent references to this work are cited by page number in the text.

8. Guy LeStrange translates the phrase as "Christians and Jews in great numbers" (*Book of Travels (Safarnama) Selection based on Nasir-i Khusrau. Diary of a Journey through Syria and Palestine*, trans. and ed. Guy LeStrange [London: Palestine Pilgrims' Text Society, 1893], 15). Subsequent references to this work are cited by page number in the text.

9. Bordeaux Pilgrim, "An Itinerary from Bordeaux to Jerusalem," trans. Aubrey Stewart, in *Anonymous Pilgrims, I–VIII* (London: Palestine Pilgrims' Texts Society, 1894), 22.

10. A Persian sect founded in the eighth century that rejected the Talmud and its interpretation of the Torah. For a time they maintained a Yeshiva in Tiberias and another in Jerusalem. Karaites who traveled to Jerusalem termed themselves as Mourners of Zion who adopted an ascetic lifestyle, including avoidance of wine and meat, frequent fasting, and intensive regimens of prayer for the coming of the Messiah.

11. Chufut-Kale (it means Jewish Fortress) was a center of the Karaites during Turkish rule (1475–1783). *Jewish Encyclopedia Online*, s.v. "Karaite Pilgrimages," http://www.jewishencyclopedia.com (accessed March 3, 2004 and December 22, 2004).

12. Mark Friedman, "Jewish Pilgrimage after the Destruction of the Second Temple," in *City of the Great King: Jerusalem from David to the Present*, ed. Nitza Rosovsky (Cambridge: Harvard University Press, 1996), 140.

13. ibn al-Qalanisi, *The Damascus Chronicle of the Crusades*, trans. H.A.R. Gibb (London: Luzac, 1932), 48.

14. Document 2874 in the Bodleian Library, Oxford, Heb. MS. b11, translated by S. D. Goitein, "Contemporary Letters on the Capture of Jerusalem by the Crusaders," *Journal of Jewish Studies* 3 (1952): 176.

15. Document in the Jewish Theological Seminar of America, New York, Elkan Nathan Adler collection, New Series 22, f. 24, reproduced and translated by S. D. Goitein, "Tyre-Tripoli-'Arqa: Geniza Documents from the Beginning of the Crusader Period," *Jewish Quarterly Review* 66 (1975): 84–85.

16. There were about 1,000 Christians in the city at the same time. *Jewish Encyclopedia Online*, s.v. "Pilgrimage."

17. These and other groups' arrivals are recorded in legal documents as the pilgrims had to pay a tax in Nablus before entering Jerusalem. Cohen, *Jewish Life*, 109, 105–106.

18. Quoted in Moshe Gil, "Aliya and Pilgrimage in the Early Arab Period (634–1009)," in "Symposium: The Relationship Between the Diaspora and the Land of Israel Under Arab Rule," ed. Lee I. Levine, special issue, *The Jerusalem Cathedra* 3 (1983): 166–167, 169, and n. 27.

19. Document 2874 in the Bodleian Library, Oxford, Heb. MS. b11, translated by Goitein, "Contemporary Letters," 176.

20. Josef W. Meri, *The Cult of Saints Among Muslims and Jews in Medieval Syria* (Oxford: Oxford University Press, 2002), 217. He cites E. ben-Yehudah, *Milon ha-Lashon ha-'Ivrit* (New York and London, 1959–60), 2:7052–3.

21. Nachmanides mentions in a letter to his son that he plans to go to Hebron "to prostrate myself, and there to dig my grave." Nachmanides, "The Letters of Moses Nachmanides to His Sons from the Holy Land," in *A Treasury of Jewish Letters*, trans. and ed. Franz Kobler, 2 vols. (Philadelphia: Jewish Publication Society, 1954), 1:226.

22. Chryssa A. Maltezou, "From Crete to Jerusalem: The Will of a Cretan Jew (1626)," in "Intercultural Contacts in the Medieval World," special issue, *Mediterranean Historical Review* 10, no. 1–2 (1996): 189–201.

23. John Sanderson, *The Travels of John Sanderson in the Levant, 1584–1602, with His Autobiography and Selections from His Correspondence*, ed. William Foster (London: Hakluyt Society, 1931), 116. Subsequent references to this work are cited by page number in the text.

24. Avraham Holtz, comp. and ed., *The Holy City: Jews on Jerusalem* (New York: W. W. Norton, 1971), 62–63.

25. Document 2874 in the Bodleian Library, Oxford, Heb. MS. b11, translated by Goitein, "Contemporary Letters," 176–177.

26. Elijah of Ferrara, "Elijah of Ferrara," in *Jewish Travellers in the Middle Ages*, ed. Elkan Nathan Adler (1930; rpt. New York: Dover, 1987), 154–155.

27. Moses Basola, *In Zion and Jerusalem: The Itinerary of Rabbi Moses Basola (1521–1523)*, ed. Abraham David, trans. Dena Ordan (Ramat Gan: C. G. Foundation; Jerusalem Project Publications of the Martin [Szusz] Department of Land and Israel Studies of Bar-Ilan University, 1999), 65. Subsequent references to this work are cited by page number in the text.

28. Petachia of Ratisbon, *Travels of Rabbi Petachia of Ratisbon*, trans. A. Benisch (London: Trubner & Co., 1856), 47. Subsequent references to this work are cited by page number in the text.

29. This spring resembles the myth of the Sambatyon River which dates from early rabbinic literature. The river flows strongly for six days and then rests on the Sabbath.

30. Rivka Tal, "Va'amartem Ko Lechai, Rabbi Shimon Bar Yochai: Lag BaOmer at Meiron," *Dei'ah ve Dibur/Information and Insight* (16 Iyar 5761–May 9, 2001), www.shemayisrael.com/chareidi/archives5761/behaaloscha.emrfeatures2.htm (accessed March 10, 2004 and December 4, 2004). The article cites this anonymous pilgrim as 525 years after Shmuel bar Simson (Samuel ben Samson) visited Meron, but we think it was only a century later, probably about 1350.

31. Obadiah Jaré da Bertinoro, "The Letters of Obadiah Jared a Bertinoro (1487–90)," in *Jewish Travellers in the Middle Ages*, ed. Elkan Nathan Adler (1930; rpt. New York: Dover, 1987), 245. Subsequent references to this work are cited by page number in the text.

32. Judah Halevi, *Selected Poems of Jehudah Halevi*, ed. Heinrich Brody, trans. Nina Salaman (1924; rpt. New York: Arno Press, 1973), 23. Subsequent references to this work are cited by page number in the text.

33. Solomon Shloemel ben Hayyim Meinsterl of Lundenberg (also called Shlomel of Dresnitz (Strassnitz), "A Godly Life," in *Roads to Zion: Four Centuries of Travelers' Reports*, ed. Kurt Wilhelm, trans. I. M. Lask (New York: Schocken, 1948), 58.

34. Reb Noson of Nemirov, "Sichos HaRan, Rebbe Nachman's Wisdom. Shevachay HaRan (The Praise of Rebbe Nachman–Part II) (Rebbe Nachman's Pilgrimage to the Land of Israel)," http://www.breslov.org/torah/wisdom/wisdom-pilgrim-a.html (accessed March 25, 2004).

35. Moses ben Israel Poryat (also known as Moses Praeger), "A Vademecum for Palestinian Travelers," in *Roads to Zion: Four Centuries of Travelers' Reports*, ed. Kurt Wilhelm, trans. I. M. Lask (New York: Schocken, 1948), 65. Subsequent references to this work are cited by page number in the text.

36. "Rabbi Isaiah Hurwitz of Prague settles in the Holy Land," in *A Treasury of Jewish Letters*, trans. and ed. Franz Kobler, 2 vols. (Philadelphia: Jewish Publication Society, 1954), 2:481.

37. Gil, "Aliya," 171. He cites TS 13 J26, f. 1a, lines 14–15, in Jacob Mann, *The Jews in Egypt and in Palestine under the Fatimid Caliphs* (rpt. New York: Ktav, 1970), 2:187.

38. Document 2874 in the Bodleian Library, Oxford, Heb. MS. b11, translated by Goitein, "Contemporary," 176–177.

39. He got lost along the way, but luck was with him and he bumped into another pilgrim, from Azerbaijan, who had already been there before. Together they went to various graves, including those of Jethro, Ezra, Job's son, Moses's mother, and Jacob's four sons.

40. Disciple of Bertinoro, "In the Footsteps of the Master," in *Roads to Zion: Four Centuries of Travelers' Reports*, ed. Kurt Wilhelm, trans. I. M. Lask (New York:

Schocken, 1948), 22. Subsequent references to this work are cited by page number in the text.

41. Abraham David, *To Come to the Land: Immigration and Settlement in Sixteenth-Century Eretz-Israel*, trans. Dena Ordan (Tuscaloosa: University of Alabama Press, 1999), 14, 16–17.

42. Gil, "Aliya," 169. Subsequent references to Sfaxi are indicated by page numbers in the text.

43. "A Letter of Introduction," in *A Treasury of Jewish Letters*, trans. and ed. Franz Kobler, 2 vols. (Philadelphia: Jewish Publication Society, 1954), 1:143. The letter was found in the Cairo Genizah. Kobler does not include the names of the Russian pilgrim or his relative.

44. "A Community, Probably in Spain, to the Communities on the Road to Palestine," in *A Treasury of Jewish Letters*, trans. and ed. Franz Kobler, 2 vols. (Philadelphia: Jewish Publication Society, 1954), 1:147–148.

45. Cohen, *Jewish Life*, 105.

46. Ibid., 184.

47. Amnon Cohen, *Ottoman Documents on the Jewish Community of Jerusalem in the Sixteenth Century* (Jerusalem: Yad Izhak Ben-Zvi, 1976), document XVIII.

48. David, *To Come to the Land*, 15.

49. Cohen, *Jewish Life*, 67.

50. Ibid., 105.

51. ". . . to promote by thus meeting and feasting together feelings of mutual affection. for it is good that they should not be ignorant of one another, being members of the same race and partners in the same institutions; and this end will be attained by such intercourse, when through sight and speech they recall those ties to mind, whereas if they remain without ever coming into contact they will be regarded by each other as absolute strangers." Flavius Josephus, *Antiquities*, in *Josephus* [*Works*], trans. H. St. J. Thackeray et al., 10 vols. (London: William Heinemann, Ltd.; Cambridge: Harvard University Press, 1926–1965), 4.203; vol. 4:573.

52. Cohen, *Jewish Life*, 185.

53. Cited in ibid., 108.

54. Dan Barag, "Glass Pilgrim Vessels from Jerusalem," *Journal of Glass Studies* 12 (1970): 35–63.

Chapter 6. Oh, Zion: Jerusalem in the Center

1. Disciple of Bertinoro, "In the Footsteps of the Master," in *Roads to Zion: Four Centuries of Travelers' Reports*, ed. Kurt Wilhelm, trans. I. M. Lask (New York: Schocken, 1948), 22.

2. Simon ben Zemah Duran, *Responsa*. Cited in *The Holy City: Jews on Jerusalem*, ed. Avraham Holtz (New York: W. W. Norton, 1971), 68. He was probably a Spanish pilgrim to the Holy Land.

3. See, for example, Lee I. Levine, ed., *Ancient Synagogues Revealed* (Jerusalem: Israel Exploration Society; Detroit: Wayne State University Press, 1982). The development of the mizrach, the decoration on the east wall of a house, may be an outgrowth of the adornment of the east wall of the synagogue. It is in clear evidence in northern European folk art (Poland, for example) by the seventeenth century as paper cuttings.

4. Holtz, *Holy City*, 60–62.

5. "Addir Hu" may have been a general festival hymn in the Avignon, France, *Mahzor* and was added specifically to the Haggadah toward the end of the fifteenth century. *Jewish Encyclopedia Online*, s.v. "Addir Hu," http://www.jewishencyclo pedia.com (accessed January 5, 2005).

6. Arie Morgenstern, "Dispersion and the Longing for Zion, 1240–1840," *Azure* (Winter 2002): 80.

7. Moshe Gil, "Aliya and Pilgrimage in the Early Arab Period (634–1009)," in "Symposium: The Relationship Between the Diaspora and the Land of Israel Under Arab Rule," ed. Lee I. Levine, special issue, *The Jerusalem Cathedra* 3 (1983): 169.

8. Samuel ben Samson, "Itinerary of Rabbi Samuel ben Samson in 1210," in *Jewish Travellers in the Middle Ages*, ed. Elkan Nathan Adler (1930; rpt. New York: Dover, 1987), 103. Subsequent references to this work are cited by page number in the text.

9. Jacob of Paris, "Jacob, The Messenger of Rabbi Jechiel of Paris," in *Jewish Travellers in the Middle Ages*, ed. Elkan Nathan Adler (1930; rpt. New York: Dover, 1987), 117. Subsequent references to this work are cited by page number in the text.

10. Nachmanides (also known as Ramban), "The Letters of Moses Nahmanides to his Sons from the Holy Land," in *A Treasury of Jewish Letters*, trans. and ed. Franz Kobler, 2 vols. (Philadelphia: Jewish Publication Society, 1954), 1:226. Subsequent references to this work are cited by page number in the text.

11. Estori Farhi (also known as ha-Parhi), [*Caftor VaFerah*], in *The Holy City: Jews on Jerusalem*, ed. Avraham Holtz (New York: W. W. Norton, 1971), 129–130.

12. Obadiah Jaré da Bertinoro, "The Letters of Obadiah Jared a Bertinoro (1487–90)," in *Jewish Travellers in the Middle Ages*, ed. Elkan Nathan Adler (1930; rpt. New York: Dover, 1987), 234. Subsequent references to this work are cited by page number in the text.

13. Casale Pilgrim, *The Casale Pilgrim: A Sixteenth-Century Illustrated Guide to the Holy Places*, trans. and ed. Cecil Roth (London: Soncino Press, 1929), 41. Subsequent references to this work are cited by page number in the text.

14. Meshullam ben Menachem of Volterra, "Meshullam ben Menachem," in *Jewish Travellers in the Middle Ages*, ed. Elkan Nathan Adler (1930; rpt. New York: Dover, 1987), 191. Subsequent references to this work are cited by page number in the text.

15. Robert L. Wilken, "Christian Pilgrimage to the Holy Land," in *City of the Great King: Jerusalem from David to the Present*, ed. Nitza Rosovsky (Cambridge: Harvard University Press, 1996), 122. He cites M. Martolioth, *Halakhoth on the Land of Israel from the Genizah* (Jerusalem, 1974), 139–141.

16. J. Berakoth 9:3, 13D. Cited by Karen Armstrong, *Jerusalem: One City, Three Faiths* (New York: Alfred A. Knopf, 1996), 169.

17. Moses Basola, *In Zion and Jerusalem: The Itinerary of Rabbi Moses Basola (1521–1523)*, ed. Abraham David, trans. Dena Ordan (Ramat Gan: C. G. Foundation, Jerusalem Project Publications of the Martin [Szusz] Department of Land of Israel Studies of Bar-Ilan University, 1999), 72. Subsequent references to this work are cited by page number in the text.

18. Jacob ben Rabbi Nathaniel ha Cohen, "Jacob ha Cohen," in *Jewish Travellers in the Middle Ages*, ed. Elkan Nathan Adler (1930; rpt. New York: Dover, 1987), 98–99. Subsequent references to this work are cited by page number in the text.

19. Gil, "Aliya," 170.

20. Ibid.

21. Bordeaux Pilgrim, "An Itinerary from Bordeaux to Jerusalem," trans. Aubrey Stewart, in *Anonymous Pilgrims, I–VIII* (London: Palestine Pilgrims' Texts Society, 1894), 22.

22. Hieronymus, *Commentarium in Sophoniam Prophetam*, in *Patrologia Latina*, ed. J.-P. Migne (Paris: J.-P. Migne, 1844–1864), 1:15–16 (28: col. 1354). St. Jerome's *sparsi crines* has a classical basis and perhaps may indicate a sign of mourning). His use of the verb *ululare* may, again, indicate his disrespect of the Jews, for in classical Latin the verb refers to the howling of wolves. It may also be an early reference to ululation, which is a basic vocal part of commemoration activities in the Maghreb.

23. John Wilkinson, *Jerusalem Pilgrims Before the Crusades*, 2nd ed. (Warminster: Aris & Phillips, 2002), 358.

24. Jacob of Paris, "Jacob, The Messenger of Rabbi Jechiel of Paris," in *Jewish Travellers in the Middle Ages*, ed. Elkan Nathan Adler (1930; rpt. New York: Dover, 1987), 119. Subsequent references to this work are cited by page number in the text.

25. Benjamin of Tudela, *The Itinerary of Benjamin of Tudela*, trans. Marcus Nathan Adler (New York: Philipp Feldheim, 1907), 36, http://chass.colostate-pueblo.edu/history/seminar/benjamin/.

26. Isaac ben Joseph ibn Chelo, "The Roads from Jerusalem," in *Jewish Travellers in the Middle Ages*, ed. Elkan Nathan Adler (1930; rpt. New York: Dover, 1987), 131. Subsequent references to this work are cited by page number in the text.

27. Francis E. Peters, *Jerusalem and Mecca: The Typology of the Holy City in the Near East* (New York: New York University Press, 1986), 126–131.

28. Gil, "Aliya," 170.

29. Ibid.

30. Ibid.

31. John Sanderson, *The Travels of John Sanderson in the Levant, 1584–1602, with His Autobiography and Selections from His Correspondence*, ed. William Foster (London: Hakluyt Society, 1931), 105.

32. Christian pilgrims, too, took note of these tombs, but in accord with their theology that saw the Jewish Bible as a prefiguration of the New Testament, related them to Christian stories. The Piacenza Pilgrim, who visited David's and Absalom's tombs in 570, for example, noted that the children that Herod slaughtered were buried there as well. Piacenza Pilgrim, "Travels," in *Jerusalem Pilgrims Before the Crusades*, trans. and ed. John Wilkinson, 143.

33. Gil, "Aliya," 169.

Chapter 7. Jewish Saints Be Praised!

1. Disciple of Bertinoro, "In the Footsteps of the Master," in *Roads to Zion: Four Centuries of Travelers' Reports*, ed. Kurt Wilhelm, trans. I. M. Lask (New York: Schocken, 1948), 20. Subsequent references to this work are cited by page number in the text.

2. Casale Pilgrim, *The Casale Pilgrim: A Sixteenth-Century Illustrated Guide to the Holy Places*, trans. and ed. Cecil Roth (London: Soncino Press, 1929), 33. Subsequent references to this work are cited by page number in the text.

3. Abraham Zacuto (circa 1452–1514), *The Complete Book of Yohassin*, trans. Abraham Haim Freimann, http://www.israelshamir.net/Talmud/227-230.shtml (accessed April 16, 2005).

4. "Epistle to Jacob ben Samuel," in *Karaite Anthology: Excerpts from the Early Literature*, trans. Leon Nemoy (New Haven: Yale University Press, 1969), 115–116.

5. Jacob ben Rabbi Nathaniel ha Cohen, "Jacob ha Cohen," in *Jewish Travellers in the Middle Ages*, ed. Elkan Nathan Adler (1930; rpt. New York: Dover, 1987), 92. Subsequent references to this work are cited by page number in the text.

6. Jacob of Paris, "Jacob, the Messenger of Rabbi Jechiel of Paris," in *Jewish Travellers in the Middle Ages*, ed. Elkan Nathan Adler (1930; rpt. New York: Dover, 1987), 115. Subsequent references to this work are cited by page number in the text.

7. Moses Basola, *In Zion and Jerusalem: The Itinerary of Rabbi Moses Basola (1521–1523)*, ed. Abraham David, trans. Dena Ordan (Ramat Gan: C. G. Foundation, Jerusalem Project Publications of the Martin [Szusz] Department of Land of Israel Studies of Bar-Ilan University, 1999), 93, emphasis ours. Subsequent references to this work are cited by page number in the text.

8. Samuel ben Samson, "Itinerary of Rabbi Samuel ben Samson in 1210," in *Jewish Travellers in the Middle Ages*, ed. Elkan Nathan Adler (1930; rpt. New York: Dover, 1987), 103. Subsequent references to this work are cited by page number in the text.

9. Petachia of Ratisbon, *Travels of Rabbi Petachia of Ratisbon*, trans. A. Benisch (London: Trubner & Co., 1856), 57. Subsequent references to this work are cited by page number in the text.

10. The work is also known as *Qivrei Avoth*. Joshua Prawer considers this the earliest example of the Crusader-era itinerary genre. The author may have been from Babylon or Damascus. It is Genizah fragment 2699 (E. Adler collection). Joshua Prawer, *The History of the Jews in the Latin Kingdom of Jerusalem* (Oxford: Clarendon; New York: Oxford University Press, 1988), 176.

11. David dei Rossi, "A Jewish Merchant Reports on Life in Palestine" [Letter], in *A Treasury of Jewish Letters*, trans. and ed. Franz Kobler, 2 vols. (Philadelphia: Jewish Publication Society, 1953), 2:339.

12. Elkan Nathan Adler, *Jewish Travellers in the Middle Ages* (1930; rpt. New York: Dover, 1987), xx.

13. Amoraïm was a term applied to interpreters of the Mishnah in the third to fifth centuries CE.

14. The custom persists in the Sephardic world. We write these words in Essaouira, Morocco, where we visited the tomb of the tzadiq Haim Pinto, which has likewise been covered with expensive draping.

15. Isaac ben Joseph ibn Chelo, "The Roads from Jerusalem," in *Jewish Travellers in the Middle Ages*, ed. Elkan Nathan Adler (1930; rpt. New York: Dover, 1987), 134. Subsequent references to this work are cited by page number in the text.

16. Some people also believed that Adam and Eve had dwelt in the cave after they were expelled from Paradise. Fifteenth- and sixteenth-century Christian pilgrims claimed to see the depressions in the rock that had served Adam and Eve as beds. Zev Vilnay, *The Sacred Land*. Vol. 2: *Legends of Judea and Samaria* (Philadelphia: Jewish Publication Society, 1975), 35–36.

17. "Travels," in *Jerusalem Pilgrims Before the Crusades*, trans. and ed. John Wilkinson, 2nd ed. (Warminster: Aris & Phillips, 2002), 143. Wilkinson contends that approximately two-thirds of the places visited by early Christian pilgrims were Jewish biblical sites.

18. Naser-e Khosraw (also written Nasir-i Khusrau or Khusraw), *Naser-e Khosraw's Book of Travels (Safarnama)*, trans. W. M. Thackston, Jr. (Albany: State University of New York Press, 1986), 35–36.

19. Benjamin of Tudela, *The Itinerary of Benjamin of Tudela*, trans. Marcus Nathan Adler (New York: Philipp Feldheim, 1907), 40–41, http://chass.colostate-pueblo.edu/history/seminar/benjamin/. Subsequent references to this work are cited by page number in the text.

20. Cited in Prawer, *History*, 176.

21. Meshullam ben Menachem of Volterra, "Meshullam ben Menachem" in *Jewish Travellers in the Middle Ages*, ed. Elkan Nathan Adler (1930; rpt. New York: Dover, 1987), 185–186. Subsequent references to this work are cited by page number in the text.

22. Obadiah Jaré da Bertinoro, "The Letters of Obadiah Jared a Bertinoro (1487–90)," in *Jewish Travellers in the Middle Ages*, ed. Elkan Nathan Adler (1930; rpt. New York: Dover, 1987), 233. Subsequent references to this work are cited by page number in the text.

23. John Sanderson, *The Travels of John Sanderson in the Levant, 1584–1602, with His Autobiography and Selections from His Correspondence*, ed. William Foster (London: Hakluyt Society, 1931), 112. Subsequent references to this work are cited by page number in the text.

24. Adomnan, "The Holy Places," and the Piacenza Pilgrim, "Travels," in *Jerusalem Pilgrims*, 142, 186–187. Circa 500, Peter the Iberian stopped to pray there (101) and the Piacenza Pilgrim noted that a church next to the shrine marked the place where Mary, Joseph, and Jesus stopped on the family's way to Egypt.

25. Several modern researchers make a strong case that Rachel's Tomb was not an active cult pilgrimage site until the mid-twentieth century. See especially Susan Starr Sered, "Rachel's Tomb: The Development of a Cult," *Jewish Studies Quarterly* 2, no. 2 (1995): 103–148.

26. Most modern scholars believe that the *Zohar* was really written—or assembled—by Moses de León in Castile between 1280 and 1286. Isaac Luria drew attention to the book in the mid-sixteenth century. It was printed in 1558–1560, and from then on it has been indisputably the guiding text of Jewish mysticism.

27. Joseph the Scribe of Beresteczko, "Of Earthquakes and Torah Scrolls," in *Roads to Zion: Four Centuries of Travelers' Reports*, ed. Kurt Wilhelm, trans. I. M. Lask (New York: Schocken, 1948), 89. Subsequent references to this work are cited by page number in the text.

28. Cited in Elchanan Reiner, "Meron's Miracle," *Eretz Weekly*, February 6, 2000, www.eretz.com/archive/feb0600.htm (accessed August 18, 2000). The grave of Honi ha-Me'agel in the Galilee and the Cave of Machpelah were also propitious sites at which to pray for relief from drought or famine. Pinchas Giller, "The Veneration of Gravesites in Kabbalah," http://www.yarzheit.com/heavensregister/galileegiller.htm (accessed April 15, 2005).

29. Recounted by Abraham Zacuto (1452–circa 1514) in his *Sefer Yohassin*. Cited in Reiner, "Meron's Miracle."

30. As we will see in Chapter 9, the holy graves at Meron still attract pilgrims for the Lag b'Omer celebration. It has become the largest annual religious pilgrimage in modern Israel. For more on the date of the festival, see Chapter 9.

31. This may be the grave of a Dosa ben Hurcanus (or Harkinas), renowned rabbi, circa 80–120 CE. Jacob of Paris mentioned the grave of Hanina ben Dosa in a town he called Araba.

32. Solomon Shloemel ben Hayyim Meinsterl of Lundenberg (also called Shlomel of Dresnitz [Strassnitz], "A Godly Life," in *Roads to Zion: Four Centuries of Travelers' Reports*, ed. Kurt Wilhelm, trans. I. M. Lask (New York: Schocken, 1948), 58.

33. Vilnay, *The Sacred Land*. Vol. 2: *Legends of Judea and Samara*, 270.

34. Amnon Cohen, *Jewish Life Under Islam: Jerusalem in the Sixteenth Century* (Cambridge: Harvard University Press, 1984), 101–103.

35. Joseph the Scribe of Beresteczko (mid-eighteenth century) remembered having seen sites related to Samson, but put them vaguely somewhere near Sidon: "I also saw the tomb of the hero Samson and the house which he brought down upon himself and the Philistines. To this day it has never been possible to build it up again" (91).

36. In competing traditions, Christians identify these sites with Saint George, and Muslims, with the holy man Al-Hadr.

37. Cited in Josef W. Meri, "Re-Appropriating Sacred Space: Medieval Jews and Muslims Seeking Elijah and al-Khadir," *Medieval Encounters: Jewish, Christian and Muslim Culture in Confluence and Dialogue* 5, no. 3 (1999): 252.

38. Jacob Mann, "Moses b. Samuel, A Jewish Katib in Damascus, and his Pilgrimage to Medinah and Mekkah," *Journal of the Royal Asiatic Society of Great Britain and Ireland* (1919): 182.

39. Judah ben Solomon Harizi (also known as Alharizi), *The Book of Tahkemoni. Jewish Tales from Medieval Spain*, trans. and ed. David Simha Segal (Portland, OR: Litman Library of Jewish Civilization, 2001), 280. Subsequent references to this work are cited by page number in the text.

40. Cited in Josef Meri, *The Cult of Saints Among Muslims and Jews in Medieval Syria* (Oxford: Oxford University Press, 2002), 23. The seventeenth-century work is entitled *Concise Pamphlet Concerning Noble Pilgrimage Sites*.

41. Petachia says the grave of Rabbi Meir is in a city called Mella (33; the editor believes it is a mistranscription [94, n. 59]).

42. Joel L. Kraemer, "A Jewish Cult of the Saints in Fatimid Egypt," in *L'Egypte Fatimide: son art et son histoire: actes du colloque organisé à Paris les 28, 29 et 30 mai 1998*, ed. Marianne Barrucand (Paris: Université de Paris–Sorbonne, 1999), 579–601.

43. Kraemer, "Jewish Cult," 580.

44. Mishneh Torah, Hilkhot Shevitat Yom Tov, VI, 19–21. Cited in Kraemer, "Jewish Cult," 587.

45. They are Rabbis Jacob ben Moses Moellin (died 1427), Elijah ben Moses Loanz (died 1636), Jair Chaim Bacharach (died 1702), and Menachem Mendel Rothschild (died 1732). Manfred Maier, *The Jewish Cemetery of Worms* (Worms: Verlag Stadtarchiv Worms, 2001), 8.

Chapter 8. The Cult of the Rebbe: Hasidic Pilgrimage

1. Cited by Debra Nussbaum Cohen, "Crowds of Followers Give Life to Rebbe's Burial Location," *Jewish News Weekly of Northern California*, November 12, 1999, http://www.jewishsf.com/content/2-0-/module/displaystory/story_id/12437/edition_id/240/format/html/displaystory.html (accessed March 25, 2004).

2. Tzvi Meir Cohn, "Journey to the Grave Site of the Ba'al Shem Tov," http://www.baalshemtov.com/pilgrim1.htm (accessed August 2, 2004).

3. John Berger, "Uman Page," http://www.johnberger.com (accessed April 15, 2005).

4. Mishneh Torah, Deut 6:2.

5. Rabbi Yonassan Gershom, "FAQ on Hasidism," http://www.pinenet.com/~rooster/Hasid1.html#HASID1-Q3 (accessed March 31, 2004).

6. Louis Jacobs, *Hasidic Prayer* (Washington: Littman Library of Jewish Civilization, 1993), 23, 129.

7. Commenting on an exhibit on tzadiqim called "To the Tombs of the Righteous: Pilgrimage in Contemporary Israel." Cited in Ilene R. Prusher, "The Who, Where, and Why of Mystic Meccas," *Christian Science Monitor* (June 29, 1999), http://search.csmonitor.com/durable/1999/06/29/p13s1.htm (accessed February 20, 2004).

8. Marcia Pally, "'Farbrengen' My Baby Back Home," *Film Comment* (1987), http://www.marciapally.com/farbreng.html (accessed March 18, 2005).

9. David Landau, "Bobover Rabbi Shlomo Halberstam Dies at 92," *Jewish News Weekly of Northern California* (August 4, 2000), http://www.jewishsf.com/content/2-0-/module/displaystory/story_id/14184/edition_id/275/format/html/displaystory.html (accessed April 12, 2004).

10. Yitschak Meir Kagan, "Seeking Farbrengen," *Farbrengen Magazine*, http://www.chabad.org/library/article.asp?AID=2216 (accessed April 10, 2004).

11. Some claim that the practice goes back to the days of Maimonides; others, that it began with the Ba'al Shem Tov. What seems probable is that it was introduced by his grandson, Rabbi Boruch'l of Medzhibozh. Menashe Unger, "The Kvittel," http://www.shemayisrael.co.il/parsha/review/archives/tezave61.htm (accessed March 28, 2004).

12. Miriam Zakon, "Four Days in Poland: Searching for Sarah Schenirer. Searching for our Heritage. Searching, Just a Little, for Myself," *Jewish Observer* 34, no. 5 (May, 2001): 19.

13. The custom of requiring contributions, whether for taking kvitlach or granting blessings, is viewed by many Jews with the same kind of anger and skepticism that reformers like Erasmus of Rotterdam and Martin Luther vented against the Catholic Church's lucrative business of selling indulgences. As Jeremy Rosen put it, on learning that his beloved rebbe was in his old age taking kvitlach, "my tears turned to anger. I was angry at the way the orthodox world has come to be dominated by a sort of mind set that once was no more than a marginal version of popular religion for the less educated masses of Eastern Europe. Together with the growth in miracle workers, mezuzah readers, ketuba decipherers, red bendelach salesmen and a host of other pious, religious miracle workers, our religion is being dragged down into the realms of superstition and hocus pocus" (http://www.somethingjewish.co.uk/columnists/ [accessed March 15, 2004]).

14. Reuben Margaliot's *Hilula de-Tzaddikaya* (Limberg, 1929), lists of dates of yahrzeit of famous tzadiqim for the purpose of visiting their graves. See also Louis Jacobs, *Holy Living: Saints and Saintliness in Judaism* (Northvale and London: J. Aronson, 1990), 119.

15. Rashi's commentary on BT Yebamoth 122a states that it was customary for the disciples and the general public to sit around the grave of a great man and otherwise honor him, on the anniversary of his death. Cited in *Jewish Encyclopedia Online*, s.v. "Jahrzeit" (by Cyrus Adler and Judah David Eisenstein), http://www.jewishencyclopedia.com (accessed April 10, 2004).

16. Michael Samuel, "Is it OK to Pray to the Soul of the Lubavitcher Rebbe?" (1998), http://jewish.com/askarabbi/askarabbi/askr2115.htm (accessed March 15, 2004).

17. Eitan Schuman, "Reflections on Poland," http://www.ohrtorahstone.org.il/features/poland.htm (accessed August 2, 2004). *Gedolim* (great men); *kippitel tehellim* (chapter of Psalms); *Kel Moleh Rachamim* (prayer for the dead).

18. Yonassan Gershom, "Journey to Uman" (1997), http://www.pinenet.com/~rooster/uman.html (accessed August 2, 2004). Gershom made his pilgrimage in 1989.

19. The Information and Analytical Edition of the Jewish Confederation of Ukraine, "Jewish Ukraine" (September 2002), http://www.jewukr.org/observer (accessed November 15, 2004).

20. Cohn, "Journey to the Grave Site of the Baal Shem Tov."

21. The Federation of Jewish Communities of the CIS, "Double Joy: Mass Bar Mitzva and Chupa Celebrated in Ukraine" (October 19, 2004), http://www.fjc.ru/news/newsArticle.asp?AID=214300 (accessed November 15, 2004).

22. The Canadian Foundation of Polish-Jewish Heritage, Montreal Chapter, "Pilgrimage," http://polish-jewish-heritage.org/Eng/pilgrimage.html (accessed August 5, 2004).

23. Antoni Ledamski, "Pilgrimage: Hasidim in Lezajsk," *Warsaw Voice* (March 17, 2002), http://www.warsawvoice.pl/archiwum.phtml/1913/ (accessed March 25, 2004).

24. Ibid.

25. Aaron Tapuchy (Jablonka), "Hassidim in the Town," trans. Jerrold Landau, http://www.jewishgen.org/yizkor/Czyzew/czy0273.html (accessed March 10, 2004).

26. Dovid Sears, "10,000 Jews Spend Rosh Hashana in Uman" (October 13, 2000), http://breslovcenter.com/article_RHinUman.html (accessed March 25, 2004). Roman Woronowycz, "Thousands Travel to Uman for Annual Pilgrimage on Rosh Hashanah," *Ukrainian Weekly* 71, no. 42 (October 19, 2003), http://www.ukrweekly.com/Archive/2003/420306.shtml (accessed March 15, 2004).

27. Reb Noson of Nemirov, "Rebbe Nachman's Wisdom," Breslov Research Institute, http://www.breslov.org/torah/wisdom/wisdom-pilgrim-a.html (accessed March 25, 2004).

28. Arthur Green, *Tormented Master: A Life of Rabbi Nahman of Bratslav* (Tuscaloosa: University of Alabama Press, 1979), 63–93.

29. Herbert Weiner, "The Dead Hasidim," *Commentary* 31, no. 3 (March 1961): 240, http://www.commentarymagazine.com/Summaries/V31I3P56-1.htm (accessed March 8, 2005).

30. For the experience in 2004 of a female rabbi who tacked a visit to the grave site onto an educational and service trip to the Ukraine, see Goldie Milgram, "The Road to Reb Nachman's Grave," http://www.rebgoldie.com/nachman.htm (accessed March 10, 2004).

31. Gershom, "Journey to Uman."

32. http://www.breslov.org/umantoday.html (accessed August 5, 2004).

33. For Sidra DeKoven Ezrahi, visits such as these are a "memetic activity of *oyle regl*, of pilgrimage, [in which each site is a] simulacrum of the Temple" (*Booking Passage: Exile and Homecoming in the Modern Jewish Imagination* [Berkeley: University of California Press, 2000], 196).

34. Debra Nussbaum Cohen, "If Only the Rebbe Were Here," *Moment* 27, no. 5 (October 2002): 49.

35. Samuel Heilman, "Still Seeing the Rebbe: Pilgrims at the Lubavitcher Grand Rabbi's Grave in Queens" (2001), http://www.killingthebuddha.com/dogma/still_seeing_rebbe.htm (accessed March 25, 2004).

36. Cited in Heilman, "Still Seeing the Rebbe." Heilman comments that "instead of one man coming to the ohel and bringing back blessings and guidance for them, as the Rebbe had once done for them, now they all could come themselves and receive the counsel and help they used to receive from their Rebbe when he was alive."

37. "Netanyahu Visits Rebbe's Gravesite," *Jewish News Weekly of Northern California* (September 20, 1996), http://www.jewishsf.com/content/2-0-/module/displaystory/story_id/4550/format/html/displaystory.html (accessed March 19, 2004).

38. Miriam Greenberg, "Pilgrimage of a Non-Believer," special issue, *Jewish Folklore and Ethnology Review* 17, no. 1–2 (1995): 40.

39. Cohen, "If Only the Rebbe Were Here," 49.

40. Charles W. Kim, "Hasidim Return to Grave Site to Honor Rebbe," *Sentinel* (North Brunswick, NJ) (July 26, 2001), http://nbs.gmnews.com/News/2001/0726/Front_Page/019.html (accessed March 5, 2004).

41. Shlomo B. Abeles, "Munkacs and Satmar Rebbes," http://www.aishdas.org/avodah/vol03/v03n161.shtml (accessed March 25, 2004).

42. *Encyclopedia Judaica,* s.v. "An Important Hasidic Dynasty," http://motlc.wiesenthal.com/text/x28/xr2864.html (accessed March 25, 2004).

43. M. Levy, "Poland Comes to Life," *Dei'ah ve Dibur/Information and Insight* (April 17, 2002), http://www.shemayisrael.com/chareidi/archives5762/achrei/AMK62features2.htm (accessed March 10, 2004). For typical Ukrainian Hasidic tours see http://www.lybid-kiev.com.ua/tour10.htm (accessed March 15, 2004) and http://www.jewishroute.kiev.ua/t/delux.html (accessed August 6, 2004). For tours to Hungary, Austria, and the Czech Republic see http://www.totallyjewishtravel.com/features/?disp_feature=zHzvGF (accessed March 5, 2004).

Chapter 9. Praying at the Tzadiq's Tomb: Sephardic Pilgrimage

1. Issachar Ben-Ami, *Saint Veneration Among the Jews in Morocco* (Detroit: Wayne State University Press, 1998), 310.

2. Issachar Ben-Ami, "Folk Veneration of Saints Among the Moroccan Jews," in *Studies in Judaism and Islam*, eds. S. Morag et al. (Jerusalem: Magnes Press, 1981), 294.

3. Ruth Fredman Cernea, "Flaming Prayers: Hillula in a New Home," in *Between Two Worlds: Ethnographic Essays on American Jewry*, ed. Jack Kugelmass (Ithaca: Cornell University Press, 1988), 178.

4. Austen Henry Layard, *A Popular Account of Discoveries at Nineveh* (New York: J. C. Derby, 1854), 165, http://mcadams.posc.mu.edu/txt/ah/Layard/DiscNineveh07.html (accessed February 20, 2004).

5. Warren Freedman, *World Guide for the Jewish Traveler* (New York: E. P. Dutton Inc, 1984), 157.

6. *Jewish Encyclopedia Online,* s.v. "Pilgrimage" (by Gotthard Deutsch et al.), http://www.jewishencyclopedia.com (accessed February 10, 2004).

7. http://www.jewishsightseeing.com/oman/salalah/tomb_of_job (accessed February 20, 2004).

8. Daniel Aldrich, "A Petra Vacation," http://www.targum.com/horizons/excerpts/Aldrich36.html (accessed February 20, 2004).

9. Stephen Schwartz, "Jewish Stolac: Sephardic Judaism, Balkan Islam, and Tomb Visitation in Bosnia-Hercegovina" (paper delivered at Haverford College, Haverford PA, November 10, 2002), http://www.haverford.edu/relg/sells/stolac/stolacrenewed (accessed January 20, 2005).

10. These graffiti are cited by Gila Hadar, "Salonika: Memoirs of a City in the Context of Diversity and Change: 1914–1943" (conference paper, Nationalism, Society

and Culture in Post-Ottoman South East Europe, St. Peter's College, Oxford University, May 29–30, 2004), 10–12, http://www.sant.ox.ac.uk/areastudies/hadar.pdf (accessed December 15, 2004). Hadar takes them from I. Immanuel, *Matzevot Saloniki* (Jerusalem: n.p., 1968): stone 599 (1:262), 1799 (1:884), 1577 (1:726), and 1408 (1:649).

11. Shlomo Deshen, *The Mellah Society: Jewish Community Life in Sherifian Morocco* (Chicago: University of Chicago Press, 1989), 82.

12. Ben-Ami, *Saint Veneration*, 308–309.

13. Harvey E. Goldberg, "The Mellahs of Southern Morocco: Report of a Survey," *The Maghreb Review* 8, no. 3–4 (1983): 61–69.

14. Edward Westermark, *Ritual and Belief in Morocco* 2 vols. (London: Macmillan, 1926), 1:195–196. Louis Voinot, *Pèlerinages judéo-musulmans du Maroc* (Paris: LaRose, 1948), 18. For more on baraka in both religions, see Eyal Ben-Ari and Yoram Bilu, *Grasping Land: Space and Place in Contemporary Israeli Discourse and Experience* (Albany: State University of New York Press, 1996), 28ff; Dale F. Eickelman, *Moroccan Islam: Tradition and Society in a Pilgrimage Center* (Austin: University of Texas Press, 1976), 160ff.

15. Norman A. Stillman, *The Language and Culture of the Jews of Sefrou, Morocco: An Ethnolinguistic Study* (Manchester: University of Manchester, 1988), 126.

16. Voinot, *Pèlerinages judéo-musulmans*, 19.

17. Taufik Canaan, *Mohammedan Saints and Sanctuaries in Palestine* (London: Luzac, 1927), 1.

18. Stillman, *Language and Culture of the Jews of Sefrou*, 23–24.

19. Deshen, *Mellah Society*, 83.

20. Ben-Ami, *Saint Veneration*, 94, 103.

21. In the 1920s in Morocco Westermark found strong rural Muslim beliefs in the polluting powers of Christians and, especially, Jews. Jews were banned from approaching holy springs, beehives, Muslim cemeteries, or tombs. They could not touch Muslim amulets. Prayers recited in Jews' houses had no power. Muslims who entered a Jew's house, or cemetery, or slept in a Jew's bed, or had intercourse with a Jewish woman were considered impure, and could not approach a saint's tomb until their ritual purity had been restored (Westermark, *Ritual and Belief*, 1:195, 229, 253–254, 534). Jewish tradition, on the other hand, generally barred from holy sites only those who were at the moment ritually impure, such menstruating women, or people who had come in direct contact with the dead (Ben-Ami, *Saint Veneration*, 162).

22. Voinot, *Pèlerinages judéo-musulmans*, 34–35, 121.

23. *Jewish Encyclopedia Online*, s.v. "Pilgrimage."

24. For Abraham ben Zmirrou, Dawid d'Dra' and Yahia ben Doussa, see Voinot, *Pèlerinages judéo-musulmans*, 16–17, 19, 31, 47–85. For Dawid ben 'Amram, see Westermark, *Ritual and Belief*, 1:195–196.

25. Westermark, *Ritual and Belief*, 1:175–177.

26. Ben-Ami, *Saint Veneration*, 190.

27. Documented by Dov Noy, in *Seventy-One Folktales of Libyan Jews* (Jerusalem: Folklore Archives [Hebrew]). Cited in Harvey E. Goldberg, "Torah and Children: Some Symbolic Aspects of the Reproduction of Jews and Judaism," in *Judaism Viewed from Within and from Without: Anthropological Studies*, ed. Harvey Goldberg (Albany: State University of New York Press, 1986), 125.

28. Expatriate development moneys benefited some relatively obscure sites like the grave of the sixteenth-century rabbi Shlomo ben Hensh in the High Atlas Ourika Valley,

covered with a white marble dome in 1976 (Bryan Schwartz, "In Morocco's Mountains, Elderly Jew Watches the Shrine of His Holy Rebbe," *Jewish News of Greater
Phoenix* 54, no. 27 [March 22, 2002], http://www.jewishsf.com/bk020322/i40.shtml
[accessed September 7, 2002]).

29. Ben-Ami, *Saint Veneration*, 125–129. Oren Kosansky, "Tourism, Charity, and
Profit: The Movement of Money in Moroccan Jewish Pilgrimage," *Cultural Anthropology* 17, no. 3 (August 2002): 366.

30. For Morocco, for example, Charles de Foucauld's survey in 1883
(*Reconnaissance au Maroc, 1883–1884*) suggests that about half of Morocco's Jews
lived in the country's large cities and half were rural. An Alliance Israélite Uni-
verselle survey, circa 1904, found that of Morocco's 88,000 Jews, roughly one-
quarter were rural. While the Jewish populations of Fez, Meknès, Sefrou,
Marrakech and other cities all grew during the early years of the twentieth century,
the largest number of Jews migrated to Casablanca (Goldberg, "Mellahs," 61–69).
By 2003 more than of Morocco's remaining Jews lived in Casablanca. (Mitchell
Bard, "The Jews of Morocco," Jewish Virtual Library, www.jewishvirtuallibrary
.org/source/anti-semitism/morocjews.html [accessed August 12, 2005]).

31. Ben-Ami, "Folk Veneration," 283.

32. Her family name is sometimes transcribed Achouel, Hatchouel, Hachuel,
Hatchuel, or Hatuel. For many years she was venerated by Muslims as well, until the
1920s (Voinot, *Pèlerinages judéo-musulmans,* 50–51).

33. Ben-Ami, *Saint Veneration*, 97, 315–318.

34. "Here lies Mademoiselle Solica Hatchouel, born in Tangier in 1817. Her re-
fusal to become a Muslim led the Arabs to murder her in Fez in 1834. Everyone
misses this holy young woman."

35. *The Road to Fez* (Washington, DC: Counterpoint, 2001), 218–219. Lalla Sol
was a hot topic in romantic times, as evidenced by the several works based on her life:
Lady Theodora Bird, *Wings of a Bird; Memoirs of a Lady Traveller in North Africa,
1832–1839*; Eugenio-María Romero, *El martirio de la joven Hatchuel o la heroína hebrea*
(Gibraltar: n.p., 1837). I. Vendan, *La heroína hebrea, Sol "la Saddika": drama histórico
en prosa y verso en cinco actos* [Larache (Morocco): n.p., n.d.]; A. Calle, *El martirio de la
joven Hachuel, o la heroína hebrea* (Seville: n.p., 1852); Henry Iliowizi, *Sol, An Epic
Poem* (Minneapolis: Tribune, circa 1882). Ben-Ami lists the other principal sources
that deal with Lalla Sol's life and legends (*Saint Veneration*, 320–321).

36. Several studies provide information about Rabbi 'Amram and his hillula. The
most useful are Ben-Ami, *Saint Veneration*, 100; *Jewish Encyclopedia Online*, s.v. "Pilgrimage"; Stillman, *Language and Culture of the Jews of Sefrou*, 22–24; Voinot,
Pèlerinages judéo-musulmans, 49. Among the several websites, see http://www.yourish
.com/archives/2003/may11-17_2003.html.

37. Voinot, *Pèlerinages judéo-musulmans*, 50.

38. Our description follows that of Taïta Umm Hnina, *Le pèlerinage de la Ghriba à
Djerba* (Charenton-le-Pont: Victor Trabelsi, 1994).

39. Panafrican News Agency (Dakar), May 17, 2001, http://www.islamfortoday
.com/jewishpilgrimage.htm (accessed February 10, 2004). Jewish Telegraphic Agency
report, May 9, 2002, http://www.jewishsf.com/content/2-0-/module/displaystory/
story_id/18160/edition_id/363/format/html/displaystory.html (accessed February
10, 2004). See also Karin Albou's 1995 documentary film, *Mon pays m'a quitté (My
Country Left Me)*.

40. Keren Friedman, "The Rabbi with the Long White Beard: A Personal

Encounter," special issue, *Jewish Folklore and Ethnology Review* 17, no. 1–2 (1995): 37–39.

41. We draw on the study by Susan Slyomovics, "The Pilgrimage of Rabbi Ephraim Al-Naqawa, Tlemcen, Algeria," *Jewish Folklore and Ethnology Review* 15, no. 2 (1993), 84–88. The rabbi's name is also transcribed as Al-Naqawa, Ankawa, Ankaoua, Enkaoua, etc.

42. Arnold van Gennep, "Le pèlerinage de Rabb," in *En Algérie* (Paris: Mercure de France, 1914), 41–58.

43. Henriette Azen, "Un haut lieu de pèlerinage du judaïsme algérien: Le Rabb de Tlemcen," *Los Muestros* (Brussels) 29 (December 1997): 21–23.

44. The French noun *remplacement* comes from the synagogue's rabbi, Salomon Tapiero (Slyomovics, "Pilgrimage of Rabbi Ephraim Al-Naqawa," 85).

45. Ben-Ami, *Saint Veneration*, 176.

46. According to Kosansky, "Tourism, Charity," 364.

47. http://www.map.co.ma/mapeng/eng.htm (accessed March 13, 2004).

48. Bard, "Jews." By 1998 the Jewish Tunisian community had dropped to 2,000. "Jewish Communities of the World," http://www.adherents.com (accessed April 2, 2005).

49. Bard, "Jews"; Kosansky, "Tourism, Charity," 366; Matti Friedman, "The End of Morocco's Mosaic of Tolerence," *Jerusalem Report* (July 14, 2003): 22–26; and Shlomo Deshen and Moshe Shokeid, *The Predicament of Homecoming: Cultural and Social Life of North African Immigrants in Israel* (Ithaca: Cornell University Press, 1974), 34.

50. Yoram Bilu, "The Role of Charismatic Dreams in the Creation of Sacred Sites in Present-Day Israel," in *Sacred Space: Shrine, City, Land*, eds. Benjamin Z. Kedar and J. Zwi Werblowsky (New York: New York University Press, 1998), 297. In a subsequent refinement of this study he splits categories 1 and 3 to create six categories (Yoram Bilu, "Moroccan Jews and the Shaping of Israel's Sacred Geography," in *Divergent Jewish Cultures: Israel and America*, ed. Deborah Moore et al. [New Haven: Yale University Press, 2001], 77–81).

51. Ben-Ami, "Folk Veneration," 176, 302–303. Yoram Bilu, "The Inner Limits of Communitas: A Covert Dimension of Pilgrimage Experience," *Ethos. Journal of the Society for Psychological Anthropology* 16, no. 3 (1988): 312–313. Stillman, *Language and Culture of the Jews of Sefrou*, 23–24.

52. Other examples are listed in Ben-Ami, *Saint Veneration*, 94.

53. See, for example, http://harissa.com/D_Souvenirs/ziarasayedelmaarabi.htm.

54. Among the many miracles attributed to this saint in Tunisia are several of alleviating barrenness and, on one notable occasion in World War II, of stopping a German tank just short of overrunning his tomb. http://harissa.com/D_Souvenirs/ziarasayedelmaarabi.htm (accessed February 12, 2004).

55. Deshen and Shokeid, *Predicament of Homecoming*, 102. This hillula was described by Friedman, "Rabbi with the Long White Beard," 37–39.

56. Deshen and Shokeid, *Predicament of Homecoming*, 105–106.

57. http://www.arbiv.com/rabishimon.htm (accessed January 21, 2005). See Chapter 7.

58. Bilu, *Without Bounds*, 26–27.

59. Edith Turner, "Bar Yohai, Mystic: The Creative Persona and His Pilgrimage," in *Creativity/Anthropology*, eds. Smadar Lavie et al. (Ithaca: Cornell University Press, 1993), 240–242.

60. Sigmund Diamond, *In Quest: Journal of an Unquiet Pilgrimage* (New York: Columbia University Press, 1980), 208.

61. Turner, "Bar Yohai," 239.

62. This is the central thesis of Bilu's critique of the Turners' theory of communitas ("The Inner Limits of Communitas"). Deshen and Shokeid, on the other hand, observed that "Moroccans and Ashkenazim, as well as other ethnic groups, intermingled and confronted one another on apparently equal terms," and that in the festival's intensified atmosphere "social and cultural barriers were removed" (*Predicament of Homecoming*, 85).

63. This custom, and the attendant ceremonies, are similar in some ways to the Muslim practice of *'akikah*, at which a male child's hair is cut at a local sanctuary on the eighth day after his birth. The family may thank the saint for having protected mother and child during the birth. They may dedicate the child to the service of God, asking that the saint keep him under his protection. Frequently the family makes a donation to the shrine, sometimes of the weight in silver or gold of the hair that has been cut off (Julian Morgenstern, *Rites of Birth, Marriage, Death, and Kindred Occasions Among the Semites* [Cincinnati/Chicago: Hebrew Union College Press/Quadrangle Books, 1966], 26, 87).

64. Based on observations in 1966 (Deshen and Shokeid, *Predicament of Homecoming*, 75).

65. Turner, "Bar Yohai," 244–245.

66. Ben-Ami, "Folk Veneration," 284; Eyal Ben-Ari and Yoram Bilu, "Saints' Sanctuaries in Israeli Development Towns: On a Mechanism of Urban Transformation," *Urban Anthropology* 16, no. 2 (1987): 253–259; Yoram Bilu, "Oneirobiography and Oneirocommunity in Saint Worship in Israel: A Two-Tier Model for Dream-Inspired Religious Revivals," *Dreaming* 10, no. 2 (2000): 89.

67. Ben-Ami, *Saint Veneration*, 176.

68. Details of this hillula, and key promotional texts, are found in Yoram Bilu, "Dreams and Wishes of the Saint," in *Judaism Viewed from Within and from Without*, ed. Harvey E. Goldberg (Albany: State University of New York Press, 1986), 289, 300–310.

69. Ben-Ami, *Saint Veneration*, 24–25, 30. There are numerous variant spellings of the family name: Abuchatsera, Abehsera.

70. For the impact of the intifada on this shrine, see Chapter 14.

71. Eliyahu Alfasi, Yechiel Torgeman, and C. T. Bari, *Baba Sali Our Holy Teacher: His Life, Piety, Teachings and Miracles. Rav Yisrael Abuchatzeirah,* trans. Leah Dolinger (New York: Judaica Press, 1986).

72. http://www.trekearth.com/gallery/Middle_East/Israel/photo30410.htm (accessed February 22, 2004).

73. Yoram Bilu and Eyal Ben-Ari term this process the "charismatization" of Baba Sali, helped along by the fact that "as a living descendent of this holy family, Baba Sali thus provided a focus for the amorphous hagiolatric sentiments which were previously directed towards other Jewish Moroccan saints, whose tombs had been left behind, and in a sense, 'deserted' upon emigrating to Israel" ("Modernity and Charisma in Contemporary Israel," *Israel Affairs* 1, no. 3 [1995]: 224–236, http://www.geocities .com/alabasters_archive/baba_sali.html [accessed February 24, 2004]).

74. Yoram Bilu and Eyal Ben-Ari, "The Making of Modern Saints: Manufactured Charisma and the Abu-Hatseiras of Israel," *American Ethnologist* 19, no. 4 (1992): 672–687.

75. Still another member of the Abuhatzeira clan has developed a kind of cult following. Baba Sali's cousin Meir Abehsera was a founder of the American macrobiotic

healing movement. Born in Morocco and educated in Paris as a civil engineer, he settled in New York. His restaurant, writings, and macrobiotic center made him a focus
of counter culture pilgrimage in the 1960s, when he was often visited by Bob Dylan
and the folksinging group Peter, Paul and Mary, among others. Eventually his Jewish
interests intensified, in part under the influence of the Lubavitcher Rebbe, and he relocated to Jerusalem.

76. Matt Rees, "Miracle Makers. Israel's Shas Party Is Tapping into Mysticism to
Give Its Politics More Potency," *Time Europe* 156, no. 13 (September 25, 2000),
http://www.time.com/time.europe/magazine/2000,0925/jerusalem.html (accessed
March 13, 2004).

77. Shifra Epstein, "Inventing a Pilgrimage: Ritual, Love and Politics on the Road
to Amuka," special issue, *Jewish Folklore and Ethnology Review* 17, no. 1–2 (1995):
25–32.

78. *Studies in the History of Biblical Culture* (Tel Aviv, 1977), as cited by Epstein,
"Inventing."

79. http://www.dangooRABBIcom/73page94.html (accessed February 21, 2004).

80. Cernea, "Flaming Prayers," 178–184.

Chapter 10. The Shrines of the Holocaust

1. Eitan Schuman, "Reflections on Poland," http://www.ohrtorahstone.org.il/
features/Poland.htm (accessed August 2, 2004).

2. Hershel Shanks, "The Strange Enrichment of Seeing Auschwitz," *Moment*
(February 1990): 4.

3. Shaul Rosenblatt, "Belzec: The Forgotten Camp," April 30, 2000, http://
www.aish.com/holocaust/issues/belzec_the_forgotten_camp_.asp (accessed March 5,
2004).

4. Mark Kurlansky, "Visiting Auschwitz-Poland—adapted from 'A Chosen Few:
The Resurrection of European Jewry,'" *Harper's Magazine* 289, no. 1733 (October
1994): 38.

5. The torah from the Czech town of Tabor, when the synagogue was razed and
the town cleansed of Jews by the Nazis, somehow survived the maelstrom, and now is
held in permanent loan by Temple Israel in Minneapolis. In 2000, Rabbi Joseph Edel-
heit, in what he describes as a personal pilgrimage, reconnected the torah to its own
roots by taking it back to Tabor for the first time in fifty-five years. http://pages
.prodigy.net/ebeebe/mktrip.htm (accessed January 15, 2004).

6. "Holocaust Memory in America," in *The Art of Memory: Holocaust Memorials in
History*, ed. James E. Young (New York and Munich: Prestel, 1944), 159–166. James
Young employs the word fetish as he talks about artifacts in museums, opening the
way for others to talk about festishization of Holocaust-related items, sometimes also
called relics (James E. Young, *The Texture of Memory: Holocaust Memorials and Meaning* [New Haven: Yale University Press, 1993], 127).

7. Abraham Palti, "Recuerdos inextinguibles," *Nunca olvidaremos. Marcha de la
vida 1992* (Mexico City: Edamex, 1992), 30. These and the other personal recollections by the Mexican participants cited here are drawn from this 35-page mimeo-
graphed souvenir booklet put together by students in the 1992 "Marcha de la Vida."
All translations from the original Spanish by David M. Gitlitz.

8. Leonardo Simpser, "No lo olvidaré," *Nunca olvidaremos*, 18.

9. Paola Hamui, "Una página de mi diario," *Nunca olvidaremos*, 19.

10. http://www.yad-vashem.org.il/download/education/conf/Bialecka.pdf (accessed January 15, 2004).

11. Leon Wieseltier, "After Memory: Reflections on the Holocaust Memorial Museum," *New Republic* 208, no. 18 (1993): 16–26.

12. Young, *Texture of Memory,* viii, 2.

13. Bialecka attempts to answer some of these questions. She acknowledges that people come to Auschwitz-Birkenau for a variety of reasons ("out of duty, on a pilgrimage, to struggle with their own past; they come out of curiosity or they make their visit a further step on their tour through Poland"). She is cognizant of the importance of generational differences ("for the third generation born after the war, their history is so remote that they do not identify with it the same way as their parents do and grandparents do"). Most of the schoolchildren who are her principal concern come because "for years it has been a kind of tradition in schools to arrange the so-called trip to the Auschwitz Museum and teachers still feel obliged." They come for educational purposes ("to learn what happened here half a century ago and how and why it was possible that it happened at all"), but are expected to apply their education ("to learn how to take precautions against the possible repetition of what happened in Auschwitz"). They also come to memorialize ("as a form of commemoration, paying tribute to the victims").

14. Later in her remarks, Bialecka sketches her view of the content of the Auschwitz-Birkenau curriculum: totalitarianism; Nazism; the extermination of Poles, Jews, and Gypsies; the administration of the camps; the fate of women; the history of the IG Farben factory. Absent are any references to anti-Semitism, to the slaughter of Jews merely because they were Jews, or any possible Polish responsibility for what happened.

15. Jackie Feldman notes the parallels between the meanings assigned to the shrines of the Shoah and to the ruins of the Second Temple in Jerusalem. "The Shoah is often referred to as a *hurban,* a term reserved for catastrophes like the Destruction of the Second Temple. . . . That ancient hurban not only precipitated fast days, dirges and apocalyptic works, but also gave rise to pilgrimage to the Temple remains a generation or two after its destruction. Just as the pilgrimage to the Temple ruins affirmed the centrality of the destroyed Temple while viewing the catastrophe as a necessary stage in the drama leading to the Messianic redemption, so, too, the current pilgrimage to Poland assigns meaning to the destruction of the Jewish past through redemptive acts in the independent State of Israel." "'It Is My Brothers Whom I Am Seeking': Israeli Youths' Pilgrimages to Poland of the Shoah," special issue, *Jewish Folklore and Ethnology Review* 17, no. 1–2 (1995): 33.

16. Young, *Texture of Memory,* 2.

17. Marek Kucia, "KL Auschwitz in the Social Consciousness of Poles, AD 2000," in *Remembering for the Future: The Holocaust in an Age of Genocide,* eds. John K. Roth et al. (Basingstoke/New York: Palgrave/Houndsmill, 2001), vol. 3, *Memory,* 643. Andreas Huyssen, "Monument and Memory in a Postmodern Age," in *The Art of Memory, Holocaust Memorials in History,* ed. James E. Young (New York and Munich: Prestel, 1994), 9–17.

18. Joseph Greenblum, "A Pilgrimage to Germany," *Judaism* 44, no. 4 (Fall 1995): 478.

19. Boris Pahor, *Pilgrim Among the Shadows: A Memoir,* trans. Michael Biggins (New York: Harcourt, Brace and Co., 1995), 2.

20. Greenblum, "Pilgrimage," 478–479.

21. Susan Slyomovics, "Rebbele Mordkhele's Pilgrimage in New York City, Tel Aviv, and Carpathian Ruthenia," in *Going Home*, ed. Jack Kugelmass (New York: YIVO and Northwestern University Press, 1993), 373.

22. Cited by Aaron Hass, "Survivor Guilt in Holocaust Survivors and Their Children," in *A Global Perspective on Working with Holocaust Survivors and the Second Generation*, ed. John Lemberger (Jerusalem: JDC-Brookdale Institute of Gerontology and Human Development, in Cooperation with the World Council of Jewish Communal Service, AMCHA, and JDC-Israel, 1995), http://www.holocaust-trc.org/glbsurv.htm (accessed March 5, 2004).

23. Daniel Singer, "A Haunted Journey," *The Nation* 269, no. 9 (September 27, 1999): 21.

24. Shanks, "Strange Enrichment of Seeing Auschwitz," 4.

25. Stuart Schoffman, "Transcendence in a Cursed Place: An Arab-Jewish Visit to Auschwitz Is a Rare Exercise in Empathy," *Jerusalem Report* (June 30, 2003): 30.

26. André Schwarz-Bart, *The Last of the Just*, trans. Stephen Becker (London: Secker and Warburg, 1961), 409.

27. Miriam Zakon, "Four Days in Poland: Searching for Sarah Schenirer. Searching for our Heritage. Searching, Just a Little, for Myself," *Jewish Observer* 34, no. 5 (May 2001): 21.

28. Bush is widely quoted as having remarked, "Boy, they were big on crematoriums, weren't they?"

29. http://www.whitehouse.gov/g8/interview5.html (accessed March 24, 2004).

30. Jean Mouttapa, "Des Arabes à Auschwitz," in "La mémoire de la Shoah," special issue, *Nouvel Observateur*, hors série (December 2003/January 2004): 84–87. See also Jean Mouttapa, *Un Arabe face à Auschwitz: La mémoire partagée* (Paris: Albin Michel, 2004) and http://www.mliles.com/melkite/abounaemileshoufani.shtml (accessed March 24, 2004).

31. Nazir Majali, quoted by Etta Prince-Gibson, "Arabic in Auschwitz," *International Jerusalem Post* (June 20, 2003): B5.

32. Schoffman, "Transcendence," 30.

33. The Peacemaker Community was founded in 1996 by Bernie Glassman and Sandra Jishu Holmes with a mission "to experience and manifest the power of diverse people connecting, linking, participating in shared experiences" while building "a global partnership among people around the world working towards social transformation." See http://www.peacemakercircle.org/ (accessed March 10, 2004). All citations from Laura Carboni are from http://www.bearingwitnessjournal.com/ (accessed March 10, 2004).

34. Similarly, an American Catholic who visited Terezin in the Czech Republic in 2000 with an ecumenical group from Minneapolis, wrote that "it was one of the most gut-wrenching experience of our lives," and that "the amazing things which happened to us there left me feeling as if my chest were being compressed by a heavy weight." Louis and Mary Kay Manning, http://pages.prodigy.net/ebeebe/mktrip.htm (accessed July 17, 2002).

35. http://www.motl.org/ (accessed March 15, 2004).

36. According to George Halasz, Australians from Sydney participate in "this sacred pilgrimage of Australian high school students . . ." (http://www.dosinc.org.au/reviews34.html). Students from Miami in 1998 join "a two week spiritual pilgrimage from Poland to Israel" (http://ftmmusic.com/benhorin.htm). Students from San Francisco take part in "the annual pilgrimage to former Nazi death camps"

(http://www.jewishsf.com/bk020322/sf12.shtml) (all accessed March 15, 2004). See also Oren Stier, "Lunch at Majdanek: The March of the Living as a Contemporary Pilgrimage of Memory," special issue, *Jewish Folklore and Ethnology Review* 17, no. 1–2 (1995): 57–60.

37. http://www.cajebroward.net/march/ (accessed March 15, 2004).

38. Silvio Bar Niv, "Regreso," *Nunca olvidaremos*, 8.

39. Dara Horn, "On Filling Shoes," *Hadassah Magazine* (November 1992): 21. All quotations from Dara Horn come from this article.

40. http://www.motl.org/reflections.htm (accessed March 15, 2004).

41. http://www.motl.org/moments.htm (accessed March 15, 2004).

42. http://www.librarygirl.org/MOTL/words.html (accessed March 15, 2004). All quotations from Sara Marks are from this source.

43. "March of the Living 1999 Diary," http://www.geocities.com/SouthBeach/1915/entry20.html (accessed March 12, 2004). All quotations from Julie Golick are from this source.

44. This and the following Canadian survivors' statements come from Eli Rubenstein's April 19, 2001, reprise of the group's experiences, http://www.marchoftheliving.org/mol2001/pages/comments.html (accessed March 18, 2004).

45. Hana Greenfield, *Fragments of Memory* (Jerusalem: Gefen Books, 1992). Ms. Greenfield's mother was deported, accompanying 1,196 children from Terezin, never to be heard of again (all were gassed upon their arrival in Auschwitz on October 7, 1943).

46. This and the following 2003 Phoenix group observations are from Rachel Block's posting at http://www.jewishaz.com/jewishnews/980605/march.shtml (accessed March 12, 2004).

47. Marna Sapsowitz, "Serving as a Rabbi in Poland," *Reconstructionism Today* 11, no. 3 (Spring–Summer 2004), http://www.jrf.org/rt/2004/rabbi-poland.htm (accessed July 28, 2004).

48. March of the Living website, cited without date of pilgrimage, http://www.motl.org/programs/highschool.htm (accessed March 15, 2004).

49. Cited by Jackie Feldman, "Voyages to Poland: Sensitizing Educators to Non-Verbal Elements," International School for Holocaust Studies Workshop (October 11, 1999): 2, http://www.yadvashem.org.il/download/education/conf/Feldman1B.pdf (accessed March 20, 2004).

50. Nili Keren, "The Influence of Opinion Leaders and of Holocaust Research on the Development of the Educational Discussion and Curriculum on the Holocaust in Secondary Schools and in Informal Education in Israel, 1948–1981" (PhD diss., Hebrew University, 1985), 143. Cited in Tom Segev, *The Seventh Million: The Israelis and the Holocaust* (New York: Hill and Wang, 1993), 478. See also Jackie Feldman, "'Above the Death-Pits and with the Flag of Israel Waving on High'—The Structure and Meaning of Israeli Youth Missions to Poland of the Shoah," in *Never Again! The Holocaust's Challenge for Educators*, ed. Helmut Schreier and Matthias Heyl (Hamburg: Krämer, 1997), 117–132, 206.

51. A Holts Tours trip to Poland in 2004 was described in its web advertising as "a journey of pilgrimage and remembrance," http://www.battletours.co.uk/2004tours/holocaust.html (accessed March 4, 2004).

52. Nob Hill Travel Service, http://www.nobhilltravel.com/jht.htm (accessed February 4, 2004). A 2004 Varsovia Tours pilgrimage to Holocaust sites includes a visit to "Cracow—Schindler's List," http://www.varsovia-tours.pl/index.php?page=773

(accessed January 4, 2004). Canada's Cascade Travel offers a tour including a pilgrimage to Terezin and later a pilgrimage to Auschwitz and Birkenau, http://surelux.com/cascade/a_jewish_heritage_tour.htm (accessed March 21, 2004).

53. Nob Hill Travel Service, http://www.nobhilltravel.com/jht.htm (accessed February 4, 2004).

54. The Commission charged with conceptualizing the Washington museum prepared itself by visiting numbers of European Holocaust-related sites. As Edward T. Linenthal notes, "The impact of these sites convinced members of the staff that museum visitors would have to experience such a trip *within* the space of the museum in order to confront the Holocaust viscerally." He further notes that the trips to collect artifacts themselves functioned for the museum staff as pilgrimages "designed to provide a spiritual transformation" (*Preserving Memory: The Struggle to Make America's Holocaust Museum* [New York: Viking, 1995], 35).

55. http://www.va-holocaust.com/learn/default.asp?id=58 (accessed July 28, 2004).

56. James Ingo Freed, "The United States Holocaust Memorial Museum," *Architecture and Urbanism* 11, no. 278 (November 1993): 92–93.

57. Ibid., 91.

58. Helen N. Fagin, "The Holocaust Memorial—In Memory of Six Million Martyrs," http://www.holocaustmmb.org/InMemoryOf.html (accessed September 4, 2002).

59. Ibid.

60. This museum is analyzed and critiqued by Oren Baruch Stier, "Virtual Memories: Mediating the Holocaust at the Simon Wiesenthal Center's Beit Hashoah–Museum of Tolerance," *Journal of the American Academy of Religion* 64, no. 4 (1996): 831–851.

61. Anne's father, who survived the war and was instrumental in setting up the museum and who saw Anne's diary as expressing a universal rather than a Jewish experience, envisaged the house as "a dynamic meeting-place for young people from all over the world . . . [to] propagate and help realize the ideals bequeathed by Anne Frank in her diary. . . . At the same time, an attempt [would] be made through international youth congresses and conferences to stimulate young people to discuss international cooperation, mutual understanding, tolerance, a confrontation of life-philosophies, world peace, modern upbringing, youth problems, modern art, the questions of race and the fight against illiteracy." Cited by James E. Young, "The Anne Frank House: Holland's Memorial 'Shrine of the Book,'" in *The Art of Memory, Holocaust Memorials in History*, ed. James E. Young (New York and Munich: Prestel, 1994), 133.

62. http://www.thechurchontheinternet.com/sermon1.htm (accessed July 17, 2002).

63. Steven Erlanger, "Israel Opens Holocaust History Museum," *San Diego Union-Tribune* (March 16, 2005).

64. Joan R. Branham, "Mapping Tragedy in the US Holocaust Memorial Museum," in "The Tragic in Architecture," special issue, *Architectural Design* 70, no. 5 (2000): 55.

65. Young, *Texture of Memory*, 133.

66. The cult of memory of the Shoah feeds into two disturbing Christian theological traditions as well. The first is that the Jews, in willfully rejecting Jesus as their Messiah, allied themselves with the forces of the Devil, and therefore both cause and deserve all of the violence and oppression to which they have been subjected. Second, the Christian foundation story conceives of Christianity as the successor to Judaism in God's plan. History has a beginning (creation), a middle (now), and an end (Christ's return at the coming end-of-time). The absorption of Judaism into Christianity—

preferably through voluntary conversion, but historically by more draconian measures as well—is a necessary precondition to this last phase. The Christian theological arguments and traditions are too complex to detail here, but at their core remains a unifying concept: Christ will return when there are no more Jews. To see Judaism only in terms of its destruction fits too neatly into this schema and reinforces the systematic dehumanization of individual Jews.

67. Steward Weiss, "The March to Nowhere," *Jerusalem Post* (March 24, 2002): 7.

Chapter 11. The Shrines of Nationhood

1. Benjamin Lee Gordon, *New Judea: Jewish Life in Modern Palestine and Egypt* (Philadelphia: Julius H. Greenstone, 1919), 1, 25–26.

2. Charles S. Liebman and Eliezer Don-Yehiya, *Civil Religion in Israel* (Berkeley: University of California Press, 1983), ix, 28.

3. Jackie Feldman, "'Above the Death-Pits and with the Flag of Israel Waving on High'—The Structure and Meaning of Israeli Youth Missions to Poland of the Shoah," in *Never Again! The Holocaust's Challenge for Educators*, ed. Helmut Schreier and Matthias Heyl (Hamburg: Krämer, 1997), 118.

4. David Cesarani, "Coming to Terms with the Past," *Today's History* 54, no. 2 (February 2004): 16–18, http://www.historytoday.com/dm_getArticle.asp?gid=19778 (accessed February 15, 2005).

5. Yael Zerubavel, *Recovered Roots: Collective Memory and the Making of Israeli National Tradition* (Chicago: University of Chicago Press, 1995), 124.

6. Mooli Brog, "From the Top of Masada to the Bottom of the Ghetto" [in Hebrew], in *Myth and Memory: Transfigurations of Israeli Consciousness*, eds. David Ohana and Robert Wistrich (Jerusalem and Tel Aviv: Van Leer Institute, 1996), 203–227, http://www.jafi.org.il/education/festivls/ZKATZ/ZK/massada.html (accessed February 15, 2005).

7. The conflictive interpretations of what happened at Masada and its relevance to the modern Jewish state are legion. Yigal Yadin's *Masada: Herod's Fortress and the Zealots' Last Stand*, trans. Moshe Pearlman (New York: Random House, 1966) is a romanticized site report widely criticized for drawing conclusions beyond what the findings warrant. G. W. Bowersock, "Ancient History and Modern Politics," *Grand Street* (Autumn 1984): 130–141, contends that Israeli archaeologists have distorted the facts. Richard Horsley, *Bandits, Prophets & Messiahs: Popular Movements in the Time of Jesus* (1985; Philadelphia: Trinity Press International, 1999), argues that Masada's defenders were largely assassins. Nachman Ben-Yehuda, *The Masada Myth: Collective Memory and Mythmaking in Israel* (Madison: University of Wisconsin Press, 1995), believes that Josephus presents Masada's last stand as a destructive revolt by terrorists and assassins, the Sicarii, and the mass suicide as something to be condemned, not praised.

8. Cited by Myron J. Aronoff, "Establishing Authority: The Memorialization of Jabotinsky and the Burial of the Bar-Kochba Bones in Israel Under the Likud," in *The Frailty of Authority*, ed. Myron J. Aronoff (New Brunswick, NJ: Transaction Books, 1986), 121.

9. Maoz Azaryahu, "Mount Herzl: The Creation of Israel's National Cemetery," *Israel Studies* 1, no. 2 (1996): 46–74, http://iupjournals.org/israel/iss1-2.html (accessed February 10, 2005).

10. David Ben-Gurion's grave in Kibbutz Sde Boker, in the Negev, has become another popular pilgrimage site.

11. In addition to Azaryahu's penetrating analysis of Mount Herzl's symbolic functions, see Yael Zerubavel, *Recovered Roots*; Barry Schwartz, "The Social Context of Commemoration. A Study in Collective Memory," *Social Forces* 82 (1982): 374–402.

12. Tamara Rachmani, in "Pilgrims' Stories," ed. Ani Zocher (2003), http://www.usy.org/programs/ip/stories/poland2.asp (accessed February 24, 2005).

13. Chris McGreal, "100,000 Call for Peace at Rabin Memorial Rally," *The Guardian* (November 3, 2003), http://www.guardian.co.uk/israel/Story/0,2763,1076432,00.html (accessed February 24, 2005).

14. Amos Ron, "A Rachel for Everyone: The Kinneret Cemetery as a Site of Civil Pilgrimage," in *Sanctity of Time and Space in Tradition and Modernity*, ed. Alberdina Houtman et al. (Leiden: Brill, 1998), 349–357.

15. Saguy Green, "Memorial for a Fallen Star," *Haaretz* (June 21, 2003), http://israel.jcca.org/Press/memorial.html (accessed February 13, 2005).

16. Roth Kolodny Bachi, *If You Go Along With Me: The Story of Olga Hankin* [in Hebrew] (Israel: Yad Ben-Zvi, 1997).

17. Margaret Larkin, *The Six Days of Yad-Mordechai* (Israel: Yad Mordechai Museum, 1970).

18. See Francis E. Peters, "The Holy Places," in *City of the Great King: Jerusalem From David to the Present*, ed. Nitza Rosovsky (Cambridge: Harvard University Press, 1996), 58; and Meron Benvenisti, *Jerusalem: The Torn City* (Minneapolis: University of Minnesota Press, 1976), Chapter 19. The human remains found at Masada in 1960 presented a similar problem. Call them Jewish martyrs and inter them in the military cemetery? Or treat them as antiquities?

19. Danielle Storper-Perez and Harvey E. Goldberg, "The Kotel: Toward an Ethnographic Portrait," *Religion* 24 (1994): 327.

20. Ibid., 326.

Chapter 12. Israel as a Shrine for the Diaspora

1. Leiah Elbaum, "Letters from Israel" (December 30, 2000), http://lulubold.tripod.com/letters/20001230.html (accessed February 11, 2005).

2. Lisa D. Grant, "Paradoxical Pilgrimage: American Jewish Adults on a Congregational Israel Trip" (PhD diss., Jewish Theological Seminary of America, 2000), 126.

3. Rossi, "My Brother Is Going to Israel," http://www.rossirant.com/archives/000032.htm (accessed September 9, 2004). Rossi is a single-name Jewish blogger who portrays herself as a sometime food and humor journalist.

4. Stuart Berman, "A Reform Jew's Perspective on Israel" (August 2, 1997), http://www.bluethread.com/imagecredits.html (accessed January 20, 2005).

5. Ronald S. Hendel, "Sacrifice as a Cultural System: The Ritual Symbolism of Exodus 24:3–8," *Zeitschrift für die alttestamentliche Wissenschaft* 101 (1989): 377, reprising Martin Noth, "Das System der zwölf Stämme Israels," *Beiträge zur Wissenschaft vom Alten und Neuen Testament* 4, no. 1 (1930): 86–100.

6. David Mittelberg, *The Israel Connection and American Jews* (Westport: Praeger, 1999), 128.

7. Congregation Beth Yeshurun, "Israel 2004 With Rabbi David and Marcie Rosen, June 14–25, 2004," http://www.bethyeshurun.org/toisrael.htm (accessed September 9, 2004).

8. The Northern California Region of the United Synagogue of Conservative Judaism, http://www.uscj.org/ncalif/Israel.htm (accessed February 27, 2005).

9. Congregation Beth Shalom, "Israel Pilgrimage," www.arzaworld.com/pdf/mission-june30-jul12-05-BethSholom.pdf (accessed February 27, 2005).

10. In a study of UJA tour participants in the 1990s, for example, 59 percent said that they expected the trip to affect their sense of personal identity or their relationship to the Jewish people (Grant, "Paradoxical Pilgrimage," 72). Grant accompanied a congregational tour in 1998 and analyzes the strategies by which the group experience met those expectations ("Paradoxical Pilgrimage," 115–173).

11. Neot Kedumim, "In a Nutshell," http://www.n-k.org.il/GeIn/nut1.html (accessed November 25, 2004).

12. National Tours' advertisement in the "Travel" section of Canoe Network's website, http://www.canoe.ca/TravelWorld/9904_pilgrims.html (accessed August 30, 2004; this specific advertisement now discontinued). National Tours maintains its own website with a page devoted to specialized, personalized bar/bat mitzvah trips: Nat-Tours-Israel, "Bar Mitzvah Tours" and "Bat Mitzvah Tours," http://nat-tours-israel.co.il (accessed March 20, 2005).

13. G & S Travel, "Bar/Bat Mitzvah in Israel: An Unforgettable Family Experience," http://www.graiver.co.il/gstravel/mitzva.htm (accessed August 30, 2004).

14. Israeli Ministry of Tourism, "Bar/Bat Mitzvah in Israel," http://www.goisrael.com/discoverisrael/jewishinterest/planbarmitzva.asp (accessed September 10, 2004).

15. The Best of Israel, Ltd., "Why a Bat/Bar Mitzvah in Israel?" http://www.bestofisrael.net/pages/tp_barmizva_netscape.html (accessed September 12, 2004).

16. Howard S. Hoffman, "From the Rabbi's Desk," *North Shore Jewish Center Bulletin* (2000), http://www.northshorejc.org/bulletin/0600/rabbi.html (accessed January 24, 2005).

17. Jonathan Bash, "Sorry, I Can't Come to Your Wedding," *Jewish World* (January 12, 2005), http://www.aish.com/jewishissues/israeldiary/Sorry3_I_Cant_Come_to_Your_Wedding.asp (accessed January 23, 2005).

18. Yechiel Fuchs, "Wedded Bliss," *Jewish Week* (January 17, 2005), http://www.thejewishweek.com/bottom/freshink_content.php3?artid=263 (accessed January 21, 2005).

19. Mittelberg, *Israel Connection*, 128–130.

20. Simone Weichselbaum, "Program Teaches U.S. Students About Jewish Heritage Abroad" (January 22, 2001), *Eagle Online* (American University), http://www.theeagleonline.com/news/2001/01/22/News/Au.Students.Spend.Break.In.Israel-682390.shtml (accessed September 9, 2004).

21. The American-Israeli Cooperative Enterprise: Jewish Virtual Library, s.v. "Charles Bronfman (1931–)," http://www.jewishvirtuallibrary.org/jsource/biography/Bronfman.html (accessed November 27, 2004).

22. Janice De Jesus, "Youths Discover Heritage on Trip to Israel," *Walnut Creek Journal* (August 26, 2004), at Contra Costa Times.com, http://www.realcities.com/mld/cctimes/news/local/states/california/counties/contra_costa_county/cities_nei ghborhoods/walnut_creek/9500731.htm (accessed September 4, 2004).

23. Weichselbaum, "Program."

24. CRB Foundation, *Attitudes Toward Travel to Israel Among Jewish Adults and Youth, Summary of a Research Report* (CRB Foundation, 1990): 52. Cited by Tamar A. Levinson and Susan Zoline, "Impact of Summer Trip to Israel on the Self-Esteem of Jewish Adolescents," *Journal of Psychology and Judaism* 21, no. 2 (1997): 95.

25. Barry Chazan and Arianna Koransky, *Does the Teen Israel Experience Make a Difference?* (New York: Israel Experience, 1997). The report includes an extensive bibli-

ography of evaluative studies of programs that bring adolescents to Israel. See also http://www.jafi.org.il/papers/2004/dec/dec21ajta.htm.

26. Julie Wiener, "Initial Skepticism about Birthright Turns into Enthusiasm . . . and Cash," http://www.jafi.org.il/papers/2000/april/jtaapr14.htm (accessed November 25, 2004).

27. Deena Yellin, "College Students on Pilgrimage to Israel in Show of Solidarity," *Florida Flambeau* (Florida State University) (March 20, 2003), http://www.fsunews .com/vnews/display.v/ART/2003/03/20/3e79598c4ff79 (accessed September 9, 2004).

28. Alexandra J. Wall, "Despite Terror, Federations, Congregants Head to Israel," *Jewish News Weekly of Northern California* (January 11, 2002), http://www.jew ishsf.com/content/2-0-/module/displaystory/story_id/17503/edition_id/347/ format/html/displaystory.html (accessed January 24, 2005).

29. Union for Reform Judaism's Online Pressroom, "Reform Movement Mission Heads to Israel Sunday/Five-Day Journey Will Affirm Reform Solidarity with the Israeli People" (July 24, 2001), http://urj.org/pr/2001/010724/ (accessed January 24, 2005).

30. http://www.goisrael.com/missions/ (accessed January 24, 2005).

31. Wendy Elliman, "Reform Judaism Creates Its Own Israeli Identity," *Jewish Post of New York* (October 1998), http://www.jewishpost.com/jp0410/jpn0410b.htm (accessed November 23, 2004); UAHC 64th Biennial Convention, "Reform Pilgrimage to Israel," http://rj.org/uahc/dallas/areso/israel.html (accessed November 23, 2004).

32. Lucille Barnes, "Retiring Sen. Jesse Helms Caved to Pro-Israel Lobby Halfway Through His Career," *Washington Report on Middle East Affairs* (March 2002), http:// www.wrmea.com/archives/march2002/0203034.html (accessed September 9, 2004).

33. Chad Peterson, "Mayor Begins 'Mission' to Israel," *Yale Daily News* (March 23, 1995), http://www.yaledailynews.com/article.asp?AID=6174 (accessed January 24, 2005).

Chapter 13. Roots Pilgrimage

1. Herbert Hadad, "All the Way Home," *Daily News Magazine* (January 24, 1998); reprinted in *Sephardic-American Voices: Two Hundred Years of a Literary Legacy*, ed. Diane Matza (Hanover, NH: Brandeis University Press, 1997), 66–67.

2. David Margolis, "Ellis Island Revisited," *Los Angeles Jewish Journal* (1993), http://www.davidmargolis.com/article.php?id=51&cat_fp=0&cat_cc (accessed March 22, 2005).

3. Victor D. Sanua, "A Return to the Vanished World of Egyptian Jewry," http://www.sefarad.org/diaspora/egypt/vie/001/0.html (accessed November 30, 2004).

4. Alex Haley, *Roots* (Garden City, NY: Doubleday, 1976).

5. Lisa D. Grant, "Paradoxical Pilgrimage: American Jewish Adults on a Congregational Israel Trip" (PhD diss., Jewish Theological Seminary of America, 2000), 55.

6. Sigmund Diamond, *In Quest: Journal of an Unquiet Pilgrimage* (New York: Columbia University Press, 1980), x.

7. Allison Block, "Remembrances of Places Past," *Indiana University Research and Creative Activity* 17, no. 1 (April 1994): 12, http://www.indiana/.edu/~rcapub/ v17n1/p12html (accessed March 15, 2004).

8. Leon Wahba, "Letter from America to Ms. Carmen Weinstein, March 2001," Bassatine News.com (Jewish Community Council of Cairo), http://www.geocities .com/RainForest/Vines/5855/leonwahba.html (accessed January 20, 2005).

9. Eitan Schuman, "Reflections on Poland," http://www.ohrtorahstone.org.il/features/Poland.htm (accessed August 2, 2004).

10. Diamond, *In Quest*, 38.

11. Maxim Biller, "See Auschwitz and Die," in *Jewish Voices, German Words: Growing up Jewish in Postwar Germany and Austria*, ed. Elena Lappin, trans. Krishna Winston (North Haven, CT: Catbird Press, 1994), 212, 222–223.

12. Alan Scher Zagier, "Centerpiece: A Journey Home. An Immigrant's Son, a Vanished Village," *Bonita Daily News* (Naples, FL) (January 19, 2003), http://www.bonitanews.com/03/01/bonita/d856798a.htm (accessed August 8, 2004).

13. Andrea Simon, *Bashert: A Granddaughter's Holocaust Quest* (Jackson: University Press of Mississippi, 2002), 123.

14. Biller, "See Auschwitz," 223.

15. Jeffrey Dekro, "First Time Home: Poland Leaves Its Mark on a Visitor," *Reconstructionist* 54 (October–November 1988): 9–14.

16. Howard Jacobson, *Roots Schmoots: Journeys Among Jews* (Woodstock, NY: Overlook Press, 1994), 500–501.

17. Jonathan Boyarin, *Storm from Paradise: The Politics of Jewish Memory* (Minneapolis: University of Minnesota Press, 1992), 6–7.

18. Hasia R. Diner, *Lower East Side Memories: A Jewish Place in America* (Princeton: Princeton University Press, 2000), 18, 20.

19. Suzanne Wasserman, "Re-creating Recreations on the Lower East Side: Restaurants: Cabarets, Cafes, and Coffeehouses in the 1930s," in *Remembering the Lower East Side: American Jewish Reflections*, eds. Hasia R. Diner et al. (Bloomington: Indiana University Press, 2000), 165–166.

20. Alan Dershowitz, "Lox on Both their Houses," *New York Times* (August 9, 1988). Cited in Wasserman, "Re-creating," 170.

21. http://www.he.net/~radtours/tours/lesi.htm (accessed January 6, 2005).

22. Marion S. Jacobson, "The Klezmer Club as Pilgrimage," special issue, *Jewish Folklore and Ethnology Review* 17, no. 1–2 (1995): 42–46.

23. Susan Slyomovics, "Rebbele Mordkhele's Pilgrimage in New York City, Tel Aviv, and Carpathian Ruthenia," in *Going Home*, ed. Jack Kugelmass (Evanston, IL: YIVO and Northwestern University Press, 1993), 369–394.

24. American Jewish Joint Distribution Community, "Bridging Generations: A Sigd Pilgrimage to Jerusalem for the Ethiopian-Israeli Community," http://www.jdc.org/p_is_ps_vulnerable_3.html (accessed January 20, 2005). See also the home page of the Israel Association for Ethiopian Jews and the explanation of the Sigd at http://www.iaej.co.il/pages/our_culture_sigd.htm.

25. Roots pilgrimage information cited in this section comes from a random sample of Jewish roots pilgrimage programs listed on the World Wide Web in September 2004. They include: Jewish Heritage Tours (http://www.heritagetoursonline.com), cited as "Heritage"; National Tours (http://www.nat-tours-israel.co.il/jewish.shtml), cited as "National"; E&M Travel Jewish Heritage tours (http://www.emcoinc.com/travel/html/JewishTravel/LithuaniaWestExpressMenu.htm), cited as "E&M"; Weber Travel Worldwide Travel Service (http://www.msnbc.msn.com/id/3081107), cited as "Weber"; and Routes to Roots (http://www.routestoroots.com), cited as "Routes to Roots."

26. http://www.elderhostel.org/programs/programdetail.asp?Rowld=1-OAMV&DateId= (accessed March 5, 2004).

27. André Levy, "Ethnic Aspects of Israeli Pilgrimage and Tourism to Morocco," special issue, *Jewish Folklore and Ethnology Review* 17, no. 1–2 (1995): 21.

28. Oren Kosansky, "Tourism, Charity, and Profit: The Movement of Money in Moroccan Jewish Pilgrimage," *Cultural Anthropology* 17, no. 3 (2002): 360, 367, 369, 371.

29. Hannah Levine, "Changing Destinations," *Jerusalem Report* (July 28, 2003): 40.

30. Daniel Soyer, "The Travel Agent as Ethnic Broker Between Old World and New: The Case of Gustave Eisner," *YIVO Annual* 21 (1933): 354, 351.

31. Ibid., 352–353.

Chapter 14. Shrine Wars

1. Keith Grimwood and Ezra Idlet (Trout Fishing in America), "Mine," in a CD entitled *Mine!* (Trout Records/troutoons [BMI], © 1993).

2. Sharon Waxman, "Shrine to Hatred," *Washington Post* (October 28, 2000): C1, http://www.library.cornell.edu/colldev/mideast/shryus.html (accessed January 31, 2005).

3. State of Israel, Ministry of Foreign Affairs, "Protection of Holy Places Law" (June 27, 1967).

4. Waxman, "Shrine to Hatred."

5. For example, the Shomron Regional Council, which acts as a municipal government for the Jewish settlements in Judea around Shechem. Margaret Dudkevitch, "Joseph's Tomb: Holy, Hotly Contested," *Jerusalem Post* (December 14, 2003), http://www.jpost.com/servlet/Satellite?pagename=JPost/JPArticle/ShowFull&cid=10713004082 (accessed February 3, 2005). Other voices proclaim Rachel's Tomb the third most important.

6. "I Cried and Asked Forgiveness: Joseph's Brothers Sold Him Again," *Arutz Sheva Israel National News* (9 Iyar, 5762/2002), cited in Shechem.org, "Joseph's Tomb in Shechem (Nablus)," http://www.shechem.org/kyos/engkyos.html (accessed February 1, 2005).

7. Prof. Moshe Maoz of the Hebrew University admitted as much when he told a group of Jewish leaders in New York in May 2001: "We invent all kinds of tombs [in Palestinian-populated areas]." Cited by Melissa Radler, "Jews Fabricate Holy Sites, They Do Not Matter," *Jerusalem Post* (May 29, 2001), http://www.themodernreligion.com/jihad/fabricate.html (accessed August 20, 2004).

8. Michael Freund, "Take Back Joseph's Tomb," Freeman Center for Strategic Studies, http://www.freeman.org/m_online/oct02/freund2.htm (accessed February 1, 2005).

9. "I Cried and Asked Forgiveness."

10. Israel Shamir, "Joseph Revisited," Fontenelles—Palestine Archive, http://home.mindspring.com/~fontenelles/shamir5.htm (accessed February 1, 2005).

11. Waxman, "Shrine to Hatred."

12. Shamir, "Joseph Revisited."

13. Waxman, "Shrine to Hatred."

14. Ariel Naton Pasko, "Israel or Palestine?" Keystone Publishing, http://www.pushhamburger.com/israel_or.htm (accessed February 1, 2005).

15. Freund, "Take Back Joseph's Tomb."

16. Leiah and Jason Elbaum, "Battle in Shechem—Eyewitness Report," e-mail message to IRIS [Information Regarding Israel's Security] (September 26, 1996), http://www.io.com/~jewishwb/iris/archives/883.html (accessed February 1, 2005).

17. Shamir, "Joseph Revisited."

18. Ibid.

19. "Trouble in the Holy Land: Arab Vandals Desecrate Joseph's Tomb, Gravestone of Biblical Patriarch Ruined Despite Palestinian Pledge," *WorldNetDaily* (February 25, 2003), http://www.worldnetdaily.com/news/article.asp?ARTICLE_ID=31203 (accessed February 1, 2005).

20. Shamir, "Joseph Revisited."

21. Dale Baranowski, "Jerusalem Mayor Olmert Presses for Security Fence Around Rachel's Tomb," http://www.rachelstomb.org/update.htm (accessed February 5, 2005); The Committee for Rachel's Tomb, "Recent History: A Year That Changed Rachel's Tomb and Our Nation," http://www.rachelstomb.org/recenthistory.html (accessed February 2, 2005).

22. Nadav Shragai, "The Palestinians Who Are Shooting at the Rachel's Tomb Compound Have Already Singled It Out as the Next Jewish Holy Site Which They Want to 'Liberate,'" *Haaretz* (October 31, 2000), citing Uzi Benziman, *Jerusalem: A City Without a Wall* (Hebrew) (Jerusalem: Sho'en, 1973).

23. Nadav Shragai, "Rachel's Tomb: Beyond or Within?" *Haaretz* (July 23, 2002), www.haaretzdaily.com (accessed February 8, 2005).

24. The Committee for Rachel's Tomb, "Recent History: A Year that Changed Rachel's Tomb and Our Nation," http://www.rachelstomb.org/recenthistory.html (accessed February 2, 2005).

25. Ibid.

26. E-mail message to Women for Israel's Tomorrow (Women in Green), May 7, 2001, http://www.rachelstomb.org/update.htm (accessed February 2, 2005).

27. Joshua Hammer, *A Season in Bethlehem: Unholy War in a Sacred Place* (New York: Free Press, 2003), Chapter 1, http://www.northshire.com/siteinfo/bookinfo/0-7432-4413-3/0/ (accessed February 6, 2005).

28. Bassem Shehada, "Mufti Claims Ownership of 'Rachel's Tomb,'" *Jerusalem Times* (September 19, 2002), http://www.jerusalem-times.net/article/news/details/detail.asp?id=2042 (accessed February 2, 2005).

29. Yuval Yoaz, "Whose Fence Is It Anyway?" *Haaretz* (February 9, 2005), http://www.haaretz.co.il/marketing/mediakit/pop.html (accessed Februay 10, 2005).

30. "Court Decrees No Change in Security Fence Route," *Jerusalem Post* (February 3, 2005), http://www.jpost.com/servlet/Satellite?pagename=JPost/JPArticle/ShowFull&cid=1107400718858&p=1078397702 (accessed February 8, 2005).

31. Nadia Abou El-Magd, "A Contentious Birthday Celebration," *Al-Ahram Weekly Online* 516 (January 11–12, 2001), http://weekly.ahram.org.eg/2001/516/eg5.htm (accessed February 5, 2005).

32. Ibid.

33. Amil Khan, "Court Rejects Jewish Shrine as Cultural Site," *Middle East Times* 37 (2001), http://www.metimes.com/2K1/issue2001-37/eg/court_rejects_jewish.htm (accessed February 5, 2005).

34. El-Magd, "Contentious Birthday Celebration."

35. "Shrine Revisited," *Al-Ahram Weekly Online* 536 (May 31–June 6, 2001), http://weekly.ahram.org.eg/2001/536/eg3.htm (accessed February 5, 2005). *Yated Ne'eman* staff, "Few Attend Hillula of HaRav Abu Chatzeirah," shema Yisrael Torah Network, January 17, 2001, http://www.shemayisrael.com/chareidi/archives5761/shemos/abuchtz.htm (accessed February 23, 2004).

36. "Shrine Revisited."

37. Ambassador David Welch, "Remarks at a Luncheon of the Egyptian European

Council, Farah Boat Restaurant," January 18, 2005, http://cairo.usembassy.gov/usis/sp011805.h (accessed February 5, 2005).

38. *Jerusalem Report* (December 26, 1996), cited in http://www.ourjerusalem.com/opinion/story/opinion20040628b.htm (accessed February 14, 2005).

39. Steward Weiss, "Strangers in a Familiar Land," *Jerusalem Post* (November 2, 2003), http://www.freeman.org/m_online/November03/ (accessed January 24, 2004).

40. The comments are chronicled by the GPO News Department and the IDF Spokesman's Office, Information Branch, http://www.mfa.gov.il/MFA/RSS/ (accessed February 2, 2005).

41. *Report of the Commission Appointed by His Majesty's Government in the United Kingdom of Great Britain and Northern Ireland, with the Approval of the Council of the League of Nations, to Determine the Rights and Claims of Moslems and Jews in Connection with the Western or Wailing Wall at Jerusalem* (London: HMSO, 1931), 57–58. Reprinted by the United Nations as an addendum to document A/7057-S/8427.

42. Amos Elon, *Jerusalem, Battlegrounds of Memory* (New York: Kodansha International, 1995), 110.

43. "Israel to Dig New Tunnel Under Aqsa Mosque" (March 1, 2004), http://www.pna.gov.ps/subject_details2.asp?DocId=1257 (accessed February 24, 2005).

44. Ikrima Sabri, "Interview," *Makor Rishon* (May 22, 1998), cited in Jerusalem Fund of Aish Hatorah, "Palestinian Denial of Religious Freedom," aish.com, http://www.aish.com/Israel/articles/Palestinian_Denial_of_Religious_Freedom.asp (accessed March 1, 2005).

45. William A. Orme, "Construction at 2,000-Year-Old Religious Site Unleashes a Tempest," *International Herald Tribune* (December 23, 1999): B2.

BIBLIOGRAPHY

Ackerman, Susan. *Under Every Green Tree: Popular Religion in Sixth-Century Judah*. Atlanta: Scholars Press, 1992.

Adler, Elkan Nathan, ed. *Jewish Travellers in the Middle Ages: 19 Firsthand Accounts*. 1930. Rpt. New York: Dover, 1987.

Adomnan. "The Holy Places." In *Jerusalem Pilgrims Before the Crusades*. Trans. and ed. John Wilkinson. Jerusalem: Ariel, 1977. 2nd ed. Warminster: Aris & Phillips, 2002. 167–206.

Albertz, Rainer. *A History of Israelite Religion in the Old Testament Period*. Trans. John Bowden. 2 vols. Louisville: Westminster/John Knox Press, 1994.

Albou, Karin. *Mon pays m'a quitté*. Video, 50 minutes, 1995.

Alfasi, Eliyahu, Yechiel Torgeman, and C. T. Bari. *Baba Sali Our Holy Teacher. His Life, Piety, Teachings and Miracles. Rav Yisrael Abuchatzeirah*. Trans. Leah Dolinger. New York: Judaica Press, 1986.

American Israeli Cooperative Enterprise. Jewish Virtual Library. http://www.jewishvirtuallibrary.org.

Aristeas. *Aristeas to Philocrates (Letter of Aristeas)*. Trans. and ed. Moses Hadas. New York: Harper & Brothers, 1951.

Armstrong, Karen. *Jerusalem: One City, Three Faiths*. New York: Alfred A. Knopf, 1996.

Aronoff, Myron J. "Establishing Authority: The Memorialization of Jabotinsky and the Burial of the Bar-Kochba Bones in Israel Under the Likud." In *The Frailty of Authority*. Ed. Myron J. Aronoff. New Brunswick, NJ: Transaction Books, 1986. 5:105–130.

Avi-Yonah, Michael. *The Jews of Palestine: A Political History from the Bar Kokhba War to the Arab Conquest*. New York: Schocken, 1976.

Azaryahu, Maoz. "Mount Herzl: The Creation of Israel's National Cemetery." *Israel Studies* 1, no. 2 (1996): 46–74. http://iupjournals.org/israel/iss1-2.html.

Azen, Henriette. "Un haut lieu de pèlerinage du judaïsme algérien: Le Rabb de Tlemcen." *Los Muestros* (Brussels) 29 (December 1997): 21–23.

The Babylonian Talmud. Ed. I. Epstein. 35 vols. London: Soncino Press, 1961.

Bachi, Roth Kolodny. *If You Go Along with Me: The Story of Olga Hankin* [in Hebrew]. Israel: Yad Ben-Zvi, 1997.

Barag, Dan. "Glass Pilgrim Vessels from Jerusalem." *Journal of Glass Studies* 12 (1970): 35–63; 13 (1971): 45–63.

Barker, Margaret. *The Gate of Heaven: The History and Symbolism of the Temple in Jerusalem*. London: SPCK, 1991.

Barnes, Lucille. "Retiring Sen. Jesse Helms Caved to Pro-Israel Lobby Halfway Through His Career." *Washington Report on Middle East Affairs* (March 2002). http://www.wrmea.com/archives/march2002/0203034.html.

Bash, Jonathan. "Sorry, I Can't Come to Your Wedding." *Jewish World* (January 12, 2005). http://www.aish.com/jewishissues/israeldiary/Sorry3_I_Cant_Come_to_Your_Wedding.asp.

Ben-Ami, Issachar. "Folk Veneration of Saints Among the Moroccan Jews." In *Studies in Judaism and Islam*. Eds. S. Morag, Issachar Ben-Ami, and Norman A. Stillman. Jerusalem: Magnes Press, 1981. 283–344.

——. *Saint Veneration Among the Jews in Morocco*. Detroit: Wayne State University Press, 1998.

Ben-Ari, Eyal, and Yoram Bilu. "Saints' Sanctuaries in Israeli Development Towns: On a Mechanism of Urban Transformation." *Urban Anthropology* 16, no. 2 (Summer 1987): 243–272.

——, eds. *Grasping Land: Space and Place in Contemporary Israeli Discourse and Experience*. Albany: State University of New York Press, 1996.

Ben-Yehuda, Nachman. *The Masada Myth: Collective Memory and Mythmaking in Israel*. Madison: University of Wisconsin Press, 1995.

Benjamin of Tudela. *The Itinerary of Benjamin of Tudela*. Trans. and ed. Marcus Nathan Adler. New York: Philipp Feldheim, 1907. http://chass.colostate-pueblo.edu/history/seminar/benjamin/benhamin1.htm.

Benvenisti, Meron. *Jerusalem: The Torn City*. Minneapolis: University of Minnesota Press, 1976.

Biller, Maxim. "See Auschwitz and Die." In *Jewish Voices, German Words: Growing up Jewish in Postwar Germany and Austria*. Ed. Elena Lappin. Trans. Krishna Winston. North Haven, CT: Catbird Press, 1994. 210–225.

Bilu, Yoram. "Dreams and the Wishes of the Saint." In *Judaism Viewed from Within and from Without: Anthropological Studies*. Ed. Harvey E. Goldberg. Albany: State University of New York Press, 1986. 285–313.

——. "The Inner Limits of Communitas: A Covert Dimension of Pilgrimage Experience." *Ethos. Journal of the Society for Psychological Anthropology* 16, no. 3 (1988): 302–325.

——. "Moroccan Jews and the Shaping of Israel's Sacred Geography." In *Divergent Jewish Cultures: Israel and America*. Eds. Deborah Dash Moore and Selwyn Ilan Troen. New Haven: Yale University Press, 2001. 72–86.

——. "Oneirobiography and Oneirocommunity in Saint Worship in Israel: A Two-Tier Model for Dream-Inspired Religious Revivals." *Dreaming* 10, no. 2 (2000): 85–101.

——. "The Role of Charismatic Dreams in the Creation of Sacred Sites in Present-

Day Israel." In *Sacred Space: Shrine, City, Land*. Eds. Benjamin Z. Kedar and J. Zwi Werblowsky. New York: New York University Press, 1998. 295–315.

Bilu, Yoram, and Eyal Ben-Ari. "The Making of Modern Saints: Manufactured Charisma and the Abu-Hatseiras of Israel." *American Ethnologist* 19, no. 4 (1992): 672–687.

———. "Modernity and Charisma in Contemporary Israel." *Israel Affairs* 1, no. 3 (1995): 224–236.

Binder, Donald D. *Into the Temple Courts: The Place of the Synagogues in the Second Temple Period*. Atlanta: Society of Biblical Literature, 1999.

Bird, Lady Theodora. *Wings of a Bird: Memoirs of a Lady Traveller in North Africa, 1832–1839*. N.p.: n.p., n.d.

Bivin, David. "Synagogue Guest House for First-Century Pilgrims." *Jerusalem Perspective Online*. http://www.jerusalemperspective.com.

Block, Allison. "Remembrances of Places Past." *Indiana University Research and Creative Activity* 17, no. 1 (April 1994). http://www.indiana/.edu/~rcapub/v17n1/p12html.

Bordeaux Pilgrim. "An Itinerary from Bordeaux to Jerusalem." In *Anonymous Pilgrims, I–VIII*. Trans. Aubrey Stewart. London: Palestine Pilgrims' Texts Society, 1894. 6:1.

Bowersock, G. W. "Ancient History and Modern Politics." *Grand Street* (Autumn 1984): 130–141.

Boyarin, Jonathan. *Storm from Paradise: The Politics of Jewish Memory*. Minneapolis: University of Minnesota Press, 1992.

Branham, Joan R. "Mapping Tragedy in the US Holocaust Memorial Museum." In "The Tragic in Architecture." Special issue, *Architectural Design* 70, no. 5 (2000): 54–59.

Brog, Mooli. "From the Top of Masada to the Bottom of the Ghetto" [in Hebrew]. In *Myth and Memory: Transfigurations of Israeli Consciousness*. Eds. David Ohana and Robert Wistrich. Jerusalem and Tel Aviv: Van Leer Institute, 1996. 203–227. http://www.jafi.org.il/education/festivls/ZKATZ/ZK/massada.html.

Calle, A. *El martirio de la joven Hachuel, o la heroína hebrea*. Seville (Spain): n.p., 1852.

Canaan, Taufik. *Mohammedan Saints and Sanctuaries in Palestine*. London: Luzac, 1927.

Casale Pilgrim. *The Casale Pilgrim: A Sixteenth-Century Illustrated Guide to the Holy Places Reproduced in Facsimile*. Trans. and ed. Cecil Roth. London: Soncino Press, 1929.

Cernea, Ruth Fredman. "Flaming Prayers: Hillula in a New Home." In *Between Two Worlds: Ethnographic Essays on American Jewry*. Ed. Jack Kugelmass. Ithaca: Cornell University Press, 1988. 162–191.

Cesarani, David. "Coming to Terms with the Past." *Today's History* 54, no. 2 (February 2004): 16–18. http://www.historytoday.com/dm_getArticle.asp?gid=19778.

Chazan, Barry, and Arianna Koransky. *Does the Teen Israel Experience Make a Difference?* New York: Israel Experience, Inc., 1997.

Cohen, Amnon. *Jewish Life Under Islam: Jerusalem in the Sixteenth Century*. Cambridge: Harvard University Press, 1984.

———. *Ottoman Documents on the Jewish Community of Jerusalem in the Sixteenth Century*. Jerusalem: Yad Izhak Ben-Zvi, 1976.

Cohen, Debra Nussbaum. "Crowds of Followers Give Life to Rebbe's Burial Location." *Jewish News Weekly of Northern California* (November 12, 1999). http://www.jewishsf.com/content/2-0-/module/displaystory/story_id/12437/edition_id/240/format/html/displaystory.html.

———. "If Only the Rebbe Were Here." *Moment* 27, no. 5 (October 2002): 48–49.

Cohen, Erik. "Pilgrimage Centers: Concentric and Excentric." In "Pilgrimage and Tourism: The Quest in Guest." Ed. Valene Smith. Special issue, *Annals of Tourism Research* 19, no. 1 (1992): 33–50.

"Court Decrees No Change in Security Fence Route." *Jerusalem Post* (February 3, 2005). http://www.jpost.com/servlet/Satellite?pagename=JPost/JPArticle/ShowFull&cid=1107400718858&p=1078397702.

Crow, Loren D. *The Songs of Ascents (Psalms 120–134): Their Place in Israelite History and Religion*. Atlanta: Scholars Press, 1996.

Dan, Joseph. "Jerusalem in Jewish Spirituality." In *City of the Great King: Jerusalem from David to the Present*. Ed. Nitza Rosovsky. Cambridge: Harvard University Press, 1996. 60–73.

David, Abraham. *To Come to the Land: Immigration and Settlement in Sixteenth-Century Eretz-Israel*. Trans. Dena Ordan. Tuscaloosa: University of Alabama Press, 1999.

David dei Rossi. "A Jewish Merchant Reports on Life in Palestine" [Letter]. In *A Treasury of Jewish Letters*. Ed. Franz Kobler. 2 vols. 1952. 2nd ed. Philadelphia: Jewish Publication Society, 1953. 2:337–340.

Davidson, Linda Kay, and David M. Gitlitz. *Pilgrimage: From the Ganges to Graceland: An Encyclopedia*. Santa Barbara, CA: ABC-CLIO, 2002.

Davies, W. D. *The Territorial Dimension of Judaism*. Berkeley: University of California Press, 1982.

Dekro, Jeffrey. "First Time Home: Poland Leaves Its Mark on a Visitor." *Reconstructionist* 54 (October–November 1988): 9–14.

Deshen, Shlomo. *The Mellah Society: Jewish Community Life in Sherifian Morocco*. Chicago: University of Chicago Press, 1989.

Deshen, Shlomo, and Moshe Shokeid. *The Predicament of Homecoming: Cultural and Social Life of North African Immigrants in Israel*. Ithaca: Cornell University Press, 1974.

Dever, William H. *Did God Have a Wife?: Archaeology and Folk Religion in Ancient Israel*. Grand Rapids, MI: Eerdmans Press, 2005.

Diamond, Sigmund. *In Quest: Journal of an Unquiet Pilgrimage*. New York: Columbia University Press, 1980.

Diner, Hasia R. *Lower East Side Memories: A Jewish Place in America*. Princeton: Princeton University Press, 2000.

Disciple of Bertinoro. "In the Footsteps of the Master." In *Roads to Zion: Four Centuries of Travelers' Reports*. Ed. Kurt Wilhelm. Trans. I. M. Lask. New York: Schocken, 1948. 15–28.

Dudkevitch, Margaret. "Joseph's Tomb: Holy, Hotly Contested." *Jerusalem Post* (December 14, 2003). http://www.jpost.com/servlet/Satellite?pagename=JPost/JPArticle/ShowFull&cid=10713004082.

Eickelman, Dale F. *Moroccan Islam: Tradition and Society in a Pilgrimage Center*. Austin: University of Texas Press, 1976.

El-Magd, Nadia Abou. "A Contentious Birthday Celebration." *Al-Ahram Weekly Online* 516 (January 11–12, 2001). http://weekly.ahram.org.eg/2001/516/eg5.htm.

Eliade, Mircea. *The Sacred and the Profane: The Nature of Religion*. Trans. Willard R. Trask. New York: Harcourt, Brace, 1959.

Elijah of Ferrara. "Elijah of Ferrara." In *Jewish Travellers in the Middle Ages*. Ed. Elkan Nathan Adler. 1930. Rpt. New York: Dover, 1987. 151–155.

Elijah of Pesaro. "On the Way." In *Roads to Zion: Four Centuries of Travelers' Reports*. Ed. Kurt Wilhelm. Trans. I. M. Lask. New York: Schocken, 1948. 39–56.

Elliman, Wendy. "Reform Judaism Creates Its Own Israeli Identity." *Jewish Post of New York* (October 1998). http://www.jewishpost.com/jp0410/jpn0410b.htm.

Elon, Amos. *Jerusalem, Battlegrounds of Memory*. New York: Kodansha International, 1995.

Encyclopaedia Judaica. 16 vols. Jerusalem: Macmillan, 1972.

Epic of Gilgamesh. Trans. N. K. Sanders. Baltimore: Penguin, 1960.

Epstein, Shifra. "Inventing a Pilgrimage: Ritual, Love and Politics on the Road to Amuka." Special issue, *Jewish Folklore and Ethnology Review* 17, no. 1–2 (1995): 25–32.

Erlanger, Steven. "Israel Opens Holocaust History Museum." *San Diego Union-Tribune* (March 16, 2005).

Estori Farhi. *[Caftor VaFerah.]* In *The Holy City: Jews on Jerusalem*. Ed. Avraham Holtz. New York: W. W. Norton, 1971. 126–150.

Ezrahi, Sidra DeKoven. *Booking Passage: Exile and Homecoming in the Modern Jewish Imagination*. Berkeley: University of California Press, 2000.

Feldman, Jackie. "'Above the Death-Pits and with the Flag of Israel Waving on High'—The Structure and Meaning of Israeli Youth Missions to Poland of the Shoah." In *Never Again! The Holocaust's Challenge for Educators*. Eds. Helmut Schreier and Matthias Heyl. Hamburg: Krämer, 1997. 117–132, 206.

———. "La circulation de la Tora: les pèlerinages au second Temple." In *La Société juive à travers l'histoire*. Ed. S. Trigano. Trans. John-Christoph Ettias. 4 vols. Paris: Fayard, 1992–1993. 4:161–178.

———. "'It Is My Brothers Whom I Am Seeking': Israeli Youths' Pilgrimages to Poland of the Shoah." Special issue, *Jewish Folklore and Ethnology Review* 17, no. 1–2 (1995): 33–37.

———. "Voyages to Poland: Sensitizing Educators to Non-Verbal Elements." International School for Holocaust Studies Workshop, October 11, 1999. http://www.yadvashem.org.il/download/education/conf/Feldman1B.pdf.

Foucauld, Charles de. *Reconnaissance au Maroc (1883–1884)*. Paris: n.p., 1888.

Freed, James Ingo. "The United States Holocaust Memorial Musesum." *Architecture and Urbanism* 11, no. 278 (1993): 88–127.

Freedman, Warren. *World Guide for the Jewish Traveler*. New York: E. P. Dutton, 1984.

Friedman, Keren. "The Rabbi with the Long White Beard: A Personal Encounter." Special issue, *Jewish Folklore and Ethnology Review* 17, no. 1–2 (1995): 37–39.

Friedman, Mark. "Jewish Pilgrimage after the Destruction of the Second Temple." In *City of the Great King: Jerusalem from David to the Present*. Ed. Nitza Rosovsky. Cambridge: Harvard University Press, 1996. 136–146.

Friedman, Matti. "The End of Morocco's Mosaic of Tolerance." *Jerusalem Report* (July 14, 2003): 22–26.

Fuchs, Yechiel. "Wedded Bliss." *Jewish Week* (January 17, 2005). http://www.the jewishweek.com/bottom/freshink_content.php3?artid=263.

Gafni, Isaiah M. *Land, Center and Diaspora: Jewish Constructs in Late Antiquity*. Sheffield: Sheffield Academic Press, 1997.

Gao Xingjian. *Soul Mountain*. Trans. Mabel Lee. New York: HarperCollins, 2000.

Gennep, Arnold van. "Le pèlerinage de Rabb." In *En Algérie*. Paris: Mercure de France, 1914. 41–58.

———. *The Rites of Passage*. Chicago: University of Chicago Press, 1961.

Gil, Moshe. "Aliya and Pilgrimage in the Early Arab Period (634–1009)." In "Symposium: The Relationship Between the Diaspora and the Land of Israel Under Arab Rule." Ed. Lee I. Levine. Special issue, *The Jerusalem Cathedra* 3 (1983): 163–173.

Goitein, S. D. "Contemporary Letters on the Capture of Jerusalem by the Crusaders." *Journal of Jewish Studies* 3 (1952): 162–177.

———. "Tyre-Tripoli-'Arqa; Geniza Documents from the Beginnings of the Crusader Period." *Jewish Quarterly Review* 66 (1975): 84–85.

Goldberg, Harvey E. "The Mellahs of Southern Morocco: Report of a Survey." *The Maghreb Review* 8, no. 3–4 (1983): 61–69.

———. "Torah and Children: Some Symbolic Aspects of the Reproduction of Jews and Judaism." In *Judaism Viewed from Within and from Without: Anthropological Studies*. Ed. Harvey E. Goldberg. Albany: State University of New York Press, 1986. 107–130.

Goodman, Martin. "Nerva, the *Fiscus Judaicus* and Jewish Identity." *Journal of Roman Studies* 79 (1989): 40–44.

———. "The Pilgrimage Economy of Jerusalem in the Second Temple Period." In *Jerusalem: Its Sanctity and Centrality to Judaism, Christianity, and Islam*. Ed. Lee I. Levine. New York: Continuum, 1999. 69–76.

Gordon, Benjamin Lee. *New Judea: Jewish Life in Modern Palestine and Egypt*. Philadelphia: Julius H. Greenstone, 1919.

Graburn, Nelson H. "Tourism: The Sacred Journey." In *Hosts and Guests: The Anthropology of Tourism*. Ed. Valene Smith. Philadelphia: University of Pennsylvania Press, 1977. 17–31.

Grant, Lisa D. "Paradoxical Pilgrimage: American Jewish Adults on a Congregational Israel Trip." PhD diss., Jewish Theological Seminary of America, 2000.

Green, Arthur. *Tormented Master: A Life of Rabbi Nahman of Bratslav*. Tuscaloosa: University of Alabama Press, 1979.

Green, Saguy. "Memorial for a Fallen Star." *Haaretz* (June 21, 2003). http://israel.jcca.org/Press/memorial.html.

Greenberg, Miriam. "Pilgrimage of a Non-Believer." Special issue, *Jewish Folklore and Ethnology Review* 17, no. 1–2 (1995): 40–41.

Greenblum, Joseph. "A Pilgrimage to Germany." *Judaism* 44, no. 4 (Fall 1995): 478–485.

Greenfield, Hana. *Fragments of Memory*. Jerusalem: Gefen Books, 1992.

Grimwood, Keith, and Ezra Idlet (Trout Fishing in America). "Mine!" In *MINE!* Trout Records/troutoons (BMI), ©1993.

Gruen, Erich S. *Diaspora: Jews Amidst Greeks and Romans*. Cambridge: Harvard University Press, 2002.

Hadad, Herbert. "All the Way Home." *Daily News Magazine* (January 24, 1998). Rpt. in *Sephardic-American Voices: Two Hundred Years of a Literary Legacy*. Ed. Diane Matza. Hanover, NH: Brandeis University Press, 1997. 66–67.

Hadar, Gila. "Salonika: Memoirs of a City in the Context of Diversity and Change: 1914–1943." Conference Paper, *Nationalism, Society and Culture in Post-*

Ottoman South East Europe. St. Peter's College, Oxford, England. May 29–30, 2004. http://www.sant.ox.ac.uk/areastudies/hadar.pdf.

Haley, Alex. *Roots*. Garden City, NY: Doubleday, 1976.

Hammer, Joshua. *A Season in Bethlehem: Unholy War in a Sacred Place*. New York: Free Press, 2003. http://www.northshire.com/siteinfo/bookinfo/0-7432-4413-3/0/.

Haran, Menahem. *Temples and Temple-Service in Ancient Israel. An Inquiry into the Character of Cult Phenomena and the Historical Setting of the Priestly School*. Oxford: Clarendon, 1978.

Harizi, Judah ben Solomon. *The Book of Tahkemoni. Jewish Tales from Medieval Spain*. Trans. and ed. David Simha Segal. Portland, OR: Litman Library of Jewish Civilization, 2001.

Hass, Aaron. "Survivor Guilt in Holocaust Survivors and Their Children." In *A Global Perspective on Working with Holocaust Survivors and the Second Generation*. Ed. John Lemberger. Jerusalem: JDC-Brookdale Institute of Gerontology and Human Development, in Cooperation with the World Council of Jewish Communal Service, AMCHA, and JDC-Israel, 1995. 163–184.

Hendel, Ronald S. "Sacrifice as a Cultural System: The Ritual Symbolism of Exodus 24:3–8." *Zeitschrift für die alttestamentliche Wissenschaft* 101 (1989): 366–390.

Hoffman, Howard. "From the Rabbi's Desk." *North Shore Jewish Center Bulletin* (2000). http://www.northshorejc.org/bulletin/0600/rabbi.html.

Holtz, Avraham, comp. and ed. *The Holy City: Jews on Jerusalem*. New York: W. W. Norton, 1971.

Horn, Dara. "On Filling Shoes." *Hadassah Magazine* (November 1992): 16–22.

Horsley, Richard. *Bandits, Prophets & Messiahs: Popular Movements in the Time of Jesus*. 1985. Philadelphia: Trinity Press International, 1999.

Huyssen, Andreas. "Monument and Memory in a Postmodern Age." In *The Art of Memory: Holocaust Memorials in History*. Ed. James E. Young. New York and Munich: Prestel, 1994. 9–17.

"I Cried and Asked Forgiveness: Joseph's Brothers Sold Him Again." *Arutz Sheva Israel National News* (9 Iyar 5762/2002). http://www.shechem.org/kyos/engkyos.html.

ibn al-Qalanisi. *The Damascus Chronicle of the Crusades*. Trans. H.A.R. Gibb. London: Luzac, 1932.

Iliowizi, Henry. *Sol, An Epic Poem*. Minneapolis: n.p., circa 1882.

Isaac ben Joseph ibn Chelo. "The Roads from Jerusalem." In *Jewish Travellers in the Middle Ages*. Ed. Elkan Nathan Adler. 1930. Rpt. New York: Dover, 1987. 130–150.

Jacob, the Messenger of Rabbi Jechiel of Paris, 1238–44. "[Jacob, The Messenger of Rabbi Jechiel of Paris]." In *Jewish Travellers in the Middle Ages*. Ed. Elkan Nathan Adler. 1930. Rpt. New York: Dover, 1987. 115–129.

Jacob ben Nathaniel ha Cohen. "[Jacob ben R. Nathaniel ha Cohen]." In *Jewish Travellers in the Middle Ages*. Ed. Elkan Nathan Adler. 1930. Rpt. New York: Dover, 1987. 92–99.

Jacobs, Louis. *Hasidic Prayer*. Washington: Littman Library of Jewish Civilization, 1993.

———. *Holy Living: Saints and Saintliness in Judaism*. Northvale, NJ and London: J. Aronson, 1990.

Jacobson, Howard. *Roots Schmoots: Journeys Among Jews*. Woodstock, NY: Overlook Press, 1994.

Jacobson, Marion S. "The Klezmer Club as Pilgrimage." Special issue, *Jewish Folklore and Ethnology Review* 17, no. 1–2 (1995): 42–46.

Jeremias, Joachim. *Jerusalem in the Time of Jesus: An Investigation into Economic and Social Conditions During the New Testament Period.* Trans. F. H. and C. H. Cave. Philadelphia: Fortress Press, 1962.

Jerome. *Commentarium in Sophoniam Prophetam*, in *Patrologia Latina*. Ed. J.-P. Migne. Paris: J.-P. Migne, 1844–1864. 28:1337–1356.

———. "Letter 108 to Eustochium." In *Jerusalem Pilgrims Before the Crusades*. Trans. and ed. John Wilkinson. Jerusalem: Ariel, 1977. 2nd ed. Warminster: Aris & Phillips, 2002. 79.

Jewish Encyclopedia Online. http://www.jewishencyclopedia.com.

Johnsson, William G. "The Pilgrimage Motif in the Book of Hebrews." *Journal of Biblical Literature* 97, no. 2 (June 1978): 239–251.

Joseph the Scribe of Beresteczko. "Of Earthquakes and Torah Scrolls." In *Roads to Zion: Four Centuries of Travelers' Reports*. Ed. Kurt Wilhelm. Trans. I. M. Lask. New York: Schocken, 1948. 85–94.

Josephus, Flavius. *Josephus [Works]*. Trans. H. St. J. Thackeray et al. 10 vols. London: William Heinemann, Ltd.; Cambridge: Harvard University Press, 1926–1965.

Judah Halevi. *Selected Poems of Jehudah Halevi*. Ed. Heinrich Brody. Trans. Nina Salaman. 1924. Rpt. New York: Arno Press, 1973.

Kagan, Yitschak Meir. "Seeking Farbrengen." *Farbrengen Magazine*. http://www.chabad.org/library/article.asp?AID=2216.

Kaufmann, Yehezkel. *History of the Religion of Israel, from the Babylonian Captivity to the End of Prophecy*. Trans. Clarence Efroymsen. New York: Ktav, 1976.

Keren, Nili. "The Influence of Opinion Leaders and of Holocaust Research on the Development of the Educational Discussion and Curriculum on the Holocaust in Secondary Schools and in Informal Education in Israel, 1948–1981." PhD diss., Hebrew University, 1985.

Khan, Amil. "Court Rejects Jewish Shrine as Cultural Site" and "Jewish Pilgrimage Banned in Northern Egypt." *Middle East Times* (2001). http://www.metimes.com/2K1/issue2001-37/eg/court_rejects_jewish.htm.

Kim, Charles W. "Hasidim Return to Grave Site to Honor Rebbe." *Sentinel* (North Brunswick, NJ) (July 26, 2001). http://nbs.gmnews.com/News/2001/0726/Front_Page/019.html.

Kobler, Franz, ed. *A Treasury of Jewish Letters*. 2 vols. Philadelphia: Jewish Publication Society, 1954.

Kollek, Teddy, and Moshe Pearlman. *Pilgrims to the Holy Land*. New York: Harper, 1970.

Kosansky, Oren. "Tourism, Charity, and Profit: The Movement of Money in Moroccan Jewish Pilgrimage." *Cultural Anthropology* 17, no. 3 (August 2002): 359–401.

Kotker, Norman. *The Earthly Jerusalem*. New York: Charles Scribner's Sons, 1969.

Kraeling, Carl H. *The Synagogue*. New Haven: Yale University Press, 1956.

Kraemer, Joel L. "A Jewish Cult of the Saints in Fatimid Egypt." In *L'Égypte Fatimide: son art et son histoire: actes du colloque organisé à Paris les 28, 29 et 30 mai 1998*. Ed. Marianne Barrucand. Paris: Université de Paris–Sorbonne, 1999. 579–601.

Kraus, Hans-Joachim. *Worship in Israel: A Cultic History of the Old Testament*. Richmond: John Knox Press, 1965.

Kucia, Marek. "KL Auschwitz in the Social Consciousnes of Poles, A.D. 2000." In *Remembering for the Future: The Holocaust in an Age of Genocide*. Eds. John K. Roth et al. Vol. 3, *Memory*. Basingstoke/New York: Palgrave/Houndsmill, 2001. 632–651.

Kurlansky, Mark. "Visiting Auschwitz-Poland—Adapted from 'A Chosen Few: The Resurrection of European Jewry.'" *Harper's Magazine* 289, no. 1733 (October 1994): 35–38.

Landau, David. "Bobover Rabbi Shlomo Halberstam Dies at 92." *Jewish News Weekly of Northern California* (August 4, 2000). http://www.jewishsf.com/content/2-0-/module/displaystory/story_id/14184/edition_id/275/format/html/displaystory.html.

Larkin, Margaret. *The Six Days of Yad-Mordechai*. Israel: Yad Mordechai Museum, 1970.

Layard, Austen Henry. *A Popular Account of Discoveries at Nineveh*. New York: J. C. Derby, 1854. http://mcadams.posc.mu.edu/txt/ah/Layard/DiscNineveh07.html.

Ledamski, Antoni. "Pilgrimage: Hasidim in Lezajsk." *Warsaw Voice* (March 17, 2002). http://www.warsawvoice.pl/archiwum.phtml/1913/.

Levine, Haninah. "Changing Destinations." *Jerusalem Report* (July 28, 2003): 40.

Levine, Lee I., ed. *Ancient Synagogues Revealed*. Jerusalem: Israel Exploration Society; Detroit: Wayne State University Press, 1982.

Levinson, Tamar A., and Susan Zoline. "Impact of Summer Trip to Israel on the Self-Esteem of Jewish Adolescents." *Journal of Psychology and Judaism* 21, no. 2 (Summer 1997): 87–119.

Levy, André. "Ethnic Aspects of Israeli Pilgrimage and Tourism to Morocco." Special issue, *Jewish Folklore and Ethnology Review* 17, no. 1–2 (1995): 20–24.

Levy, M. "Poland Comes to Life." *Dei'ah ve Dibur/Information and Insight* (April 17, 2002). http://www.shemayisrael.com/chareidi/archives5762/achrei/AMK62 features2.htm.

Liebman, Charles S., and Eliezer Don-Yehiya. *Civil Religion in Israel*. Berkeley: University of California Press, 1983.

Linenthal, Edward T. *Preserving Memory: The Struggle to Make America's Holocaust Museum*. New York: Viking, 1995.

Lives of the Prophets. Trans. Charles Cutler Torrey. Philadelphia: Society of Biblical Literature and Exegesis, 1946.

Maier, Manfred. *The Jewish Cemetery of Worms*. Worms: Verlag Stadtarchiv Worms, 2001.

Maltezou, Chryssa A. "From Crete to Jerusalem: The Will of a Cretan Jew (1626)." In "Intercultural Contacts in the Medieval World." Special issue, *Mediterranean Historical Review* 10, no. 1–2 (1996): 189–201.

Mann, Jacob. "Moses b. Samuel, A Jewish Katib in Damascus, and His Pilgrimage to Medinah and Mekkah." *Journal of the Royal Asiatic Society of Great Britain and Ireland*, 3rd series (1919): 155–184.

Margolis, David. "Ellis Island Revisited." *Los Angeles Jewish Journal* (1993). http://www.davidmargolis.com/article.php?id=51&cat_fp=0&cat_cc.

Marmorstein, A., ed. "*Sefer Qabbalath Sadiqei Eretz Israel*." *Maasef Zion* 2 (1926): 31–39.

Marx, Emanuel. "Communal and Individual Pilgrimage: The Region of Saints' Tombs in South Sinai." In *Regional Cults*. Ed. Richard P. Werbner. London: Academic Press, 1977. 29–51.

McGreal, Chris. "100,000 Call for Peace at Rabin Memorial Rally." *The Guardian* (November 3, 2003). http://www.guardian.co.uk/israel/Story/0,2763, 1076432,00.html.

Meri, Josef W. *The Cult of Saints Among Muslims and Jews in Medieval Syria*. Oxford: Oxford University Press, 2002.

———. "Re-Appropriating Sacred Space: Medieval Jews and Muslims Seeking Elijah and al-Khadir." *Medieval Encounters: Jewish, Christian and Muslim Culture in Confluence and Dialogue* 5, no. 3 (1999): 237–252.

Meshullam ben Menachem of Volterra. "[Meshullam ben Menachem of Volterra]." In *Jewish Travellers in the Middle Ages*. Ed. Elkan Nathan Adler. 1930. Rpt. New York: Dover, 1987. 156–208.

Midrash Rabbah. Trans. H. Freedman and Maurice Simon. London: Soncino, 1977.

Mishnah. Trans. Herbert Danby. 1933. London: Oxford University Press, 1958.

Mittelberg, David. *The Israel Connection and American Jews*. Westport: Praeger, 1999.

Montgomery, James A. *A Critical and Exegetical Commentary on the Books of Kings*. Edinburgh: T. & T. Clark, 1967.

Morgenstern, Arie. "Dispersion and the Longing for Zion, 1240–1840." *Azure* (Winter 2002): 71–132.

Morgenstern, Julian. *Rites of Birth, Marriage, Death, and Kindred Occasions Among the Semites*. Cincinnatti/Chicago: Hebrew Union College Press/Quadrangle Books, 1966.

Moses Basola. *In Zion and Jerusalem: The Itinerary of Rabbi Moses Basola (1521–1523)*. Ed. Abraham David. Trans. Dena Ordan. Ramat Gan: C. G. Foundation; Jerusalem Project Publications of the Martin (Szusz) Department of Land of Israel Studies of Bar-Ilan University, 1999.

Moses ben Israel Poryat. "A Vademecum for Palestinian Travelers." In *Roads to Zion: Four Centuries of Travelers' Reports*. Ed. Kurt Wilhelm. Trans. I. M. Lask. New York: Schocken, 1948. 65–72.

Mouttapa, Jean. "Des Arabes à Auschwitz." In "La mémoire de la Shoah." Special issue, *Nouvel Observateur*, hors série (December 2003/January 2004): 84–87.

———. *Un Arabe face à Auschwitz: La mémoire partagée*. Paris: Albin Michel, 2004.

Myers, Jacob Martin. *The World of the Restoration*. Englewood Cliffs, NJ: Prentice-Hall, 1968.

Nachmanides. "The Letters of Moses Nahmanides to His Sons from the Holy Land." In *A Treasury of Jewish Letters*. Ed. Franz Kobler. 2 vols. Philadelphia: Jewish Publication Society, 1954. 1:225–228.

Naser-e Khosraw. *Book of Travels (Safarnama)*. Trans. W. M. Thackston, Jr. Albany: State University of New York Press, 1986.

———. *Book of Travels (Safarnama) Selection Based on Nasir-i Khusrau. Diary of a Journey Through Syria and Palestine*. Trans. and ed. Guy LeStrange. London: Palestine Pilgrims' Text Society, 1893.

"Netanyahu Visits Rebbe's Gravesite." *Jewish News Weekly of Northern California* (September 20, 1996). http://www.jewishsf.com/content/2-0-/module/display story/story_id/4550/format/html/displaystory.html.

The New Oxford Annotated Bible. Ed. Michael D. Coogan. 3rd ed. New York: Oxford University Press, 2001.

Niebuhr, Richard. "Pilgrims and Pioneers." *Parabola* 9, no. 3 (1984): 6–13.

Novick, Peter. "Holocaust Memory in America." In *The Art of Memory: Holocaust Memorials in History*. Ed. James E. Young. New York and Munich: Prestel, 1994. 159–166.

Nunca olvidaremos. Marcha de la vida 1992. Mexico City: Edamex, [1992].

Obadiah Jaré da Bertinoro. "The Letters of Obadiah Jaré da Bertinoro (1487–90)." In *Jewish Travellers in the Middle Ages*. Ed. Elkan Nathan Adler. 1930. Rpt. New York: Dover, 1987. 209–250.

Oesterley, W.O.E., and Theodore H. Robinson. *Hebrew Religion: Its Origin and Development*. 2nd ed. New York: Macmillan, 1937.

Orme, William A. "Construction at a 2,000-Year-Old Religious Site Unleashes a Tempest." *International Herald Tribune* (December 23, 1999): B2.

Pahor, Boris. *Pilgrim Among the Shadows: A Memoir*. Trans. Michael Biggins. New York: Harcourt, Brace & Co., 1995.

Pally, Marcia. "'Farbrengen' My Baby Back Home." *Film Comment* (1987). http://www.marciapally.com/farbreng.html.

Petachia of Ratisbon. *Travels of Rabbi Petachia, of Ratisbon, Who, in the Latter End of the Twelfth Century, Visited Poland, Russia, Littly Tartary, the Crimea, Armenia, Assyria, Syria, the Holy Land, and Greece*. Trans. and ed. A. Benisch. London: Messrs. Trubner & Co., 1856.

Peters, Francis E. "The Holy Places." *City of the Great King: Jerusalem from David to the Present*. Ed. Nitza Rosovsky. Cambridge: Harvard University Press, 1996. 37–59.

——. *Jerusalem and Mecca: The Typology of the Holy City in the Near East*. New York: New York University Press, 1986.

Peterson, Chad. "Mayor Begins 'Mission' to Israel." *Yale Daily News* (March 23, 1995). http://www.yaledailynews.com/article.asp?AID=6174.

Philo Judaeus. *Philo*. Trans. F. H. Colson. 10 vols. London: William Heinemann, Ltd; Cambridge: Harvard University Press, 1929–1962.

Piacenza Pilgrim. "Travels." In *Jerusalem Pilgrims Before the Crusades*. Trans. and ed. John Wilkinson. Jerusalem: Ariel, 1977. 2nd ed. Warminster: Aris & Phillips, 2002. 129–151.

Prawer, Joshua. *The History of the Jews in the Latin Kingdom of Jerusalem*. Oxford: Clarendon; New York: Oxford University Press, 1988.

Price, Jonathan J. "The Jewish Diaspora of the Graeco-Roman Period." *Scripta Classica Israelica* 13 (1994): 169–186.

Prince-Gibson, Eetta. "Arabic in Auschwitz." *International Jerusalem Post* (June 20, 2003): B5. http://www.jpost.com/International.

Prusher, Ilene R. "The Who, Where, and Why of Mystic Meccas." *Christian Science Monitor* (June 29, 1999). http://search.csmonitor.com/durable/1999/06/29/p13s1.htm.

Radler, Melissa. "Jews Fabricate Holy Sites, They Do Not Matter." *Jerusalem Post* (May 29, 2001). http://www.themodernreligion.com/jihad/fabricate.html.

Rees, Matt. "Miracle Makers. Israel's Shas Party Is Tapping into Mysticism to Give Its Politics More Potency." *Time Europe* 156, no. 13 (September 25, 2000). http://www.time.com/time.europe/magazine/2000,0925/jerusalem.html.

Reiner, Elchanan. "Meron's Miracle." *Eretz Weekly* (February 6, 2000). http://www.eretz.com/archive/feb0600/htm.

Report of the Commission Appointed by His Majesty's Government in the United Kingdom of

Great Britain and Northern Ireland, with the Approval of the Council of the League of Nations, to Determine the Rights and Claims of Moslems and Jews in Connection with the Western or Wailing Wall at Jerusalem. London: HMSO, 1931.

Romero, Eugenio-María. *El martirio de la joven Hatchuelo la heroína hebrea*. Gibraltar: n.p., 1837.

Ron, Amos. "A Rachel for Everyone: The Kinneret Cemetery as a Site of Civil Pilgrimage." In *Sanctity of Time and Space in Tradition and Modernity*. Eds. Alberdina Houtman, Marcel Poorthuis, and Joshua Schwartz. Leiden; Boston: Brill, 1998. 349–359.

Rosovsky, Nitza, ed. *City of the Great King: Jerusalem from David to the Present*. Cambridge: Harvard University Press, 1996.

Rowley, H. H. *Worship in Ancient Israel: Its Form and Meaning*. Philadelphia: Fortress Press; London: SPCK, 1967.

Rubenstein, Jeffrey L. *The History of Sukkot in the Second Temple and Rabbinical Periods*. Atlanta: Scholars Press, 1995.

Safrai, Shemuel. "Pilgrimage to Jerusalem at the End of the Second Temple Period." In *Studies on the Jewish Background of the New Testament*. Eds. O. Michel et al. Assen, Netherlands: Van Gorcum, 1969. 12–21.

——. "Relations Between the Diaspora and the Land of Israel." In *The Jewish People in the First Century*. Eds. Shemuel Safrai and Menahem Stern. 2 vols. Philadelphia: Fortress Press, 1974. 1:184–215.

——. "The Temple." In *The Jewish People in the First Century*. Eds. Shemuel Safrai, and Menahem Stern. 2 vols. Philadelphia: Fortress Press, 1974. 2:864–905.

Sahl ben Masiah. "Epistle to Jacob ben Samuel." In *Karaite Anthology: Excerpts from the Early Literature*. Trans. Leon Nemoy. New Haven and London: Yale University Press, 1969. 111–122.

Samuel ben Samson. "Itinerary of Rabbi Samuel ben Samson in 1210." In *Jewish Travellers in the Middle Ages*. Ed. Elkan Nathan Adler. 1930. Rpt. New York: Dover, 1987. 103–110.

Samuel Jemsel. "Samuel Jemsel the Karaïte." In *Jewish Travellers in the Middle Ages*. Ed. Elkan Nathan Adler. 1930. Rpt. New York: Dover, 1987. 329–344.

Sanderson, John. *The Travels of John Sanderson in the Levant, 1584–1602, with His Autobiography and Selections from His Correspondence*. Ed. William Foster. London: Hakluyt Society, 1931.

Sanua, Victor D. "A Return to the Vanished World of Egyptian Jewry." http://www.sefarad.org/diaspora/egypt/vie/001/0.html.

Sapsowitz, Marna. "Serving as a Rabbi in Poland." *Reconstructionism Today* 11, no. 3 (Spring–Summer 2004). http://www.jrf.org/rt/2004/rabbi-poland.htm.

Sarna, Nahum. *The Jewish Publication Society Torah Commentary: Genesis*. Philadelphia: Jewish Publication Society, 1989.

Satterthwaite, Philip E. "Zion in the Songs of Ascents." In *Zion: City of Our God*. Eds. Richard S. Hiss and Gordon J. Wenham. Grand Rapids, MI: Eerdmans, 1995. 105–128.

Scham, Sandra. "The Lost Goddess of Israel." *Archaelogy* 58, no. 2 (March/April 2005): 36–40.

Schoffman, Stuart. "Transcendence in a Cursed Place: An Arab-Jewish Visit to Auschwitz Is a Rare Exercise in Empathy." *Jerusalem Report* (June 30, 2003): 28–30.

Schwartz, Barry. "The Social Context of Commemoration. A Study in Collective Memory." *Social Forces* 82 (1982): 374–402.

Schwartz, Bryan. "In Morocco's Mountains, Elderly Jew Watches the Shrine of His Holy Rebbe." *Jewish News of Greater Phoenix* 54, no. 27 (March 22, 2002). http://www.jewishsf.com/bk020322/i40.shtml.

Schwartz, Stephen. "Jewish Stolac: Sephardic Judaism, Balkan Islam, and Tomb Visitation in Bosnia-Hercegovina." Paper. Haverford College, Pennsylvania. November 10, 2002. http://www.haverford.edu/relg/sells/stolac/stolacrenewed.

Schwarz-Bart, André. *The Last of the Just*. Trans. Stephen Becker. London: Secker and Warburg, 1961.

Segev, Tom. *The Seventh Million: The Israelis and the Holocaust*. New York: Hill and Wang, 1993.

Sered, Susan Starr. "Rachel's Tomb: The Development of a Cult." *Jewish Studies Quarterly* 2, no. 2 (1995): 103–148.

Setton, Ruth Knafo. *The Road to Fez*. Washington, DC: Counterpoint, 2001.

Shanks, Hershel. "The Strange Enrichment of Seeing Auschwitz." *Moment* (February 1990): 4.

Shehada, Bassem. "Mufti Claims Ownership of 'Rachel's Tomb.'" *Jerusalem Times* (September 19, 2002). http://www.jerusalem-times.net/article/news/details/detail.asp?id=2042.

Shragai, Nadav. "The Palestinians Who Are Shooting at the Rachel's Tomb Compound Have Already Singled It Out as the Next Jewish Holy Site Which They Want to 'Liberate.'" *Haaretz* (October 31, 2000). www.haaretzdaily.com.

———. "Rachel's Tomb: Beyond or Within?" *Haaretz*. www.haaretzdaily.com.

"Shrine Revisited." *Al-Ahram Weekly Online* (May 31–June 6, 2001). http://weekly.ahram.org.eg/2001/536/eg3.htm.

Silverberg, Robert. *Kingdoms of the Wall*. New York: Bantam, 1992.

Simon, Andrea. *Bashert: A Granddaughter's Holocaust Quest*. Jackson: University Press of Mississippi, 2002.

Singer, Daniel. "A Haunted Journey." *The Nation* 269, no. 9 (Sepember 27, 1999): 18–24.

Slyomovics, Susan. "The Pilgrimage of Rabbi Ephraim Al-Naqawa, Tlemcen, Algeria." *Jewish Folklore and Ethnology Review* 15, no. 2 (1993): 84–88.

———. "Rebbele Mordkhele's Pilgrimage in New York City, Tel Aviv and Carpathian Ruthenia." In *Going Home*. Ed. Jack Kugelmass. Evanston, IL: YIVO and Northwestern University Press, 1993. 369–394.

Smith, Mark S. *The Early History of God: Yahweh and the Other Deities in Ancient Israel*. San Francisco: Harper and Row, 1990.

———. "The Psalms as a Book for Pilgrims." *Interpretation* 46 (1992): 156–166.

Solomon Shloemel ben Hayyim Meinsterl of Lundenberg. "A Godly Life." In *Roads to Zion: Four Centuries of Travelers' Reports*. Ed. Kurt Wilhelm. Trans. I. M. Lask. New York: Schocken, 1948. 57–64.

Soyer, Daniel. "The Travel Agent as Ethnic Broker Between Old World and New: The Case of Gustave Eisner." *YIVO Annual* 21 (1993): 345–368.

State of Israel, Ministry of Foreign Affairs. "Protection of Holy Places Law." June 27, 1967.

Stier, Oren Baruch. "Lunch at Majdanek: The March of the Living as a Contemporary Pilgrimage of Memory." Special issue, *Jewish Folklore and Ethnology Review* 17, no. 1–2 (1995): 57–67.

———. "Virtual Memories: Mediating the Holocaust at the Simon Wiesenthal Center's Beit Hashoah–Museum of Tolerance." *Journal of the American Academy of Religion* 64, no. 4 (1996): 831–851.

Stillman, Norman A. *The Language and Culture of the Jews of Sefrou, Morocco: An Ethnolinguistic Study*. Manchester, UK: University of Manchester, 1988.

Storper-Perez, Danielle, and Harvey E. Goldberg. "The Kotel: Toward an Ethnographic Portrait." *Religion* 24 (1994): 309–332.

Tal, Rivka. "Va'amartem Ko Lechai, Rabbi Shimon Bar Yochai: Lag BaOmer at Meiron." *Dei'ah ve Dibur/Information and Insight* (May 9, 2001). http://www.shemayisrael.com/chareidi/archives5761/behaaloscha/EMRfetures2.htm.

Toorn, Karel van der. *From Her Cradle to Her Grave: The Role of Religion in the Life of the Israelite and the Babylonian Woman*. Trans. Sara J. Denning-Bolle. Sheffield (England): Journal for the Study of the Old Testament, 1994.

"Trouble in the Holy Land: Arab Vandals Desecrate Joseph's Tomb, Gravestone of Biblical Patriarch Ruined Despite Palestinian Pledge." *WorldNetDaily* (February 25, 2003). http://www.worldnetdaily.com/news/article.asp?ARTICLE_ID=31203.

Turner, Edith. "Bar Yohai, Mystic: The Creative Persona and His Pilgrimage." In *Creativity/Anthropology*. Eds. Smadar Lavie, Kirin Narayan, and Renato Rosaldo. Ithaca: Cornell University Press, 1993. 225–252.

Turner, Victor. "The Center Out There: Pilgrim's Goal." *History of Religions* 12, no. 3 (February 1973): 191–230.

———. "Liminality and Communitas." In *The Ritual Process: Structure and Anti-Structure*. Victor Turner. 1969. Chicago: Aldine Press, 1974. 94–130.

Turner, Victor, and Edith Turner. *Image and Pilgrimage in Christian Culture. Anthropological Perspectives*. New York: Columbia University Press, 1978.

Umm Hnina, Taïta. *Le pèlerinage de la Ghriba à Djerba*. Charenton-le-Pont: Victor Trabelsi, 1994.

Union for Reform Judaism's Online Pressroom. "Reform Movement Mission Heads to Israel Sunday/Five-Day Journey Will Affirm Reform Solidarity with the Israeli People" (July 24, 2001). http://urj.org/pr/2001/010724/.

Urman, Dan, and Paul V. M. Flesher. *Ancient Synagogues: Historical Analysis and Archaeological Discovery*. 2 vols. Leiden: Brill, 1995.

Vaux, Roland de. *Ancient Israel: Its Life and Institutions*. Trans. John McHugh. Original French edition in 2 vols. called *Les Institutions de l'Ancien Testament*. Paris: Les Editions du Cerf (n.d.). London: Darton, Longham & Todd, 1965.

———. *The Early History of Israel*. Trans. David Smith. Philadelphia: Westminster Press, 1978.

Vendan, I. *La heroína hebrea, Sol "la Saddika": drama histórico en prosa y verso en cinco actos*. Larache [Morocco]: n.p., n.d.

Vilnay, Zev. *The Sacred Land*. Vol. 2: *Legends of Judea and Samara*. Philadelphia: Jewish Publication Society of America, 1975.

Voinot, Louis. *Pèlerinages judéo-musulmans du Maroc*. Paris: LaRose, 1948.

Wall, Alexandra J. "Despite Terror, Federations, Congregants Head to Israel." *Jewish News Weekly of Northern California* (January 11, 2002). http://www.jewishsf.com/content/2-0-/module/displaystory/story_id/17503/edition_id/347/format/html/displaystory.html.

Ward, Seth. *God's Place in the World*. London: Cassel, 1998.

Wasserman, Suzanne. "Re-creating Recreations on the Lower East Side: Restaurants,

Cabarets, Cafes, and Coffeehouses in the 1930s." In *Remembering the Lower East Side: American Jewish Reflections*. Eds. Hasia R. Diner, Jeffrey Shandler, and Beth S. Wenger. Bloomington: Indiana University Press, 2000. 155–178.

Waxman, Sharon. "Shrine to Hatred." *Washington Post* (October 28, 2000): C1. http://www.library.cornell.edu/colldev/mideast/shryus.html.

Weichselbaum, Simone. "Program Teaches U.S. Students about Jewish Heritage Abroad." *Eagle Online*, American University (January 22, 2001). http://www.theeagleonline.com/news/2001/01/22/News/Au.Students.Spend.Break.In.Israel-682390.shtml.

Weiner, Herbert. "The Dead Hasidim." *Commentary* 31, no. 3 (March 1961). http://www.commentarymagazine.com/Summaries/V31I3P56-1.htm.

Weiss, Steward. "The March to Nowhere." *Jerusalem Post* (March 24, 2002): 7.

———. "Strangers in a Familiar Land." *Jerusalem Post* (November 2, 2003). http://www.freeman.org/m_online/November03/.

Werblowsky, J. Zwi. "The Meaning of Jerusalem to Jews, Christians, and Muslims." In *Jerusalem in the Mind of the Western World, 1800–1948. With Eyes Toward Zion*. Eds. Yehoshua Ben-Arieh and Moshe Davis. Westport: Praeger, 1997. 7–21.

Westermark, Edward. *Ritual and Belief in Morocco*. 2 vols. London: Macmillan, 1926.

Wieseltier, Leon. "After Memory: Reflections on the Holocaust Memorial Museum." *The New Republic* 208, no. 18 (May 3, 1993): 16–26.

Wilhelm, Kurt, ed. *Roads to Zion: Four Centuries of Travelers' Reports*. Trans. I. M. Lask. New York: Schocken, 1948.

Wilken, Robert L. "Christian Pilgrimage to the Holy Land." In *City of the Great King: Jerusalem From David to the Present*. Ed. Nitza Rosovsky. Cambridge: Harvard University Press, 1996. 117–135.

Wilkinson, John. *Jerusalem Pilgrims Before the Crusades*. Jerusalem: Ariel, 1977. 2nd ed. Warminster: Aris & Phillips, 2002.

Wolf, E. "The Virgin of Guadalupe: A Mexican National Symbol." *Journal of American Folklore* 71, no. 1 (1958): 34–39.

Woronowycz, Roman. "Thousands Travel to Uman for Annual Pilgrimage on Rosh Hashanah." *Ukrainian Weekly* 71, no. 42 (October 19, 2003). http://www.ukrweekly.com/Archive/2003/420306.shtml.

Yadin, Yigal. *Masada: Herod's Fortress and the Zealot's Last Stand*. Trans. Moshe Pearlman. New York: Random House, 1966.

Yellin, Deena. "College Students on Pilgrimage to Israel in Show of Solidarity." *Florida Flambeau*, Florida State University (March 20, 2003). http:// www.fsunews.com/vnews/display.v/ART/2003/03/20/3e79598c4ff79.

Yoaz, Yuval. "Whose Fence Is It Anyway." *Haaretz* (February 9, 2005). http://www.haaretz.co.il/marketing/mediakit/pop.html.

Young, James E. "The Anne Frank House: Holland's Memorial 'Shrine of the Book.'" In *The Art of Memory: Holocaust Memorials in History*. Ed. James E. Young. New York and Munich: Prestel, 1994. 131–138.

———. *The Texture of Memory: Holocaust Memorials and Meaning*. New Haven: Yale University Press, 1993.

Zacuto, Abraham. *The Complete Book of Yohassin* [*Yuhasin ha-shalem*]. Trans. Abraham Haim Freimann. http://www.israelshamir.net/Talmud/227-230.shtml.

Zagier, Alan Scher. "Centerpiece: A Journey Home. An Immigrant's Son, a Vanished

Village." *Bonita Daily News* (Naples, FL) (January 19, 2003). http://www.bonitanews.com/03/01/bonita/d856798a.htm.

Zakon, Miriam. "Four Days in Poland: Searching for Sarah Schenirer. Searching for Our Heritage. Searching, Just a Little, for Myself." *Jewish Observer* 34, no. 5 (May 2001): 18–22.

Zerubavel, Yael. *Recovered Roots: Collective Memory and the Making of Israeli National Tradition*. Chicago: University of Chicago Press, 1994.

INDEX

About the Authors

DAVID M. GITLITZ is Professor of Languages at University of Rhode Island. His book *Secrecy and Deceit: The Religion of the Crypto-Jews* won a National Jewish Book Award.

LINDA KAY DAVIDSON is an instructor at University of Rhode Island and has written four books on aspects of the pilgrimage to Santiago de Compostela.

Together, Gitlitz and Davidson have co-authored *A Drizzle of Honey: The Lives and Recipes of Spain's Secret Jews*, which won a National Jewish Book Award as well as the International Association of Culinary Professionals Prize for Scholarship; *The Pilgrimage Road to Santiago: The Complete Cultural Handbook*; and *Pilgrimage from the Ganges to Graceland: An Encyclopedia*, selected by the *Library Journal* as a Best Reference Source for 2002.